BERTRAND RUSSELL'S AMERICA

1896 *German Social Democracy*
1897 *An Essay on the Foundations of Geometry* (Constable)
1900 *The Philosophy of Leibniz*
1903 *The Principles of Mathematics*
1910 *Philosophical Essays*
1912 *Problems of Philosophy* (Oxford U.P.)
1910–13 *Principia Mathematica* 3 vols. (with A. N. Whitehead) (Cambridge U.P.)
1914 *Our Knowledge of the External World*
1916 *Justice in Wartime*
1916 *Principles of Social Reconstruction*
1917 *Political Ideals*
1918 *Roads to Freedom*
1918 *Mysticism and Logic*
1919 *Introduction to Mathematical Philosophy*
1920 *The Practice and Theory of Bolshevism*
1921 *The Analysis of Mind*
1922 *The Problem of China*
1923 *The Prospects of Industrial Civilization* (with Dora Russell)
1923 *The ABC of Atoms* (out of print)
1924 *Icarus or the Future of Science* (Spokesman Books)
1925 *The ABC of Relativity*
1926 *On Education*
1927 *An Outline of Philosophy*
1927 *The Analysis of Matter*
1928 *Sceptical Essays*
1929 *Marriage and Morals*
1930 *The Conquest of Happiness*
1931 *The Scientific Outlook*
1932 *Education and the Social Order*
1934 *Freedom and Organization: 1814–1914*
1935 *In Praise of Idleness*
1935 *Religion and Science* (Oxford U.P.)
1936 *Which Way to Peace?* (out of print)
1937 *The Amberley Papers* (with Patricia Russell)
1938 *Power*
1940 *An Inquiry into Meaning and Truth*
1945 *History of Western Philosophy*

1948 *Human Knowledge: Its Scope and Limits*
1949 *Authority and the Individual*
1950 *Unpopular Essays*
1951 *New Hopes for a Changing World*
1952 *The Impact of Science on Society*
1953 *The Good Citizen's Alphabet* (Gaberbocchus)
1953 *Satan in the Suburbs* (out of print)
1954 *Nightmares of Eminent Persons* (out of print)
1954 *Human Society in Ethics and Politics*
1956 *Logic and Knowledge* (ed. by R. C. Marsh)
1956 *Portraits from Memory*
1957 *Why I Am Not a Christian* (ed. by Paul Edwards)
1957 *Understanding History and Other Essays* (USA only) (out of print)
1958 *Vital Letters of Russell, Khrushchev, Dulles* (out of print)
1958 *Bertrand Russell's Best* (ed. by Robert Egner)
1959 *Common Sense and Nuclear Warfare*
1959 *Wisdom of the West* (ed. by Paul Foulkes) (Macdonald)
1959 *My Philosophical Development*
1960 *Bertrand Russell Speaks His Mind* (out of print)
1961 *Fact and Fiction*
1961 *Has Man a Future?*
1961 *The Basic Writings of Bertrand Russell* (ed. by R. E. Egner & L. Denonn)
1963 *Unarmed Victory*
1967 *War Crimes in Vietnam*
1967 *The Archives of Bertrand Russell* (ed. by B. Feinberg, Continuum) (out of print)
1967 *Autobiography 1872–1914*
1968 *Autobiography 1914–1944*
1969 *Autobiography 1944–1967*
1969 *Dear Bertrand Russell . . .* (ed. by B. Feinberg & R. Kasrils)
1972 *The Collected Stories of Bertrand Russell* (ed. by B. Feinberg)
1973 *Essays in Analysis* (ed. by Douglas Lackey)

BERTRAND RUSSELL'S AMERICA

1896–1945

BY

BARRY FEINBERG

AND

RONALD KASRILS

A RICHARD SEAVER BOOK

THE VIKING PRESS • NEW YORK

TO EDITH, COUNTESS RUSSELL

ACKNOWLEDGEMENTS

Except where otherwise stated and described, all Russell's writings appearing in this volume have been unpublished and are reproduced with the joint permission of The Bertrand Russell Estate, Hollybush House, Hadley Green, Barnet, Hertfordshire, and the Bertrand Russell Archives at McMaster University, Hamilton, Ontario.

Special thanks are due to Edith, Countess Russell, for her encouragement and invaluable assistance and to the following individuals who helped in many and various ways during the preparation of this volume: Christopher Farley and Kenneth Coates of The Bertrand Russell Peace Foundation, Anton Felton of The Bertrand Russell Estate, Kenneth Blackwell and his staff at the Bertrand Russell Archives, Michael Burn, Professor Harry Ruja, Professor Abraham Edel, Professor Barrows Dunham, Richard Seaver, Georgette Felix, Anne Fremantle, Jack Black, Ronald Clark, Rayner Unwin, Ronald Eames, Caroline Bell, Janice Ogg, Joan Dawes.

Thanks are also due to Russell's publishers: George Allen & Unwin Ltd; Atlantic-Little, Brown & Co.; W. W. Norton & Co.; Liveright Publishing Corporation; Humanities Press; *Tribunal*; the *New Republic*; *New Leader*; the *Nation and the Athenaeum*; *The New York Times Magazine*; New York *Herald Tribune Magazine*; *Forward*; *Outlook & Independent*; the *Virginia Quarterly Review*; the *New York American*; *Survey Graphic*; *Common Sense*; the *American Mercury*; *Saturday Evening Post*; *Horizon*.

For permission to include certain of their papers we are indebted to the following individuals and institutions: Edith, Countess Russell, for excerpts from her biography, *Carey Thomas of Bryn Mawr*, and for the letters of her friend Lucy Donnelly; Otto Nathan on behalf of The Estate of Albert Einstein; Bernard Perry on behalf of the Estate of Ralph Barton Perry; the Harvard Corporation for the letters of A. Lawrence Lowell and James Woods; Valerie Eliot, Faber and Faber Ltd and Harcourt Brace Jovanovich, Inc. for T. S. Eliot's poem 'Mr. Apollinax' from *Collected Poems 1909-1962* by T. S. Eliot, Copyright, 1936, by Harcourt Brace Jovanovich, Inc.; copyright © 1963, 1964 by T. S. Eliot; Frida Laski for Harold Laski's letters; Isador M. Sheffer for Henry Sheffer's letter; Margot Cory for George Santayana's letters; The Controller of H.M.S.O. for facsimiles of Crown-copyright records in the Public Record Office; The New York Times Company (© 1916/29/31/37/38); Museum Press for extract from *Great Companions,* U.K. edition (original edition, Max Eastman, U.S.A.) ; Professor Paul Edwards; Professor Daniel J. Bronstein; Professor Y. H. Krikorian; Professor Victor F. Lenzen; Professor Barrows Dunham; Professor William M. Armstrong; Scott Nearing.

CONTENTS

CONTENTS

INTRODUCTION

Bertrand Russell's association with the United States, a country he grew to know well, was both fascinating and important and encompassed the whole of his adult life. At a time when his right to comment on American affairs was being challenged, Russell wrote in reply to an American correspondent:

'My first lectures in your country were in 1896, and my last in 1951, so I have had a fairly long experience of the United States.'[1]

Russell's interest in America began from childhood in a period when 'young people who hoped to reform the world went to America to discover how to do so'.[2] Inspired by America's example of democracy and freedom Russell's parents, who were Victorian radicals, visited the United States in 1867, shortly after the Civil War, and made friends with leading liberals. 'They could not foresee,' Russell commented exactly 100 years later in his *Autobiography*, 'that the men and women whose democratic ardour they applauded and whose triumphant opposition to slavery they admired were the grandfathers and grandmothers of those who murdered Sacco and Vanzetti.'[3]

Nurtured on liberal Whig traditions, which presented him with John Stuart Mill as a 'godfather', the young Russell came to admire the ideals embodied in the writings of Jefferson and Paine, and regarded America as 'a romantic land of freedom'.[4] These early feelings, however, were in marked contrast to the opinions he was to hold in the latter part of his life. By the time of his death in 1970, Russell's views were so transformed that he had become a vigorous opponent of American policies: regarding the United States as the greatest threat to world peace and her actions in Vietnam 'at least as bad as the Nazis'.[5] The American and British press, while praising Russell as the supreme mathematician and master of logic, described him as being irrationally hostile to the United States. *Time* magazine accused him of 'obsessive' anti-Americanism,[6] and *The Times*, in a lengthy obituary, claimed that his public undertakings 'became increasingly bizarre' and 'obscured in his final years the extraordinary achievements of his long life'.[7]

Russell visited the United States on nine occasions, including a period of extended residence during the Second World War. He lectured at numerous colleges and universities and held professorships at the universities of Harvard, Chicago and California. As early as 1912, George Santayana was informing Russell that 'there is no one whom the younger school of philosophers in America are more eager to learn of than you'.[8] His experience of America, however, was not only from the vantage point of academic institutions. Apart from his impact as a philosopher, he became famous as a populariser of socio-political ideas through public lectures and debates across the country. Russell's activities, including the publication of his numerous journalistic writings and books, brought him into close touch with the American public and with the forces shaping American society. From England Russell kept abreast of developments in the U.S. through correspondence with many American friends. Throughout his life he continued to lay great store by contact of this kind and in 1916 indicated his debt to transatlantic communications which enabled him to assess public feeling in America towards the war.

Russell's early romantic notions about America barely survived his first visit. The First World War caused a major transformation in his outlook. For the first time, Russell became totally involved in social and political concerns. The broadening of his interests, at a time when the United States was emerging as a dominant world power, made him turn his attention to America's role in international affairs. 'The hopes and fears of the world, probably for the next fifty years at least,' he wrote in 1922, 'depend upon the use which America makes of her vast power.'[9] By 1924, he had become an outspoken critic of American capitalism, and conducted an extensive socialist propaganda tour of the U.S. He was convinced that a socialist America was a necessary step towards solving the world's problems.

As Russell's association with America developed, and he became more intimate with problems facing the American people, so the scope of his activities widened. He found, in the land where the rights of man were idealised, gross inequalities in wealth and power, authoritarian interference with academic freedom and civil liberties, racism and the persecution of minorities. Russell recognised that radicalism in America was very weak; one of his main concerns, therefore, was to help promote liberal and tolerant attitudes. His emphasis on education as a powerful vehicle for reshaping society led him to express advanced views on the family and sexual morality which provoked great hostility towards him; and in the 1940s he found himself the subject of a fierce witch-hunt in which a coalition of his clerical and political opponents attempted to drive him from the country. However, Russell was also viewed as an outstanding symbol of reason and hope by wide sections of American opinion, including the peace and civil-rights movements, students and academics, and was already in the early 1920s being described as 'an inspiration to progressive forces in America'.[10]

As Russell developed his critique of the American power structure ('Oil and Morgan rule you', he informed American audiences in 1924) he was careful to distinguish between United States government policy and the interests of the American people. 'I am speaking to you,' he broadcast on National Liberation Front radio in 1966 to American soldiers in Vietnam, 'in order to explain how your government has abused your rights . . .'[11]

Russell's first wife was an American, and so was Edith Finch, whom he married in 1952. When accused of anti-Americanism he liked to quip: 'Anti-American? Half my wives have been American' (a retort which *Time* magazine found 'astonishing').[12] Russell was very aware of American sensitivity to outside criticism, especially English, but nevertheless his outspoken views succeeded, like no other foreign voice, in arousing Americans to the crisis of their society.

Russell's social ideals and his struggle for world peace and justice are clearly conveyed through his long association with the United States. An account of this association has never before been attempted. Russell himself suggested that an epitaph reading: 'He lived for six years in America, and did *not* write a book about it',[13] should be inscribed on his tombstone. In his biography of Russell, Alan Wood comments that this omission 'can be repaired by some diligent research among his forgotten journalistic writings, and among scattered references to America in his books'.[14]

Russell's writings on America began in earnest shortly before America's entry into the First World War. His contributions to American periodicals commenced at this time and became extensive over the years. The subject of his writings ranges from serious polemic on politics and sociology to light-hearted journalism, which includes his impressions of such American institutions as the cinema, Prohibition, psychoanalysis, the telephone, railroads, boxing, and the penchant for lectures 'which is, to an Englishman, quite unintelligible'.[15] These writings, which reflect the development of Russell's views on America, became more prolific in the 1950s and 1960s as the threat of nuclear war emerged and the crises of the United States became more profound.

A further source of rich material reflecting Russell's interest in the United States, is his collection of letters to and from American and English friends which reveals his most personal views and moods at various times. Taken together with seven decades of American press coverage of Russell, and the epigrammatic accounts of his visits contained in his *Autobiography*, a detailed picture emerges of Russell's relationship with the United States. This picture, it should be pointed out, does not include Russell's contribution to American philosophical thought, as an exposition on his technical philosophy was considered to be outside the scope of this book.

When our research began in 1969, it soon became apparent that Alan Wood had, perhaps, under-estimated the extent of relevant data available. Because of the enormous quantity of material, and in order to present it in an integrated and readable form, it has been necessary to produce this work in two volumes, covering the periods 1896–1945, and 1945–1970, respectively. The end of the Second World War, when Russell had returned to England after his six-year stay in the United States, provided a suitable dividing point, since the development and use of the Atomic Bomb foreshadowed a new era in his life. Volume One is in two parts; the first part presents in biographical and documentary form an account of Russell's involvement with the United States, with special reference to the seven visits he made in this period. The most representative of Russell's journalistic writings are highlighted throughout the narrative, and the full text of these appears in the second part.

This method of presentation was considered essential for continuity of narrative and ease of reference. Most of the articles selected have hitherto been practically inaccessible, published, as they were, many years ago in widely dispersed and now almost unobtainable journals. One third of the articles have not, to our knowledge, been published before, and much of the correspondence is published here for the first time. Many of the letters have required considerable editing, so as to retain only those extracts which are of importance to the theme of this book. News reports, covering the American tours, have been similarly dealt with. Those articles and other relevant material consulted in the course of research, but not reproduced, are referred to in the bibliography at the end of the book. We do not claim, however, to have uncovered all Russell's writings on America, nor have we consulted all America's writings on Russell. Our intention has been to assemble sufficient data to provide an understanding of Russell's deep and many-sided involvement with the United States. We believe that Bertrand Russell emerges as a man who had much knowledge of, and interest in, the United States and its people. His attitudes stemmed not from irrational hostility to the United States but from an overriding concern for the well-being of mankind, which led him to oppose all those ideas and practices he considered contrary to the interests of the American people.

We have, as far as possible, endeavoured to prevent our own personal views from intruding in this work, so as to allow Russell to speak for himself. Had this book consisted only of a selection of Russell's important writings on America, our task would have been relatively simple. But, in order to reveal the history of Russell's relationship with America, the task became much more complex involving, as it did, the assemblage of a myriad of elements which were then moulded into a literary form. Such an approach inevitably leaves traces of our own preferences and sympathies, but we feel, nonetheless, that this work presents a true and representative picture of Bertrand Russell's association with the U.S.A. A picture which, we hope, will be complete with the publication of Volume Two.

NOTES

London = George Allen & Unwin Ltd; Boston = Atlantic-Little, Brown & Co., throughout the Notes, unless otherwise stated.

[1] B. Feinberg and R. Kasrils (eds), *Dear Bertrand Russell* (London, 1969), pp. 183–4 (Houghton Mifflin, Boston, 1969), p. 154.

[2] From 'Can Americans and Britons be Friends?' (see below, p. 328).

[3] B. Russell. *Autobiography* (London, 1967), Vol. I, p. 16; (Boston, 1967), p. 9.

[4] Ibid., p. 76; p. 104.

[5] *Time* magazine (16 February 1970).

[6] Ibid.

[7] *The Times* (3 February 1970).

[8] Letter from George Santayana to Russell (see below, p. 33).

[9] From 'Hopes and Fears as Regards America' (see below, p. 220).

[10] Letter from Harry W. Laidler to Russell (see below, p. 91).

[11] B. Russell, *War Crimes in Vietnam* (London, and Monthly Review Press, New York, 1967), p. 107.

[12] *Time* magazine (16 February 1970).

[13] Alan Wood, *Bertrand Russell, the Passionate Sceptic* (London, 1957), p. 145 (Simon & Schuster, New York, 1957).

[14] Ibid.

[15] From 'Impressions of America' (see below, p. 228).

PART I

CHAPTER 1

AMERICA IN 1896

Bertrand Russell's early views on America were shaped by his family's lively interest in that country and their admiration for the spirit of liberty embodied in the Declaration of Independence. America in the nineteenth century 'was thought to be a strange, wild, revolutionary country'; Russell wrote: 'it was beloved by young radicals and hated by old conservatives'.[1]

Russell as a boy was particularly shy and retiring. He had little social contact outside his own family circle. In 1889, at the age of 17, he was introduced by his Uncle Rollo Russell to the Pearsall Smiths, an enlightened and outgoing family of Philadelphia Quakers who had settled in the Sussex countryside. Russell was delighted with the introduction and was especially struck by the younger daughter, Alys, who was studying at Bryn Mawr, an American college, and was home for the holidays. He found her 'more emancipated than any young woman I had known, since she was at college and crossed the Atlantic alone, and was, as I soon discovered, an intimate friend of Walt Whitman.'[2]

Alys was very beautiful, five years older than Russell, and he fell in love with her at once. In subsequent years he spent many happy hours in the company of her family and later described how 'they would make a camp fire in the woods, and sit round singing Negro spirituals, which were in those days unknown in England'.[3] Russell recorded that he 'found among them an absence of many prejudices which hampered me at home' and 'Above all I enjoyed their emancipation from good taste.'[4]

Russell's grandmother displayed a rather conventional English attitude towards American women when she was confronted by her ward's growing relationship with Alys. She wished him to mix in circles more suited to his class and she variously described Alys as a 'baby snatcher, a low-class adventuress, a designing female'.[5] Nevertheless, Russell persisted in seeing Alys and they were married in 1894.

Prompted largely by Alys's wish to introduce him to her relatives, they planned a trip to America in 1896. At 24, and fresh from his early successes as a mathematician at Cambridge, Russell was highly elated at the prospect of his first transatlantic crossing. He wished to lecture while in America and as he was not well known outside Cambridge he and Alys contacted certain members of her family who had connections with American colleges. Alys's cousin, Dr Martha Carey Thomas, was President of Bryn Mawr, a women's college in Pennsylvania, and her uncle was associated with Johns Hopkins, a university for men in Baltimore. Arrangements were made to visit Bryn Mawr, and, with a view to securing a similar appointment at Johns Hopkins, Russell wrote to Alys's uncle, Dr James Thomas, on 3 July 1896:[6]

'I am expecting to deliver a course of six lectures at Bryn Mawr College this autumn, on the philosophical foundations of geometry, as they appear in the light of non-Euclidean theories. I learn that much interest is taken in this subject in the Johns Hopkins University and I should be willing in the event of an opportunity offering itself, to deliver the same or a similar course there. My lectures would be an expansion of a dissertation which I submitted when I was elected a Fellow of Trinity College, Cambridge; since my election, I have continued to work at the same subject, and I hope that the Cambridge University Press will publish a book by me on the subject, during the course of the next year.'

Thomas approached the President of Johns Hopkins, Daniel Coit Gilman, on Russell's behalf and passed on references from leading Cambridge philosophers attesting to Russell's ability as a mathematician and lecturer.[7] Gilman referred the matter to several scholars associated with his college, seeking their opinion. The response was unencouraging. Simon Newcomb, the celebrated astronomer, commented: 'I have never heard of Mr Bertrand Russell. . . . I cannot imagine that there is anything of real value in the theme that cannot be developed in two lectures.'[8]

In a spirit of humbug and suspicion, similar to that which Russell was to encounter among the American academic hierarchy many years later, Thomas Craig, editor of the *American Journal of Economics*, advised Gilman against employing Russell. Craig questioned whether there were 'a dozen mathematicians outside of Cambridge' who knew of Russell, and was of the opinion that 'the strong endorsements that he has received are due to the fact that his friends want to find him a position.' The course of lectures that Russell proposed was dismissed by Craig as 'a sort of dilettante affair at best'. Craig indicated his preference for employing young Americans instead.[9] However, family ties proved sufficient, and Gilman chose to ignore these objections. Russell was duly invited to lecture at Johns Hopkins as well as at Bryn Mawr.

The Russells arrived in America early in October 1896, for a visit which was to last three months, and the first thing they did was to pay homage to Walt Whitman, whom they both greatly admired, by visiting his house in Camden, New Jersey. Whitman, who died in 1893, had thought very highly of Alys: 'She is the handsomest, healthiest best balanced young woman in the world known to me,' he commented in a letter to a friend.

Before travelling on to Bryn Mawr, Russell had a unique opportunity to experience small-town America at the turn of the century, when he and Alys visited a cousin of hers who lived in Millville, New Jersey. The cousin's wife always carried a revolver, and used to take Russell on 'long drives over dirt tracks in a buggy.' The town had 10,002 inhabitants, and the couple 'used to say that they were the two.'[10]

The month of November was spent at Bryn Mawr as guests of Carey Thomas, the college's president, whom Russell later remembered as 'a lady who was treated almost with awe by all the family. She had immense energy, a belief in culture which she carried out with a businessman's efficiency, and a profound contempt for the male sex. . . . I was never able myself, however, to take her quite seriously, because she was so easily shocked. . . . However, at Bryn Mawr she was Zeus, and everybody trembled before her.'[11]

At Bryn Mawr Russell delivered his lectures on non-Euclidean geometry, which proved very successful. Alys lectured on temperance and women's suffrage and gave private talks in favour of free love. According to Russell 'this caused a scandal and we were practically hounded out of the college.'[12] Nevertheless, their time at Bryn Mawr was on the whole happy, and Russell compared the college favourably with Girton and Newnham.

Russell's lectures were not confined to mathematics. He took the opportunity to air his views on socialism and delivered a discourse on 'Socialism as the Consummation of Human Liberty'.[13] It is not well known that social problems featured strongly in Russell's life at that time. It is widely assumed that until the First World War he was almost wholly occupied with mathematical philosophy. Yet, his two expeditions to Germany with Alys in 1895 had been in order to study the German Social Democratic movement, and his first book was on that subject.[14] It appears that his latterday political passions were being shaped at this early period.

While the Russell's were at Bryn Mawr, the McKinley–Bryan presidential election was in progress. Russell's letters to friends and family in England reveal a lively and critical insight into the machinations of the American political system, as well as an intense interest in America and its people. He wrote to Graham Wallas, the Fabian socialist, on 13 November 1896:[15]

'I have been meaning to write to you ever since the presidential election, on account of a specimen ballot paper which I am sending you by book-post. This document, I am told, is more complicated than in any other State: certainly it is a triumph. It seems to me to contain within it the whole eighteenth-century theory of the free and intelligent demos, and the whole nineteenth-century practice of bossism. Imagine using such a phrase as "straight ticket" on a ballot-paper, and imagine the stupendous intellect of a man who votes anything else on such a ballot-paper! I have never seen a document more replete with theory of politics, or illustrating more neatly the short road from bad metaphysics to political corruption. The whole interest, in Philadelphia, centred about the election of the sheriff: Crow, the independent Republican, was making a stand against bossism, and strange to say, he got in, tho' by a very narrow majority.

'I am sending you also some rather transparent boss's devices for allowing fictitious voters to vote. You will see that the vouchers I enclose enable a man to vote without being on the register. I was taken to a polling-booth in Philadelphia, and there stood, just outside, a sub-deputy boss, named Flanagan, instructing the ignorant how to vote, illegally watching them mark their ballot-paper, and when necessary vouching for the right to vote. A Republican and a Democrat sat inside to see that all was fair, it being supposed they would counteract each other: as a matter of fact they make a deal, and agree to keep up their common friends, the bosses, even if they have to admit fraudulent votes for the opposite party. Americans seem too fatalistic and pessimistic to do much against them: I was taken by a man appointed as official watcher for the Prohibitionists, but tho' he observed and pointed out the irregularities, he merely shrugged his shoulders when I asked why he did not interfere and make a row. The fact is, Americans are unspeakably lazy about everything but their business: to cover their laziness, they invent a pessimism, and say things can't be improved: tho' when I confront them, and ask for any single reform movement which has not succeeded, they are stumped, except one who mentioned the Consular service—naturally not a very soul-stirring cry. One of them, who prides himself on his virtue, frankly told me he found he could make more money in business than he could save in rates by fighting corruption—it never seemed to enter his head that one might think that a rather lame excuse. However, everything seems to be improving very fast, tho' nothing makes the lazy hypocritical Puritans so furious as to say so. They take a sort of pride in being the most corrupt place in the Union: everywhere you go they brag of the peculiar hopelessness of their own locality. The fall of Altgeld[16] and the defeat of Tammany seem to irritate them: it might so easily have been otherwise, they say, and will be otherwise next election. Altogether I don't see that they deserve better than they get. The Quakers and Puritans, so far as I have come across them, are the greatest liars and hypocrites I have ever seen and are as a rule totally destitute of vigour. Here's a Philadelphia story. Wanamaker is the local Whitely,[17] enormously rich and religious. The protective tariff is dear to his soul. In the election of 1888, when New York was the critical State, it was telegraphed to the Phila. Republican Committee that 80,000 dollars would win the election. Wanamaker planked down the sum, New York State was won by a majority of 500, and Wanamaker became Postmaster General. Here's a New York tale. Jay Gould[18] in 1884 offered a huge sum to the Republicans. This became known to the Democrats, who next day had a procession of several hours past his house, shouting as they marched: "Blood! Blood! Jay Gould's Blood!" He turned pale, and telegraphed any sum desired to the Democrats. Cleveland was elected.—However, individual Americans are delightful: but whether from lack of courage or from decentralisation, they do not form a society of frank people, and all in turn complain that they would be universally cut if they ever spoke their minds. I think this is largely due to the absence of a capital. A similar cause I think accounts for the religiosity and timidity of the universities. Professor Ely was dismissed from Johns Hopkins for being Xtian Socialist!—There are possibilities tho': everybody is far more anxious to be educated than in England, the level of intelligence is high, and thoughtful people admit—though only within the last few years, I am told, apparently since Bryce—that their form of government is not perfect. I think you will have, as we have, a very good time here. We probably sail 30 December, and strongly urge you to arrive before then. We shall be in New York, and want very much to see you, as also to introduce you to several nice people who will be there. If you have not yet written about the date of your arrival, please write soon.—The College is a fine place, immeasurably superior to Girton and Newnham; the Professor of Pol. Econ. oddly enough is a socialist and a Free Silver Man, and has carried all his class with him, tho' many of them are rich New Yorkers. Those I have met are intelligent and generous in their views of social questions.'

Russell wrote to his Uncle Rollo on 20 November 1896, giving his views of the election and news of his stay at Bryn Mawr:[19]

'I should have written to you before about America and all the people and things that have interested me here, but I have been so occupied, what with my lectures, and with perpetually meeting new people and seeing new places, that I have scarcely had a moment to spare. The country is full of interest, and it was especially fortunate to be here at the time of such an exciting presidential election. Almost every one met was in favour of McKinley, but oddly enough, the one Bryanite I have met is

23

the Prof. of Political Economy at this College, a very intelligent man, who persuaded me there must be more in Bryan's point of view than most people would allow one to believe. However, tho' he was the poor man's candidate, and should have represented radicalism, his whole attitude did seem rather foolish and pernicious.—This college is a very nice place: it seems to me much better than Girton and Newnham, especially in the greater freedom it allows to the girls. Also those girls that I have met seem to have more independence of mind, more spirit and more originality, than most of the girls at Cambridge.—I give my last lecture today: I have had an extraordinary number of people at them—about thirty, I think—many of them teachers and professors, from this and neighbouring colleges. Tomorrow I am giving a lecture which I have called "Socialism as the Consummation of Individual Liberty"—I doubt whether I shall convert anybody, as Americans seem very much more opposed to socialism than English people.—Alys too has been busy: the other day she gave an excellent speech on temperance, urging the importance of study and of indirect and less obvious methods of dealing with drunkenness. Next week she is giving a lecture on the history of the movement for women's suffrage in England and Germany. After that we go to Baltimore, for me to repeat my lectures at the Johns Hopkins. Then we shall go to Boston, which I look forward to very much, as it seems to be the most interesting place in America. On the whole tho' I have met many Americans who are as nice as any English people, I think this would be a depressing country to live in, if only on account of the politics. For tho' politics seem to be improving, there is still an immense deal to be done, as the best people still hold too much aloof from them. . . .'

Soon after leaving Bryn Mawr, Alys, whose talks on Free Love had caused a minor controversy at the college, wrote to Carey Thomas on 26 November 1896:[20]

'It is quite impossible to impress in any way how grateful we feel to thee for all thy kindness, but we really have appreciated it. It was a perfectly delightful month, and we both enjoyed ourselves *immensely*, and found it exceedingly profitable as well. Bertie feels that thee and all the academic people were most kind, and he was delighted to have such a splendid opportunity of lecturing and to such a splendid audience. He enjoyed all the social things, too, for the first time in his life.

'I feel as if I must thank thee for myself for allowing me to speak to the students on Monday. I do most sincerely hope that it will not get thee into trouble with the trustees, because thee certainly did not know how I was going to put the thing. I shall never again have such an intelligent audience.

'We are getting on very well here, but it does not compare to Bryn Mawr! With love from us both. . . .'

In her biography of Carey Thomas, Edith Finch wrote of the Russells' visit to Bryn Mawr:[21]

'With their markedly unconventional statements, radical theories, and probing questions, they set the college, and in particular the trustees, by the ears. However right she [Carey Thomas] thought them—and their flaming indiscretions seem tame old saws now—and however much she approved the mental ferment they engendered, she was sorely put to it to explain and justify.'

Russell wrote to Carey Thomas, in appreciation of her hospitality, on 1 December 1896:[22]

'. . . I should like . . . to thank you most warmly for all your kindness while we were with you, both in private and in regard to my lectures. If the Johns Hopkins people are a quarter so kind, I shall have a very pleasant stay there. I enjoyed immensely seeing all the people at the college, and it was most interesting to get some knowledge of the workings of such an institution. . . .'

Before leaving for Baltimore the Russells visited Alys's rich maiden-aunt in Philadelphia and dined with her on Thanksgiving Day. Russell recalled her as 'a very greedy old lady', who 'had supplied a feast which required a gargantuan stomach', and, 'just as we were about to eat the first mouthful, she said: "Let us pause and think of the poor." Apparently she found this thought an appetizer.'[23] Russell found her to be fairly typical of Philadelphia Quakers whose old families he described as having 'all the effeteness of a small aristocracy. Old misers of 90 would sit brooding over their hoard while their children of 60 or 70 waited for their death with what patience they could command. Various forms of mental disorder appeared common. Those who must be accounted sane were apt to be very stupid.'[24]

The Baltimore branch of the family was more to Russell's liking. While at Johns Hopkins, Russell and Alys were the guests of her uncle, Dr James Thomas, whose family Russell found interesting:[25]

'There was a son at Johns Hopkins who was very brilliant in brain surgery; there was a daughter, Helen, at Bryn Mawr, who had the misfortune to be deaf. She was gentle and kind, and had very lovely red hair. I was very fond of her for a number of years, culminating in 1900. Once or twice I asked her to kiss me, but she refused. . . . There was another daughter who had remained a pious and very orthodox Quaker. She always alluded to those who were not Quakers as "the world's people."

They all of them used "thee" in conversation, and so did Alys and I when we talked to each other.'

From Baltimore the Russells went to Boston and on to Harvard, where they stayed with William James, the eminent philosopher. They spent their last days in New York before leaving for England. Looking back on his first experience of America, Russell wrote:[26]

'America in those days was a curiously innocent country. Numbers of men asked me to explain what it was that Oscar Wilde had done. In Boston we stayed in a boarding-house kept by two old Quaker ladies, and one of them at breakfast said to me in a loud voice across the table: "Oscar Wilde has not been much before the public lately. What has he been doing?" "He is in prison", I replied. Fortunately on this occasion I was not asked what he had done. I viewed America in those days with the conceited superiority of the insular Briton. Nevertheless, contact with academic Americans, especially mathematicians, led me to realise the superiority of Germany to England in almost all academic matters. Against my will, in the course of my travels, the belief that everything worth knowing was known at Cambridge gradually wore off. In this respect my travels were very useful to me.'

NOTES

[1] From 'Can Americans and Britons be Friends?' (see below, pp. 328–37).

[2] B. Russell, *Autobiography* (London, 1967,) Vol. I, pp. 75–6 (Boston, 1967), pp. 103–4.

[3] Ibid.

[4] Ibid.

[5] Ibid., p. 82; p. 113.

[6] First published in William M. Armstrong, 'Bertrand Russell Comes to America, 1896', *Studies in History and Society*, II (1970), Nos 1 and 2, p. 30.

[7] Ibid., pp. 30–2; the testimonials were from: H. Montagu Butler, Master of Trinity College; James Ward, the Kantian philosopher; Henry Sidgwick, Knightsbridge Professor of Moral Philosophy in Cambridge.

[8] Ibid., p. 34.

[9] Ibid., pp. 34–5.

[10] B. Russell, *Autobiography*, Vol. I, p. 130; pp. 192–3.

[11] Ibid., p. 131; pp. 193–4.

[12] Ibid., p. 132; p. 195.

[13] As far as has been ascertained, no written version of this lecture is extant; it is referred to, however, in Russell's letter to his Uncle Rollo Russell (see below, pp. 23–4).

14 B. Russell, *German Social Democracy* (Longmans, Green, London and New York, 1896); Alys contributed an appendix on 'Social Democracy and the Woman Question in Germany'.

15 B. Russell, *Autobiography*, Vol. I, pp. 139–41; pp. 206–9.

16 John P. Altgeld, governor of Illinois and a supporter of Bryan.

17 John Wanamaker, who, like William Whitely in England, developed department stores in America.

18 Prominent financier.

19 This letter was made available to The Bertrand Russell Estate by Mrs Margaret Lloyd, Rollo Russell's daughter.

20 This letter was made available to The Bertrand Russell Estate by Bryn Mawr College.

21 Edith Finch, *Carey Thomas of Bryn Mawr* (Harper, New York, 1947), p. 194.

22 This letter was made available to The Bertrand Russell Estate by Bryn Mawr College.

23 B. Russell, *Autobiography*, Vol. I, p. 133; p. 196.

24 Ibid.

25 Ibid., p. 132; p. 196.

26 Ibid., p. 133; pp. 196–7.

CHAPTER 2

LUCY DONNELLY OF BRYN MAWR

Eighteen years were to pass before Russell's second trip to the U.S.A. They were eventful years, dominated by intensive work on *Principia Mathematica*—which was to revolutionise thinking in its field—and his first political campaigns.

On his return to England early in 1897, Russell had his *Foundations of Geometry* published, which was based on his Cambridge dissertation and his lectures at Bryn Mawr and Johns Hopkins. In 1900 he published *The Philosophy of Leibniz*, and in 1903, after several years' work, he completed *The Principles of Mathematics*. In a short interlude before becoming totally absorbed in *Principia Mathematica*, he renewed his contact with two young women he had befriended while at Bryn Mawr when they were preparing themselves to teach English literature at the college. The one was Dr James Thomas's daughter Helen, for whom Russell had expressed a romantic interest, and the other was Lucy Donnelly, whom Russell observed as having a 'passionate friendship' with Helen; 'at least on Lucy's part it was passionate'. When Helen married and moved to New York, Lucy was plunged into despair from which Russell 'tried to rescue her by offering the consolations of philosophy'.[1] A warm friendship developed between them, marked by a frequent correspondence which they were to maintain until Lucy's death almost fifty years later.

His correspondence with her kept Russell in touch with the developments in America that interested him. Extracts from his early letters to Lucy offer some fascinating comments on and references to America.[2]

Russell to Lucy Donnelly 6 July 1902
'Many thanks . . . for the excellent account of Harvard and Barrett Wendell. What an astonishing thing that a University should teach journalism! I thought that was only done at Oxford. . . . I suppose Wendell is better than his books: I was disappointed in his American literature. For, though I agree with him that America, like the Australian marsupials, is an interesting relic of a bygone age, I care little for the great truth that American writers have all been of good family, and that

Harvard is vastly superior to Yale. And his failure to appreciate Walt Whitman to my mind is very damaging. He talks of "Brooklyn Ferry" and so on, and quite forgets "Out of the Cradle Endlessly Rocking", and "When Lilacs Last in the Dooryard Bloom'd". This seems to me to show a deplorable conventionality, both in taste generally, and in judgement of Whitman specially. . . . The Past is an awful God, tho' he gives Life almost the whole of its haunting beauty. I believe those whose childhood has been spent in America can scarcely conceive the hold which the Past has on us of the Old World: the continuity of Life, the weight of tradition, the great eternal procession of youth and age and death, seem to be lost in the bustling approach of the future which dominates American life. And that is one reason why great literature is not produced by your compatriots.'

Russell to Lucy Donnelly 1 September 1902
'Real life means a life in some kind of intimate relation to other human beings. . . . It seems to me that your difficulty comes from the fact that there are no real people to speak of in your world. The young are never real, the unmarried very seldom. Also, if I may say so, the scale of emotion in America seems to me more frivolous, more superficial, more pusillanimous, than in Europe; there is a triviality of feeling which makes real people very rare. I find, in England, that most women of 50 and upwards, have gone through the experience of many years' voluntary endurance of torture, which has given a depth and richness to their natures that your easy-going, pleasure-loving women cannot imagine.'

Russell to Lucy Donnelly 29 July 1903
'Seeing Grace [Carey Thomas's sister] just before her departure, the other day, seemed to bring America nearer. Usually, when I write to you or Helen, I feel almost as if I were writing to dead people whom I have read about in books—the whole place seems so remote, so plunged in memories of an utterly different person who occupied my body seven years ago, that I can hardly believe it to be real or inhabited by real people. . . . We are all wildly excited about Free Trade; it is to me the last piece of sane internationalism left, and if it went I should feel inclined to cut my throat.'

Russell's commitment to social causes had added a further dimension to his reputation. Between 1903 and 1904 he campaigned for Free Trade (in opposition to official government policy), made his first public political speeches, and wrote articles on the subject. His activity was not going unnoticed in America and one of the first of many letters he was to receive from the American public in the course of his life came from a Mr A. Nyckoff of New Jersey who inquired in October 1904:

'The . . . purpose of this note is to ask how I may secure what you have written and published on the Free Trade controversy during the past year or two. . . . And I shall be grateful, too, for any suggestions of other publications in that connection that seem to you important. Some of us over here are beginning to prepare for an active Free Trade campaign, and I should like to make sure of getting hold of the best that has been called out by the present campaign in England.'

Championing a cause espoused by his parents, Russell fought an election on behalf of the women suffragists in 1907. Alys, who had long been in the forefront of feminist causes, assisted him in a bitter campaign. 'When, in later years, I campaigned against the First World War', Russell recalled, 'the popular opposition I encountered was not comparable to that which the suffragists met in 1907.'[3]

An indication of the interest he was arousing in America was the press coverage he received. The *New York American* of 3 June 1907, commented on the election campaign but gave little indication of the ferocity of Russell's opponents. Revelling in the vision of a home-grown girl standing up to the English establishment the report was headlined:

'American Girl Spoils a Walkover for Parliament. Hon. Bertrand Russell's Wife Gets Woman Suffragists to Aid Her Husband.'

The report was datelined London, 2 May, and continued:

'Determined that Honorable Bertrand Russell, whose wife was Miss Alys Smith, the daughter of Robert Pearsall Smith, the Philadelphia millionaire, shall be elected to the House of Commons from Wimbledon, an army of women suffragists has been mobilised to defeat Henry Chaplin, a bitter enemy of the suffragist movement. . . . Chaplin thought he could gain the office without any difficulty. He reckoned without the woman suffragists. Today these women announced their intention of beating Chaplin and seating Russell, who is the brother and heir-presumptive of Earl Russell. There is a belief that Russell will win, as his American wife, so long identified with the fight for "woman's rights", is at the head of the crusade, and her word practically has become law among the devotees of the cause. Her practical, effective work among the poor of London has won her thousands of friends, who believe in her ideas concerning the emancipation of woman. She once donned the garb of a working girl and labored in factories, studying conditions. As a result she wrote many brilliant essays on the conditions existing among workers, and greatly aided in numerous reforms. With the aid of the future Countess, it is said there is little doubt of her husband's success in the battle with the veteran anti-suffragist, Chaplin.'

Despite Alys and the optimism of the *New York American*'s correspondent, Russell was defeated. He returned to his work on *Principia* but not before he had written to Lucy Donnelly giving an account of his electoral bid. Lucy wrote back on 18 June 1907, describing the effect of his campaign on America:

'Thank you for writing me in detail about Wimbledon. . . . More and more I care supremely about "the cause", and about the bettering and broadening of women's lives—though I do all too little myself in our behalf. Your generous example has roused a number of us here to the wrong we are doing through our inertia, and will, I sincerely think, make us better workers in future. Our American problem is of course very different from your English one, and immensely much more difficult, both because we have made so much less headway at the present time and because the whole question of the franchise at large becomes here yearly more complicated. Everyone's cry is: "Don't say anything about women, until we have solved the problem for men." My own part in it all is of course with my undergraduates. And they, young as they are, are in the rank and file discouraging. Their minds already at 17 seem closed, or so prejudiced, that after a long and interesting and lucid argument or a very moving speech they will answer with tales of the dowdiness and unattractiveness (forgive the Americanism: it is both mine and my students), the lack of charm of "women's rights women" or the unsuitability of election-booths for ladies and so on. They are as little affected by eloquence or proof and as irrelevant and personal in their remarks as those women at that extraordinary meeting in some London suburb to which I went with you years back.

'One must have patience I suppose. In truth I am passing through a period of discouragement over the American girl—a mood that Mr Creswell, who has the best girls' school in New York, confirmed when I lunched beside him at Commencement.

'The girls of today are hopelessly conventional and immensely much more in the hands of their parents, in the grip of the parental point of view than they were ten or twenty years back. I long for the old revolting daughters. Extreme though that may have been too. No one revolts now whether she should or not, she "comes out" or she "goes to college" as her Mama wills: she gives you her father's physical force argument against the suffrage with just his finality and is perplexed when you disagree with him. How can a well brought up child question her father's decision. Year by year my difficulties in dealing with Desdemona and Cordelia grow greater and more laughable. But the older women who live about me are worse. Their point of view is fairly Turkish. What else can one call it? Sometimes I wonder is it the exaggeration natural to women who have been too long cloistered—ugly thought this be; then

I remember Kate Kinsella and am something reassured about ourselves in especial if not about women in general. I beg you send me some sane advice and if you can some good cheer.'

Principia Mathematica was published in three volumes between 1910 and 1913, after ten years' work and collaboration with A. N. Whitehead. International acclaim followed and Russell's reputation was assured. In the U.S.A., in particular, his efforts to give a scientific basis to mathematics won him an admiring following among the young philosophers who were active in the 'neo-realist' school, struggling against the tradition-bound, European style of philosophy. As early as 1905 Lucy Donnelly had informed him of Marion Reilly, a follower of his and a lecturer in philosophy at Bryn Mawr. Russell responded on 10 November:

'I am interested to hear that I have a disciple at Bryn Mawr. Two young men, Huntington at Harvard and Veblen at Princeton, have written works in which they make pleasing references to me. The latter, at least, is brilliantly able.'

In 1910 Russell became a lecturer in the Principles of Mathematics at Trinity College, Cambridge. The following year he and Alys separated; their marriage had proved unsatisfactory since 1901—when he found he no longer loved her—although they were only to be divorced in 1921. It was about this time that he began to receive many letters from American academics exhorting him to lecture at their colleges. Russell was no longer an unknown entity but a scholar of considerable repute, and in great demand. Harvard was extremely keen to obtain Russell, and Professor Ralph Barton Perry, Chairman of the Philosophy Department, and one of the founders of the 'neo-realist' school, wrote to him on 17 May 1911. Perry inquired whether Russell would be prepared to spend a year at Harvard giving 'what lectures you saw fit' both in the philosophy of mathematics and a more popular course. Perry informed Russell that on President Lowell's authorisation he would also be invited to give the Lowell Institute Lectures in Boston. He went on to add:

'I need not say that I most eagerly hope that you will come. I have not forgotten that you once told me that you were not wholly disinclined to a year in America. And since then you have become one of our great men! There is a considerable body of graduate students here each year with an interest in your special field—and to all of our students you have come to be one of the leaders in a new movement of thought. The younger men on this side of the Atlantic are everywhere inclining to realism—and you are one of its most august prophets.'

This was followed by a personal approach from George Santayana of

Harvard who was a close friend of Russell's elder brother, Frank, and who once informed Russell that: 'People are not intelligent. It is very unreasonable to expect them to be so, and that is a fate my philosophy reconciled me to long ago. How else could I have lived for forty years in America?'[4] Santayana, who was visiting England, wrote to Russell on 8 February 1912, encouraging him to accept the Harvard offer:[5]

'. . . . there is no one whom the younger school of philosophers in America are more eager to learn of than of you. You would bring new standards of precision and independence of thought which would open their eyes, and probably have the greatest influence on the rising genera-tion of professional philosophers in that country.'

Russell accepted the invitation from Harvard and it was decided that the spring of 1914 would be an appropriate time to lecture there. The news of his Harvard post travelled fast and he was plied with invitations to lecture at a host of clubs, colleges and universities, prominent amongst which were the universities of Columbia, Chicago, Wisconsin, Michigan, Johns Hopkins and Smith College. When he had accepted the Harvard position, he wrote to Lucy on 19 December 1912, giving her the news:

'I have accepted an invitation to go to Harvard in the spring of 1914. . . . My time will not be so taken up as to make it impossible to see you—particularly if you are ever able to get away to New York. I dare say I may lecture at Columbia some times. Will Carey admit me within the sacred portals of Bryn Mawr, or am I too wicked? . . . I find myself full of ideas and projects and vast schemes of work—whether I shall have energy to carry them out remains to be seen. I feel as if I had just discovered what philosophy is and how it ought to be studied. I look forward to setting forth my ideas when I come to America.'

The prestige which Russell enjoyed among America's foremost philo-sophers was indicated by Josiah Royce of Harvard, whom Russell had first met in 1896 while staying with William James. Royce, on a visit to England, had arranged a meeting with Russell, and wrote to him on 2 February 1913: 'It will be a satisfaction to talk over your coming Harvard work with you. I need not say that we are all expecting a great many good times as a part and as a result of your visit to America.'

Whereas on his previous visit it was family connections that had secured his invitations to lecture at Bryn Mawr and Johns Hopkins, on the occasion of his second visit Russell was not too sure whether he would be welcome at Bryn Mawr, since Carey Thomas, out of loyalty to her cousin Alys, was prejudiced against him. Lucy was delighted at the prospect of Russell's visit, and in spite of Carey Thomas's reluctance to extend an invitation, she was determined to bring Russell to Bryn Mawr and assured him that 'we shall do all in our power for the sake of the college to arrange it.' Russell was undeterred by Carey Thomas's attitude, which he felt was unnecessary and not 'what Alys would desire'. He wished to see Lucy and renew his association with Bryn Mawr. On 18 April 1913, he wrote to Lucy:

'Certainly I will come to Bryn Mawr, even if Carey does not ask me officially. . . . I am much excited by your Tariff Question. Wilson looks splendid from here; how does he look to you? Is Carey ashamed of having given him the sack?[6] Is she going to invite him to Commencement? . . .

'I shall be at Harvard, March, April and May. I am to give six lectures a week and eight lectures altogether for the Lowell Institute. . . . Most of my spare time from now till then will be taken up preparing my lectures, as they will be quite unlike my lectures here, and I want them to contain new thought. I am very happy and very fit—full of energy and joy of life—with every cause for contentment, inward and outward. It is wonderful how much one can live through and come up smiling.'

Although Russell was happy about his Lowell appointment, he experienced some difficulty in preparing the lectures: 'I announced the subject of my Lowell lectures, but could not think of anything to say. I used to sit in the parlour of the "Beetle and Wedge" at Moulsford, wondering what there was to say about our knowledge of the external world. . . .'[7] Part of Russell's problem might have been due to certain restrictions imposed by President Lowell, who wrote to him on 6 June 1913:

'Owing to a provision of the will of the founder of the Lowell Institute, I should prefer that you take some subject not so distinctly religious; for he did not want any disbelief expressed in the Divine origin of the Old and New Testament, and although we cannot carry out his intention in just the way he expressed it, I try not to run counter to his wishes any more than I can help. Could you not take some subject of a more scientific character and less bordering on religion? For Harvard, you will say what you think best in your chair, but the Lowell Institute is somewhat limited by the intent of the founder, as expressed in his will.'

Lucy, in a letter of 22 June 1913, continued to inform Russell of America's mounting interest in his visit and of the atmosphere of expectation at her college:

'Bryn Mawr people are immensely looking forward to your coming. I was amused the other day by one of our scholars in philosophy who wanted to borrow my Jowett's *Plato* for the summer and, when I asked her why she felt it necessary to "read *Plato* all through" in the next months, replied, "because Mr Russell is coming". Of course I lent my *Plato* all the more gladly and was not surprised to hear the week following in New York, at the other extreme, that the Rockefellers want to meet you. . . .

'So many people will be claiming your attention everywhere I do not expect to see a great deal of you myself, but I count on your visit to Bryn Mawr and on perhaps an occasional meeting in New York. And it will be a great thing just to have you on this side of the Atlantic. I am delighted to hear that you are to give the Lowell lectures and I dare say by this time you have added Princeton to your list, as I heard there in May they were hoping to get you to speak to them.

'. . . A week ago I travelled West over the Great Lakes with Edith Hamilton—all to see America I don't know [sic] of vague expanses of land and water and low lying islands, an America so bright and clear-aired it blinds my eyes to look at it. The streets of its towns are untidy, its clerks all in their shirtsleeves, its manners are utterly casual and democratic, the servants even are "pleased to meet you". Here in Mackinac the Chicago pork packers and politicians live in "a Millionaire Row" of wooden palaces painted strawberry pink and lemon yellow, set side by side within talking distance with great flower beds, gaudier than the houses themselves, in front of them instead of gardens. I find myself bristling with Eastern prejudices, though I make a struggle to cure my provincialism.'

Russell replied on 3 July 1913:

'I am interested always, and a little surprised, by what you say of my reputation in America. The funny thing is that none of the philosophers take the trouble to find out my opinions, even on the points I have most emphasised. That is just the same here. . . . I am terribly hard up, and am looking to America to re-establish my finances. I shall therefore be glad to undertake anything *paid* that is compatible with my duties at Harvard. I imagine Carey won't want me officially at Bryn Mawr. I suppose, tho', she won't object to my paying you a friendly visit? It would interest me very greatly to meet the Rockefellers. Nothing is arranged yet about Princeton.

'. . . . It is interesting that you have taken to exploring America, and that you are full of Eastern prejudices. Democracy is a fine thing, but not for those who would otherwise be at the top.'

The year's end found Russell holidaying in Italy. He was still undecided as to the content of his Lowell lectures. On his return to Cambridge, on New Year's Day 1914, with scarcely two months in hand, he

35

'arranged for a shorthand typist to come next day, though I had not the vaguest idea what I should say to her when she came. As she entered the room my ideas fell into place, and I dictated in a completely orderly sequence from that moment until the work was finished.'[8] Russell, still rather shy as a speechmaker, tried out the subject matter of his Lowell lectures on his own Cambridge students. The lectures were received with enthusiasm, and from that moment on his future audiences would never come to suspect his earlier diffidence.

As the time for his departure drew near he informed Lucy of his plans to sail and inquired: 'Will America be shocked if I come second class? I am so hard up that I should be glad of the saving.'[9] On 20 February 1914, he wrote Lucy his last letter before sailing:

'I sail 7 March on the *Mauretania*, so I suppose I shall land in New York quite early Friday 13th (doubly unlucky date!) and go to Boston by the 1 o'clock train. I must get to Boston that night, as I lecture at Harvard on Saturday 14th. My address will be Colonial Club, Cambridge, Mass. . . . I shall be very much occupied while I am in America—I know a good many week-ends I shall have engagements—so we must fix up things as soon after I land as possible. . . . At Xmas I went to Rome. . . . Since then I have done an unspeakable amount of new work—my brain has been wonderfully fit. I shall pour it all out on America. I am reading a paper to a philosophical club in New York of which poor Micher (whom I remember from Bryn Mawr days) is secretary—I wrote it in the first days of the year just after returning from Rome. It is 11,000 words and took me three days—don't tell them, or they will think it worthless, whereas it is one of the best things I ever did! I am giving a course of lectures here on "our knowledge of the external world", at which I have a great crowd, as they are semi-popular. I found they were taking every word I spoke as gospel, so I solemnly besought them not to believe anything I said, as I felt sure it was all wrong. So then they believed that too. . . .'

Shortly before his departure Russell received a letter from his 'disciple' Marion Reilly, which confirmed that Carey Thomas had persisted to the end in her 'prejudices' and that he would have to visit Bryn Mawr informally:[10]

'I am just realising that March is approaching very rapidly and that you will soon be on your way to America. . . . My mother and I live in a small house on the college campus and it will be a great pleasure if you will stay with us for at least a few days. . . . I am so sorry that it is not going to be possible for you to speak at Bryn Mawr. I should like, however, to have the privilege of presenting some of our faculty to you. . . .

If I can be of any service to you while you are in America I hope that you will let me know.'

Lucy Donnelly persisted in her efforts to gain some formal recognition for Russell's anticipated visit to Bryn Mawr, although the following letter to Carey Thomas did not succeed in its objective:[11]

'As Bertie Russell is arriving shortly, I thought I should like to tell you that I am asking him to come to Bryn Mawr for a week-end in April or May, as best suits his engagements. If I understand Miss Reilly right, you do not wish him to meet any of the students, and I will of course observe your directions in the matter very exactly.

'I want, however, to ask if you would not approve his speaking perfectly formally in the philosophical seminary to the graduate students in philosophy? I ask because I know that the students have been working on his books and articles and would be greatly interested and stimulated by a lecture from him, and because I feel sure so small and academic a meeting could give rise to no publicity or gossip of any kind. I think Bertie would be willing to speak there informally, if I told him we would like to have him, but of course he is too full of engagements to be in any way eager for an extra lecture and above all would not wish to speak unless it is desired by you that he should do so.

'My personal interest in the matter is, only, the good of the graduate school. I do not like to have Bryn Mawr students miss what students in other colleges are getting and prizing, and I think that we have had here this year unusually few speakers of real intellectual eminence.

'If you thought better of a meeting of the philosophical school elsewhere than in the Library, doubtless Miss Reilly would lend her big room, or my own study might be large enough for so small a group of persons, but I should suppose the philosophical seminary would be the best place and would impose just the right degree of formality desirable.'

Although Russell's second visit to America was occasioned by his Harvard appointment, every spare moment was taken up with engagements to lecture at other colleges. This was in marked contrast to his first visit when family ties had enabled him to secure the only two invitations he had. Paradoxically, it was those same ties that now created difficulties at Bryn Mawr. Had it not been for his close friendship with Lucy Donnelly, and her and her colleagues' determination to provide private facilities for his lecture, Russell would probably not have undertaken to revisit the college.

NOTES

[1] From Russell's holograph note which he attached to his collection of correspondence with Lucy Donnelly and Helen Flexner (née Thomas).

[2] For the letters in full, see B. Russell, *Autobiography* (London, 1967), Vol. I, pp. 164–7, 170 (Boston, 1967), pp. 248–52, 257–8.

[3] Ibid., p. 153; p. 231.

[4] From Santayana's letter of December 1917, in B. Russell, *Autobiography* (London, 1968), Vol. II, p. 51 (Boston, 1968), p. 57.

[5] Ibid., p. 50; p. 55.

[6] Woodrow Wilson; associate professor at Bryn Mawr 1884–7. See Edith Finch, *Carey Thomas of Bryn Mawr* (Harper, New York, 1947), for an account of Wilson's resignation from Bryn Mawr.

[7] B. Russell, *Autobiography*, Vol. I, p. 210; pp. 324–5.

[8] Ibid.

[9] From Russell's letter of 14 November 1913.

[10] Undated, February 1914.

[11] 8 March 1914; this letter was made available to The Bertrand Russell Estate by Bryn Mawr College.

CHAPTER 3

THE HARVARD TERM, 1914

The *Mauretania* docked in New York on the morning of 13 March 1914. In contrast to the young stranger who arrived in 1896, Russell was now 42, and famous. Noting his arrival *The New York Times* of 14 March referred to him as 'one of the foremost lecturers on philosophy'. On disembarkation, he was welcomed by Lucy Donnelly and Helen Flexner (née Thomas), and he spent a few hours in their company, arranging with Lucy his visit to Bryn Mawr for the following month, before taking a train to Boston. Harvard was famous throughout the Western world for its philosophy faculty, but Russell, as he later wrote, was not over-impressed with its professors who had recently been deprived of their three most able colleagues:[1]

'At Harvard I met all the professors. I am proud to say that I took a violent dislike to Professor Lowell [the President of Harvard], who sub-sequently assisted in the murder of Sacco and Vanzetti. I had at that time no reason to dislike him, but the feeling was just as strong as it was in later years, when his qualities as a saviour of society had been mani-fested. Every professor to whom I was introduced in Harvard made me the following speech: "Our philosophical faculty, Dr Russell, as doubt-less you are aware, has lately suffered three great losses. We have lost our esteemed colleague, Professor William James, through his lamented death; Professor Santayana, for reasons which doubtless appear to him to be sufficient, has taken up his residence in Europe; last *but* not least, Professor Royce, who, I am happy to say, is still with us, has had a stroke." This speech was delivered slowly, seriously, and pompously. The time came when I felt that I must do something about it. So the next time that I was introduced to a professor, I rattled off the speech myself at top speed. This device, however, proved worthless. "Yes, Dr Russell", the professor replied: "As you very justly observe, our philo-sophical faculty . . ." and so the speech went on to its inexorable conclusion. I do not know whether this is a fact about professors or a fact about Americans. I think, however, that it is the former. I noticed another fact about Harvard professors: that when I dined with them, they would always tell me the way home, although I had had to find their house without this assistance. There were limitations to Harvard culture. Schofield, the Professor of Fine Arts, considered Alfred Noyes a very good poet.'

Russell was more in sympathy with Harvard students, and commented: 'Anyone who has attempted to present a new philosophy to Oxford and the Sorbonne and the universities of America, will have been struck by the greater readiness of the Americans to think along unfamiliar lines.'[2] His lectures were highly successful and because he felt that 'really advanced teaching of clever people is best done in personal talk', he extended his classes into weekly discussions over tea at his residence. Of the students who attended, two particularly impressed him and one of them was T. S. Eliot. According to Russell:[3]

'I did not know at that time that Eliot wrote poetry. He had, I think, already written "A Portrait of a Lady" and "Prufrock", but he did not see fit to mention the fact. He was extraordinarily silent, and only once made a remark which struck me. I was praising Heraclitus, and he observed: "Yes, he always reminds me of Villon." I thought this remark so good that I always wished he would make another.'

The other student was Raphael Demos:[4]

'He was a Greek whose father, having been converted by the missionaries, was an evangelical minister. Demos had been brought up in Asia Minor, and had risen to be librarian of some small library there, but when he had read all the books in that library he felt that Asia Minor had nothing further to offer him. He therefore saved up until he could afford a passage, steerage, to Boston. Having arrived there, he first got a job as a waiter in a restaurant, and then entered Harvard. He worked hard, and had considerable ability. In the course of nature he ultimately became a professor.'

Another of Russell's students was Victor F. Lenzen, currently Emeritus Professor of Physics at the University of California, who has recalled some details of the Harvard visit:[5]

'At this time in the history of the United States, the principal philosophical interest was the New Realism, or Neo-Realism. . . . In view of the realistic basis of Russell's *Principles of Mathematics*, the latter work was a foundation of the realistic philosophy. Thus Russell's visit to Harvard excited extraordinary interest. Professor Royce was still lecturing on Absolute Idealism, but he was one of the proponents of mathematical logic in the nation and welcomed Russell as a logician. Indeed, Professor

Royce said to me about Russell: "He has received more attention than any logician since Aristotle." To the students, Mr Russell was an almost superhuman person. I can not adequately describe the respect, adoration, and even awe which he inspired. He was very kind and hospitable to students. He had an apartment in a house a few blocks from Harvard Square, and once a week he was at home for tea for us students. His witty remarks, uttered with a quizzical smile, were heard with delight. I especially recall one remark in his first meeting with the small class in Logic . . . he said: "A fact is not a thing. When I say that I am talking nonsense. Nevertheless, I want you to take it as a profound truth." This paradoxical statement manifested the influence of Wittgenstein. Mr Russell told us about the latter, his genius, and his original ideas. . . .

'The class in Logic was a small class for special students in the field. The course in Theory of Knowledge was of more general interest and was attended practically by all students. Even the chairman of the department, whose essay in the *New Realism* exhibited the influence of Russell's *Principles*, attended the class. On one occasion when Mr Russell was expounding his dualism between mind and matter, a question raised by Raphael Demos, who was an incisive questioner, caused Professor Perry to be drawn into defense of his behavioristic theory of mind. . . .

'Mr Russell at the time was especially interested in applying the methods of mathematical logic to problems of philosophy, as scientific method of philosophy. He set forth the new method of extensive abstraction, the invention of which he attributed to Whitehead. During his residence at Harvard, he gave a series of lectures under the auspices of the Lowell Institute in Boston. Of course, we students attended those lectures.'

After one week at Harvard, Russell gave Lucy Donnelly his first impressions of the place. He wrote on 20 March 1914:

'My pupils here seem to me very good, able and well-informed in my sort of stuff. Everybody is kind, and the place is admirable in a thousand ways. I enjoy my lecturing here (not the Lowell lectures, which I only give for pay and think futile), but I miss in the professors the atmosphere of meditation and absent-mindedness which one associates with thought— they all seem more alert and business-like and punctual than one expects very good people to be. And they are all overworked; President Lowell, whom I find *utterly loathsome*, is determined to get his money's worth out of them, and throw them on the scrap heap when they are used up. . . .

'My pupils are very international: Chinese, Japanese, Greek, Indian, German, etc. They make me feel it was worth while coming.'

He also informed Lucy that he would be revisiting Washington of which he remembered 'chiefly the white ties and spittoons by which your legislators show their sympathy with the people'.

To a friend in England, Margaret Llewellyn Davies, he wrote on 12 April 1914:

'I wonder what is happening to you and what you are thinking—of politics, etc. . . .

'Here I am very busy, too busy to have time to think or get impressions. I like my pupils at Harvard, who seem to me able and well-trained, and some of them very nice. But otherwise Americans are so much on a pattern—after 100 people have said: "Very happy to make your acquaintance, Professor Russell", I feel inclined to yell.

'Boston prides itself on virtue and ancient lineage—it doesn't impress me in either direction. It is musty, like the Faubourg St Germain. I often want to ask them what constitutes the amazing virtue they are so conscious of—they are against Wilson, against Labour, rich, over-eating, selfish, feeble pigs. . . .

'Do let me have a line from you some time if you can take pity on an exile.'

Russell's first break from Boston came on Saturday, 18 April, when he travelled by train to Bryn Mawr for a week-end visit. Lucy had arranged for his informal talk to be given in her rooms at the college over Sunday tea. Although the lecture was confined to her study, Russell's presence was felt throughout the college and his visit was considered a tremendous success. Lucy wrote to him on 24 April, describing the effect of the visit:

'Miss Thomas might just as well have let you speak to the whole body of students, for the praise and "inspiration" of your lecture has spread like wild fire and the people you moved intellectually are moving others in some sort at least. My happiness is in no degree malicious, believe me. There is nothing I have cared for so much as to have you get hold of the place, as I have never known anyone else to get hold of people, intellectually as well as personally. You were like a wizard weaving your subtle wonderful spells that evening in my study. Indeed this is no partial judgement, for I have heard the best people speak here—William James and Santayana had nothing like your magic or intellectual potency with their audience—and I am critical to a fault, as you know, even of people I most admire and love.

'I could not have believed even you could have effected so much in so short a time with such a handful of people and my joy for my college is as great as was my bitterness that you couldn't speak to all the undergraduates.

'Well, the philosophers are taking your material . . . for their discussion for the rest of the year and the starveling students are pathetic fairly in their sense of what you gave them and they are unlikely to get again. Marion Reilly is still on fire, as everybody noticed, she will stop in the corridors with anyone learned enough to discuss your points. Rhys Carpenter—who was kept from tea on Sunday by a typhoid inoculation against a journey to Greece, came to express his regret for having missed what he "heard was the best thing of the year," and Mrs Wright to reproach me for my not having arranged for you to speak to the college at large! . . .

'P.S. Miss Thomas made Marion Reilly and me another scene on Wednesday, this time about scholarships and so forth. She is utterly confused and putting her mind on nothing and increasingly autocratic. She just thumps the table and answers: "I am President of this college." '

Following the lecture at Bryn Mawr, Russell went to Johns Hopkins and then to Princeton. Katherine Gerould, a writer, who had known Russell in Oxford in 1909, was present at the Princeton lecture, and described her impressions of Russell's visit in a letter to Lucy:

'I feel a desire to tell you in two words how delightful it was to see Mr Russell again, and what a vivid pleasure his passing gave, I believe, to everyone who saw him in Princeton. . . . There was for Princeton an excellent audience, in spite of two other lectures the same evening. The room was not large, but was packed full, and he told Gordon[6] that he liked the audience very much—thought the students extremely intelligent.'

Katherine Gerould went on to describe a dinner party given in Russell's honour at Princeton:

'The dinner was so small as to be almost *intime*—I fancy, with the halo of B. R.'s reputation for brilliancy hanging round him, Mrs Hibben plain funked Mrs Spaulding and Mrs Robert Bruce Cash Johnson. The men had their chance at him after the lecture; and B. R. came back saying he had had "rare sport" in their hot discussion.'

After Princeton, Russell visited the Flexners in New York, and then travelled to Northampton to lecture at Smith College. When Russell returned to Harvard, he was exhausted by a week of concentrated work and travel, and complained bitterly to Lucy about the superficiality of university social life. He wrote on 20 April 1914:

'I have a blessed day of leisure with no engagements except to address the Mathematical Club here in the evening and dine with them first, so I will seize the moment to write to you. Thank you for sending me Mrs

Gerould's letter, by which I was duly flattered. Thank you still more for all the kind things in your own letter. . . .

'By the time I got back here Sunday night I was exhausted. I had promised to stay at Northampton till 6 in the hope of a walk in the hills—but it rained continuously, and my hosts . . . were awful bores—"fancy" bores, with woolly pretentious ideas of their own. Helen will have told you of my adventures in New York—I was very happy with her. Now that I am not to see either you or her again I feel that there is no more enjoyment for me in America, and I merely clench my teeth and count the days. The ugliness and stridency of things and of people's minds are very trying.

'It is pleasant to be praised, but with most people here I feel that they regard one externally—they have not in themselves the same impulses which produce what they praise. There is an absence of artistic conscience about their work—it seems done to please men rather than to please God. They remind one of the rule in football: "Observe the rules so long as the umpire is looking." What is lacking here is the non-social side of the good life—the blind instinctive devotion to ideals dimly seen, regardless of whether they are useful or appreciated by others. This is what makes me feel lonely here. It is rare enough in Europe, but not so rare as here. There are *two* commandments, to love God and to love your neighbour—and I feel love of God is forgotten here. But I dare say it will grow up again when the country is full and material things are less absorbing. I don't feel any lack in my pupils, only in older people.'

Lucy continued to write Russell glowing accounts of the effect of his visit on her Bryn Mawr colleagues and students. Russell, while enjoying his success, did not allow it to influence his judgement. With the exception of Demos and Eliot, whose qualities he had perceived, he remained uncompromising in his criticism of American academics. He wrote on 11 May 1914:

'Ever since I got your letter I have been meaning to answer it—but here, when I get leisure, the sheer desire to do nothing overpowers me. I have by a little idleness got over the fit of spleen that came from fatigue after my trip. And my Greek pupil Demos, with whom I went on a walk the other day, turned out to be so full of courage and of passion for philosophy that he really brightened the world for me. The spectacle of courage and high passion is the most consoling that life affords. . . . What you tell me of Mr Connor pleases me very much—it is never a matter of indifference to me to get praise from people who are in earnest. . . .

'I have just been spending Sunday in the country at a lovely place with one of the philosophy instructors, an Oxfordised Harvardian, cultivated, full of the classics, talking as like an Englishman as he can, full of good nature, but feeble—quite without the ferocity that is needed to redeem culture. One of my pupils, named Eliot, was there too—a very similar type, proficient in Plato, intimate with French literature from Villon to Vildrach, very capable of a certain exquisiteness of appreciation, but lacking in the crude insistent passion that one must have in order to achieve anything. However, he is the only pupil of that sort that I have; all the others are vigorous intelligent barbarians. . . .'

Russell wrote a similar letter to Lady Ottoline Morrell, who later remarked about it: 'I imagine it was during this week-end visit or in consequence of it that T. S. Eliot wrote "Mr Apollinax"'.[7] Eliot's poem celebrated Russell's visit to America, and observed the society which sought to cultivate him:

Mr Apollinax[8]

Ω τῆς καινότητος. Ἡράκλεις, τῆς παραδοξολογίας.
εὐμήχανος ἄνθρωπος.

LUCIAN

When Mr Apollinax visited the United States
His laughter tinkled among the teacups.
I thought of Fragilion, that shy figure among the birch-trees,
And of Priapus in the shrubbery
Gaping at the lady in the swing.
In the palace of Mrs Phlaccus, at Professor Channing-
     Cheetah's
He laughed like an irresponsible fœtus.
His laughter was submarine and profound
Like the old man of the sea's
Hidden under coral islands
Where worried bodies of drowned men drift down in the
     green silence,
Dropping from fingers of surf.
I looked for the head of Mr Apollinax rolling under a chair

Or grinning over a screen
With seaweed in its hair.
I heard the beat of centaur's hoofs over the hard turf
As his dry and passionate talk devoured the afternoon.
'He is a charming man'—'But after all what did he mean?'—
'His pointed ears. . . . He must be unbalanced,'—
'There was something he said that I might have challenged.'
Of dowager Mrs Phlaccus, and Professor and Mrs Cheetah
I remember a slice of lemon, and a bitten macaroon.

Towards the end of May, Russell concluded his Harvard appointment. Before returning to England he undertook a short lecture tour of
Chicago and the Mid-West. While on his way to Chicago, Russell wrote
to Lucy from the train, on 26 May, summing up his views of Harvard:

'This morning I gave two lectures and left Boston at 12.30—everybody
at Harvard has been amazingly nice to me—some of the philosophy
department might well have been jealous or in some way ungenerous,
but none were. And I liked the students to the last. On the whole, I
think very well of what I have seen of Harvard. The only real defects to
my mind are those it shares with all other universities here—the institution of the President and the Board of Overseers. The fact that universities are not self-governing makes the career of a teacher less attractive
and respected than with us. . . .

'My time has been terribly full, and will be in Chicago and Wisconsin,
so train journeys are my only time for writing. My final impression of
Harvard was good enough to moderate my future diatribes on the
United States.

'Do send a line to my ship—*Megantic*—leaving Montreal daybreak 6
June. Then I can answer on the ship, to Brown Shipley, if only Columbus had gone there, how much trouble he would have saved himself.'

In the three days available to him at Chicago, Russell delivered
several lectures at the university. He was the guest of Dr Dudley, a well-
known gynaecologist who had 'written a book on the diseases of women
containing a coloured frontispiece of the uterus. He presented this book
to me, but I found it somewhat embarrassing, and ultimately gave it to a
medical friend.'[9] Dudley had four daughters, one of whom, Helen,
particularly impressed Russell.

She met him at the station and he 'at once felt more at home with her
than I had with anybody else that I had met in America. . . . I spent
two nights under her parents' roof, and the second I spent with her. Her
three sisters mounted guard to give warning if either of the parents approached'.[10] Helen promised to follow Russell to England where they
hoped to live together and eventually marry, if he could obtain a divorce
from Alys.

After Chicago, in the short time left to him, he lectured at the University of Wisconsin and then at the University of Michigan at Ann Arbor
where:[11]

'. . . the President showed me all the new buildings, more especially the
library, of which he was very proud. It appeared that the library had
the most scientific card-index in the world, and that its method of
central heating was extraordinarily up-to-date. While he was explaining

46

all this, we were standing in the middle of a large room with admirable desks. "And does anybody ever read the books?" I asked. He seemed surprised, but answered: "Why yes, there is a man over there now reading." We went to look, and found that he was reading a novel.'

Russell's final activity before leaving America was a visit to Niagara Falls. When he arrived in Montreal, his port of embarkation, he received a last letter from Lucy wishing him *bon voyage* and commenting:[12]

'Your American visit has been such a happiness I must mark its end as I welcomed its beginning. It was a pleasure both nationally and personally to hear you left Harvard with such a good opinion of the place—I hope it may bring you back again.'

Russell sailed for home on the *Megantic* on 6 June, and on the same day he wrote a letter of farewell to Lucy:

'I wonder whether I shall ever come back. America has treated me very kindly, but I do not think its output in philosophy will be very important for some time to come—the conditions, financially and mentally, are too adverse. For this reason, I would rather have European pupils.

'Niagara gave me no emotion, but this river is very beautiful, and I am glad to fill my memory with it. Much of the Canadian country, as I passed through in the train, seemed to me to have a good deal of wild beauty.'

Keenly anticipating his return home, Russell wrote, on 9 June, to Margaret Llewellyn Davies, who had been complaining about life in England:

'. . . Do try a dose of America before you curse your native land. Everybody was kind and appreciative, and treated me as a big-wig, so that I became persuaded I was becoming an elderly incubus. What troubles me most there is the absolutely unbelievable conventionality. . . .

'I enjoyed my week in the West. It seems to me Boston is the worst place in America, but perhaps that is only because it is the place I saw most of. I am devoutly thankful to have escaped, but I feel I must have caught some of their prosiness. Meanwhile I am enjoying the holiday on the sea. I have just this moment seen an iceberg—the first I ever saw— sticking up in a conical shape, just as they do in pictures. Otherwise, there is nothing to do but eat and sleep. . . .

'It has been hateful being out of things so long, and I was too busy to keep up even as much as one could in America. I hope to get home on the 14th. . . .

'P.S. I have now seen four icebergs!'

NOTES

1 B. Russell, *Autobiography* (London, 1967), Vol. I, p. 211 (Boston, 1967), pp. 325–6.

2 Alan Wood, *Bertrand Russell, the Passionate Sceptic* (London, 1957), p. 94 (Simon & Schuster, New York, 1957).

3 B. Russell, *Autobiography*, Vol. I, p. 212; p. 327.

4 Ibid.

5 Victor F. Lenzen, 'Bertrand Russell at Harvard, 1914', in *Russell: The Journal of the Bertrand Russell Archives* (Autumn, 1971), No. 3.

6 Katherine Gerould's husband, a professor at Princeton.

7 Robert Gathorne-Hardy (ed.), *Ottoline, The Early Memoirs of Lady Ottoline Morrell* (Faber & Faber, London, 1963), p. 257. Of additional interest concerning 'Mr Apollinax' is a comment by George Santayana in his letter to Russell of 21 July 1914: ' . . . friends of mine have written about having had great pleasure in seeing you in America. One sagacious person observes that you were [in Boston] "a great success among the high-brows" and adds "However I doubt if he enjoyed himself." '

8 T. S. Eliot, *Collected Poems, 1909–1935* (Faber & Faber, London, 1936).

9 B. Russell, *Autobiography*, Vol. I, p. 213; pp. 328–9.

10 Ibid.

11 Ibid., p. 212; p. 328.

12 From Lucy Donnelly's letter of 3 June 1914.

CHAPTER 4

FIRST WORLD WAR

On returning to England, Russell went directly to Cambridge from where he had obtained leave of absence for the Easter term. He was happy to be back in England, and wrote to Lucy Donnelly on 25 June 1914:

'. . . Ten days now I have been back in this country—very happy in the complexities and diversifications of old Europe. In America one gets so few surprises—it is all as one expects. I am reminded of Dora Sanger's uncle, who going to Palestine, arranged a cabling code with his family in which one word meant "the flora and fauna of the Holy Land have surpassed even my expectations." So I might have arranged to cable that the skyscrapers surpassed my expectations or that Niagara fell below them. I saw Niagara in company with a German doctor who knew no English. I asked him if he had seen the Rockefeller Institute and he replied: "*Ach nein, das haben wir ja alles viel besser in Frankfurt.*" Insufferable race.

'England is as usual in a political turmoil; no one knows what the outcome will be. As for the suffragettes, no issue is possible except to give them the vote. They are ready to die, but the government dare not let them die. . . .'

The suffrage issue was to be swept aside by the imminence of war; its prospect was the subject of acrimonious debate at Cambridge, and Russell at once involved himself on the anti-war platform. By August, Helen Dudley arrived from Chicago to join Russell but the outbreak of war, and his intense involvement with the pacifist movement, diverted his feelings, and he lost his interest in her. Some years later she 'fell a victim to a rare disease which paralysed her and then made her insane. If the war had not intervened, the plan which we formed in Chicago might have brought great happiness to us both. I feel still the sorrow of this tragedy.'[1]

At the outbreak of hostilities, Lucy conveyed to Russell the feeling in America towards the war:[2]

'What a terrible calamity, what incredible suffering and waste to fall upon this age of the world! and how wicked of Germany! Here, too, the war overshadows everything and sobers us all. It is all our thought and talk, it fills the first pages of our papers to the exclusion of all American news, and "extras" are cried constantly in the streets. The sympathies of the people and press are much with the Allies, for all our technical neutrality, even to many German-Americans who, if reluctantly, blame the Kaiser. Others, like Münsterberg at Harvard, explain it as Teuton against Slav, or like Kuno Franke say there must be explanations we have not yet got, and send indignant letters to the papers to say their news is prejudiced because it comes all from England, France, and Belgium—brave little Belgium!

'I can imagine how terribly exciting and distressing and preoccupying it must all be to you and I wonder if you were at all with the non-interventionists, or thought England *must* go in to protect Belgium. Here we are pretty bloodthirsty and longing to have you kick the Kaiser out of militarism for ever. . . .

'I left Mackinac a week ago and am glad to sniff the Atlantic again and to get the news from Europe at the earliest moment. I travelled East with a train full of drummers whose big importing houses had telegraphed them to stop sales and return to New York. Prices are already rising here and a mercantile marine planning. My father tells me the big Remington typewriters Trust who are his clients are closing their factories, dismissing employees, and planning to pass their dividends. My father is so depressed by the war I do not know if I shall get him off for his holiday. He lives through his own battles of the civil war again in it, when as a mere boy he was decorated for gallantry at Chancellorsville. I think he wants to send over American generals to aid you! . . .

'I must tell you that a Chicago Mrs Barling who was staying at the Hamiltons too, told me of the pleasure you gave her set by snubbing, at a dinner at the Dudleys, a smart woman who has too long posed as Chicago's literary dictator to them. I have forgotten her name . . . but when she told you she should read your books if she liked you, you replied that they would be much too hard for her, to the infinite joy of her friends and the paying off of many scores. . . .

'I send this letter betimes for the American liner that promised to sail on Friday and beg you to write me back about England and yourself in this crisis which seems to make all the ordinary business of life stand still. . . .'

The advent of the First World War transformed Russell's life. His social and political concerns, which in the past had been sporadic, were now to become paramount. Already, at this stage, Russell was looking hopefully towards President Woodrow Wilson and neutral America. His state of mind is expressed in his reply to Lucy on 22 August 1914:

'Thank you for your letter. What I think about the war you will see from the enclosed,[3] Germany is less guilty, and we are less innocent, than news from London would make you think. It is plain (tho' under the influence of war-fever people here deny it) that Germany and Austria thought they could punish Servia without causing Russian intervention, and that they arrived at a *diplomatic* humiliation of Russia. They did not expect war, but were hurried into it by the Russian general mobilisation. As for Belgium, that was, for us, merely a pretext: it has long been universally known that Belgium neutrality would be violated in the next Franco–German war. All the Great Powers except France are to blame, but not Germany only: it is terror of Russia that has produced Germany's apparent madness.

'It is impossible to convey to you anything of the horror of these past weeks. Events of a month ago seem to belong to a previous existence. All our hopes and faiths and foolish confidences are gone flaming down into Hell. The little sheltered nook in which we tried to live by thought and reason is swept away in a red blast of hate: nothing seems worth while except to kill and be killed. In Cambridge there are at this moment about 20,000 troops: we have officers to dine in Hall, and Nevile's Court has been taken over by the War Office to be a hospital till the end of the war. Over 1,000 undergraduates have gone to fight. I met an advanced socialist two days ago, who told me he was enlisting because he could imagine no greater joy than to see a German fall to his rifle. Wells writes that he is "enthusiastic" for this war; Shaw favours it; secretaries of peace societies welcome it; vegetarians and anti-vivisectionists support it to a man. Hardly any one seems to remember common humanity—that war is a mad horror, and that deliberately to cause the deaths of thousands of men like ourselves is so ghastly that hardly anything can justify it. Last night I met Marsh, who is Winston's private secretary, and spends his days and nights at the Admiralty—he looked blooming and happy, delighted with his importance, wholly untroubled by the thought that he was organising the killing and mangling of brave men. And if we succeed, the only Power that will ultimately profit is Russia—the land of the knout. However, we shall have established the great principle that it is proper to assassinate the sons of emperors, which is the point in dispute between the two sides. For this at least let us be thankful. . . .

'Military people think the war may last years; I believe starvation must end it before that, especially if Wilson succeeds in preventing loans from America, as I hope he will. However the Germans may succeed at first, I cannot believe they have any chance of ultimate victory.

'I don't remember the incident at Chicago that you mention, tho' I remember a dinner-party at the Dudleys. . . .'

Russell soon became prominent within the pacifist movement. This caused him to be isolated from his friends and colleagues who, almost without exception, were caught up in the rampant national chauvinism of the time. America seemed to Russell the only hope for ending the war. He was convinced that without American participation the war could not last long and that President Wilson as a neutralist could exert pressure to bring the war to an early end.

In September 1914, he had discussions with Elizabeth Perkins from Boston, a writer and lecturer on art and religion, who was on an extended visit to England. She had friends both in the United States administration and in the publishing world. Impressed by Russell's views she tried to arrange for him a political lecture tour of America and a meeting with President Wilson. She wrote on 11 October 1914:

'There is no doubt that you could see Dr Wilson satisfactorily. Would it not be well for me to write to William Phillips, one of the Secretaries of State, asking him to arrange a meeting after Christmas and telling him in a general way of your plan? . . . As to meetings and lectures, I have had some experience in arranging for them in the Eastern cities. . . . Once inaugurated and properly advertised you would be certain to succeed as everyone in America would be interested in the subject. But all arrangements must be made beforehand. There should be a large meeting at Faneuil Hall in Boston, another at the Cooper Union in New York. I can write to the 20th Century Club in Boston which is very active, all important persons there being members—and I feel sure that they would help as well in getting up other meetings as in having you to talk to them. Also you should secure one of the Ford Hall Sunday evening meetings—a sort of "people's" forum, which is always crowded and questions are asked from the floor. . . .

'Of one thing I am sure, much must be pre-arranged before you start to have the thing succeed.'

With Russell's agreement, Elizabeth Perkins contacted William Phillips, the Assistant Secretary of State, with a view to sounding out the prospects for a peace mission by Russell to America. Although she had been optimistic, her inquiries led her to inform Russell that 'the outlook does not seem encouraging'.

She forwarded to Russell an article by Theodore Roosevelt which, together with other evidence from American newspapers, convinced her that 'the public temper is either suspicious or silly at the mention of peace. . . . This makes your work all the more difficult and the more necessary.'[4] She also sent Russell a copy of a letter dated 2 November 1914, which she had received from William Phillips in response to her inquiry about Russell meeting President Wilson:

'Surely I have met Bertrand Russell when he came to Harvard last year, and I am very much interested to hear of his contemplated trip to the United States. His interview with the President should not be difficult to arrange, provided he can come in touch with his own Embassy. Unfortunately, the rule here is very strict in that no foreigner may be presented to the President except by his own Ambassador or Minister—a rule which is maintained in nearly all countries at the present time.

'The present is not the time to discuss peace and I fear that Russell will find a very small audience in this country at the present moment, but the time will come, undoubtedly, when everything he has to say will be listened to with intense interest.'

As an alternative to visiting America, Elizabeth Perkins proposed that Russell concentrate on publicising his views through the United States press. She offered to put Russell in touch with friends who were editors of leading journals, including Henry Holt of *Unpopular Review* and Ellery Sedgwick of the *Atlantic Monthly*, as well as various newspaper people in Boston.

Since the climate seemed unsuited to an early visit, Russell agreed to take advantage of Elizabeth Perkins's publishing connections and began writing for American journals. One of the first of a stream of articles was transmitted to the *Atlantic Monthly* with Elizabeth Perkins's assistance. The article, entitled 'Is a Permanent Peace Possible?', examined the causes of militarism in Europe and put forward the steps Russell thought necessary towards achieving a lasting peace. He maintained that 'unless America undertakes the championship of mankind against the warring governments', those who profited from the war would be able to 'postpone the inauguration of a happier age'. He stressed the importance of American participation at any peace congress which, he felt, should take place 'in the neutral atmosphere of Washington with Mr Wilson as its President.'[5] In this and other articles Russell began to advance his view that an international authority with wide powers was necessary to urge the just settlement of disputes between nations.

After arranging for the *Atlantic Monthly* to publish the article, Elizabeth Perkins commented on 11 December 1914:

'The *Atlantic* article will be in sympathy with so many American hopes and ideas, that it should be well received. I think it quite the best presentation of the special "case" so far. Even if the people of the U.S. are only to be "a convenient telephone between different interests" (according to the *Morning Post* editorial) the line must be put and kept in order. . . .'

In an effort to keep pace with the increasing demand of anti-war work, Russell arranged to have his academic duties at Cambridge suspended. Harvard, always predisposed to obtaining Russell's services, wrote to him on 2 February 1915, in the person of Professor Perry, inquiring: 'Does that mean that you would be free to come to us for the year (or part of it) if the way should be open?' In his letter Perry, who was pro-Ally in sentiment, also stated:

'I have just read your article in the *International Journal of Ethics*. I both admire and disapprove it. I hope to find time to write a brief discussion of it for the same periodical. Here we are all hotly pro-Ally—all, that is, save Münsterberg and one or two others. We believe that Germany is most guilty of the war and that all good things will best be served by her defeat. . . .

'. . . Woods has assumed the chairmanship [of the Philosophy Department] and I may at last spend uninterrupted consecutive hours in my study. I have a good seminary in Epistemology, with Demos, Lenzen, Blake and others whose minds you stimulated and nourished last year.'

The article which Perry referred to was 'The Ethics of War', published in January 1915. In it Russell questioned 'whether war is ever justified, and if so under what circumstances'. He argued that while certain wars undoubtedly contributed towards human betterment, most had the opposite effect. He characterised the present European war as having 'a double effect in retarding social progress' as it not only caused vast chaos and destruction but served 'to distract men's minds from the claims of social justice'.[6]

Russell replied to Perry on 21 February 1915:

'I am sorry you disapprove my article. One lives here in such an atmosphere of humbug, hypocrisy and self-righteousness that any person with a spark of honesty is driven nearly mad with disgust. The effect on Shaw has been displayed to the world; no doubt something of the same spleen appears in my article. I am sorry. You in America, not having followed diplomacy since 1904, are probably less aware than some of us of the weak points of our case. . . .

'How happy, in retrospect, the times seem when I was in Harvard! Your mentioning Demos, Lenzen, Blake and the others, brings them back very vividly to my mind. Please give my kindest remembrances to all who were in my logic class. I retain a very affectionate memory of them, and a wish to see them again. . . .

'Woods very kindly cabled to ask about my coming to Harvard—I should love it, but I want to be here while the war is on and immediately after it. I am doing speaking and writing—of a sort, I fear, that you dislike—and I want to be free to give all my time to it. . . .'

Russell was soon to receive further news of the impact of his ideas on American readers. His article, 'Is a Permanent Peace Possible?', was published in early March by the *Atlantic Monthly* and provoked considerable response. One of many encouraging letters he received was from Nancy Toy with whom he had been friendly while at Harvard the previous year. She was an acquaintance of Woodrow Wilson and wrote to Russell on 9 March 1915: 'I have just sent off your *Atlantic Monthly* article to the President, and wish now that I hadn't so that I might thank you more intelligently by reference to it. I wish the whole world could be as convinced by it as it is really convincing. . . .'

Through his writings Russell continued to win sympathy in America for his views. But, on 7 May 1915, the *Lusitania* was attacked and sunk by a German submarine. It seemed likely that the *Lusitania* disaster would wreck the case for neutrality and precipitate America's entry into the war. Certainly, Russell's American friends were much affected by the tragedy. Elizabeth Perkins wrote on 9 May 1915:

'We have been in the midst of the *Lusitania* tragedy and one of the maids had a brother on board. The telegram has just come saying that he has been saved.

'It looks as though the U.S. might be forced into war—and again as in the case of the *Maine*—a ship sunk becomes the direct *casus belli*. Your words about the difficulty of living through all this—if one does not die through it as a soldier—are much in my mind today. We knew enough persons on the ship to make half a dozen separate tragedies and one's egoism is such that even an acquaintance focuses interest to a great degree.'

Concerned about its timing, Russell immediately withdrew an article which had been set up in type for the July issue of the *Atlantic Monthly*. The article, entitled 'How America Can Help to Bring Peace', set forth Russell's views on a neutral America's role in achieving peace.[7] In the article Russell made clear his debt to American correspondents and asserted:

'It is difficult at all times to gauge the public opinion of a country not one's own, and it is especially difficult in time of war, when the desire to attain truth is almost wholly extinct, and newspapers contain only such news as is thought likely to stimulate the wish to kill. But if it is possible to judge from some acquaintance with America, and from many correspondents and close friends in the United States, I think it is safe to believe that there is a very large and potentially powerful body of opinion which desires the war to end as soon as is compatible with justice, and wishes the United States administration to use all possible means to that end short of actually taking up arms. The difficulty which faces this body of opinion is the difficulty of discovering any line of action which will further peace; for the moment, it might seem as though the United States were powerless to do more than watch passively while the nations slowly approach the time when peace is brought by the death or disablement of all their manhood. I believe that this is a mistake, and that it is possible for America without joining in the struggle to take action which would very materially shorten the war. This is possible through America's importance as a source of loans, supplies, and ammunitions of war, provided this leverage is skilfully used. . . .'

He concluded the article with this plea:

'America as the greatest of the neutrals, and as a pioneer in liberal and pacific principles, has the opportunity of playing a great and noble part, by a wise choice of the means and the moment. Will this opportunity be seized? Or will official caution allow it to pass by? Upon the answer to this question depends, perhaps, the whole future of our civilisation.'

America's reaction to the *Lusitania* disaster was as Russell had anticipated. Neutralism was under attack, and Wilson was sending strongly worded notes to Germany. Lucy Donnelly described the mounting hatred for Germany in a letter of 21 May 1915:

'We have felt ourselves, indeed, on the brink of war since the *Lusitania* disaster and are very restless here until we get Germany's reply. You will have seen in your papers how high public feeling has run over the outrage to humanity, not merely to America. The best of our German–Americans to Herman Riddes himself have been deeply shocked and Wilson had a tremendous ovation in New York on Monday, at the naval review, after sending off his note to Germany. There seems to be no doubt he will stand by it. If we could shorten the war and bear our share by going in, many of us would do so willingly. . . .'

Although Russell was preoccupied with the war issue, his academic reputation continued to soar, particularly in America. At a time when he was becoming unpopular in England, Columbia University honoured him, in June 1915, with the Nicholas Murray Butler Medal for the most outstanding work in philosophy over the previous five years. However, it was Russell's writings on the war that commanded most attention in America, as in Britain. Professor Perry had written an article for the April issue of the *International Journal of Ethics* attacking Russell's views on 'The Ethics of War'. Russell continued the argument in the August issue of the *Atlantic Monthly* with his article, 'War and Non-Resistance',[8] and wrote to Perry on 3 August 1915:

'I realise that all sensible men agree with you against me, but I hold to my opinion. I wish I could argue it with you face to face; I believe I could convince you. I have learnt many things about the underground parts of human nature since the war began—partly from introspection, for the instinctive part of me is as fiercely patriotic as any Junker. I think people in America cannot really judge, since they do not feel the hot breath of fierceness. An American lately landed described it to me as being like stepping into an oven. . . .'

Elizabeth Perkins, who had by this time returned to Boston, informed Russell on 9 November 1915, of the *Atlantic Monthly* editor's view of his articles:

'The Sedgwicks dined here last night and it was good to listen to Ellery's pleasure in the articles you sent to the *Atlantic*. The fact that many disapproving letters both from the U.S. and England had been received about the Non-Resistance article, only seems to increase his satisfaction. . . .

'In the ten weeks since our return, we have had many emotions. The effort to realise what the war was doing to us here has at best resulted in a few conclusions. Not only Wilson, but the country at large remains unalterable for peace. . . .

'I have been doing a little work in Jamaica Plains for the elections. Most of the wards contain 50 per cent of German names—and in a play now running in Boston, the Kaiser is repeatedly cheered by an apparently mixed audience. The Republican gains in Massachusetts, New York, and Pennsylvania are significant—also the German/American hatred of Wilson. It seems clear that he will never have another term. . . .

'If the U.S. is to be useful in Europe, it must look to its human coherence rather than to the defense program. The Germans have alarmed many of us without a single raid, and the moving pictures show New York and Boston bombarded and in flames. To spirit the peaceful citizen!'

In January 1916, Professor James Woods of the Harvard Philosophy Department wrote to Russell renewing their offer of a lectureship.

Woods expected that 'many of the cleverest of the youth with predilections for logic would flock to Harvard'[9] as a consequence of Russell's presence there. Although Russell's commitments had prevented him from taking up the earlier invitation for 1916, he was quite prepared to go there in the following year, especially as Woods had offered to include in the appointment a course based on Russell's political views of the war. Woods had drawn attention to the growing danger of war hysteria and the need for Russell's presence to help counteract it. Russell immediately cabled his acceptance. Harvard was delighted to have again obtained his services and there followed an exchange of letters in which Woods arranged the guide-lines for the courses which Russell was to give. These included a formal logic course, a course on 'Social Psychology and Ethics' (which Russell tactfully suggested as the title for his political lectures), and an informal course based on the fact that in 1914, according to Woods, 'the hour in your den in Craigie Hall was one of the most fruitful hours that the men spent'. In his letter of 21 March 1916, Woods, commenting on the political course, informed Russell:

'. . . . I have, however, laid the matter before the president [Lowell], who, you remember, is far from being a pacifist, and whose nationalistic feeling is vigorous. He quite agrees with me that there can be nothing but good in the course, and, in fact, I know he would be delighted to have the benefit of your fresh treatment of these problems on which we need so much light in America. Royce, in spite of an entirely different ethical point of view, says the course will be heartily welcomed and so do all the others. I wish to say myself that I think you have an extraordinary opportunity in America, due to the fact that our thinking on the political presuppositions has been so hopelessly optimistic and infantile. Just now we are aware that all that has been in the main stream in the tradition must be recast. Accordingly, instead of thinking that we should approve your course, it would be more fitting if you counted it as creating and satisfying a need of which we were only dimly aware. . . .'

Russell had in the meantime sent Woods the syllabus for his lectures in 'Social Psychology and Ethics'. These lectures had been written in 1915, and Russell was currently delivering them in London. (They were later to be published in America as *Why Men Fight: A Method of Abolishing the International Duel* and in Britain as *Principles of Social Reconstruction.*) Woods was in great sympathy with Russell's outlook on the war, and, judging from their correspondence, learnt a great deal from Russell. 'What you have written me about the political situation', he confided in a letter of 22 March, 'is most illuminating and if you can write a few words once more, I should be very grateful. Every word you write has a bearing upon our political attitude here.' By the end of May, Woods was able to send Russell details of his itinerary, which included engagements to lecture at half-a-dozen other colleges. Amongst these, the University of Michigan had indicated to Woods their preference for purely philosophical subjects, 'owing to the strong local feeling for the Allies'. Perry, who had been patiently anticipating Russell's return to Harvard ever since his invitation in February 1915, added a final note of encouragement on 8 June 1916, notwithstanding his own views on the war:

'. . . I want you to know how delighted we all are at the prospect of having you with us next year again—the memory of 1914 is good, the prospect of 1917 is better. We shall quarrel about peace and war but I have no fear that it will divide us fundamentally. I dare say that if you had been in America and I in England our roles would have been exchanged. You are disgusted with the humbuggery of the British Liberal Government. What would you think of a soppy sentimentalism, and a worldly complacency that calls itself "The American vision"? The great fault over here is shortsightedness, or the lack of sufficient inspiration to offset our physical remoteness from what is going on. I pray Heaven that when you are here, the end of the war may be in sight, but the promise is not hopeful. . . .'

NOTES

[1] B. Russell, *Autobiography* (London, 1967), Vol. I, p. 214 (Boston, 1967), p. 330.

[2] The letter is undated; Britain declared war on 4 August 1914.

[3] 'The Rights of the War', Russell's letter to the *Nation* (London, 15 August 1914).

[4] From Elizabeth Perkins's letter of 12 November 1914.

[5] Published in the *Atlantic Monthly* (March 1915); reprinted in B. Russell, *Justice in Wartime* (London and Open Court, Chicago, 1916).

[6] Reprinted in *Justice in Wartime*.

[7] It remains unpublished.

[8] Reprinted in *Justice in Wartime*.

[9] From Woods's letter of 5 January 1916.

CHAPTER 5

A LETTER TO THE PRESIDENT

The introduction of conscription in Britain, early in 1916, threatened the activity of anti-war militants. This occurred at the time when Russell was finalising his arrangements with Harvard to lecture there from February 1917. In April 1916, Russell had written a leaflet for the No-Conscription Fellowship protesting against the imprisonment of a conscientious objector.[1] When six pacifists were in their turn imprisoned for distributing the leaflet, Russell, in a famous letter to *The Times* of 17 May 1916, declared himself to be the author and invited his own prosecution as the 'person primarily responsible'.[2]

Meanwhile, Harvard, concerned that Russell might be refused permission to leave Britain, contacted Sir Cecil Spring Rice, the British Ambassador in Washington, inquiring about Russell's position. Spring Rice referred the matter to the British Foreign Office, and suggested that Russell 'be warned that Germans will circulate any anti-British utterances he may make here'. Spring Rice's notification was circulated among Foreign Office officials, and the following comments are revealed by Foreign Office records:

'I do not think that such a warning [as suggested by Spring Rice] would have any effect in moderating Mr Russell's utterances. He has lately publicly announced that he is the author of a No-Conscription pamphlet for which some other people have been prosecuted and convicted, so that the Home Office may well be considering whether steps should be taken against him. He ought by all means to be prevented from going.' *S.G.* (*29 May*)

'I think his effect would be disastrous in the United States just now with so much peace talk about. . . .' *G.B.* (*29 May*)

'First let us ask the Home Office confidentially if any steps are contemplated against him. If so, it will pave the way for refusing to issue a passport—which is the only real means I know of by which we can stop him from leaving the country.' [?] (*29 May*)

'We already have him on our "blacklist".' *H.S.M.* (*30 May*)

'This is one of the most mischievous cranks in the country and I submit that it would be folly to let him go to America.' *N.* (*31 May*)

Following his admission in *The Times*, Russell was summonsed to appear in court, and on 5 June was found guilty and fined £100 under the Defence of the Realm Act for 'statements likely to prejudice the recruiting and discipline of His Majesty's Forces'. The Foreign Office informed Ambassador Spring Rice of Russell's conviction and of the decision that 'no passport will be issued to him to proceed to the United States.' Spring Rice wrote to President Lowell on 8 June:[3]

'I am sorry to say that Russell has been convicted under "Defence of the Realm Act" for writing an undesirable pamphlet. Under these circumstances it would be impossible to issue a passport to him to leave the country.

'I am sorry . . . that it is impossible to meet your wishes but I trust that you will understand the necessity of which my government is placed.

'Oddly enough I was at the Berlin Embassy when we got into trouble owing to Russell's attitude when on a visit to Berlin as the German government strongly objected to his language.'

Russell heard for the first time of the British government's decision through Professor Woods, who wrote to him on 23 June 1916 enclosing the Spring Rice letter:

'In reply to a request that you be given permission to come to this country, the letter which I enclose was returned. It is a grievous disappointment to us. We have tried to think that some way of circumventing the government might be discovered, but apparently there is little chance for altering the decree.

'Under these circumstances, I suppose we must announce that your courses cannot be given, however bitter it is to us to make this statement. The compensation is, however, that the next year and the years following, the welcome will be even greater here. . . .'

While Russell found sympathy from Harvard, this was not the case at his own college. His reply to Woods of 30 July 1916 carried news of his dismissal from Trinity College, Cambridge:[4]

'Your letter and the ambassador's were not wholly a surprise to me. I cabled to you on receiving them, but I doubt if the cable ever reached you. Your letter was most kind. The allusion to my doings in Berlin was misleading. I was there in 1895 for the purpose of writing a book on

German socialism; this led me to associate with socialists, and therefore to be excluded from the Embassy. I did nothing publicly all the time I was there. The Kaiser was having socialists imprisoned in large numbers for their opinions, which gave me a hatred for him that I retain to this day. But unless in quite private conversations I never expressed my feelings all the time I was there. I have never been in Berlin since 1895.

'I should be glad to know whether you have seen or received the verbatim report of my trial. It has been sent you, but may have been stopped by the Censor, who is anxious that America should not know the nature of my crime. You will have heard that I have been turned out of Trinity for the same offence. The sum total of my crime was that I said two years' hard labour in prison was an excessive punishment for the offence of having a conscientious objection to participation in war. Since then, the same offence has been punished by the death-sentence, commuted to ten years' penal servitude. Anyone who thinks that I can be made to hold my tongue when such things are being done is grossly mistaken. And the government only advertises its own errors by trying ineffectually to punish those of us who won't be silent. Working men are sent to prison when they commit the crime that I committed. And when they come out, no one will employ them, so that they are reduced to living on charity. This is a war for liberty.

'This letter will no doubt never reach you, but it may be found interesting by the Censor. If it does reach you, please let me know by return of post. It is a matter of some public interest to know what is allowed to pass, and if I don't hear from you within six weeks I shall assume that this letter has been stopped.

'These are fierce times. But there is a new spirit abroad, and good will come out of it all in the end. I wish your country had not embarked upon the career of militarism.'

Neither this letter nor the cable to which Russell referred ever reached Woods. The report of Russell's trial met a similar fate: all were intercepted by the Censor and ended up in the Foreign Office files.

Russell, concerned that America should know the truth about his trial, cabled Harvard seeking consent to publicise his correspondence with it. Although Woods was willing to allow Russell use of the letters, President Lowell instructed him to reply that 'nothing would be gained by publishing them.'[5]

But news of Russell's trial had not escaped the attention of the American press. An item from a Boston newspaper which Elizabeth Perkins sent to Russell is evidence of the interest America was showing in his clash with English authority:

'The case of the Hon. Bertrand Arthur William Russell, who has been refused a passport to visit the United States, is of especial interest to Bostonians, and many of them will read of the prohibition with surprise. When he was in this city a little more than two years ago he was known mainly as an authority on mathematics and philosophy. His series of Lowell Institute lectures on 'Our Knowledge of the External World as a Field for Scientific Method in Philosophy' was an event in the intellectual life of the community, and his admirers have been looking forward with a good deal of interest to a further series of addresses on similar themes planned for him next year by Harvard University.

'That a scholar of his meditative type should have entered ardently into the issues of the war seemed little likely. Yet on its outbreak he openly opposed his country's participation in it, indicating his opposition in writings published on both sides of the Atlantic. When the issue of British conscription came up, he espoused the cause of the conscientious objectors, and did so with utter disregard of consequences. At least one of the leaflets which were issued to dissuade from enlistment was written by him.

'He might have escaped all responsibility in the matter, but he voluntarily went into court with a complete avowal of the authorship, telling the magistrate that as distributors of the leaflet were being fined he also had a right to share in the punishment meted out to them. And the results of his frankness did not end with the heavy penalty which was immediately imposed by the judge. Cambridge University, where he had been a lecturer for a number of years, took up his "case", held Council as to the facts, and dismissed him from its faculty. . . .'

Russell received many letters of support from America in the weeks following his trial and his dismissal from Cambridge. 'I wish to express to you the sympathy which I and most of my university colleagues throughout the United States feel for your stand for humanity', one of his well-wishers wrote, and added: 'It is a great source of distress to us to see free England in the grasp of martial law, which is no law at all, sliding back into the days of the press gang and the Stuarts!'[6]

In England, reaction to the pacifist campaign grew fiercer. Undeterred by public condemnation and official censure, Russell continued his anti-war work. Thrown out of Trinity and denied the opportunity of earning money in America, he found himself in financial difficulties, since he had previously given away most of his inheritance to hard-up friends. Russell was forced to live with his brother, Frank, in London and began to lecture on political theory in various parts of England and Wales on a professional basis. In September, these activities were curtailed by a government order restricting his movements. An interview with the War Office made clear that he was regarded as a security risk and he was no longer able to move freely about the country.

Russell protested about his treatment, and as a consequence this issue, including the government's refusal to permit him to visit America, was sharply raised in Parliament. A liberal M.P., Philip Morrell,[7] in a defence of Russell, attacked the action that had prevented him from taking up the Harvard appointment, and stated:[8]

'. . . Mr Russell would now be on his way to America to deliver this course of lectures. His passport was refused. It was a heavy loss to him in every way, pecuniary and otherwise. It naturally aroused a great deal of comment in the United States. He has received letters from the university regarding the action of the government, and the matter has been commented on again and again in the American newspapers. Here you have one of the most distinguished living mathematicians, one of the best known philosophers in this country, not allowed to go to deliver a course of lectures on mathematics at Harvard University!'

Herbert Samuel, the Home Secretary, claimed that the government had been willing to lift the restrictions on Russell's movements provided that his lectures were free of anti-war propaganda. Samuel implied that such an undertaking would have enabled Russell to travel to America.[9] As a result, Russell wrote the following letter to *The Times* and it appeared on 27 October 1916:

'*Sir.* Will you allow me to correct a misapprehension, which is liable to arise out of Mr Herbert Samuel's answers in the House of Commons on 19 and 25 October, as regards the government's refusal to permit me to go to America? No correspondence of any kind, and no verbal communication, official or unofficial, ever passed between me and any government office on this subject. The only communication of which I have any knowledge is a letter from our ambassador in the United States to the president of Harvard stating that a passport could not be granted to me because of my conviction at the Mansion House under the Defence of the Realm Act. This letter was dated 8 June, at a time when the Mansion House decision was still not *judice*, as I had appealed to quarter-sessions. I was never asked whether I would give such an undertaking as Mr Samuel now says would be sufficient. Throughout my recent correspondence with the War Office, I not only did not know, but did not in any way suspect, that the undertaking demanded would carry with it permission to go to America. It is now too late for me to fulfil my engagement at Harvard, as the Harvard authorities have been compelled to make other arrangements as I have also. Mr Samuel stated on 25 October that "Mr Russell could at any time have obtained a permit to go to America on giving such an undertaking." Not the faintest hint of this was given to me, and I neither knew nor guessed that it was the case.'

In America the presidential election had resulted in victory for Woodrow Wilson. In Russell's view this improved the prospects for peace, and he wrote to Ellery Sedgwick, editor of the *Atlantic Monthly*, on 25 November 1916:

'I am very glad that Wilson has been re-elected. I suppose one ought to have no views on the politics of a foreign country but I cannot help thinking it is to the good of mankind that he remains at the White House.'

Russell was growing despondent and began to doubt the efficacy of his anti-war work. 'I was having the greatest difficulty in believing that anything at all was worth doing', he wrote. 'At the height of my winter despair, however, I had found one thing to do, which turned out as useless as everything else, but seemed to me at the moment not without value. America still being neutral, I wrote an open letter to President Wilson, appealing to him to save the world.'[10]

Russell to President Woodrow Wilson 4 December 1916[11]

'You have an opportunity of performing a signal service to mankind, surpassing even the service of Abraham Lincoln, great as he was. It is in your power to bring the war to an end by a just peace, which shall do all that could possibly be done to allay the fear of new wars in the near future. It is not yet too late to save European civilisation from destruction; but it may be too late if the war is allowed to continue for the further two or three years with which our militarists threaten us.

'The military situation has now developed to the point where the ultimate issue is clear, in its broad outlines, to all who are capable of thought. It must be obvious to the authorities in all the belligerent countries that no victory for either side is possible. In Europe, the Germans have the advantage; outside Europe, and at sea, the Allies have the advantage. Neither side is able to win such a crushing victory as to compel the other to sue for peace. The war inflicts untold injuries upon the nations, but not such injuries as to make a continuance of fighting impossible. It is evident that however the war may be prolonged, negotiations will ultimately have to take place on the basis of what will be substantially the present balance of gains and losses, and will result in terms not very different from those which might be obtained now. The German government has recognised this fact, and has expressed its willingness for peace on terms which ought to be regarded at least as affording a basis for discussion, since they concede the points which involve the honour of the Allies. The Allied governments have not had the courage to acknowledge publicly what they cannot deny in private, that the hope of a sweeping victory is one which can now scarcely be entertained. For want of this courage, they are prepared to involve Europe in the horrors of a continuance of the war, possibly for another two or three years. This situation is intolerable to every humane man. You, Sir, can put an end to it. Your power constitutes an opportunity and a responsibility; and from your previous actions I feel confident that you will use your power with a degree of wisdom and humanity rarely to be found among statesmen.

'The harm which has already been done in this war is immeasurable. Not only have millions of valuable lives been lost, not only have an even greater number of men been maimed or shattered in health, but the whole standard of civilisation has been lowered. Fear has invaded men's inmost being, and with fear has come the ferocity that always attends it. Hatred has become the rule of life, and injury to others is more desired than benefit to ourselves. The hopes of peaceful progress in which our earlier years were passed are dead, and can never be revived. Terror and savagery have become the very air we breathe. The liberties which our ancestors won by centuries of struggle were sacrificed in a day, and all the nations are regimented to the one ghastly end of mutual destruction.

'But all this is as nothing in comparison with what the future has in store for us if the war continues as long as the announcements of some of our leading men would make us expect. As the stress increases, and weariness of the war makes average men more restive, the severity of repression has to be continually augmented. In all the belligerent countries, soldiers who are wounded or home on leave express an utter loathing of the trenches, a despair of ever achieving a military decision, and a terrible longing for peace. Our militarists have successfully opposed the granting of votes to soldiers; yet in all the countries an attempt is made to persuade the civilian population that war-weariness is confined to the enemy soldiers. The daily toll of young lives destroyed becomes a horror almost too terrible to be borne; yet everywhere, advocacy of peace is rebuked as treachery to the soldiers, though the soldiers above all men desire peace. Everywhere, friends of peace are met with the diabolical argument that the brave men who have died must not have shed their blood in vain. And so every impulse of mercy towards the soldiers who are still living is dried up and withered by a false and barren loyalty to those who are past our help. Even the men hitherto retained for making munitions, for dock labour, and for other purposes essential to the prosecution of the war, are gradually being drafted into the armies and replaced by women, with the sinister threat of coloured labour in the background. There is a very real danger that, if nothing is done to check the fury of national passion, European

66

civilisation as we have known it will perish as completely as it perished when Rome fell before the Barbarians.

'It may be thought strange that public opinion should appear to support all that is being done by the authorities for the prosecution of the war. But this appearance is very largely deceptive. The continuance of the war is actively advocated by influential persons, and by the press, which is everywhere under the control of the government. In other sections of society, feeling is quite different from that expressed by the newspapers, but public opinion remains silent and uninformed, since those who might give guidance are subject to such severe penalties that few dare to protest openly, and those few cannot obtain a wide publicity. From considerable personal experience, reinforced by all that I can learn from others, I believe that the desire for peace is almost universal, not only among the soldiers, but throughout the wage-earning classes, and especially in industrial districts, in spite of high wages and steady employment. If a plebiscite of the nation were taken on the question whether negotiations should be initiated, I am confident that an over-whelming majority would be in favour of this course, and that the same is true of France, Germany and Austria–Hungary.

'Such acquiescence as there is in continued hostilities is due entirely to fear. Every nation believes that its enemies were the aggressors and may make war in a few years unless they are utterly defeated. The United States government has the power, not only to compel the European governments to make peace, but also to reassure the populations by making itself the guarantor of the peace. Such action, even if it were resented by the governments, would be hailed with joy by the populations. If the German government, as now seems likely, would not only restore conquered territory, but also give its adherence to the League to Enforce Peace or some similar method of settling disputes without war, fear would be allayed, and it is almost certain that an offer of mediation from you would give rise to an irresistible movement in favour of negotiations. But the deadlock is such that no near end to the war is likely except through the mediation of an outside Power, and such mediation can only come from you.

'Some may ask by what right I address you. I have no formal title; I am not part of the machinery of government. I speak only because I must; because others, who should have remembered civilisation and human brotherhood, have allowed themselves to be swept away by national passion; because I am compelled by their apostasy to speak in the name of reason and mercy, lest it should be thought that no one in Europe remembers the work which Europe has done and ought still to do for mankind. It is to the European races, in Europe and out of it, that the world owes most of what it possesses in thought, in science, in art, in ideals of government, in hope for the future. If they are allowed to destroy each other in futile carnage, something will be lost which is more precious than diplomatic prestige, incomparably more valuable than a sterile victory which leaves the victors themselves perishing. Like the rest of my countrymen I have desired ardently the victory of the Allies; like them, I have suffered when victory has been delayed. But I remember always that Europe has common tasks to fulfil; that a war among European nations is in essence a civil war; that the ill which we think of our enemies they equally think of us; and that it is difficult in time of war for a belligerent to see facts truly. Above all, I see that none of the issues of the war are as important as peace; the harm done by a peace which does not concede all that we desire is as nothing in comparison to the harm done by the continuance of the fighting. While all who have power in Europe speak for what they falsely believe to be the interests of their separate nations, I am compelled by a profound conviction to speak for all the nations in the name of Europe. In the name of Europe I appeal to you to bring us peace.'

The letter was smuggled into America by Katherine Dudley, Helen Dudley's sister, who had been on a visit to England. It was distributed by American pacifists and given nationwide press coverage at a time when pressures against neutralism were mounting. *The New York Times* of 23 December gave front page prominence to the story under the headline: 'Mysterious Girl Brings Russell's Peace Plea Here; Famous English Philosopher and Mathematician Asks Wilson to "Stop War Ere Europe Perishes".' Reproducing the full text of Russell's letter, *The New York Times* reported:

'An unnamed and otherwise unidentified passenger from England, a girl, walked into the Hotel Astor yesterday while members of the American Neutral Conference Committee were in session and handed to the committee a letter from Bertrand Russell, British pacifist, philosopher and mathematician, appealing to President Wilson to end the war in Europe.

'Hamilton Holt, president of the conference, introduced the messenger, the letter was read, and at midnight a committee left for Washington to present the document to Mr Wilson. It was explained in the conference's behalf, that having slipped out of England with the letter, avoiding British censorship, it was undesirable to make the messenger's name public. She had arrived here on Wednesday, it was added, and had come purposely to deliver the letter. She was described officially by the conference merely as "a confidential agent" of Mr Russell. The meeting at which she presented the letter was a private luncheon.

'It could not be ascertained that night whether members of the

Neutral Conference Committee had advance knowledge of the girl messenger's mission. The committee named to take the letter to Washington consisted of George Foster Peabody, Paul U. Kellogg, and Miss Emily Green Balch. It was explained that the letter would be placed in the President's hands as soon as he should care to receive the committee.

'Russell, who is the heir of Earl Russell, and was a lecturer and fellow of Trinity College, Cambridge, recently was fined $500 for having written a pamphlet opposing conscription in England. He also was prohibited from coming to the United States to lecture at Harvard, and was forbidden to enter any prohibited area in England.'

Giving further details of Russell's career, *The New York Times* described him as 'one of England's most extreme pacifists whose misadventures, because of his belief, have attracted widespread attention not only in England but here as well. . . .' Russell believed, the newspaper reported, that an early peace 'could be obtained without weakening seriously any of the Great Powers involved, and for the future has advocated a central world government "able and willing to secure obedience by force" and, therefore, a guarantee of future peace.' Katherine Dudley's identity intrigued the press, and *The New York Times* of 24 December revealed, 'Russell Courier an American Girl', and continued with its sensational story of the previous day:

'The young woman who delivered Bertrand Russell's peace letter to the Neutral Conference Committee . . . was an American, who has lived in England, according to a member of the conference. He said yesterday that her identity must continue to remain a secret, for she expected shortly to return to England. . . . Russell, she explained to the conference here, had considered making use of the mails to send his letter to President Wilson, as well as a number of articles which he wanted delivered to a magazine editor, but he abandoned this plan on the theory that nothing he wrote would pass the censors in its entirety.'

When the letter was delivered to the White House, the President was out, and it was left with his secretary. Although it did not ultimately achieve its purpose, it gave great heart to the American neutralist cause. Harry Dana, of Columbia University, wrote to Russell on 24 December:

'Your letter to President Wilson which was brought to our Neutral Conference Committee yesterday and has today appeared in the newspapers throughout the country has made a profound impression everywhere. At the Faculty Club of this university, to cite but one instance, it has helped many men to see things at last as they are. It could not have come at a more opportune moment. . . .'

During 1917, Russell intensified his literary barrage against the war, mainly through regular weekly articles for the *Tribunal*, the official organ of the No-Conscription Fellowship. On 1 February, he wrote a leader article for the *Tribunal*,[12] defending President Wilson's call for a just peace, 'a peace without victory', which *The Times* had attacked. Russell commented: 'In leading us to understand and respect this neutral view, President Wilson is performing the inestimable service of contributing to heal the bitterness that the war has produced.' Despite Wilson's pronouncements, America's neutralist position was deteriorating and, as her entry into the war grew imminent, Russell received scores of letters from his American readers. Not all of these were complimentary. A letter from Indiana suggested that 'the authorities ought to . . . bundle you off to Germany, bag and baggage, provided Germany would undertake to keep you for life.' A correspondent from Oregon commenting on the Wilson letter declared: 'I am surprised that an Englishman could be found to write such a letter . . . you and men like you if there are any ought to stand solid with your fellow Britons.'

The American version of *The Principles of Social Reconstruction*, entitled *Why Men Fight*, was being widely read and reviewed. The New York *Tribune* of 28 February 1917 published a tribute to the book and its author in the form of a poem by Irwin Edman, the philosopher:

> *To Bertrand Russell*
> After Reading *Why Men Fight*
> There is a facile and familiar way
> To courage; one in comradeship may be
> Herded in the habitual array
> Of flushed and furious humanity.
> There is the close, warm fellowship of fear,
> Huddled with many friends, one may rejoice
> To laud the scarlet idols they hold dear,
> To be their favoured unprophetic voice.
> Or one may choose the graceless, strenuous vision,
> Gazing with spacious and eternal view,
> Clear eyed and terrible through men's derision,
> To sting them with a cleansing faith, as you
>   Up friendless and forbidden paths have fought
>   To wave white truths from lonely peaks of thought.

Shortly after America broke off diplomatic relations with Germany, Russell heard from Lucy Donnelly who had just read *Why Men Fight*, and who wrote on 8 March:

'I have read nothing with so much interest and happiness since the war began as your book. Indeed it is quite one of the finest books that I have ever read.

'. . . Your publishers I suppose send you the American reviews, or I would fill my envelope with them, as I would like to send you all that I hear said in praise of you and your book. . . . I have been wanting, too, since mid-winter to express my entire admiration of your letter to the President.

'Here in America of course we are just living from day to day. Our uncertainty will, I suppose, be at an end when this letter reaches England. I myself trust more and more to Wilson, where we have doubted him he has so often been proved right in the light of later events and fuller information. . . .'

Russell, encouraged by events in Russia, particularly the February Revolution and the emergence of Kerensky's provisional government, replied to Lucy Donnelly on 23 March:

'Very many thanks for your letter. I am immensely glad you like my book—it has been impossible to explain things in letters, and I am glad of your understanding. I have seen only one American review. I should be grateful if you would keep those you come across and let me see them when the war is over—in these days it is not worth while to send things, as there are so many chances of their not arriving.

'The Russian Revolution is a stupendous event. Although one can't tell yet how it will work out, it can hardly fail to do great good. It has been more cheering than anything that has happened since the war began. Of course we are all watching America with intense interest. I wonder what will happen. . . .'

On 6 April 1917, America declared war on Germany. In an editorial for the *Tribunal*, entitled 'America's Entry Into the War',[13] Russell argued that whereas the February Revolution in Russia brought peace nearer, America's intervention in the war could, very likely, lengthen it since 'without America, universal exhaustion might have driven all the nations to a compromise peace.' Looking back seven years later, Russell analysed the causes of America's participation in the war:[14]

'If you examine American policy since 1914, you will find one confident principle by which it can be all explained. Practically everything that has been done has furthered the interests of Standard Oil and the house of Morgan. Sometimes these interests have been in harmony with those of mankind, sometimes not; in both cases equally they have prevailed.

'If the war had ended with the victory of the central Powers, it would have hit Morgan hard, as they had financed England and France.

'After they had lent England and France as much as they thought safe, America enforced the war, and for once loans were made by the American government, to the great advantage of previous private lenders. In the spring of 1917, both sides were prepared for peace. Kerensky's government knew that Russia could not hold out much longer and adopted the slogan, "No annexations and no indemnities". France and England had exhausted their credit and would have agreed to peace on those terms if America had remained neutral. Germany was sufficiently exhausted to have accepted the Kerensky formula if America had vigorously championed it. At this movement, however, the German government, with almost inconceivable folly, adopted the unlimited submarine campaign. This gave American high finance the opportunity it needed, and enabled it to bring America into the war, directly bringing the American taxpayers to the rescue of previous private lenders.'

More than ever before, anti-war Americans turned towards Russell, and he was besieged by appeals to sponsor and support new radical journals and organisations. Individuals, too, found in him a source of comfort and inspiration during this time of great national crisis. James Bronson Reynolds, who had met Russell in New York in 1896, wrote on 9 July 1917:

'I write now to express my warm appreciation of your writings, particularly of *Justice in Wartime*, though I think I have read everything else that you have published in America on that and allied subjects within the past few years. Your profound comprehension of the fundamental issues raised by war, your high mental integrity, your illuminating discussion of historical facts and forces have been to me and many others in America both a refreshment and an uplift. When the hideous waste and slaughter of this war are ended I am confident that the immense spiritual value of your message will be understood as is perhaps not possible in the blinding storm of today. . . .

'I share the view of many in this country that not only must we make, as President Wilson declares, "the world safe for democracy" but that we must make democracy safe for the world. . . .'

Russell replied on 3 September 1917:

'Letters such as yours are a great encouragement to anyone engaged in an unpopular cause, and I am grateful to you for having written.

'I well remember the times when we met twenty years ago. It is odd to think how cheerfully superficial one's outlook was in those days. What you say about making democracy safe for the world is very true: I wish there were more realisation of it, but for the present the outlook remains very gloomy.'

Despite America's involvement in the war and the traumatic setback this had created for the pacifist cause, Russell continued to look to the United States as the best hope, in the long-term, for achieving a permanent solution to the problems of war. In October 1917, The *Seven Arts* magazine of New York published an article by Russell entitled 'Is Nationalism Moribund?' Russell, declaring that 'I do not wish to dogmatise about America in the confident fashion to which Europeans are prone', doubted whether United States participation in the war would 'produce anything like that unity of national feeling in America' which had been produced in Europe.

Russell hopefully argued that nationalism, which 'almost wholly' inspired the war that was then being fought, would lose its influence in the future and that America, of all nations, was best suited to play an internationalist role. He wrote:

'There seems little doubt that America is embarked upon a great military career. It seems reasonable to expect that America will become the greatest of all military powers. This does not mean that she will necessarily become militarist in spirit. It is quite possible that the military power of America may be used for the purpose of securing a universal diminution of armaments by international agreement. . . . But it will do this through internationalism rather than through nationalism, through the attempt to realise a family of nations with a common, supernational government rather than through the attempt to become itself a dominant nation. The mixture of races and the comparative absence of a national tradition make America peculiarly suited to the fulfilment of this task.'

Towards the end of 1917, Russell decided to resign his chairmanship of the No-Conscription Fellowship. He had, for many months, been convinced that the pacifist cause was too limited in its political objectives to help bring an end to the war. He was still prepared to write for the *Tribunal* and on 3 January 1918, the journal ran an article written by him, entitled 'The German Peace Offer'.[15] The article drew attention to the willingness of Germany to make peace, provided the Allies agreed to the Bolshevik proposals which excluded annexations and indemnities. Commenting on the offer Russell held that:

'If they [the Allies] refuse the German offer, they are unmasked before the world and before their own Labour and Socialist parties [as] . . . continuing the war for purposes of territorial aggrandisement. If they accept the offer, they afford a triumph to the hated Bolsheviks and an object lesson to democratic revolutionaries everywhere as to the way to treat with capitalists, imperialists and war-mongers.'

Russell argued that the Western Powers hoped to gain from the continuation of the war in the belief that under the conditions of prolonged suffering and starvation 'the sane constructive effort required for a successful revolution will be impossible.' Russell believed that such an approach might prove feasible because:

'The American garrison which will by that time be occupying England and France, whether or not they will prove efficient against the Germans, will no doubt be capable of intimidating strikers, an occupation to which the American army is accustomed when at home.'

For the second time in the course of the war Russell was charged and brought to trial. The reference to the American garrison was seized upon by the authorities as the reason for his arrest. For his trial Russell prepared a defence based on material extracted from the U.S. Congress 'Final Report of the Commission on Industrial Relations' (1915) which dealt with the use of U.S. troops in industrial disputes. The report showed that in recent years soldiers had helped to suppress strikers in West Virginia, Colorado and Idaho. The report stated: 'in cases arising from labor agitations, the judiciary has uniformly upheld the power exercised by the military and in no case has there been any protest against the use of such power or any attempt to curtail it. . . .' He was prevented from citing this material, found guilty and sentenced to six months' imprisonment. In passing sentence Sir John Dickinson, the magistrate, commented: 'Mr Russell seems to have lost all sense of decency and fairness and has gone out of his way to insult by a deliberate and designed sneer the army of a great nation which is closely allied to us . . . the offence is a very despicable one.' There can be little doubt that the 'insult' to the American army provided the authorities with a convenient excuse to deal with a man who had been unrelenting in his criticism of them since the first days of the war.

The New York *World* of 11 February 1918, applauded the sentence:

'Scholar and heir to an earldom, the Hon. Bertrand Russell is nevertheless a depraved liar—since he knows better—when he asserts that "the American garrison" in England and France "will no doubt be capable of intimidating strikers, an occupation to which the American army is accustomed at home." Six months in prison for this pacifist of a poisoned pen is a fit sentence.'

After an appeal against his conviction failed, Russell was committed in May to Brixton Prison where he served four months of his sentence. On his release, early in September, he was able to read the many letters which were sent from America during his imprisonment. Scott Nearing, the famous American socialist, summed up the feelings of many of his compatriots in a letter of 16 August 1918:

'I am writing this line to tell you how much it means to us, here across the sea, to have a man in England stand up, as you have stood up, in these impossible, heroic times, and face the music of life as you have faced it. We all get fresh courage from you. It puts upon you the greater responsibility, but it gives, at the same time, a feeling of world consciousness that is so much needed.

'There are thousands in America that feel as I do, and if they do not write, it is because they do not know where to address you, or because the pressure of life is too hard, or because they would spare you. We are with you, however—legions of spirits with the vision of a new day for the world.'

In the final weeks of the war, Russell was mainly concerned about the achievement of a constructive peace settlement and found that 'in common with most other people, I based my hopes upon Woodrow Wilson.'[16] However, as a result of his own activities during the war, many, especially the young, saw Russell as the focal point of their hope for the future. A student, Ramon Coffman, wrote from Newark Academy on 22 October 1918:

'As a young American liberal, I write to you to express if I can something of the esteem which I and my fellows hold for you. From the beginning of the war we have listened to your voice lifted above the maddened strife and sounding like a clear-toned bell above a turbulent sea. Your words have given us new hope, new life, new confidence in a world redeemed. They inspire us to determined activity toward so reshaping human society as to make a repetition of this war impossible.'

On Armistice Day, Lucy Donnelly wrote to Russell and expressed a hope for his return to America:

'I cannot let the day end without writing you, as my first thoughts were of you and England when the whistle and bells called us from our beds at half past 4 this morning to rejoice that the war was ended. As the students sang songs and built a great bonfire I wandered about under the stars and into the dawn thinking on and on of you and Europe with the pain and suffering you have endured. We know only the joy of victory but it would be better for us as well as you, could we have shared alike the pain and happiness. The war has only touched the surface of America, for all our will to do our part and to understand. But it is characteristic that through a newspaper fake we were informed and believed that armistice was signed on Thursday last and spent Friday in celebration. Today we have done it all over again, more lavishly and loudly than ever! But thank heaven, it is Peace this time and the fighting is stopped. . . .

'It is unbelievably good to write in this new world, we can write letters again and someday I shall see England again, and you perhaps come to America.'

NOTES

1 See B. Russell, *Autobiography* (London, 1968), Vol. II, pp. 63–4 (Boston, 1968), pp. 77–8.

2 Ibid., pp. 64–5; pp. 78–9.

3 Ibid.

4 Ibid., pp. 65–6; pp. 80–1.

5 Woods cabled Russell to this effect on 1 August 1916.

6 From David Starr Jordan, Stanford University, California. The letter was dated 15 August 1916.

7 Husband of Lady Ottoline Morrell; Russell had campaigned for him in the 1910 general election.

8 *The C.O.'s Hansard* (reprinted from official parliamentary reports), published by the No-Conscription Fellowship (26 October 1916), p. 88.

9 Ibid., pp. 94–5.

10 B. Russell, *Autobiography*, Vol. II, pp 21–2; pp. 27–8.

11 Ibid., pp. 22–5; pp. 28–31; the letter originally appeared in *The New York Times* (23 December 1916); see Illustrations, Plate 3, p. 211.

12 From 'President Wilson's Statement' (see below, pp. 215–16).

13 See below, pp. 217–19; see also Illustrations, Plate 4, p. 211.

14 From 'What is Wrong with Western Civilisation?', a lecture to the League for Industrial Democracy on 3 April 1924 in New York (see below, pp. 94–5).

15 Reprinted in B. Russell, *Autobiography*, Vol. II, pp. 79–81; pp. 103–6.

16 Ibid., p. 34; p. 37.

CHAPTER 6

CONTROVERSY AT HARVARD

Early in the war Russell had become a socialist, resigned from the Liberals and joined the Labour party. The war had caused him to write on socio-political themes. But during his imprisonment he was permitted to deal only with subjects related to his earlier philosophical work. In his four months at Brixton Prison, he completed *Introduction to Mathematical Philosophy* and began work on *The Analysis of Mind*. Looking back on the war years, Russell observed that he 'ceased to be academic and took to writing a new kind of books'.[1] He was encouraged in this by the favourable response given to his propagandist lectures and articles, selections of which had been published in book form during the war.[2] In the last days before his imprisonment he had hastily completed *Roads to Freedom* which was published in 1918. The book analysed the doctrines of socialism, anarchism and syndicalism, which were being fiercely debated at the time, and was to have a profound impact on American radicals during a period of great social unrest. Russell himself was impressed with the growth of labour agitation in America, particularly the rise of the International Workers of the World (Wobblies), and in *Roads to Freedom* noted with approval that 'industrial unionism, spreading from America, has had a considerable influence in Great Britain.'[3]

Many Americans who had lost touch with Russell during his imprisonment began to renew contact with him. Elizabeth Perkins had been attempting to reach him, and when she did she described the rapid rise of democratic feeling in the post-war months, and inquired whether Russell remembered telling her in 1915 that 'Wilson would be the peacemaker and reorganiser.' She commented: 'Few persons had this prophetic vision then—but even your intuition could not have foreseen the extraordinary events of the last months—or such a rapid growing of Democratic control.'[4]

Henry Sheffer, who had studied under Russell at Cambridge on the recommendation of Josiah Royce,[5] and was lecturing at Harvard, wrote to Russell on 17 May 1919:

'For three years I have watched your courageous intellectual honesty. Be assured that the liberal forces in America—forces of all sorts and conditions of men—have been and are with you. And, whether or not a "neutralist" like myself may be called a liberal, my admiration for your rugged fearlessness is as great as that of the most "advanced" of radicals.

'And now that the Great Crisis is at least partly over, I am glad to find you back in the fold of active mathematical logicians. I have read your *Introduction to Mathematical Philosophy*, and wish it had appeared a few months earlier, so that I could have used it in one of the classes. I was "more than" pleased with your paper on Dewey;[6] and your series of articles on "Logical Atomism" is the clearest presentation of the subject I have seen. You may be interested to know that for next fall I am offering a course entitled "The Philosophy of Logical Atomism, with special reference to Russell and Whitehead". . . .'

The democratic spirit which surged across America in the immediate post-war period soon lost ground to conservative reaction. Harvard was no exception, and those among its faculty who were at all liberal or non-conformist found themselves increasingly on the defensive. This was no surprise to Russell, who had criticised the lack of autonomy of American universities. His close connection with Harvard was to involve him in a campus controversy which reflected more significant confrontations taking place nationally. Harold Laski, the English socialist, who was teaching at Harvard wrote to Russell on 29 August 1919, drawing attention to the predicament of Sheffer, who had become an early target of discrimination at the university:[7]

'. . . I know from your *Introduction to Mathematical Logic* [*sic*] that you think well of Sheffer who is at present in the Philosophy Department here. . . . He is a Jew and he has married someone of whom the university does not approve; moreover, he hasn't the social qualities that Harvard so highly prizes. The result is that most of his department is engaged on a determined effort to bring his career here to an end . . . the whole thing is a combination of anti-Semitism and that curious university worship of social prestige which plays so large a part over here...'

Since Russell was so highly regarded at Harvard, Laski, in consort with Professor Hoernle, the Chairman of the Philosophy Department, asked Russell to provide a testimonial in support of Sheffer's ability. Russell responded with a letter to Laski in which he stated:[8]

'I know Sheffer well. He was a pupil of mine and I saw much of his work both at that time and later. He has published discoveries in the algebra of logic which appear to me very important, as I have had occasion to state in print. He has work on hand now which, from what I know of it, appears likely to constitute a very notable advance. In my opinion, both from the point of view of ability and fruitfulness of research, any faculty in the world would be fortunate to include him. I suppose Harvard realises its good fortune in having him.'

Russell also suggested to Laski that Perry be approached as a possible ally. Laski wrote back on 29 September 1919, giving news of the campaign he had initiated on Sheffer's behalf:[9]

'. . . I am . . . grateful for your word on Sheffer. I have given it to Hoernle who will show it to the members of the Philosophy Department and, if necessary, to Lowell. And I have sent copies to two members of the Corporation who will fight if there is need. I don't think there is anything further to be done at the moment. It would do no good to write to Perry. These last years, particularly twelve months in the War Department of the U.S., have made him very conservative and an eager adherent of "correct form". He is the head and centre of the enemy forces and I see no good in trying to move him directly. He wants respectable neo-Christians in the department who will explain the necessity of ecclesiastical sanctions; or, if they are not religious, at least they must be materially successful. I don't think universities are ever destined to be homes of liberalism; and the American system is in the hands of big business and dominated by its grosser ideals. Did you ever read Veblen's *Higher Learning in America*?

'You may be interested to know that I have a graduate class at Yale this term reading *Roads to Freedom*. I've never met Yale men before; but it was absorbingly interesting to see their amazement that Marx and Bakunin and the rest could be written of without abuse. . . .'

Laski, who was coming under attack for his outspoken political views, wrote to Russell on 2 November 1919, giving him some idea of the mounting difficulties faced by a radical educator in America:[10]

'. . . I find that when one presents syndicalism or socialism namelessly, they take it as reasonable and obvious; attach the name and they whisper to the parents that nameless abominations are being perpetrated. I spoke for the striking police here the other day—one of those strikes which makes one equally wonder at the endurance of the men and the unimaginative stupidity of the officials. Within a week, two papers and two hundred alumni demanded my dismissal—teaching sovietism was what urging that men who get $1,100 and work seventy-three hours are justified in striking after thirteen years agitation was called. As it happens Lowell does believe in freedom of speech, so that I stay; but you get some index to the present American state of mind.'

While Laski was fighting for Sheffer, his own position was becoming precarious. He wrote to Russell on 4 December 1919:[11]

'. . . . Things here are in a terrible mess. Injunctions violating specific government promises; arrest of the miners' leaders because the men refused to go back; recommendation of stringent legislation against "reds"; arrest of men in the West for simple possession of an I.W.W. [Wobblies] card; argument by even moderates like Eliot[12] that the issue is a straight fight between labour and constitutional government; all these are in the ordinary course of events. And neither Pound[13] nor I think the crest of the wave has been reached. Some papers have actually demanded that the Yale University Press withdraw my books from circulation because they preach "anarchy". On the other hand Holmes and Brandeis[14] wrote (through Holmes) a magnificent dissent in defence of freedom of speech in an espionage act case. . . . This sounds very gloomy; but since America exported Lady Astor to England there's an entire absence of political comedy.'

Sheffer's position at Harvard had become dependent upon a paper he had completed claiming new discoveries in mathematical logic which, he announced, would make portions of *Principia Mathematica* superfluous. Hoernle requested Russell's opinion on the quality of the work as 'we philosophers are none of us sufficiently expert in mathematical logic to feel competent to express an opinion.'[15] After reading Sheffer's treatise, Russell notified Harvard of his very high opinion of the work and informed Hoernle that his judgement had not been biased 'on account of Sheffer's situation'.[16]

Soon afterwards, the fight to win Sheffer a faculty appointment succeeded. There is no doubt that Russell's support was the decisive factor in the campaign. Sheffer wrote to Russell in appreciation on 6 March 1920, informing him that 'mainly, if not solely, on the basis of your letters to Hoernle the opposition . . . has been overcome.'

Laski, who had played such an important role in the Sheffer incident and who was instrumental in seeking Russell's support, had, in the meantime, become the subject of a full-scale witch-hunt. He informed Russell on 5 January 1920:[17]

'. . . Harvard is determined to be socially respectable at all costs. I have recently been interviewed by the Board of Overseers to know: (a) whether I believe in a revolution with blood; (b) whether I believe in the Soviet form of government; (c) whether I do not believe that the American form of government is superior to any other; (d) whether I believe in the right of revolution.

'In the last three days they have arrested 5,000 socialists with a view to deportation. I feel glad that Graham Wallas is going to try and get me home!'

In contrast to Harvard, the academic situation at Cambridge had improved and Russell was reinstated there. Among the first to congratulate him from America was Laski, who commented on his own position: 'I am heartily sick of America and I would like to have an atmosphere again where an ox does not tread upon the tongue.'[18]

A few years later, after Laski had returned to England, Russell wrote in an article, entitled 'Freedom Versus Authority':[19]

'A teacher of economics in America is expected to teach such doctrines as will add to the wealth and power of the very rich; if he does not he finds it advisable to go elsewhere, like Mr Laski, formerly of Harvard, now one of the most valuable teachers in the London School of Economics.'

NOTES

[1] B. Russell, *Autobiography* (London, 1968), Vol. II, p. 38 (Boston, 1968), p. 36.

[2] B. Russell, *Principles of Social Reconstruction* (London, 1916) as *Why Men Fight* (The Century Co., New York, 1916); *Justice in Wartime* (London and Open Court, Chicago, 1916), *Political Ideals* (The Century Co., New York, 1917).

[3] B. Russell, *Roads to Freedom* (London, 1918) as *Proposed Roads to Freedom* (Henry Holt, New York, 1919), p. 90.

[4] From Elizabeth Perkins's letter of 15 February 1919.

[5] Royce in a letter to Russell of 29 June 1910 had written of Sheffer: 'I may call him a disciple of yours. I think also that we have, in America, no more promising research student of the new logic. . . . I expect important results from him.'

[6] Russell's review of Dewey's *Essays in Experimental Logic* appeared in the *Journal of Philosophy* (2 January 1919).

[7] For the full text of this letter see B. Russell, *Autobiography*, Vol. II, pp. 111–12; pp. 154–6.

[8] Undated, September 1919.

[9] B. Russell, *Autobiography*, Vol. II, pp. 112–13; pp. 156–7.

[10] Ibid., pp. 113–14; pp. 157–8.

[11] Ibid., p. 114; pp. 158–9.

[12] Charles William Eliot, the educator, who was President of Harvard 1869–1909.

[13] Roscoe Pound, Dean of Harvard Law School.

[14] Oliver Wendell Holmes and Louis D. Brandeis, prominent jurists.

[15] From Hoernle's letter of 28 November 1919.

[16] From Russell's letter of 30 December 1919.

[17] B. Russell, *Autobiography*, Vol. II, pp. 114–15; pp. 159–60.

[18] From his letter of 18 February 1920 in ibid.

[19] Reprinted in B. Russell, *Sceptical Essays* (London, 1928), p. 198 (W. W. Norton, New York, 1928), p. 202.

CHAPTER 7

HOPES AND FEARS

Russell was not to take up his appointment at Cambridge. Although he had formally accepted a position to lecture at Trinity, on 27 November 1919, he hinted, in a letter to Lucy Donnelly, at his reluctance to return to a purely academic existence:

'. . . now that the war is over I no longer feel like a ghost, an impotent spectator of activities in which I cannot share. It is possible I may go back to Cambridge, tho' probably not for long. I don't think I could stand the academic atmosphere now, having tasted freedom and the joys of a dangerous life.'

Russell was interested to influence the shape of the emerging post-war world. As a socialist, he seized the opportunity of accompanying a British Labour delegation to Soviet Russia in May 1920. The fruit of that visit was *The Practice and Theory of Bolshevism*, which was critical of the methods used by the Bolsheviks in forcing the transition from capitalism to socialism. As with the First World War, when he felt America's role to be crucial, so he felt the attainment of socialism in Europe could not 'succeed until America is either converted to socialism, or at any rate willing to remain neutral'.[1]

Russell held that any successful socialist revolution depended on economic self-sufficiency which, in his view, Russia did not possess. This he applied to all countries except America, which, he felt, lacked the necessary 'psychological conditions' to achieve revolution: 'There is no other civilised country where capitalism is so strong and revolutionary socialism so weak as in America.'[2] Russell eschewed 'the arguments of hatred and universal upheaval', which he ascribed to the Third International, and advocated instead:[3]

'It is by slower and less showy methods that the new world must be built: by industrial efforts after self-government, by proletarian training in technique and business administration, by careful study of the international situation, by a prolonged and devoted propaganda of ideas rather than tactics, especially among the wage-earners of the United States.'

As if to confirm his own thoughts, a letter from Lucy Donnelly, declaring: 'Heaven knows all America needs liberalising at the moment!', was waiting for him on his return from Russia. The letter was dated 6 June 1920, and Lucy, who was abroad at the time, continued:

'I need not tell you in what a black night of prejudice and political intrigue I left it [America]. And Hoover to whom some of us have been clinging for help out of our immediate muddle has now become a very forlorn hope with the Republican Convention.'

Another letter waiting for Russell invited him to lecture in China on behalf of the Chinese Lecture Association. He accepted the invitation and in October 1920 arrived in China to take up a position as a Visiting Professor of Philosophy at Peking University. Russell was impressed with China; the culture and civilisation especially delighted him, despite spending several months of his stay convalescing after a severe attack of double pneumonia. When he was well enough, he travelled to Japan for a brief visit but not before some Japanese newspapers reported that he had died. The rumours soon spread to America, and thence to England, and the 21 June issue of the *Atlantic Monthly* commented:

'Bertrand Russell has recently, we now hope wrongfully, been reported dead in China. Gifted with a mind of extraordinary brilliancy, he gained early in life a great reputation as a mathematician. To the larger public he is known chiefly as a political philosopher of radical tendencies, whose intellect is never overridden by his sympathies: witness his extraordinarily candid little volume on the principles of communism and socialism.'

On his return to England in September 1921, he married Dora Black, who had accompanied him on the trip as his secretary.

Russell had now visited and gained first-hand experience of the three countries whose developing world roles and interrelationships were to occupy his attention in the years ahead; Russia, China and the U.S.A. He was particularly anxious about the future and fate of China, which was then being decided at the Washington Conference, where America, Britain, France and Japan were seeking agreement on their respective areas of control. Russell contributed several articles to English and American periodicals on the subject of Anglo–American involvement in China, hoping to influence government policy and the outcome of the Washington Conference. His article, 'How Washington Could Help China', was published in the British Labour paper, the *Daily Herald*, on 16 December 1921, and *The New York Times* carried excerpts from the article on the same day, under the sensational heading, 'War Is Predicted by Bertrand Russell'.[4]

In it, Russell stated that the Washington Conference could serve a useful purpose only it if succeeded in curbing Japanese ambitions. This, he held, was possible because British and American interests were dependent upon stability in China and the ending of Japanese territorial aggression. Russell foresaw a war with Japan if her activities in China remained unchecked. This would result in the destruction of Japan:

'. . . and following upon this there will be a slow destruction of the civilisation of China, not by war, but by Americanisation. The big towns will become like Chicago, and the small towns like Main Street. America would feel that they were conferring a boon in effecting this transformation, but no person with any receptivity or aesthetic sense would share their view. . . .'

Robert Young, an American journalist and editor of the *Japan Weekly Chronicle*, wrote to Russell on 2 January 1922 on the outcome of the Washington Conference. Russell had befriended Young the previous year in Japan and considered his paper to be 'the best newspaper I have ever known'.[5] Young declared:[6]

'. . . What a farce the Washington Conference is. From the first I doubted the sincerity of this enthusiasm for peace on the part of those who made the war. . . . Japan has sulkily accepted the ratio proposed by America, but is supporting the French demand for more submarines. France is showing herself a greater danger to Europe than Germany ever was. China has been betrayed at the Washington Conference, as we expected. The Anglo–Japanese alliance has been scrapped, to be replaced by a Four-Power agreement which is still more dangerous to China. Her salvation, unhappily, lies in the jealousies of the Powers. United, the pressure on her will be increased. But I doubt whether the Senate will endorse the treaty, once its full implications are understood....'

The Washington Conference and its consequences was one of the subjects dealt with by Russell in his book, *The Problem of China*, published in 1922. Of the parties to the Conference, Russell was most concerned about America. Despite his acceptance of America's foreign policy which, relative to the other Powers, he regarded as liberal, he was troubled about the role she was likely to play:[7]

'. . . I begin with America, as the leading spirit in the conference and the dominant Power in the world. American public opinion is in favour of peace, and at the same time profoundly persuaded that America is wise and virtuous while all other Powers are foolish and wicked. The pessimistic half of this opinion I do not desire to dispute, but the optimistic half is more open to question. Apart from peace, American public opinion believes in commerce and industry, Protestant morality, athletics, hygiene, and hypocrisy, which may be taken as the main ingredients of American and English *Kultur*. Every American I met in the Far East, with one exception, was a missionary for American *Kultur*, whether nominally connected with Christian missions or not. . . .'

And further:[8]

'. . . American ambitions in China are economic, and require only that the whole country should be open to the commerce and industry of the United States. The policy of spheres of influence is obviously less advantageous to so rich and economically strong a country as America, than the policy of the universal Open Door. We cannot therefore regard America's liberal policy as regards China and naval armaments as any reason for expecting a liberal policy when it goes against self-interest.

'In fact, there is evidence that when American interests or prejudices are involved, liberal and humanitarian principles have no weight whatever. . . .'

On the consequences of the Washington Conference, Russell wrote:[9]

'The Four Powers—America, Great Britain, France and Japan—have agreed to exploit China in combination, not competitively. There is a consortium as regards loans, which will have the power of the purse and will therefore be the real government of China. As the Americans are the only people who have much spare capital, they will control the consortium. As they consider their civilisation the finest in the world, they will set to work to turn the Chinese into muscular Christians. As the financiers are the most splendid feature of the American civilisation, China must be so governed as to enrich the financiers, who will in return establish colleges and hospitals and Y.M.C.A.s throughout the length and breadth of the land, and employ agents to buy up the artistic treasures of China for sepulture in their mansions. Chinese intellect, like that of America, will be, directly or indirectly, in the pay of the Trust magnates, and therefore no effective voice will be raised in favour of radical reform. . . .'

Russell had become a political propagandist in the course of the First World War. When he had experienced the difficulties of influencing people who were caught up by national emotion in war-time, he gradually became convinced of the long-term need to educate and prepare people against future wars. His travels immediately after the war persuaded him that the constructive peace which he had hoped for was in fact elusive, and that the rivalry between the Great Powers contained the seeds of a future war. His writings on Russia and China indicate his awareness of America's growing role as the dominant world power, and thus her key position in shaping international policies. He saw the great weakness of radical forces in America, and realised that his main efforts should be directed towards strengthening them. Consequently, his work as publicist was stimulated and his contributions to American journals increased.

A key article in this period was his 'Hopes and Fears as Regards America',[10] published in two parts by the *New Republic* on 15 and 22 March 1922, in which he stated:

'Apart from the Russian Revolution, the most striking result of the war has been the world-supremacy of the United States. . . . Therefore, the hopes and fears of the world, probably for the next fifty years at least, depend upon the use which America makes of her vast power.'

Russell was intent to point out to Americans the dangers of national self-esteem, and the need for Americans to 'become more critically minded towards their government and their financiers'. He was particularly concerned that American radicals should be made aware of these dangers: 'If I could bring them to share my fears, my fears would be much diminished.' He saw the need to expose the atmosphere of deception surrounding American politics, which lead to the theory that 'American economic despots would never use their power against the public interest.'

Russell argued that the only way of securing social justice was through democracy:

'But if democracy is to be effective, it requires two extensions beyond the present American practice. . . . The first of these . . . economic power is now at least as important as political power, owing to the growth of vast industrial organisations; therefore democracy must be extended to economics, which can only be done by socialism. The second point is that democracy will not be genuinely established until it is international, which requires some sacrifice of sovereignty on the part of separate States. Until there is international government, strong States can bully weak ones, and will do so whenever it is to their interest. To this rule I see no reason to admit exceptions.'

Russell's interest in America was increasing. He had begun to study and read extensively on America, and in his quest for information became interested in the works of Upton Sinclair. He wrote to Sinclair on 19 November 1922:

'I am an admirer of your books, and have got into trouble with various Americans by quoting them as an authority on American conditions.

'I wish I knew of similar books that I could quote as to similar conditions here. Would you be so kind as to send me the following three books—*100 per cent*, *The Brass Check*, *The Profits of Religion*, for which I enclose $1.80.'

Sinclair, who had been arrested for attempting to read the Constitution of the United States in public during a longshoremen's strike at the harbour of Los Angeles, kept Russell well supplied with his novels and plays. Russell read *Hell* 'with the greatest pleasure', and, considering its message useful for the Independent Labour party, asked for Sinclair's views on its dramatisation.[11] Russell also inquired:

'Is it true you have got into trouble with the authorities because they take the same view of the Declaration of Independence as George III took? If so, you have my warmest sympathy and good wishes.'

Russell's forthright views on America, and the workings of American capitalism, were beginning to annoy many of his readers in the United States. His 'Hopes and Fears as Regards America' had proved particularly provocative, and Russell was taken to task by Ellery Sedgwick of the *Atlantic Monthly* who also criticised Russell for citing Upton Sinclair as an authority on American affairs. Russell replied to Sedgwick on 7 February 1923:

'As regards whether the article you criticise is "reasonably impartial", of course I have not the knowledge I should have if I had been in America lately, so I have a hesitation in defending myself. At the same time, I must confess that I am not convinced. Americans tell me, as you do, that Sinclair is not an authority, but nobody has told me of any single false statement in his book. If there were any, he would presumably have been sued for libel. Therefore I feel justified in believing what he says.

'You think my criticisms of Bolshevism just, but my criticisms of America biased. A Bolshevik would think exactly the contrary. I could have rested my whole case (if I had been writing now) upon what the Attorney-General of the U.S. has been saying in the *New Republic* about Mooney.[12] His position, in a nutshell, is that, when a communist has been convicted of murder on the evidence of a perjurer, anyone who says there may have been a miscarriage of justice must be a Red. In other words, no one except the Reds cares twopence about justice. Please don't think I am criticising America as such; I am criticising capitalist industrialism, of which America is the most advanced specimen, showing what all the other nations are moving towards. When I read Sinclair, my feeling was: "I wish someone would do the same for the Northcliffe Press"; but as no one has, I go to Sinclair for facts which could be paralleled in any "civilised" country. There are things, however, which cannot *yet* be paralleled in England, though they soon will be; I mean the treatment of Debs,[13] Mooney, and radicals generally. . . .'

Russell concerned himself with the plight of Mooney and years later was to write to him in prison:[14]

'With interest and the deepest sympathy I have followed your case from its beginning, and have mentioned it, as an outside example of injustice, in some of my books. Now, at last, a widespread realisation of the un-merited character of your condemnation seems to be coming about, and I earnestly hope that your liberation is at hand.'

In 1923 Russell published a major work, *The Prospects of Industrial Civilisation*, written in collaboration with his wife Dora. In a chapter dealing with 'Socialism in Advanced Countries', they elaborated on the theme of America's pre-eminent position and the prospect for socialism:[15]

'If America advances smoothly upon the path of capitalistic imperialism which is indicated by present tendencies and opportunities, there will be a gradually increasing oppression of the rest of the world, a widening gulf between the wealth of the New World and the poverty of the Old, a growing hatred of America among the exploited nations, and at last, under socialist guidance, a world-wide revolt involving repudiation of all debts to America.'

In the course of such a struggle, the authors foresaw the destruction of European civilisation, 'while America itself would be reduced to poverty and might experience at home the socialism which had been crushed elsewhere.' Thus according to the Russells:

'. . . a not improbable outcome would be a class war in America, leading to the destruction of industrialism, the death by starvation and disease of about half the population of the globe, and ultimately the return to a simpler manner of life. After reverting for centuries to the life of Red Indians, the Americans might be re-discovered by a second Col-umbus, hunting wild beasts with bows and arrows on Manhattan Island.'

The Russells believed that a 'complete collapse of civilisation' could only be averted if 'the American belief in capitalism can be shaken'. They felt that socialism was possible in America because:[16]

'The organisation of production in America is already such as scientific socialism requires. The main industrial products are produced mono-polistically by the Trusts, with a high degree of technical efficiency and an almost complete elimination of the waste involved in competition. Indeed, what Lenin calls State capitalism may be said to exist already, since the State, for all practical purposes, is big business.'

Giving an account of the domination of America by big business, they stated:

'. . . Take first the legislature. A Standard Oil multimillionaire who desired a divorce went to live in Florida, had a very easy divorce law passed, was divorced under it, and then had the law repealed. The Tsar in the plenitude of his power could not have done so well, since the Church would have opposed him; but in America such instances abound. Take next the executive. It is customary in labour disputes for the employers to hire private armies to fight strikers, and to employ armoured trains to bomb the villages inhabited by the wives and children of strikers. Nor is the regular army unamenable to the orders of the magnates. An official government inquiry reports a prosecution where a certain decision was desired by the champions of law and order, and where United States troops surrounded the court house and trained cannon upon it in order to secure a verdict conformable to 100-per-cent Americanism. (This was before America's participation in the war.) As for the judiciary, the way in which the big interests have been able to use it has long been notorious. And public opinion, being manufactured by the press, is almost always on the side of the capitalists who control the newspapers. Thus the true government of the United States, at the present time, is an oligarchy of energetic multimillionaires which controls an admirably efficient unified system of production. This system may fairly be described as State capitalism. It differs from socialism in two respects: one, that it is aristocratic; the other, that it is run for the private profit of those who control it, not primarily for the profit of the community.'

Although the system caused some discontent, Americans were relatively satisfied with their conditions because of a high level of prosperity. Since the prosperity was likely to continue, the Russells foresaw 'no widespread discontent . . . during the next few decades'. Nevertheless, 'in spite of these considerations', they expected 'a gradual spread of socialism'. The vigorous growth of capitalism in America had enabled very rich men to rise from humble beginnings, but:[17]

'The American capitalist system is rapidly crystallising, and the opportunities of emerging from the ranks of the wage-earners grow less every year. As they grow less, men who have the same mentality as the Trust magnates without the same advantages will tend increasingly to criticise the capitalist system, and to regard as unfair the concentration of immense wealth and power in the hands of men whom they feel to be no better than themselves. Such men may be expected in time to rouse the ordinary wage-earner to a similar sense of injustice.'

As a result, the Russells predicted a managerial revolution:[18]

'When the capitalists at the head of the big Trusts have become the sons or grandsons of the able men who created them, when they merely draw a huge income which they spend in idle dissipation, the work will have to be done by the administrative staff, who may be expected to despise their lazy masters. Socialism, at that stage, will merely mean turning the administrative staff into civil servants, and distributing the income of the useless millionaires among the employees.'

To the Russells it therefore appeared that the administrative stratum of American society held the key to an advance towards socialism. They were most concerned to address themselves to this group in order to break down its misconceptions about socialism:[19]

'At present the word "socialism" terrifies them, because they see visions of anarchy, murder and red rapine; they imagine gangs of hooligans invading their houses and nationalising their wives, and they fear that they would have to live on *kasha* and black bread for the rest of their lives. But although human stupidity is certainly immense, it can hardly be sufficiently immense for such absurdities to go on being believed for ever. Without being formally renounced, they will lose their terrors, as hell-fire has done. Sooner or later, reason and self-interest combined must get the better of purely imaginary bogeys.'

The Russells argued that if socialist propaganda was to succeed in the United States, it was not sufficient to direct it solely at the industrial workers:[20]

'It must be possible so to present the case for it that, apart from tradi-tional prejudice, all but that infinitesimal section [of plutocrats] shall feel the force of the argument. It is in this way, and in this way only, that socialism can be made to prevail in a country like the United States.'

The Prospects of Industrial Civilisation had a great impact in Britain and America. Russell's studies defined for him his role as socialist pro-pagandist and educator, particularly with regard to America. Although his writings were being widely published in the United States, he did not wish to limit his activity to writing. Lecturing in America was normally a favourable vehicle for purveying ideas, and he decided to undertake a tour involving public lectures on socialist themes. Such a tour would also alleviate the financial strain he had endured since the war. The birth of his first son, John, and his resignation from Trinity College, had made urgent the solution of his finances. After an unsuccessful parlia-mentary election attempt in 1923, he began to plan a trip to America for January 1924. The response from the United States was encouraging. Much of the interest in Russell's projected visit had been stimulated by *The Prospects of Industrial Civilisation*. Scott Nearing, in a letter of 24 August

1923, wrote: 'it will do us a world of good if you will come over here and go at things straight from the shoulder.' He informed Russell of speaking arrangements at the League for Industrial Democracy and at the Rand School of Social Science, 'a socialist institution[21] [which] . . . will profit greatly by an injection of a bit of libertarianism.'

However, in December Russell became ill with pneumonia again and was forced to postpone his visit. The League for Industrial Democracy had organised a massive testimonial dinner for Russell and were particularly disappointed as they had already sold over 700 tickets. In a letter of 19 December 1923, Harry W. Laidler, the Director of the League, expressed his regret, and pointed out that he knew of no other instance during the last few years, 'when the announcement of the visit of a citizen of Great Britain has been as much of an inspiration to progressive forces in America as when we all heard that you were about to visit this country'.

Russell engaged an American agent to deal with the many cancellations, and to make alternative arrangements for April 1924. He soon regained his health and an excited American audience awaited his arrival. The tour was to last until early June, and involved a busy schedule covering areas of America which he had never seen before.

Under the headline, 'Bertrand Russell, British Socialist, Is Here Next Week', the *New Leader* of 29 March 1924 ran the following report:

'Bertrand Russell, the well-known English philosopher, writer, lecturer and publicist, whose trip to the United States as planned for January last was postponed because of a severe attack of pneumonia, has entirely recovered and will arrive in New York on 30 March.

'Russell will give two lectures for the Rand School of Social Science, in the Debs Auditorium—the first, on "European Chaos", on Saturday afternoon, 5 April, at 3.15 p.m.; the second, on 3 May, on "Mechanism and Life". In view of the limited capacity of the auditorium, those who desire tickets are urged to purchase them in advance. Very few tickets now remain, even for the second lecture, and most of those which do remain will undoubtedly be sold before the day of the lecture.

'Russell will remain until early June lecturing at Columbia, Cornell, Northwestern and Brown universities; Dartmouth, Bowdoin, Smith, Gambier and Oxford colleges, and at the universities of Wisconsin and Michigan. He is booked for fifty other lectures in New York, Boston, Philadelphia, Washington, Pittsburgh, Buffalo, Cincinnati, St Louis, Louisville, Chicago, Milwaukee, St Paul and Minneapolis on "European Chaos" and other subjects.

'Bertrand Russell does not regard the Macdonald government as socialistic, he said recently.

'"We haven't socialism and can't get it until America adopts that system", Russell said, in an address at Oxford recently. "If Britain really had adopted socialism, America could prohibit the export of wheat to her. It will be many years before socialism is a reality in England."

'"If we had socialism and through it lost our empire, we could get no oil and would eventually all be proletarians working for America."'

NOTES

[1] B. Russell, *The Practice and Theory of Bolshevism* (London, 1920), p. 181; as *Bolshevism: Practice and Theory* (Harcourt, Brace, New York, 1920).

[2] Ibid.

[3] Ibid., p. 186.

[4] Also published in the *New Republic* (2 January 1922).

[5] B. Russell, *Autobiography* (London, 1968), Vol. II, p. 134 (Boston, 1968), p. 191.

[6] Ibid., pp. 142–3; pp 205–7.

[7] B. Russell, *The Problem of China* (London, 1922), pp. 159–60 (The Century Co., New York, 1922).

[8] Ibid., p. 162.

[9] Ibid., p. 179.

[10] See below, pp. 220–7.

[11] Russell to Sinclair, 20 June 1923.

[12] Thomas J. Mooney, trade union organiser, widely held to have been wrongfully convicted for a San Francisco bomb outrage in 1916. Mooney was condemned to death, a sentence which was later commuted to life imprisonment after an international protest. The protest was sparked off by a demonstration, led by Lenin, outside the American Embassy in Petrograd on 23 April 1917. *See also* pp. 278–9.

[13] Eugene V. Debs, leading socialist and a presidential candidate, who was imprisoned in 1918 under the Espionage Act for publicly acclaiming the Bolshevik revolution.

[14] 22 December 1931.

[15] B. Russell and D. Russell, *The Prospects of Industrial Civilisation* (London, 1923), pp. 125–6 (The Century Co., New York, 1923).

[16] Ibid., p. 129.

[17] Ibid., p. 133.

[18] Ibid., pp. 133–4.

[19] Ibid., p. 134.

[20] Ibid., p. 139.

[21] The Rand School was the educational centre of the Socialist party.

CHAPTER 8

SOCIALIST TEACHER, 1924

Russell's third trip to America, in April 1924, was very different from those he had previously undertaken. In 1914 he had reached the pinnacle of his philosophical achievement, and in America had seen 'mainly universities and university teachers'.[1] After the war he emerged as a political publicist, and his primary interest in the 1924 visit was to propagate the cause of socialism and world peace. Because he wished to be as effective as possible, and reach the widest audience, he engaged William B. Feakins, a self-styled 'transcontinental tour agent for lectures by Men of Fame', to attend to his programme. Although this arrangement was advantageous to Russell it created certain problems. An American socialist interested in arranging speaking dates for Russell in Washington and Baltimore complained to him shortly before the tour:[2]

'The fee of $200 rather threw cold water on the project and I confess that until I discovered Brother Feakins abducted 50 per cent thereof I myself thought it exorbitant for a man interested in ideas rather than in lsd.'

Russell sailed on the *Celtic*, and his arrival on 1 April was announced in *The New York Times* the next day. The report giving prominence to the arrival on the same day of Robert Bridges, the English Poet Laureate, mentioned Russell as 'another passenger on the *Celtic*'. While in New York, Russell was the guest of Dr Horace M. Kallen, a philosopher friend. His first lecture was at the New York Banker's Club on 'World Peace' and it was followed by a talk on 'Education in Relation to World Peace', before the Teachers' Union Auxiliary.

Russell outlined his views in an interview with *The New York Times*, published on 3 April. 'Bertrand Russell declares that United States alone can solve Europe's troubles', it proclaimed. The report continued:

'"The ultimate solution of all problems of the world is in a proper and all-embracing League of Nations," said Mr Russell. "The present League is France under another name. The United States, Germany,

Russia and all of the other powers must be members of the new League, which must be able to decide things by majority vote. . . . There is one simple measure which America could take which would solve all European troubles at once . . . the United States should ask France to pay the interest on her debt."'

Russell went on to describe the 'French menace' in Europe as a threat to the balance of power. Almost at once Russell's comments created unease in Britain. An anonymous letter from England, addressed to Dr Kallen, stated:

'An article in *The New York Times* of 3 April has attracted the attention of influential Americans here. It seems that Bertrand Russell has insulted them by dictating what they should do as if they were in ignorance of their duty and in need of his destructive services. They prefer to have him return to his own business, and to govern their affairs without his officious interference or base attacks against France, so I thought it better to have you informed of this so that you would protect yourself from embarrassment and complicated matters by advising Bertrand Russell to give up lectures that will only stir up strife and bring him back in disgrace, unless you can manage to convince him that Americans are able to see what is right and that *they will not be forced to adopt English views*, so detrimental to their honour.'

On 3 April, Russell delivered one of his most important and keenly awaited lectures of the tour, when he spoke to the League for Industrial Democracy on 'What is Wrong with Western Civilisation?' The following day, *The New York Times* featured an account of Russell's speech, under the heading 'Bertrand Russell Sees Dark Future; Predicts Control of the Rest of the World by "America Financial Empire"', and reported:

'In the presence of several hundred liberals, radicals, social workers, university professors and students of sociology, Mr Russell declared that the deep-seated evils of our civilisation might be summed up in "militarism and competitive industrialism".'

Giving an account of Russell's prediction that a future war would result in immense destruction, the report stated that Russell did not place faith in the League of Nations, for it would not attempt to coerce France or England, 'much less restrain Russia and America from acts of aggression'. According to the report, Russell continued:

'Very reluctantly I have come to the conclusion that the first formation of a world government, if one is ever formed, will be by way of imperialism, not by the way of voluntary federation. . . . In this process, America will play the chief role. In spite of the immense amount of ignorant goodwill in America, American policy since 1914 can be explained in terms of interest. Practically everything that has been done has furthered the oil interests and the house of Morgan. . . . I foresee at no distant date an extension of the American financial empire over the whole American continent, the whole of Western Europe and also the Near East . . . in Persia it is already established. The empire of American finance will be in the highest degree illiberal and cruel. It will crush trade unionism, control education, encourage competition among the workers while avoiding it among the capitalists. It will make life everywhere ugly, uniform, laborious and monotonous. Men of ability in all countries will be purchased by high salaries. The world will enjoy peace, broken only by the dropping of bombs from airplanes on strikers, but it will look back to the old days of war as a happy memory almost too bright to be true.

'The only hope so far as I can see lies in a great development of liberal feeling and thought in America. The power of a financial magnate rests, in the last analysis, on opinion. Opinion in America supports the present system for several reasons. First, fear of violent revolution: the sooner Western socialists have done with talk of violence the better. Second, there are immense numbers of people who will suffer in their pocket if they offend the plutocrats. Only self-respect can make journalists, professors, parsons and others cease to be lackeys. Third, the proletariat in America are mainly foreigners. This will grow less with time.

'But the fundamental reason for the acquiescence of the average American citizen in the system under which he lives is that it suits his philosophy. Americans are still devoted to a conception of life which results from the impact of machines on decaying Puritanism.

'The question is one of psychology. Will industrial nations in the end weary of worshipping the machine? I believe they will, and in that day industrialism will become a boon. Until then it is a curse, like every false god.'

Another important and well-publicised engagement was a public debate with Scott Nearing, under the auspices of the League for Public Discussion. Nearing argued that 'the Soviet form of government is applicable to Western civilisation', and Russell opposed him. (The speeches for and against the motion were later published, in debate form, under the title *Bolshevism and the West*.) The debate was conducted in fluid and brilliant style before a packed and appreciative audience. The gist of Russell's argument was that socialism would come to the West through the slow process of education and not through revolution. He was in effect reiterating his standpoint on social transformations which

95

he had developed in the immediate post-war years. Russell was ful-filling the role he had defined for himself, and everywhere was acclaimed by audiences interested to hear his views on socialism.[3]

Russell felt very strongly about the plight of Sacco and Vanzetti, who had been in prison since 1920, and in his lectures in America never lost the opportunity of arousing his audience to what he considered a grave miscarriage of justice. In a lecture on 'The Danger of Creed Wars', Russell stated that in the conflict between East and West 'propaganda will cause each side to know the cruelties of the other, but not its own.' For example:[4]

'Very few Americans . . . know the truth about Sacco and Vanzetti: condemned to death for a murder to which another man confessed, and the evidence for which has been acknowledged by policemen engaged in collecting it to have been a "frame-up". A new trial was refused to these men partly on the grounds that the man who confessed to the murder was a bad character. Apparently, in the opinion of American judges, only persons of good character commit murders. The real crime of Sacco and Vanzetti was that they were anarchists.'

It was inevitable that Russell's views would create hostility. His forth-right critique of the American system, summed up in his widely publicised assertion that 'oil and Morgan rule you', was bound to bring him into conflict with certain interests. Over the years Russell had deplored the control exercised over American universities by big busi-ness. In the course of his tour, it was brought to Russell's attention that the Harvard Board of Trustees had barred Scott Nearing, and two other American radicals, from speaking at the Harvard Student Union. On 11 April, the *Crimson*, a Harvard student newspaper, interviewed Russell, who attacked what he considered was the establishment of an 'intellectual quarantine' by the Harvard authorities. Russell declared:

'Such a situation as this would be impossible in an English university. It can be attributed in part to the greatest misfortune with which your American colleges are afflicted—boards of trustees. When an institution of learning is governed by a group of financiers and businessmen, any interests are served but those of liberalism. Of course, it is true that our younger English universities are managed in much the same way, but each college of Oxford and Cambridge is owned by its professors and consequently managed to suit their interests—interests which, you must admit, are more liberal than those of a group of successful merchants.

'America is not ruled by the Washington government. It is oil and Morgan that rule you. America is on the crest of a worship of machine and industrial efficiency. An empire of American finance over the whole world, illiberal and cruel to the highest degree, is the nightmare prospect before the world.'

President Lowell immediately sent a letter of protest to Russell which was published, with an account of the controversy, in *The New York Times* of 12 April. The letter, appearing under the heading 'Counters on Briton Assailing Harvard; Lowell Denies Bertrand Russell's Charge', stated:

'If correctly reported in your interview in the *Crimson* this morning, I think you must be laboring under a misapprehension. You speak as if the trustees—at Harvard we call them Governing Boards—decided who should speak at the Harvard Union. The Harvard Union is an association of students and graduates over which the Governing Boards exercise no more control than the authorities of Oxford and Cambridge do over the question of who shall speak, or what shall be said, in the Oxford and Cambridge Unions.

'You speak also as if there were more academic freedom in English universities than here. That seems to me also a misapprehension. At Oxford not long ago, if I am right, a students' publication, the *New Oxford*, was suppressed on account of remarks that it contained. Nothing of the kind has, I believe, occurred here within the memory of man.

'During the war you lost your fellowship at Cambridge on account of your opinions. No such thing happened at Harvard. Throughout the war we kept and protected a German subject in our instructing staff. In spite of outcries for their dismissal, from alumni and others, Professor Münsterberg and Mr Laski were unflinchingly maintained in their positions.'

Russell's reply to Lowell was featured on 10 May in the *New Student*, a national university weekly concerned with student rights, under the heading: 'Harvard Fight Carried to President; Bertrand Russell Hits Back'. The report gave background details to the controversy and continued:

'Mr Russell said that his statement about "intellectual quarantine" applied to the authorities of the Harvard Union, and not of the university. He recalled his pleasant memories of Harvard University. But he repeated his assertion about American colleges in general. "The greater freedom of English universities is a fact which I think you will find no neutral person willing to deny. Ask, for example, Mr Laski, who, as you say, has experienced the utmost liberalism to be found in academic America." As for the suppression of the *New Oxford*, he stated: "In America its author would have been sentenced to ten years in prison; yet even so its suppression was regarded by most Oxford opinion as absurd, and was due to a quite exceptionally reactionary vice-chancellor. . . . My own case calls for similar comments. No one at Cambridge objected to my opinions, until I was condemned in the criminal courts; then the younger men being at the front, the older men declared that criminals were inconvenient as teachers. After the armistice, when the young men (who are on the governing board) returned from the front, they expressed indignation at the action of the older men, and restored me to my post. As for what you say about keeping Germans on the staff, that was done among us as a matter of course." Harvard students who were asked what would have happened to Mr Russell if he had been at Cambridge, Mass., during the war, agreed that he would probably have fared far worse; only the fact that no such case came up at Harvard saved her from such a "flaw".'

Although American students responded very favourably to Russell the political publicist, this was not the case with the university hierarchy for whom Russell had become too controversial. With few exceptions he was officially ignored and no honours were conferred upon him; a surprising fact in view of his philosophical eminence. Notwithstanding this virtual boycott by the universities and colleges, Russell's appointments were numerous, and although his activities were mainly centred on New York, he travelled as far West as St Paul, Minnesota. During these travels, Russell lectured to a number of women's clubs; his trip to China figured prominently in the talks he gave. One of his impressions of these lectures is conveyed by the following anecdote:[5]

'There was always one elderly woman who appeared to be sleeping throughout the lecture, but at the end would ask me, somewhat portentously, why I had omitted to mention that the Chinese, being heathen, could of course have no virtues. I imagine that the Mormons of Salt Lake City must have had a similar attitude when non-Mormons were first admitted among them.'

On several occasions Russell lectured to the Rand School of Social Science in New York, and in his last lecture of the tour chose as his topic 'How to be Free and Happy'.[6] He provoked a great deal of laughter by stating:

'In America, I have spent most of my time by preaching idleness. I made up my mind when I was young that I would not be restrained from preaching a doctrine merely because I have not practiced it. I have not been able to practice the doctrine of idleness, because the preaching of it takes up so much time.'

Russell explained that idleness 'is simply work or activity which is not part of your regular professional job'. He deplored the excessive subservience of Americans to the ethic that 'what we do is get on in our business, and get a fortune which we can leave to our descendants.' Russell advocated that people should have larger interests in life, and maintained that under socialism 'we ought none of us have to work more than four hours a day.' When his audience applauded he rejoined:

'Well, I am very glad to get that response from you, but when I made this remark to some other audiences in America a thrill of horror went through them and they said to me: "What on earth should we do with the other twenty hours?" I felt, after that, that this gospel very much needed preaching.'

Unlike his previous tours, Russell was so busy that he hardly had time to see Lucy Donnelly. He sailed for home on 31 May on the *Celtic*, and on 3 June wrote Lucy a farewell letter:

'Never in all my life have I been so busy. I had no time to get those impressions of America for which everybody asked me. It seemed to me to be a country containing many trains and many lecture halls, but beyond that I am vague about it. I preached leisure but had no chance to practise it.'

With the tour concluded, *Unity*, a Chicago journal, summed up Russell's visit and bitterly criticised the attitude of the press and universities:

'Bertrand Russell has returned to England, and one of the most impressive tours ever made in this country by a distinguished foreigner has thus come to an end. Everywhere Professor Russell spoke, he was greeted by great audiences with rapturous enthusiasm, and listened to with a touching interest and reverence. At most of his meetings, admission was charged, frequently at regular theatre rates, but this seemed to make no difference in the attendance. Throngs of eager men and women crowded the auditoriums where he appeared, and vied with one another in paying homage to the distinguished man whom they so honored. From this point of view, Bertrand Russell's visit was a triumph. From another and quite different point of view, it was a failure and disgrace! What was the great public at large allowed to know about this famous Englishman and the message which he brought across the seas to us Americans? Nothing! The silence of our newspapers was wellnigh complete. Only when Mr Russell got into a controversy with President Lowell, of Harvard, which gave opportunity to make the eagle scream, did his name or words appear in any conspicuous fashion in our public prints. The same journals which publish columns of stuff about millionaires, actors, singers, prizefighters and soldiers from abroad, and blazon forth their most casual comments about anything from women to the weather, reported almost nothing about this one of the most eminent Europeans of the day. But this is not the worst. Turn from the newspapers to the colleges and universities! Here is Mr Russell, the ablest and most famous mathematical philosopher of modern times—for long an honored Fellow of Cambridge, England—author of learned essays and treatises which are the standard authorities in their field—at least, a great scholar, at the most, one of the greatest of scholars! But how many colleges in America officially invited him to their halls? How many gave him degrees of honor? So far as we know, Smith College was the only institution which officially received him as a lecturer, though we understand that he appeared also at the Harvard Union. Practically speaking, Professor Russell was ignored. A better measure of the ignorance, cowardice and Pharisaism of American academic life we have never seen!'

Once he was back in England, Russell was able to find time to reflect on his tour and wrote 'Impressions of America'[7] for the *New Leader*, of 22 August 1924. In the article, Russell described various aspects of American society, among which was 'the general feeling that Socialism is something "foreign," advocated chiefly by alien Jews.' Russell touched on America's religious and racial troubles and stated: 'The worst, of course, is the Negro question. The way in which Southerners speak of Negroes, to this day, is so horrible that it is difficult to stay in the room with them.' Returning to his theme of America's future development he found hope among the youth, where, he believed, there existed, 'a very definite revolt against the ideals of business success which have been the curse of civilisation in the Western hemisphere.'

He wrote a second article, entitled 'The American Intelligentsia',[8] for the *Nation and the Athenaeum*, of 11 October, in which he compared the universities of 1914 with those of 1924. He noted the proliferation of administrative work, and the increasing control of the individual, and commented: 'If Einstein had been an American . . . he would have been put on to so many boards and committees that he would have had no time to do original work.'

From a personal point of view, the tour for Russell was a great success. He had found American audiences receptive to his ideas, vindicating his chosen role as a socialist educator. Financially, too, the tour had been rewarding, Russell recording that he 'earned a good deal'[9] by it.

NOTES

1 'The American Intelligentsia', first published by *Nation and the Athenaeum* (11 October 1924) (see below, pp. 232–5.)

2 T. Swann Harding, in a letter to Russell of 14 January 1924.

3 On 5 May, before a crowded auditorium at the Rand School of Social Science, Russell argued the negative in a debate on 'Is the British Labour Party Revolutionary?' with Morris Hillquit, leader of the American Socialist party.

4 Reprinted in B. Russell, *Sceptical Essays* (London, 1928), p. 215 (W. W. Norton, New York, 1928), p. 219.

5 'Ideas that have Harmed Mankind', first published by Haldeman-Julius in 1946, reprinted in B. Russell, *Unpopular Essays*, (London, 1950), p. 205 (Simon & Schuster, New York, 1950), p. 160.

6 Published by the Rand School of Social Science (New York, 1924).

7 See below, pp. 228–31.

8 See below, pp. 232–5.

9 B. Russell, *Autobiography* (London, 1968), Vol. II, p. 152 (Boston, 1968), p. 222.

CHAPTER 9

MARRIAGE AND MORALS

Russell's concern about America's growing power was reflected in a 1925 article entitled 'Is America Becoming Imperialistic?'[1] The article demonstrates the thoroughness of his researches. Quoting from contemporary studies of government policy, Russell traced the extent of American economic penetration and consequent political control of Latin America. He reiterated his view that the tendency for America to dominate and oust her rivals in the Far East and China would lead to a war with Japan. While condemning U.S. government policy, Russell was careful to point out that the American people themselves were kept unaware of what was happening. For this reason he was intent upon attacking the altruistic notion that American involvement abroad was by way of 'conferring a favour on "backward" nations'. Russell's view was that power corrupted, and 'now that America is supreme, the palm of evil doing must soon pass to America'.

Because he saw a need to change people's attitudes in order to create a better society, Russell began to investigate the theory and practice of education. In the first years after the war he had explored this field, studying the works of prominent educationalists and psychologists, including the Americans, John Dewey and J. B. Watson.[2] In 1926, Russell published *On Education: Especially in Early Childhood*, which was his first major work on this subject. The demands of parenthood—Kate, his second child was born in 1923—led him to try to develop a rational system of education. With his wife, he established, in 1927, an experimental school at Telegraph House, which he rented from his brother, Frank. The school was designed to allow children to develop free of the harmful restrictions which, he felt, characterised education in conventional schools. In Russell's view, the evils of society were perpetuated by established educational practice. His commitment to education as a long-term method for changing society was to replace his earlier role as political propagandist. His sociological concerns were, for the time being, to override his political activities.

Russell was faced with the problem of financing the school, which was non-profit-making. Based on the earnings derived from his writings in America, and the financial success of the 1924 tour, he saw America as a source of funds which could help him overcome the problem. Russell's fourth trip to America took place in 1927, during the first term of the new school. This was his most professional tour to date, and was mainly concerned with earning money to run the school. Although he was due to arrive in America at the end of September, Feakins, his tour agent, had with typical alacrity announced the tour very early in the year. A nationwide rush to book Russell for lectures and debates began and was deftly handled by Feakins, who, by 20 June, was able to inform Russell that his itinerary was almost complete and that 'you will take home with you a lot more money than you did last time.' Despite Feakins, many societies and individuals continued to approach Russell directly, but he insisted on leaving all arrangements in the hands of his agent. On 24 May 1927 he wrote to a Mrs Lena Jalfe:

'Unfortunately I am under contract with Mr Feakins to make no engagements except through him. Of course I should like to speak to a Labour audience, but you will appreciate that while in America I wish to earn enough money to finance an educational experiment that I think important and I cannot do this except by earning high fees. So I must leave the matter to Mr Feakins. If he agreed, well and good; if not, I can do nothing.'

Russell arrived in New York on 29 September, having travelled on the *Caronia*. He was immediately beset by reporters on board ship, and gave an interview in which *The New York Times* of the following day reported him as stating that although democracy had made greater strides in America than in any other land, the English had greater personal liberty. Whereas Russell had been largely ignored by the press and universities in 1924, he was now generally welcomed. There is no doubt that the emphasis he was placing on educational reform, at the expense of socialist agitation, caused him to be more restrained towards American politics, and must in part explain his new-found respectability. Ironically, in later years, his views on child-rearing and sexual ethics were to prove even more difficult to tolerate in America than his politics.

After disembarkation, Russell gave a press conference at the Town Hall Club, where 'between rather biting epigrams on political and social questions, he admitted that education was what he was "most keen about".' *The New York Times* of 30 September reported the conference under the rather misleading heading, 'Russell Envisions Childless Cities', and stated:

'The city of the future will be without children if education is to become what it should, in the opinion of Bertrand Russell, who arrived on the *Caronia* yesterday for a lecture tour. Children should be not only in the country, but out-of-doors, Mr Russell said, and consequently New York's array of costly school buildings might better be razed. . . . His contention that a child's character is largely set by the time it is five years old, and consequently the education before that age is all-important, presented difficult problems, he admitted, for it would be a definite misfortune for children to be placed in formal institutions at too tender an age.

'Mr Russell suggested that co-operative groups of about ten families might prove the best method of educating young children. They might "pool" their children, he said, and then take turns in looking after them. No great amount of looking after is required by his theories, for he considers not more that two hours of lessons to be the proper balance, with the rest of the time spent in "running wild."

'Mr Russell answered occasional questions on topics other than education. Bolshevism, he said, was really an Americanising process, and as such useful in backward countries. It was in no sense, he thought, a threat to more advanced nations. Fascism, on the other hand, was a thing for which he thought no liberal-minded person could feel anything but hatred.'

In the course of the tour, Russell lectured at colleges throughout the country. He outlined his views on the role of college students as a liberalising force in America, in an interview with the *New Student* of 19 October, which reported:

'"If you cannot liberalise the student there is no hope for America." This is Bertrand Russell's word to the colleges. More than that, it is a challenge to the students in these colleges, for the British philosopher placed the growth of American liberalism in the light of the world's one great hope for peace. "Liberals in the United States need realise," he added, "that America dominates the world. To liberalise the United States is to liberalise the world. Liberals elsewhere feel this keenly and it explains their intense interest in the Sacco–Vanzetti case. . . . American liberalism must show the way, and liberalism's greatest hope is in the colleges."'

Russell lectured on a variety of topics. He drew an audience of 1,800 when he appeared at the Community Church, New York, to speak on the causes of war. He debated with Will Durant on 'Is Democracy a Failure?', under the auspices of the Discussion Guild, and argued for democracy, maintaining that the United States and Great Britain were among the happier countries in the world. He also debated with Max

Eastman on 'The Road to Freedom' at the Cooper Union on 21 November. In an essay entitled 'The Two Bertrand Russells,' Eastman gave an account of the debate:[3]

'I approached the meeting in Cooper Union somewhat awed by the honour of being associated in conflict with so great a mind.

'*Proposed Roads to Freedom* was the title of a book that Russell had published, and my opening speech . . . was as thoughtful a criticism of it as I knew how to make. Indeed, for those in the audience with a taste for proletarian revolution, it must have seemed quite conclusive. I took a backward glance at all the great advocates of a better social system, and pointed out that none of them, from Plato to Russell, had ever even looked for *the road* to freedom. They had merely told us what a free society might be like when we got there. Karl Marx, I declaimed— and I was then immature enough to regard this as very wise—did not bother his head about what it would be like when we got there. He concentrated on finding the road: the working-class struggle, namely, for the conquest of political power.

'Russell replied . . . that this was all very much more neat than convincing, that it was impossible to treat human history as though it were a process taking place in a laboratory—words, at least, to that effect. And he remarked how many years had passed since Marx predicted the revolutionary change I was still waiting for, and spoke of the folly of any man's imagining that he could predict the course of history over a long period of time.

' "Not one of us can tell right now what is going to happen in the next seven years", he exclaimed.

'Towards the end of his speech—which was not a speech, but just brilliant inconsecutive talking—he happened accidentally, as any impromptu speaker might, to get to telling us, rather explicitly, what might be expected of the rest of the twentieth century. It was a bad accident, and I made some good fun in my rebuttal out of the striking contrast between the prophetic genius of Karl Marx and of Bertrand Russell. His answer was magnanimous, and also clever. He acknowledged that with this lucky crack I had probably won the debate, but remarked that this did not prove the validity of the theory of progress through class struggle.

'We walked across town together after the debate, and I tried to get him to say something illuminating about my teacher, John Dewey, towards whose instrumental philosophy I was still struggling to orient myself.

' "I find him such a dull writer," was all I could get out of him.'

It was Russell's views on child education that created the most interest.

He noted, on several occasions, that American parents devoted far more attention to the subject than their English counterparts. In an address on 'Education and the Good Life', delivered before members of the Child Study Association of America, he proposed principles for the education of children based upon observations in his school. 'One of the worst mistakes made by parents in their desire to bring up children properly is the effort to provide variety for the child', *The New York Times* of 27 November reported Russell as stating. The report continued:

'"Parents impose upon children by rushing them around to shows, entertainments and spectacles", he said. "Children are, in the long run, happiest in monotony. The love of monotony is deep-rooted in every animal and is the basis of man's love of home. We believe in homes because we love uniformity and an abrupt breaking of uniformity for the child creates fear and anxiety. This is what produces the adolescent mental strain which is generally attributed to other causes."

'Modern educators face a new problem in the diminishing size of the home, the speaker said. By the time a child has reached the age of three years, it is time for him to be given contacts outside the home where children of his own age will teach him the things formerly obtained from brothers and sisters within the family, Mr Russell said. Formerly these essential bits of human knowledge were picked up by the child in his companionship with other members of the family. But now, when families are so small this is impossible, he said. The actual teaching, "the imparting of abstract intelligence" can be begun when the child is seven years old, he asserted.'

One of Russell's last engagements was a lecture on 'Companionate Marriage', given to the American Public Forum, in New York, on 3 December.[4] Russell's moral outlook was rational and humane; he advocated divorce by mutual consent, as well as trial marriage for young people not yet ready to assume the responsibilities of parenthood. He concluded his lecture with the words:

'I hope and believe that the greater sexual freedom now prevailing among the young is bringing into existence a generation less cruel than that which is now old, and that a rational ethic of sex matters will, therefore, during the next twenty years, more and more prevail over the doctrines of taboo and human sacrifice which pass traditionally as "virtue".'

Opposition to moral reform was extremely fierce in America at the time and President F. B. Robinson of the City College of New York prevented moves by his faculty to invite Russell to speak at the college.[5] The chief exponent of companionate marriage and enlightened sexual ethics was Judge Ben B. Lindsey, of Denver, who had corresponded with Russell over the previous year and shown great interest in his writings. Lindsey had been under savage attack by the fundamentalist clergy and Ku-Klux-Klan which succeeded in ousting him from office on account of his views. In his Public Forum lecture, Russell began with a tribute to Lindsey 'whose courage and humanity I cannot sufficiently admire'. Russell added:

'Having long used his office for the unprecedented purpose of promoting human happiness, he has, not unnaturally, been ousted by a combination of sadists of all parties. But what Denver has lost the world has gained. If I understand aright his advocacy of "companionate marriage", his purpose is, in the highest and best sense, conservative, not subversive.'

Russell continued to communicate with Lindsey and on one occasion wrote:[6]

'I am much disgusted by the injustice and persecution to which you have been subjected. . . . I continue to be surprised by the fact that America persecutes Americans for the opinions which it hires foreigners at great expense to express.'

The 1927 tour was extremely successful. Russell left for home aboard the *Berengaria* on 15 December, having earned more than $10,000. Despite these earnings, the school was proving far costlier to run than anticipated. Russell continued to look to America as the chief source of revenue, and wrote to H. G. Wells, on 24 May 1928, asking if he would be willing to write an appeal for funds 'which might influence progressive Americans' to contribute to the running of the school. Russell informed Wells that the school was costing him about £2,000 a year, 'that is to say very nearly the whole of my income . . . [which] is precarious since it depends upon the tastes of American readers who are notoriously fickle, and I am therefore very uncertain as to whether I shall be able to keep the school going'.[7]

In 1928 Russell published *Sceptical Essays*, a collection of articles, most of which had appeared in American journals such as *Outlook and Independent*, *Harper's Bazaar* and *Dial* over the previous six years. Included in the selection was 'The Recrudescence of Puritanism' in which Russell describes American Puritanism as being a transplant from Cromwell's England with the result that 'the greatest Power in the world is controlled by men who inherit the outlook of Cromwell's Ironsides.' Giving examples of the contradictions of Puritan legislation Russell stated:[8]

'In America . . . though it is not illegal to keep a mistress, it is illegal to travel with her from one State to another; a New Yorker may take his mistress to Brooklyn but not to Jersey City. The difference of moral turpitude between these two actions is not obvious to the plain man.'

Russell described Prohibition as 'the most noteworthy victory of Puritanism'. In 'Optimistic America',[9] an article for the New York *Herald Tribune Magazine* of 6 May 1928, he attributed America's economic prosperity largely to Puritanism, and forecast that the crisis for America would arrive when Puritanism decayed. At that stage, 'the mechanical civilisation will grow at once less successful and less satisfying'.

Russell, while conscious of America's defects, wrote in his article, 'The New Philosophy of America',[10] published in the *Fortnightly Review*, May 1928, that he found its merits 'more interesting, more novel and more important'. Russell believed:

'America is achieving certain things of great moment which have never been achieved before, and is developing a philosophy of life which, whether we like it or not, is obviously more suited to the modern world than that of most Europeans.'

Russell described this philosophy as 'industrial philosophy', and defined it as 'the belief that man is the master of his fate'. Among America's many achievements he felt that 'the best work that has been done anywhere in philosophy and psychology during the present century has been done in America.' Describing the impact of industrialism on culture, Russell felt that America would overcome her 'artistic barrenness' and 'will be the first to create the new forms appropriate to modern life'.

Americans were interested in Russell's views on a variety of subjects. The *Literary Digest* of 17 March 1928 reported that 'Benny Leonard disagrees with Bertrand Russell on Boxing'. Russell admitted that he had never been to a 'prize-fight' but nevertheless regarded America's preoccupation with boxing as 'sadistic'. He added: 'I am constantly struck with the fact that there is a great deal of sadism in America.' Benny Leonard, the undefeated lightweight champion of the world, retorted: 'I wish Dr Russell would be my guest at some big bout in Madison Square Garden. . . . I venture the prediction that it would require . . . the special police to keep him in his seat when . . . one of the boxers starts to sag and his opponent measures him for the finishing punch.'

'When Bertrand Russell Goes to the Movies'[11] was the headline to an article by Russell on the cinema, especially written for the 24 March edition of *Forward*. In Russell's view, the cinema was 'perhaps the most heart-rending of all the many examples of artistic barbarism'. Although he felt the potential of the cinema was enormous, he deplored its control by 'stupid' men. As a result, American films 'have persuaded the populations of all other civilised countries . . . that Americans are silly'. As for his own tastes, Russell admitted that they were simple:

'I like to see a race between a motor-car and an express train; I enjoy the spectacle of the villain gnashing his teeth because he has just failed to pick off the engine driver; I delight in men tumbling off skyscrapers and saving themselves by telegraph wires; I am thrilled by a sheriff's posse galloping through a sandstorm in the alkali desert. And the enjoyment of these unsophisticated delights is enhanced by the feeling that in that matter at least one is in harmony with the great world democracy.'

Russell was to use his knowledge of the American cinema in his book *The Scientific Outlook*. Discussing the influence of modern techniques in promoting uniformity of opinion, he wrote:[12]

'. . . perhaps the most important of all the modern agents of propaganda is the cinema. Where the cinema is concerned, the technical reasons for large-scale organisations leading to almost world-wide uniformity are overwhelming. The costs of a good production are colossal, but are no less if it is exhibited seldom than if it is exhibited often and everywhere. The Germans and the Russians have their own productions, and those of the Russians are, of course, an important part of the Soviet government's propaganda. In the rest of the civilised world the products of Hollywood preponderate. The great majority of young people in almost all civilised countries derive their ideas of love, of honour, of the way to make money, and of the importance of good clothes, from the evenings spent in seeing what Hollywood thinks good for them. I doubt whether all the schools and churches combined have as much influence as the cinema upon the opinions of the young in regard to such intimate matters as love and marriage and moneymaking. The producers of Hollywood are the high-priests of a new religion. Let us be thankful for the lofty purity of their sentiments. We learn from them that sin is always punished, and virtue is always rewarded. True, the reward is rather gross, and such as a more old-fashioned virtue might not wholly appreciate. But what of that? We know from the cinema that wealth comes to the virtuous, and from real life that old So-And-So has wealth. It follows that old So-And-So is virtuous, and the people who say he exploits his employees are slanderers and troublemakers. The cinema therefore plays a useful part in safeguarding the rich from the envy of the poor. . . .

'What would Western Europeans do if deprived of their nightly drug from Hollywood? The moral of this for Western European governments is that they must keep on good terms with America. In the American imperialism of the future it may turn out that the producers of cinemas have been the pioneers.'

Radical Americans were interested to obtain Russell's support on burning political issues. Sacco and Vanzetti had been executed in August 1927, and on 28 September 1928 Gardner Jackson, who had been prominent in the campaign to free them, sent Russell a copy of Sacco and Vanzetti's published letters and commented: 'You'll note in one of Sacco's a reference to your *Why Men Fight*. He found it difficult but labored till he understood and enthused over it.'

Russell was concerned that Sacco and Vanzetti should not be forgotten, and when invited by Jackson to speak at a rally in America, sent the following message on 28 May 1929:[13]

'I am sorry I shall not be in America at the time of your meeting on 23 August, the more so as I shall be there not so very long after that. I think you are quite right to do everything possible to keep alive the memory of Sacco and Vanzetti. It must, I think, be clear to any unprejudiced person that there was not such evidence against them as to warrant a conviction, and I have no doubt in my own mind that they were wholly innocent. I am forced to conclude that they were condemned on account of their political opinions and that men who ought to have known better allowed themselves to express misleading views as to the evidence because they hold that men with such opinions have no right to live. A view of this sort is one which is very dangerous, since it transfers from the theological to the political sphere a form of persecution which it was thought that civilised countries had outgrown. One is not so surprised at occurrences of this sort in Hungary or Lithuania, but in America they must be matters of grave concern to all who care for freedom of opinion.'

Russell had arranged to visit America for the fifth time, and arrived in New York on 25 September 1929, for a lecture tour organised by Feakins. *The New York Times*, of the following day, announced:

'Among the notable foreign visitors who arrived yesterday on the White Star liner, *Homeric*, was Bertrand Russell, English philosopher and sociologist, who comes here after an absence of two years to debate with Will Durant on the subject "Is Education a Failure?" in Mecca Temple on 6 October. Mr Russell will take the affirmative.

'In a talk with newspaper men on board the liner, the English philosopher said he agreed with Professor Robert E. Rogers of the Massachusetts Institute of Technology that one of the defects of the modern educational system was the scarcity of men teachers, especially for the younger students. Mr Russell said it was his opinion that it tended to feminise boy pupils, but more important than that, he said, is the fact that, in his opinion, women do not take the same interest in hard facts and mix sentimentality with their teaching.

'"We need in the schools, both here and abroad", he continued, "a greater robustness in facing hard facts. The scientific attitude toward life can scarcely be learnt from women.

'"Everyone living today could have come much nearer to being a first-rate human being if the system of education were better. One great defect is that education is not designed to teach truth, but to circulate propaganda that those in power wish the children to learn.

'"Children are taught right-thinking instead of thinking. Education is largely in the hands of influential businessmen and of religious sects instead of in the hands of learned men. America has more respect for businessmen than it has for learned men.

'"The economic opportunities in America are so tremendous that the businessman is bound to have far more prestige than the learned man. When the time comes in America that money-making will be more difficult and earnings will be less, then I think we will see that the people will turn to education."

'Mr Russell said that in the matter of sex education he thought the Churches were doing much harm by standing in the way of general circulation of such knowledge.

'"Any group that lives according to dogma", he declared, "is a menace to educational progress if it interferes politically. There is more religious interference in America than in any other country except Tibet. Your fundamentalist laws in certain parts of the United States are almost incredible to Europeans.

'"The United States is in for a period of financial imperialism", he declared. "America is becoming world conscious", he added, "in a commercial sense rather than in the militaristic sense."

'On his previous visit to America two years ago, Mr Russell was not favorably inclined towards the League of Nations. He said yesterday that his views on that subject had since undergone a change. He said he had formerly felt that France dominated the League at Geneva and all its policies were then for her benefit. Now, he said, things had changed and England was not "subservient" to the League of Nations. . . .'

Russell lectured on the East Coast and also, for the first time, crossed America to the West Coast. He spent a good half of the tour out West; lecturing and debating in Los Angeles, San Francisco, San Diego and Dallas. As well as debating with Will Durant on 'Is Modern Education a

Failure?' Russell debated with John Cowper Powys on 'Is Modern Marriage a Failure?',[14] in which he affirmed that 'the present relaxation of family ties is in the interest of the good life.' The publication of Russell's *Marriage and Morals* earlier in the year had stimulated in America, as in England, much interest and controversy in his views on sexual ethics. This book, in which Russell asserted that the institution of marriage was declining and that 'complete fidelity was not to be expected in most marriages'[15]—which is not to say that Russell advocated infidelity— was to provide the grounds for a vicious campaign against his appointment to a New York college in 1940. In his book, Russell was concerned to propound a new code of sexual behaviour which would help to promote human happiness:[16]

'The doctrine that there is something sinful about sex is one which has done untold harm to individual character—a harm beginning in early childhood and continuing throughout life. By keeping sex love in a prison, conventional morality has done much to imprison all other forms of friendly feeling, and to make men less generous, less kindly, more self-assertive and more cruel. Whatever sexual ethic may come to be ultimately accepted must be free from superstition and must have recognisable and demonstrable grounds in its favour.'

Far from being libertarian, Russell's sexual ethic was grounded in social responsibility. 'The doctrine that I wish to preach is not one of licence; it involves nearly as much self-control as is involved in the conventional doctrine',[17] he stated. Explaining his approach, Russell wrote:[18]

'Sex morality has to be derived from certain general principles, as to which there is perhaps a fairly wide measure of agreement, in spite of the wide disagreement as to the consequences to be drawn from them. The first thing to be secured is that there should be as much as possible of that deep, serious love between man and woman which embraces the whole personality of both and leads to a fusion by which each is enriched and enhanced. The second thing of importance is that there should be adequate care of children, physical and psychological. Neither of these principles in itself can be considered in any way shocking, yet it is as a consequence of these two principles that I should advocate certain modifications of the conventional code. Most men and women, as things stand, are incapable of being as wholehearted and as generous in the love that they bring to marriage as they would be if their early years had been less hedged about with taboos. They either lack the necessary experience, or they have gained it in furtive and undesirable ways. Moreover, since Jealousy has the sanction of moralists, they feel justified in keeping each other in a mutual prison. It is of course a very good thing when a husband and wife love each other so completely that neither is ever tempted to unfaithfulness; it is not, however, a good thing that unfaithfulness, if it does occur, should be treated as something terrible, nor is it desirable to go so far as to make all friendship with persons of the other sex impossible. A good life cannot be founded upon fear, prohibition, and mutual interference with freedom. Where faithfulness is achieved without these, it is good, but where all this is necessary it may well be that too high a price has been paid, and that a little mutual toleration of occasional lapses would be better. There can be no doubt that mutual jealousy, even where there is physical faithfulness, often causes more unhappiness in a marriage than would be caused if there were more confidence in the ultimate strength of a deep and permanent affection.'

Russell anticipated there would be difficulties in gaining acceptance for his ideas, and declared that 'those who advocate any ethical innovation are invariably accused, like Socrates, of being corrupters of youth.'[19] Already in 1929 these views were under attack. Dr William T. Manning, the Protestant Episcopal Bishop of New York, was notably outspoken. An expatriate Englishman, Manning was concerned to protect America's youth from Russell's doctrines. He condemned the invitation extended to Russell to lecture at nine American schools and colleges, which he saw as evidence of a world-wide anti-Christian conspiracy[20] and persuaded, among others, Nicholas Murray Butler, the President of Columbia University, to withdraw an invitation to Russell to lecture at that institution.[21] In agreeing to this action, Butler appeared to have forgotten that, in 1915, he had awarded Russell the Nicholas Murray Butler gold medal, in recognition of his outstanding contribution to philosophy. Manning's attitude was in marked contrast to the enthusiastic reception accorded *Marriage and Morals* by the majority of New York book reviewers. Typical of the latter view was a description of the book as 'the most humane and persuasive volume in the recent books on marriage.' And the statement that the author was 'a humanist, defending the happiness of man against many moral prejudices'.[22]

Wherever Russell travelled, the local press clamoured for interviews. At Berkeley, a reporter with a perspicacious eye was present at one of these ordeals and wrote a report headlined 'The Ladies Interview Russell' for the *Californian* of 9 November 1929:

'When we arrived at the interview that Russell was granting to the press, late as is our habit, we found that the topic had already turned to sex, without wasting time on sensational topics of greater import but less reader-interest.

'"Now don't you think that if you taught your boys and your girls the same thing, they would grow up in the same way?" asked one of the militant mothers among the pencil-pushers. "I believe that: I believe it *so* hard." Mr Russell did not, but that made no difference to the woman. She had been told that by a woman who had looked up a report at "our club", and besides what did Russell know about it. He was only bringing up twenty children in his experimental school, and you couldn't draw a rule from that. This she confided to her next-door neighbor in a hoarse masculine undertone.

'One of the women fidgeted with her cigarettes, but did not smoke, "because," she confided to us, "perhaps Mr Russell would want to smoke his pipe if he saw me smoking, and I know that he wouldn't *think* of smoking in the presence of ladies."

'The conversation passed from topic to topic, with reporters rapidly formulating shotgun paragraphs disconnected and ill-digested statements which they were to garble for the next day's prints. Soviet Russia was dismissed with a sentence; Germany was treated with a monosyllable. The reporters did not care why Russell thought what he did; they only wanted a few sensational statements.

'The siren in Oakland signified 12 o'clock. A woman reporter grabbed her hat. "Oh, Mr Russell," she interrupted, "its 12 o'clock and we have a deadline for pictures almost right away and the city editor will be just *wild* if we're late. Would you mind standing over there in that corner. . . . Now, boys, try to catch that elfin twinkle when he smiles", she giggled engagingly. The flashlight smoke filled the room: Russell blinked. "Just one more, please."

'We sought out Russell after everyone else had left. "What do you think of American interviewers", we asked him. An appreciative venom lit his eye for a passing moment, but he merely said: "Well, they're not quite as bad as the Japs, but that's as much as I can say for them." We smiled in agreement, blissfully forgetting that we were included in his generality.

'"You can't blame them," he continued. "They're not interested in any books. I had to sign several copies of my works for them this afternoon, but they were obviously all unread. If the American people wanted to find out what I thought they wouldn't ask me questions or come to my lectures. They would read my books. Fortunately for me they do buy them."

'Up bustled a member of the Oakland Forum. "You're having lunch with us, you know, Mr Russell," she declared. "Do come along now. It will be such a nice relaxation for you, riding with a few of our members in the limousine." She said limousine with pardonable pride; Russell did not even sigh.

'The next time I saw him it was on the stage of Oakland. He was to give a speech on "My Philosophy of Life". Rabbi Louis Newman, introducing him, said: "If anybody doubts whether America is genuinely interested in philosophy, let him gaze at this assemblage here tonight." Dowagers beamed inwardly, drew themselves up in their fur coats and felt that they had received their dollar's worth of satisfaction. Russell did not smile, but I detected a slight tightening of the upper lip.'

Before Russell left America, he arranged with Feakins the possibility of a return visit for 1931. He arrived back in England on 20 December, and wrote to a friend:[23]

'. . . it is delicious to be at home. One feels very far off in California and such places. I went to Salt Lake City and the Mormons tried to convert me, but when I found they forbade tea and tobacco I thought it was no religion for me.'

In another letter he wrote:[24]

'. . . on my travels I had breakfast at a place called El Reno in Oklahoma. There was a large sign at the station saying: "El Reno is good enough for us. We believe you would like it." After that I was not surprised that they believe in God and the Democratic party. There seems no limit to what people will believe.'

In between his American tours, Russell was extremely occupied with running his school and writing. 'Life here is arduous', he wrote from his school to an American friend, '—more so than a lecture tour in America.'[25]

His visits to America prompted many Americans to write to him, and as always he was meticulous about replying:

Russell to Dr [?] Grudin 3 January 1930
'It is quite true that I regard America as peculiarly indifferent to fact. I attribute this to the prominence of the advertiser, who penetrates even the intimate thoughts and mid-night dreams of most Americans. On the promenade deck of the *Berengaria* there is a notice saying: "Five times round this deck is 1,755 yards, one mile is 1,760 yards." If she were an American ship, the notice would say: 'Five times round this deck is a mile.'

Russell to Miss R. G. Brooks[26] 5 May 1930
'I am not sure whether you are right in saying that the problem of America is greater than that of China. It is likely that America will be more important during the next century or two, but after that it may

well be the turn of China. I think America is very worrying. There is something incredibly wrong with human relations in your country. We have a number of American children at our school, and I am amazed at their mothers' instinctive incompetence. The fount of affection seems to have dried up. I suppose all Western civilisation is going to go the same way, and I expect all our Western races to die out, with the possible exception of the Spaniards and Portuguese. Alternatively, the State may take to breeding the necessary citizens and educating them as Janissaries without family ties. Read John B. Watson on mothers. I used to think him mad; now I only think him American; that is to say, the mothers that he has known have been American mothers. The result of this physical aloofness is that the child grows up filled with hatred against the world and anxious to distinguish himself as a criminal, like Leopold and Loeb.'

Russell to Miss [?] Millay 18 April 1931
'There is no interest in modern education in England whatever. I think that in England people acquire more *knowledge* in the course of education than they do in America, but in all other respects education in England is worse than in your country. I say this not from any admiration of American educational institutions. It is hardly true that the children in our school have not yet learnt to put on clothes, as we do not wish them all to die of pneumonia, but they wear clothes for the purpose of warmth and not for their original purpose of arousing erotic feelings.'

Not infrequently, Russell found that American correspondents enclosed postage stamps in their letters so as to cover the cost of his reply. He consequently liked to append to his replies a postscript along the following lines:[27] 'You may remember that the use of English stamps in America was one of the causes of the War of Independence; the use of American stamps in England has not yet been authorised.'

One of the first articles Russell wrote on returning to England had been commissioned by the magazine *Outlook and Independent*, and was published in February 1930 under the title 'Homogeneous America'.[28] The editors in introducing the article drew attention to Russell's recent tour and commented: 'He is impressed by the prevailing similarity of outlook, of the tendency towards uniformity, and the consequent persecution of minorities. . . .' Another fruit of Russell's trip was an article assessing the prospects for the American labour movement entitled 'Thirty Years from Now'.[29] It was published by the *Virginia Quarterly Review* in October 1930. Also published in 1930 was his book, *The Conquest of Happiness*, which sold well in America.

Russell returned to the United States in late October 1931, undertaking his third lecture tour in four years. On this occasion he visited

America as the 3rd Earl Russell. His brother, Frank, had died earlier in the year and Russell inherited the title, although he preferred to be known simply as Bertrand Russell. The death of Frank did not result in financial benefit for Russell; in fact it increased his obligations. Although he inherited Telegraph House, he was legally bound to support Frank's dependants. Before he left England, he wrote to his American publisher, Warder Norton of W. W. Norton:[30]

'It is nice to think that you will be on the dock when I reach New York . . . and it will be a great pleasure to me to come to you when I first land, if you can endure the bustle that always occurs during my first day or two in America.'

Russell arrived in New York on 23 October, having sailed on the *Bremen*. *The New York Times* of 24 October, describing him as 'the English socialist writer and peer of the realm', reported:

'Bertrand Russell appeared in New York again yesterday, gloomy about the state of civilisation in Europe and the state of the home in New York. Both are in a pretty bad way. There was the inference that America might help civilisation, but only lower rents can help New York. Earl Russell has been here before, and he knows . . .'

Russell had quipped to the press aboard ship: 'When the rents are high, the home goes. Perhaps it is more gone in New York City than anywhere else!' A columnist of *The New York Times* reported on 26 October, that: 'Bertrand Russell is here again to aid Americans in the Conquest of Happiness', and went on to compare certain discrepancies in the press coverage of Russell. He noted that the *Herald Tribune* had described him as 'a ruddy little man with a gnomelike face under a thatch of white hair and a voice like a phonograph record', while the *New York Times* news report had pictured 'a rather tall man with a mass of flowing white hair, a thin face and the voice of a schoolmaster'. According to the columnist, these differences arose because Russell radiated 'such a multicolored glitter and dazzle and interplay of brightness that even his hard-boiled observers and questioners couldn't see him or caught but one facet of his benign and dancing presence'. The columnist enthused over Russell: 'He is a harbinger of Christmas. He is Christmas. He is better than Christmas.'

One of the highlights of the tour was a debate with Sherwood Anderson, the novelist, on 'Shall the State Rear Our Children?',[31] which was chaired by John B. Watson. Over 2,500 people packed the Mecca Temple to hear the debate, which took place on 1 November, under the auspices of the Discussion Guild of New York. According to *The New York Times* of 2 November:

'Dr Russell declared that children require physical care and freedom rather than affection and that "most love is a prison, mother love not the least so." Maternal solicitude, he said, is designed by nature to be adequate for a family of ten and becomes excessive when concentrated upon one or two, the usual number of children in a modern family.

'. . . Both speakers made it plain that they considered themselves to be dealing almost wholly in theories. Dr Russell said in the course of the talk: "I am a moderate man, a Whig, and all I am suggesting is that it might be better if children were sent to boarding-school for a while." Dr Russell had remarked before coming to the platform that he "hoped to get back to England by 19 December to help set up my children's Christmas tree".

'Dr Russell based his advocacy of State child-rearing on seven points. His first dealt with the bad physical environment of cities for children.

' "Children need light, air, freedom of movement and freedom to make a noise", he said. "Large cities and small apartments do not give them a proper environment. Schools in the country do.

' "Second, children require the companionship of other children. In the old days of large families they could get this at home. Nowadays, in most cases, they cannot.

' "Third, maternal solicitude is designed by nature to be strong enough to preserve ten children at once from accident. The mothers of one or two concentrate upon them an amount of anxiety which is five or six times too great, with the result that they tend to become timid and are oppressed by the sense of being constantly under observation.

' "Fourth, parental feeling inevitably contains an element of possessiveness and love of power, which leads parents to wish their children to remain infantile and dependent longer than they should.

' "Fifth, the emotional attachment of children to their parents is often unduly strong.

' "Sixth, wherever the home life of the parents is not happy, children are very liable to suffer from nervous disorders as a result of the emotional conflicts produced. This is one of the most frequent sources of the problem child, and it is best cured by providing the child with a larger and freer environment.

' "Seventh, the need of the child is activity and freedom to grow. His emotions should be as little stirred as possible. The desire of many adults to obtain from children an affection with an adult emotional intensity is, without intention, cruel and harmful. Practical help without emotional intensity is more easily given by teachers than by parents, and it is this that children need." '

Russell had a message for American communists too. He argued the negative in a debate with Jay Lovestone of the Communist party on 'Is Proletarian Dictatorship the Road to Freedom?' The debate was held at the Central Opera House in New York and was arranged by the New Workers School. *The New York Times* of 28 November sensationalised its report of the meeting under the heading: 'Russell Warns Reds of Violence', and estimated the attendance at 500. According to *The New York Times*:

'. . . he warned the communists that in proclaiming violence to gain their ends, they gave the other side a real justification to take the same attitude. "If you start a revolution before you are strong enough," Mr Russell said, "the struggle is apt to be so long and so ferocious that both capitalists and communists will be destroyed and you will have only a few savages running around." He advised the communists to press their case in the legal manner rather than by force.'

As a consequence of his lecture tour, Russell began his four-year series of weekly articles for the Hearst Press. One of the first of these, 'Christmas at Sea',[32] he wrote on his return voyage to England. Many of these articles—more than 150 in all—were topical and light-hearted, and demonstrated Russell's flair for imparting wisdom through popular journalism. Among the diverse subjects treated were: 'Who May Use Lipstick?', 'On Tourists', 'Love and Money', 'Furniture and the Ego', 'On Sales Resistance', 'The Minor Troubles of Feminists', 'On Wife-Beating', 'Should Socialists Smoke Good Cigars?', 'On the Fierceness of Vegetarians', etc. His more serious articles dealt with topics arising out of crucial social issues, but some were not published. His article, 'On Equality',[33] dealt with the need for collective control over economic affairs. 'On States' Rights'[34] examined the abuses of Federal law arising out of the autonomy of State governors. In 'The Root Causes of the Depression',[35] Russell applauded 'the gallant attempt now being made in America to promote economic recovery' under President Roosevelt, and condemned 'the very rich who were in control throughout Mr Hoover's administration'.

The 1931 tour was Russell's last trip in association with the running of the school. Soon after his return to England, the break-up of his second marriage occurred and he left the school in Dora's charge. Also the depression meant the end to lecture tours in America as a source of income and affected the sale of his books. In a letter to his American publisher, Russell observed that it was not very cheering 'to receive exactly nothing for half a year's work. I cannot help thinking that America has now touched bottom, and that things will soon get better.'[36]

In his *Autobiography* Russell recorded:[37]

'. . . my income had diminished catastrophically. This was due partly to the depression, which caused people to buy much fewer books, partly to the fact that I was no longer writing popular books, and partly to my having refused to stay with Hearst in 1931 at his castle in California. My weekly articles in the Hearst newspapers had brought me £1,000 a year, but after my refusal, the pay was halved, and very soon I was told the articles were no longer required.'

Commenting on Russell's recent tour, a leader article in the *Nation* of 30 December 1931 reported that he 'promises never to return to the United States. Americans are too hospitable, he declares; they feted him to death and, he undoubtedly might have added, urged on him too constantly indifferent liquor and dull sociability.' Russell was concerned that his statement on America should not be misinterpreted, and his letter of explanation appeared in the *Nation* on 3 February 1932:

'I find in your issue of 30 December a note about myself which might give the impression that I have been finding fault with American hospitality. If in some moment of fatigue I have said anything capable of this interpretation, I apologise to my many American friends. A lecture tour in America is unavoidably rather strenuous, and advancing years have made me feel that it might be unwise to attempt another in the future. But I do not feel that Americans are responsible for this strenuousness, which is due to the desire of visitors like myself to get through a great deal in a short time.

'I have much gratitude for the kindness which I have experienced in your country, and I should not wish to be added to the number of those Englishmen who have indulged in unjust and ill-natured criticism.'

While Russell was conscious of the good treatment he received from many Americans, he was also aware of the rage his ideas provoked among the illiberal. In September 1932 '100 prominent citizens of North Carolina' petitioned the State governor demanding that he forbid 'further predatory acts by so-called modern educators' at the institutions of higher learning. Citing as examples Russell and Langston Hughes, the black poet, both of whom had lectured at the University of North Carolina the previous year, the petitioners described Russell's philosophy as 'the incarnation of paganism, dressed up in inveigling and seductive non-biblical terms, and properly branded as neo-paganism.'[38]

Russell reacted strongly to the rise of Hitler and the threat of war in Europe, which he felt should be avoided at all costs. He advocated pacifism and supported President Roosevelt's neutralist policy as he had Woodrow Wilson's during the First World War. He also championed

Roosevelt's domestic programme and in 'Can the President Succeed?',[39] written for but unpublished by the Hearst Press, supported the New Deal which he described as 'attempting, without abolishing the capitalist system, to subject it to regulations which will cause it to work in accordance with the public interest. . . .' Russell questioned whether Roosevelt's actions would be sufficient to pull the country back from depression, or whether it would be found that 'the motive of private profit needs to be wholly suspended as the motive in production.'

He also wrote approving the abolition of Prohibition which, in his Hearst article 'The End of Prohibition',[40] he described as a 'resounding defeat' for the 'restrictive morality inspired by envy'.

In a letter to Warder Norton of 7 January 1934, Russell commented on the revival of American optimism based on New Deal legislation:

'. . . I doubt whether any permanent recovery is possible so long as the profit motive remains. Roosevelt pays people *not* to grow cotton and wheat; I don't say he is wrong as things are, but obviously an economic system which demands such things is fundamentally insane. I am hoping he will gradually move to the left, but I fear that at some point the forces of reaction will revive.'

In this period, Russell continued his sociological writings, publishing in 1932 *Education and the Social Order*, and in 1934 *Freedom and Organisation, 1814–1914*, the latter of which he had contracted with W. W. Norton on his last tour.[41] The first part of this major historical work is devoted to an exposition on the development of American democracy, regarding which Russell wrote:[42]

'Throughout the first seventy-two years of its existence as an independent nation, the United States was interesting to Europeans chiefly as the most complete and important example of democracy then in existence. Opinion was divided as it now is about Russia: it was treason among radicals to admit defects in America, and among conservatives to admit merits. Nor was this view confined to Europe. With the exception of the federalists in early days, Americans felt themselves the bearers of progress. . . .'

And further:[43]

'In America, freedom was facilitated by the fact that there was room for expansion. Those who disliked the restraints of crowded cities could move westward; those who had criminal impulses could fight the Indians or the Mexicans. Jefferson's conception of democracy was agricultural; he feared the growth of great cities, and partly on that ground was opposed to tariffs on manufactures. The bulk of his political party were small freeholders, who disliked urban capitalism. From his day to our own, progressive politics in America has been mainly agricultural, largely because there is nothing in his type of liberalism that is of any use to the industrial wage-earner. . . .'

Russell was always interested in the peculiar status of women in America and in the book observed:

'The influence of women has been greater in the United States than in any other country, and in frontier communities their influence was on the side of civilisation. This was due partly to the fact that they did not drink whisky, partly to a desire for social distinction, partly to maternal affection, and partly to the fact that they were less imbued than their husbands with the tough adventurer's desire to be rid of the trammels of an artifical society. . . .'[44]

'Another result of the pioneering period has been that the non-utilitarian parts of culture have come to be regarded as almost exclusively the concern of women. Since most women have not pursued painting or literature or philosophy professionally, but only taken an intelligent interest in all of them, there has come to be a certain superficiality in regard to all such subjects, which, from an early date, was ministered to by lectures. The East, almost as much as the West, left culture to women, because business absorbed Eastern men; but the business that absorbed them was very largely concerned with the opening of the West. . . .'[45]

'To this day, America has remained on the cultural side chiefly a nation of appreciators, mainly female, while on the utilitarian side it has achieved high excellence. America is good in medicine, in law, in architecture, in mechanical invention, but in such studies as mathematics and theoretical physics almost all the advances have been European. . . .'[46]

One of Russell's main preoccupations with America was the industrialising process and its impact on labour:

'The gospel of America, as of industrial England, was competition. But whereas England, through the adoption of free trade, had proclaimed the doctrine in an international form, America, whose industries were still in their infancy, confined capitalistic competition, to a continually increasing extent, within national limits by means of the tariff. Cheap labour from Europe was admitted, but cheap goods from Europe, after the alliance of West and East in the Republican party, were taxed to an extent which gradually became prohibitive. It might have been thought that American labour would have objected to this one-sided form of competition, but American labour was intent on acquiring a homestead, and was content to leave wage-earning to foreigners. . . .'[47]

'From the wage-earners' point of view, the system established by the plutocrats was far from pleasant. In spite of democracy, in spite of protection, in spite of the rapidly increasing wealth of the country, hours were long, and wages, though better than in Europe, were infinitesimal as compared with the rewards of financial magnates. In 1872, when Commodore Vanderbilt was rapidly approaching his hundredth million, he lowered the wages of drivers and conductors on the surface line on Fourth Avenue from $2.25 a day to $2, and that for a fifteen-hour day. In steel, until well into the present century, the men who attended to the blast furnaces had to work twelve hours a day, and once a fortnight, when they changed from day to night work, they had to work for twenty-four hours on end. Trade unions were more difficult to establish than in England, because of the mixture of races; among the unskilled, they were almost non-existent before 1900. Employers were able to refuse to treat with unions, and in some cases—for instance, Carnegie after the strike in 1892—they refused altogether to employ union men. In cotton mills, especially in the South, child labour was very prevalent, and attempts to prevent it were, until lately, declared unconstitutional by the Supreme Court. . . .'[48]

Regarding the future, Russell advocated socialism, as he had for over a decade, as the only solution for America:

'The radical who believes in competition is doomed to defeat in any contest with modern corporations. Their power is analogous to that of armies, and to leave them in private hands is just as disastrous as it is to leave armies in private hands. The large-scale economic organisations of modern times are an inevitable outcome of modern technique, and technique tends increasingly to make competition wasteful. . . . The solution, for those who do not wish to be oppressed, lies in public ownership of the organisations that give economic power. For so long as this power is in private hands, the apparent equality conferred by political democracy is little better than a sham.'[49]

Russell's analysis of America in *Freedom and Organisation* was the culmination of more than three decades of involvement with that country. During his work on the book, he informed Norton of the tremendous amount of reading and research the subject had demanded.[50] The American aspect of the book reflected, also, the fruits of his several tours. It is clear that despite his preoccupation with education and social morality in the late 1920s and early 1930s, his dominant concern remained political.

Russell maintained his pacifist position throughout the 1930s and explained his standpoint in *Which Way to Peace?*, published in 1936. Despite his passionate anti-war feelings Russell saw humour in his situation: 'It always amuses me,' he remarked in a letter to Warder Norton,[51] 'that when I earn money by pacifist activities, 8 per cent goes to building American battleships and 30 per cent to building British battleships, so that I do more harm than good.'

NOTES

[1] Previously unpublished, but see below, pp. 236–43.

[2] For Russell on Dewey see *History of Western Philosophy* (London, 1946, and Simon & Schuster, New York, 1945), and for Russell on Watson see *An Outline of Philosophy* (London and W. W. Norton, New York, as *Philosophy*, 1927) and also 'Behaviourism and Values' in *Sceptical Essays* (London and W. W. Norton, New York, 1928)

[3] Max Eastman, *Great Companions* (Museum Press, London, 1959), pp. 139–40.

[4] Published in the *Forum* (July 1928).

[5] Information from Frederick B. Robinson's letter to Bishop Manning of 19 August 1929; see also p. 113.

[6] Russell to Lindsey, 14 January 1930.

[7] For the full text of this letter see B. Russell, *Autobiography* (London, 1968), Vol. II, pp. 180–1. (Boston, 1968), pp. 265–7.

[8] Russell, *Sceptical Essays* (London, 1928), p. 126 (W. W. Norton, New York, 1928), p. 129.

[9] See below, pp. 249–52.

[10] See below, pp. 244–8.

[11] See below, pp. 253–5; see also Illustrations, Plate 8, p. 211.

[12] B. Russell, *The Scientific Outlook* (London, 1931), pp. 199–201 (W. W. Norton, New York, 1931), pp. 194–5.

[13] Published in the *Lantern* (August 1929).

[14] The former reported in *The New York Times* (7 October 1929), and the latter published by the Discussion Guild (New York, 1930); see Illustrations, Plate 11, p. 211.

[15] B. Russell, *Autobiography*, Vol. II, p. 156; p. 227.

[16] B. Russell, *Marriage and Morals* (London, 1929), p. 241 (Horace Liveright, New York, 1929), p. 309.

[17] Ibid., p. 249; p. 319.

[18] Ibid., pp. 246–7; pp. 315–16.

[19] Ibid., p. 242; p. 310.

[20] From an undated, unidentified New York newspaper clipping.

21 Manning raised this matter with Butler in a letter of 30 August 1929; Butler replied on 4 September 1929.

22 John Dewey and Horace M. Kallen (eds), *The Bertrand Russell Case* (Viking Press, New York, 1941); quoted by John Dewey in his essay, p. 57.

23 Letter to Charles Sanger of 23 December 1929; for the full text see B. Russell, *Autobiography*, Vol. II, pp. 188–9; p. 280.

24 Letter to Charles Sanger of 29 December 1929.

25 Letter to Miriam Reichl of 15 March 1928.

26 Rachel Gleason Brooks, a writer on China; see B. Russell, *Autobiography*, Vol. II, p. 179; pp. 263–4.

27 See also, B. Feinberg and R. Kasrils (eds), *Dear Bertrand Russell* (London, 1969), p. 175 (Houghton Mifflin, Boston, 1969), p. 145.

28 See below, pp. 256–61.

29 See below, pp. 262–9.

30 From Russell's letter of 3 June 1931.

31 Published as 'Shall the Home be Abolished?' in the *Literary Digest* (28 November 1931). See Illustrations, Plate 9, p. 211.

32 B. Russell, *Autobiography*, Vol. II, pp. 156–8; pp. 229–30.

33 See below, pp. 272–3.

34 Previously unpublished, but see below, pp. 278–9.

35 Previously unpublished, but see below, pp. 274–5.

36 From Russell's letter to W. W. Norton of 10 March 1933.

37 B. Russell, *Autobiography*, Vol. II, p. 191; p. 286.

38 The New York *Evening Post* (8 September 1932).

39 See below, pp. 276–7.

40 See below, pp. 270–1.

41 Into this volume, Russell incorporated notes originally intended for a book on America which Norton had encouraged him to undertake.

42 B. Russell, *Freedom and Organisation, 1814–1914* (London, 1934), p. 259 (W. W. Norton, New York, 1934), p. 226.

43 Ibid., p. 267; p. 233.

44 Ibid., p. 284; p. 248.

45 Ibid., p. 287; p. 251.

46 Ibid., p. 288; p. 252.

47 Ibid., p. 343; p. 300.

48 Ibid., p. 354; p. 310.

49 Ibid., p. 356; pp. 311–12.

50 From Russell's letter of 8 November 1932.

51 From Russell's letter of 29 August 1932.

CHAPTER 10

RETURN TO AMERICA, 1938

After more than a decade of popular writing, Russell decided to return to work on technical philosophy, and delivered a course of lectures at Oxford on 'Words and Facts.' He had married again and a son, Conrad, was born to his third wife, Patricia, in 1937. *The New York Times*, repeating certain wide-spread myths about Russell, noted on 18 April:

'White-haired Bertrand Russell, whom sophisticates know for his unique views on sex, marital relations, how to bring up children, and international affairs, was proud tonight after becoming a father at the age of 64. "I'm very pleased—very," the philosopher said at his country home after announcing the birth of a son. "The mother and the baby are doing extremely well."

'But Earl Russell, whose pen has flowed freely to advise other fathers how to rear their families, insisted the upbringing of his family was "a private affair".

'He once ran a school where the children could do just what they pleased—go naked when they felt the urge, swear and attend classes as the spirit moved them.

'Bertrand Russell succeeded to an earldom in 1931, when an elder brother died, but he has taken little part in the deliberations of the House of Lords. Besides being a pacifist, he favors total disarmament and the surrender of all Great Britain's colonies to the League of Nations. These ideas are not very popular with most of the peers. . . .'

Russell was beset by growing financial problems, since he was already providing for Frank's dependants as well as for Dora and their two children. This caused Logan Pearsall Smith, Alys's brother, to observe: 'the burden of life on his aging shoulders sometimes weighs heavily, and he talks of being forced to return to Brixton Prison, owing to his inability to pay his legal obligations.'[1]

Because Russell had been having great difficulty in securing a permanent academic position in England, he had, in 1936, asked Warder Norton to inquire into the possibilities of a post at an American university. In his letter of 28 December 1936, Russell explained to Norton his reasons for wanting to work in America:

'My feelings are threefold: (a) I have a lot of ideas in my head that I long to work at and believe to be important. (b) I am faced with the likelihood of such poverty that I may be unable to give a proper education to the child that is coming. (c) That Europe is no place for children, with the imminent risk of war—particularly England, which is likely to suffer most in the next war.'

When the University of Chicago approached Russell in April 1937, offering an appointment as Visiting Professor of Philosophy for the winter term of the following year, he gladly accepted. Together with his wife and infant son, he sailed for America in September 1938.

On arriving in New York, Russell gave his usual press conference, and reporters were particularly interested in his views on events in Europe. *The New York Times* reported on 26 September: 'Bertrand Russell here; says world will be "mad" after the next great war.' The report continued:

'Earl Russell, English author and philosopher, said on his arrival from Europe yesterday that after the next great war the entire world will be as "mad" as part of it is today. He arrived on the Cunard White Star liner, *Britannic*, accompanied by his wife and their 17-month-old son, Conrad, to lecture on semantics at the University of Chicago throughout the winter.

'Lord Russell said that he had never held a very high opinion of Neville Chamberlain as Prime Minister, but after Mr Chamberlain's dramatic decision to meet Hitler personally he began to think his judgment had been faulty.

'Lord Russell said that he was "an extreme pacifist," but he realised that there were occasions "when it is very difficult to keep out of war.

'"I am afraid war would do an extraordinary amount of harm to the world", he continued. "Even if we win, after the war I am afraid we would be just as mad as Hitler is. You go into such a thing believing that you are going to accomplish something, but you get so angry that all proportion is lost."'

Russell was met by Norton and Feakins; the latter hoped to arrange a lecture tour after Russell had completed his term at the University of Chicago. In his *Autobiography*, Russell recalled his time in Chicago:

'. . . I had a large seminar, where I continued to lecture on the same subject as at Oxford, namely, "Words and Facts". But I was told that Americans would not respect my lectures if I used monosyllables, so I altered the title to something like "The Correlation between Oral and

Somatic Motor Habits". Under this title, or something of the sort, the seminar was approved. It was an extraordinarily delightful seminar. Carnap and Charles Morris used to come to it, and I had three pupils of quite outstanding ability—Dalkey, Kaplan, and Copilowish. We used to have close arguments back and forth, and succeeded in genuinely clarifying points to our mutual satisfaction, which is rare in philosophical argument. Apart from this seminar, the time in Chicago was disagreeable. The town is beastly and the weather was vile. President [Robert M.] Hutchins, who was occupied with the Hundred Best Books, and with the attempt to force neo-Thomism on the philosophical faculty, naturally did not much like me, and when the year for which I had been engaged came to an end was, I think, glad to see me go.'[2]

Temporarily cut off from England, Russell was anxious about the growing threat of war. He continued to maintain a pacifist position: 'I still thought that there was some possibility of war being avoided, and that, if war came, it would again, as in 1914–18, be an imperialist war on *both* sides.'[3] After Chamberlain's Munich agreement with Hitler, he wrote home to Dora Sanger, from Chicago, on 5 November 1938, about the Czechoslovakian crisis:[4]

'I was immensely glad when the crisis passed, but I don't know how soon it may come up again. Here in America, nine people out of ten think that we [the British] ought to have fought but America ought to have remained neutral—an opinion which annoys me.'

Russell kept in touch with Lucy Donnelly, writing to her on 31 January 1939 from Chicago:

'I am here till 20 March, then I go touring under the auspices of Feakins. . . . I find this university very good in philosophy and I have some remarkably able pupils. The intellectual level is very markedly higher than at Oxford, so I enjoy my work.'

Russell had considered returning to England that spring, but when his contract with Chicago terminated, he was offered a professorship in philosophy with the University of California at Los Angeles, to run for three years, from September 1939. At the age of 66, the prospect of being continually on the move, debating, interviewing and lecturing was not a happy one and, above all, the life of a freelance lecturer with the uncertain income entailed, was not conducive to the serious writing he wished to do. These factors influenced his decision to remain in America and accept the California post. Russell moved to California at the end of March, renting a house in Santa Barbara. 'After the bleak hideousness of Chicago, which was still in the grip of winter,' he observed, 'it was delightful to arrive in the Californian spring.' Before commencing duties at the University of California, Russell undertook the lecture tour arranged by Feakins. Of this he remembered only two things:[5]

'One is that the professors at the Louisiana State University, where I lectured, all thought well of Huey Long,[6] on the ground that he had raised their salaries. The other recollection is more pleasant: in a purely rural region, I was taken to the top of the dykes that enclose the Mississippi. I was very tired with lecturing, long journeys, and heat. I lay in the grass, and watched the majestic river, and gazed, half hypnotised, at water and sky. For some ten minutes I experienced peace, a thing which very rarely happened to me, and I think only in the presence of moving water.'

In the course of his lecture tour Russell visited Boston, where he was interviewed for a college newspaper. Many years later the interviewer recalled the occasion:[7]

'We had tea at the Ritz in Boston, and then we had dinner there, too—just the two of us. I still can't quite believe it. He was sixty-six and famous, obviously with an empty evening to fill, and I was a freshman and I didn't know *anything*. I don't remember what we talked about, but he kept the conversation going and saw to it that I got a good story for the paper, and he paid for the dinner, too. Looking back on it afterwards, I realised, of course, that *he* had interviewed *me*. And then, years later, I began to understand that he had been willing to spend all that time with me simply because he was far more interested in my mind than I was. I think this is the ultimate compliment.'

Russell continued to write for American journals. Three important articles, apparently unpublished and written before the outbreak of war were 'The American Mind',[8] 'Individual Freedom in England and America',[9] and 'America: The Next World Centre'.[10] In the second article, he contrasted the casual impressions of an English visitor to the United States with the reality learnt from long experience. Russell showed how traditional freedoms were undermined by the working of American capitalism, again reiterating his support for President Roosevelt and the New Deal:

'The power of the leading men in finance and industry in America is astounding. At present they do not control the Federal government, but they have done so at most times since the Civil War. They still control most of the State governments, and can invoke the aid of the State militia in labour disputes except where the governor is exceptionally liberal. Most of the great newspapers support them. All the best universities live on their benefactions and have powerful motives for not offending them. The outlook of the very rich is so reactionary and dictatorial that they look askance at any approximately impartial treatment of economics and social questions and suspect all supporters of the New Deal of communism. Their hostility to the President is inconceivably bitter.'

In an article 'Democracy and Economics',[11] published in *Survey Graphic*, February 1939, Russell discussed the consequences for America of the oligarchy of '2,000 individuals' who controlled half the country's industry. 'No attempt is made to cause them to obey the law', he wrote, 'even when, like Mr Henry Ford, they openly boast of being law-breakers.' Russell argued that this group controlled politics in America because of their hold on economic power and advocated the transference of this power 'into the hands of the democratic State'. The article, containing numerous references to contemporary statements and writings, demonstrated in particular his interest in the turbulent labour clashes of the 1930s, and leaves no doubt about his own sympathies.

In March 1939, Russell contributed an article to a forum on 'If War Comes—Shall We Participate or Be Neutral?', initiated by the journal *Common Sense*. His contribution, in which he stated 'The Case for U.S. Neutrality',[12] was described by the editors as 'particularly significant' since it came from 'an Englishman whose life has been dedicated to all that democracy implies'. As in the First World War, Russell advocated neutrality as the only way of preserving democracy in America. He argued:

'The best hope for the world, if Europe plunges into the madness of another great war, is that America will remain neutral, but will, when the fighting is over, use economic power to further sanity and liberalism, and to restore to the parent continent as much as possible of the civilisation that the war will have temporarily destroyed.'

Russell enthusiastically supported Roosevelt's attempts to avert the war in Europe, and wrote to the President on 15 April 1939:

'. . . I cannot resist expressing to you my profound gratitude and admiration for your peace plea to Hitler and Mussolini. In so far as a humble professor can, I have worked for peace before the Great War, during it, and ever since; to this cause I have sacrificed all conflicting loyalties. Never before have I felt moved to express such feelings as now master me to any possessor of power.'

Roosevelt replied briefly to Russell on 18 April: 'It was very kind of you to write me that fine letter approving the course which I took. I do appreciate it indeed.'

During the summer of 1939 John and Kate arrived in America to spend the school holidays with their father. The outbreak of war in

September dealt a harsh blow to Russell's work for peace and caused him, with much pain, to question his pacifist position. His immediate concern, however, was for his children. War made it impossible for them to return home, and Russell had to make provision for their education. John was entered at the University of California and Kate, despite her youth, followed soon after when it was discovered that the high school she was attending had 'only one subject taught that she did not already know, and that was the virtues of the capitalist system.'[13]

Although the horrors of the war and Britain's beleaguered isolation had not yet become fully apparent, Russell, who, throughout his life, expressed a deep love for England, suffered great distress at being safely ensconced in America. Until the California appointment, he had planned to stay in the United States for only eight months. As a parent, he was naturally relieved that his children were in a safe country, but it was predominantly the needs of employment that kept him away from home. His views on the war had been gradually changing, and Russell held to his pacifist convictions with increasing emotional strain. Unlike in the First World War, he was unsure of his attitude and this indecision was made all the more unbearable by his absence from home. He wrote to Robert Trevelyan, in England, from Los Angeles, on 22 December 1939:[14]

'I am established here as Professor of Philosophy in the University of California. John and Kate came out for the summer holidays, and stayed when the war came, so they are having to go to the university here. John has a passion for Latin, especially Lucretius; unfortunately your Lucretius is stored in Oxford with the rest of my books. (I had expected to come back to England last spring.)

'. . . I wonder what you are feeling about the war. I try hard to remain a pacifist, but the thought of Hitler and Stalin triumphant is hard to bear. . . .

'Americans all say "you must be glad to be here at this time", but except for the children's sake that is not how we feel. . . .

'Write when you can—it is a comfort to hear from old friends.'

A letter to Lucy Donnelly, also on 22 December 1939, hints at the anguish Russell was beginning to experience:[15]

'It is the custom of this country to keep all intelligent people so harassed and hustled that they cease to be intelligent, and I have been suffering from this custom. The summer at Santa Barbara, it is true, was peaceful, but unluckily I injured my back and was laid up for a long time, which caused me to get behind hand with my lectures. John and Kate, who came for the summer holidays, stayed when war broke out; it is a comfort

131

to have them here, but John does not find the University of California a satisfactory substitute for Cambridge. I think of sending them both East to some less recent university, but last September there was no time for that. Apart from home-sickness and war misery, we all flourish.

'I am, when I can find time, writing a book on "Words and Facts",[16] or "Semantics" as it is vulgarly called. The only thing to be done in these times, it seems to me, is to salvage what one can of civilisation, personally as well as politically. But I feel rather like a strayed ghost from a dead world.

'The visit to you was delightful. As time goes on, one values old friends more and more. Remember me to Miss Finch.[17] With love to yourself.'

Although he preferred the Californian climate to that of the Mid-West, Russell found the University of California academically 'much less agreeable' than Chicago, and dominated by a president, Robert Sproul, for whom Russell 'conceived, I think justly, a profound aversion'.[18] Describing the atmosphere at the university, Russell wrote:[19]

'If a lecturer said anything that was too liberal, it was discovered that the lecturer in question did his work badly, and he was dismissed. Where there were meetings of the faculty, the president of the university used to march in as if he were wearing jack-boots, and rule any motion out of order if he did not happen to like it. Everybody trembled at his frown, and I was reminded of a meeting of the *Reichstag* under Hitler.'

While at the university, Russell learnt a considerable amount about the economic life of California. He wrote:[20]

'During the depression most people who had land had been unable to pay the interest on their mortgages and the mortgages which were generally held by the Bank of America had been foreclosed, so that the Bank of America owned the greater part of the farming land of California. Now the Bank of America was entirely governed by a certain Italian fascist, a man of very extreme reactionary views, who, in spite of being a fascist, was universally accepted as great and grand because he was so rich. I was credibly informed that if one were to say anything against him one would be assassinated. I don't know whether this were true or not but it was certainly true that he completely governed the University of California which had to do whatever he told it. He depended largely upon migrant labour which was very cheap and very much oppressed and one man at the university made an investigation of migrant labour and suggested that the only cure for its troubles would be the formation of trade unions among the migrant labourers. As soon as he had published this document, the university decided that he did not do enough research and was a very bad teacher and he was therefore dismissed from his post. A certain number of people protested against this action but the supreme authorities in the university ruled any motion in his defence out of order, and he was sacked and destroyed as a teacher.'

A few years later, Russell, referring to the issue of migrant labour, remarked: 'At the present day, Californian fruit would taste less sweet to consumers if they realised the conditions of the migrant labour by which it has been picked.'[21]

Early in 1940, soon after it was announced that Russell would deliver the William James lectures at Harvard that autumn, an opportunity arose for him to take up a professorship at the College of the City of New York. Russell accepted and gave President Sproul notice of his resignation. Shortly afterwards, he learnt that the New York appointment was not yet official and he therefore asked Sproul to withdraw his resignation, but was informed that it was too late. Russell suspected that Sproul's attitude was occasioned by the fact that 'earnest Christian taxpayers had been protesting against having to contribute to the salary of an infidel, and the president was glad to be quit of me.'[22] Over the subsequent months, Russell was to become involved in a bitter public dispute concerning the City College appointment; this occurred at a time when the Nazi onslaught in Europe appeared invincible, and Russell was becoming preoccupied with Britain's desperate fight for survival.

NOTES

[1] From Pearsall Smith's letter to Santayana of 16 January 1938.

[2] B. Russell, *Autobiography* (London, 1968), Vol. II, p. 217 (Boston, 1968), pp. 331–2.

[3] 'Why I am not a Pacifist in this War', unpublished, *c.* 1941.

[4] For the full text of his letter, see B. Russell, *Autobiography*, Vol. II, p. 225; p. 343.

[5] Ibid., pp. 217–18; p. 332.

[6] Huey Long, the notoriously corrupt governor of Louisiana, who was assassinated.

[7] *The New Yorker* (21 February 1970), p. 29.

[8] See below, pp. 283–4.

[9] See below, pp. 280–2.

[10] See below, pp. 285–8.

[11] Issued separately in *Calling America: A Special Number of* Survey Graphic *on the Challenge to Democracy* (Harper, 1939); see below, pp. 289–95.

[12] See below, pp. 296–8.

[13] B. Russell, *Autobiography*, Vol. II, p. 218; p. 333.

[14] Ibid., p. 239; pp. 366–7.

[15] B. Russell, *Autobiography* (London, 1969), Vol. III, p. 38 (Boston, 1969), p. 36.

[16] This was eventually published under the title of *An Inquiry into Meaning and Truth* (London and W. W. Norton, New York, 1940); see also below, p. 184.

[17] Edith Finch, later Edith, Countess Russell; see below, pp. 173–4.

[18] B. Russell, *Autobiography*, Vol. II, p. 218; p. 333.

[19] Ibid.

[20] B. Feinberg (ed.), *The Collected Stories of Bertrand Russell* (London, 1972), (Simon & Schuster, New York, 1973), pp. 304–5.

[21] 'Outline of a Political Philosophy', unpublished, *c.* 1943.

[22] B. Russell, *Autobiography*, Vol. II, p. 218; p. 333.

CHAPTER 11

A NEW YORK APPOINTMENT

The College of the City of New York was a municipal-run institution controlled by the government of New York City. A series of procedural steps were therefore required before Russell's appointment could be officially finalised. Russell received a letter from Nelson Mead, the college's acting president, informing him that the Administrative Committee of City College had unanimously approved his appointment and, subject to one final step of ratification, that it would commence from February 1941. The body responsible for approving all appointments was the Board of Higher Education of the City of New York, which controlled the four tax-supported colleges of the city. At its meeting of 26 February, the Board unanimously approved the Russell appointment. As a result, Ordway Tead, Chairman of the Board of Higher Education, informed Russell on 29 February:

'It is with a deep sense of privilege that I take this opportunity of notifying you of your appointment as Professor of Philosophy at City College for the period 1 February 1941 to 30 June 1942. . . . I know that your acceptance of this appointment will add luster to the name and achievements of the department and the college, and that it will deepen and extend the interest of the college in the philosophic bases of human living.'

Russell's appointment was to carry a salary of $8,000 per annum and the faculty of the college were delighted that he would soon be joining them. One of the first letters of congratulation was from Philip Wiener on behalf of the college's Philosophy Department,[1] which had originally recommended him for the post:

'As Secretary of the new Philosophy Department, severed from the Psychology Department as of 1 March 1940, may I transmit the felicitations of our department as well as of our colleagues in other departments on your appointment to the head of Professorship of the Department of Philosophy. . . . We look forward toward your coming East with a great deal of pleasure.'

Russell was pleased to be going to City College as it had a liberal reputation, and a record of fostering the education of the lower classes and immigrant groups. However, he was well aware of the problems such institutions faced in maintaining a liberal position. According to Russell:[2]

'The College of the City of New York was an institution run by the City government. Those who attended it were practically all Catholics or Jews; but to the indignation of the former, practically all the scholarships went to the latter. The government of New York City was virtually a satellite of the Vatican, but the professors of City College strove ardently to keep up some semblance of academic freedom. It was no doubt in pursuit of this aim that they had recommended me.'

The Board of Higher Education, too, was considered for the first time in years a liberal body—moreover the mayor of New York, Fiorello La Guardia, had won office on a platform of reform aimed against city corruption. The new Board of Higher Education was seen as one of the challenges to the Tammany Hall politicians whose administrations had preceded La Guardia's.

In spite of Russell's insight into the American educational system, and his concern for academic freedom, he could not have anticipated the stormy events which were to follow. Reaction to the appointment was swift and aggressive; Russell's writings on religion and morality provided the focal point of an attack launched by his old adversary, Bishop Manning,[3] and other opponents of liberalism. It was alleged that Russell was morally unfit for a public teaching position and this created an opportunity for assailing the Board, and questioning its competence and autonomous right to make the appointment. The conservative New York *Sun* carried an editorial denouncing the Board's decision, and on 1 March, the New York press published an open letter from Bishop Manning which was an embittered outburst against Russell and the Board of Higher Education. Basing his harangue on misapplied quotations from Russell's writings, the Bishop depicted Russell as a polluter of public morals, and saw the appointment as a threat to religious life. Manning protested:[4]

'Can any of us wish our young people to accept these teachings as decent, true, or worthy of respect? What is to be said of colleges and universities which hold up before our youth as a responsible teacher of philosophy and as an example of light and leading a man who is a recognised propagandist against both religion and morality, and who specifically defends adultery. . . . Can anyone who cares for the welfare of our country be willing to see such teaching disseminated. . . . How is it that the College of the City of New York makes such an appointment as this?'

Bishop Manning's views received far wider attention and support than had been the case in 1929. This reflected the hardening of reaction, and the political polarisation in America, in the years immediately preceding the war; and it vindicated Russell's belief that a militaristic policy would require an assault on liberalism in America. Bishop Manning's attack has been described by Professor Paul Edwards, in his account of these events, as: 'The signal for a campaign of vilification and intimidation unequaled in American history since the days of Jefferson and Thomas Paine.'[5]

Edwards goes on to demonstrate the extent of bigoted reaction:[6]

'The ecclesiastical journals, the Hearst Press, and just about every Democratic politician joined the chorus of defamation. Russell's appointment, said the *Tablet*, came as a "brutal, insulting shock to old New Yorkers, and all real Americans". Demanding that the appointment be revoked, it editorially described Russell as a "professor of paganism", as "the philosophical anarchist and moral nihilist of Great Britain . . . whose defense of adultery became so obnoxious that one of his 'friends' is reported to have thrashed him." The Jesuit weekly, *America*, referred to Russell as "a desiccated, divorced and decadent advocate of sexual promiscuity . . . who is now indoctrinating the students at the University of California."'

While letters from outraged citizens and priests venting their moral indignation over Russell's appointment filled the press columns, there were other pressures mounting. The clamour was enjoined by ultra right-wing sects, pro-Nazi propagandists, and various Catholic groups sympathetic to fascism. The Knights of Columbus saw the appointment as symbolic of a rising tide of liberalism. The Chairman of the Catholic Affairs Committee of the New York State Council of the organisation described Russell as 'an articulate spearhead of the radical, atheistic and anti-religious elements of our time' and denounced the appointment as 'a disgrace to our city'.[7]

The Board of Education was under great pressure to rescind the appointment. Charles H. Tuttle, one of its members, persuaded the Board to reconsider Russell's appointment, in the light of the public outcry against it. In effect this was a call for Russell's dismissal. Tuttle stated that he was 'unaware of Earl Russell's views on religion and morality at the time the appointment was under consideration.'[8] Tuttle was a leading lay member of Manning's diocese.

The Board announced, on 7 March, a bare week after Manning's onslaught, that the whole question would be reviewed at its next meeting on 18 March. Meanwhile, Russell, the figure at the centre of the storm, was 3,000 miles away, quietly attending to his duties in Los

Angeles. He relied on newspaper reports and occasional communications from City College for information on the controversy. Both the Board and the college were determined to handle the situation with academic restraint, and were concerned not to involve Russell too deeply in the affair.

The first official reaction from the administration of the college was a statement by President Mead that Russell was appointed to teach mathematics and logic and not morals and religion. They apparently hoped to ride out the storm and it appears that the strength of the campaign, and the extent of its co-ordination, was seriously underestimated. On 9 March, Philip Wiener wrote to Russell for brief descriptions of his courses for inclusion in the college catalogue which was soon going to press. The concluding paragraph of this letter gives little idea of the ferocity of the battle raging in New York or of the ruthlessness of the antagonists:

'You may have noticed in the newspapers that your appointment has already begun to have an educational effect. Despite the clamor of certain groups, whose opposition was to be expected, there is clearly no danger of a reversal of the Board's decision.'

However, the City College students, the very people Bishop Manning sought to protect, were fully aware of the dangerous implications caused by the witch-hunt against Russell, and pointed out that in essence the attack was part of a process undermining academic freedom. The student council of the college issued a press statement on 9 March and sent a copy to Russell:

'The appointment of Bertrand Russell to the staff of City College has brought forth much discussion in the press and has evoked statements from various organisations and individuals. We do not wish to enter any controversy on Professor Russell's views on morals and religion; we feel that he is entitled to his own personal views.

'Professor Russell has been appointed to the staff of City College to teach mathematics and logic. With an international reputation, he is eminently qualified to teach these subjects. He has been lecturing at the University of California and has been appointed Visiting Professor at Harvard University before he comes to City College in February 1941. The student body, as well as the faculty, are of the opinion that the addition of Professor Russell to the faculty cannot but help to raise the academic prestige and national standing of our college. . . .

'By refusing to yield to the pressure being brought to bear, and by standing firm on the appointment of Professor Russell, the Board of Higher Education will be saving City College an academic black eye and doing its duty to the community in the highest sense. . . .

'City College has long been subject to attack from various sources seeking to modify or destroy our free higher education; the attack on Bertrand Russell is but another manifestation of this tendency.'

Russell thanked the students for their statement and wrote in reply:[9]

'. . . I am very happy to have the support of the student council in the fight. Old York was the first place where Christianity was the State religion, and it was there that Constantine assumed the purple. Perhaps New York will be the last place to have this honour.'

One of the first major organisations to come to the defence of Russell's appointment was the Committee for Cultural Freedom. On 5 March they confirmed this in a letter to the Board of Higher Education and followed up with a letter published in the New York *Herald Tribune* of 9 March. The letter was signed by Sidney Hook, Chairman of their executive committee:

'The hue and cry which has recently been raised in some quarters over the appointment of Bertrand Russell . . . carries with it a serious attack on hard-won principles of academic and cultural freedom. The ultimate implications of the organised campaign against Mr Russell's appointment menace the integrity of our intellectual life, which consists in the free and open consideration of alternatives honestly held and scientifically reasoned. . . .

'To censor Mr Russell's intellectual activity, because some of his views on matters not germane to his chief theoretical interest are objectionable to some members of the community, clearly contravenes the Statement on Academic Freedom and Tenure adopted both by the American Association of University Professors and the Association of American Colleges. . . .'

Following the Board of Higher Education's announcement that it would rediscuss Russell's appointment, the campaign to intimidate the Board was stepped up. Inevitably, the 'communist' smear was applied by the Hearst Press. By lifting convenient quotes from *Practice and Theory of Bolshevism*, Hearst's *Journal-American* referred to Russell as a spokesman for communism and demanded an investigation of the Board of Higher Education. Appeals by obscure religious sects and defenders of public virtue, such as the Sons of Xavier, the St Joan of Arc Holy Name Society, and the Empire State Sons of the American Revolution appeared regularly in the press. These called for the dismissal of Russell and those members of the Board who stood firm on the appointment.

According to Russell, 'priests lectured the police, who were practically all Irish Catholics, on my responsibility for the local criminals.'[10] Paul Edwards elaborates on this in his account of the controversy:[11]

'Speaking at the annual communion breakfast of the Holy Name Society of the New York Police Department, Monsignor Francis W. Walsh recalled to the assembled policemen that they had, on occasion, learnt the full meaning of the so-called "matrimonial triangle" by finding one corner of the triangle in a pool of blood, "I dare say, therefore," he continued, "that you will join me in demanding that any professor guilty of teaching or writing ideas which will multiply the stages upon which these tragedies are set shall not be countenanced in this city and shall receive no support from its taxpayers. . . ."'

The appeal to protect the taxpayers' money was a recurrent theme in the attacks on the Board, and was volubly taken up as the key issue by the Tammany office-holders who were constantly harassing the La Guardia administration. Most of these Democratic officials had connections with the groups calling for Russell's blood, and on 15 March, the City Council passed a resolution by sixteen votes to five calling upon the Board of Higher Education to revoke the Russell appointment. The warning was strategically timed three days before the Board was due to re-convene.

During this period, Russell's supporters were by no means inactive, even though they could not hope to match the powerful resources of their opponents. Not surprisingly, the universities and learned associations were the first to raise their voices in defence of the City College appointment. The Committee for Cultural Freedom and the American Civil Liberties Union, together with the City College Philosophy Department, were instrumental in organising support from the country's leading scholars and academics. It was clear that a determined struggle had to be waged to encourage the Board to stand by its original decision. City College was by no means immune to the tremendous pressure generated by Bishop Manning's attack, and it is to the credit of the Philosophy Department that they remained unanimous in their will to continue the fight. Dr Y. H. Krikorian, Chairman of the Philosophy Department, gave some idea of the spirit prevailing in his department, when he wrote to Russell on 13 March:

'The members of the Department of Philosophy are very glad that you have accepted their invitation. We are all looking forth for your coming. We are quite sure that the attempt to obstruct your coming will fail. President Mead has received hundreds of letters from distinguished philosophers and scholars protesting the possible revocation of your appointment. . . . We enjoy the fight, for it is for a philosopher we all admire, and for a cause we all like.'

One aspect of the agitation against Russell was the fact that he was not an American national. His detractors seized on this point to claim

A NEW YORK APPOINTMENT

that as an alien he was legally barred from teaching at a New York State college. In order to counter this technical objection, Russell was advised by City College to indicate his intention to apply for citizenship. Russell was not in favour of the suggestion and wired Acting President Mead on 12 March:

'In other circumstances I might have applied for American citizenship but cannot contemplate doing so in deference to an illiberal and nationalistic law unworthy of a great democracy. Sure you will agree that such laws hamper intellectual intercourse and co-operation between nations and should not be deferred to.'

However, after consulting its lawyers, City College was confident that the objection to Russell on grounds of citizenship was without merit, 'since there is a law adopted in 1938 which permits the Board of Higher Education to waive the requirement'. This information was conveyed to Russell by Professor Daniel Bronstein of the Philosophy Department on 15 March. Bronstein also indicated that the controversy was causing a certain amount of embarrassment at the college; not the least of which arose out of Russell's objection to applying for American citizenship:

'The annoyance your case is now causing some people at City College is of no moment. I think you are aware of the fact that the idea of your appointment originated in the Philosophy Department and that you have our unanimous support. Nor do we agree with Acting President Mead's statement to the press that "you were invited to teach courses in logic and mathematics, and not to express your personal views on other questions. . . ." I have heard that you sent a telegram to Acting President Mead in which you say that you will not become an American citizen and in which you make not altogether complimentary remarks about the United States. I hope my information is not accurate since such statements are, of course, not calculated to help our case, and may alienate members of the Board who otherwise would support you. If you can find it consistent with the canons of scientific method to refrain at this time from making predictions about your own future intentions with regard to citizenship . . . it would greatly strengthen our case.'

As a consequence of Bronstein's letter, Russell wrote to Mead explaining in more detail his attitude to the citizenship issue:[12]

'I understand with regret that my telegram to you about question of citizenship gave unintended impression of criticism of United States. I am living here and seeking employment because I wished my children to grow up in a country which appeared to me to be the hope of the world. But on hearing that my appointment might possibly be rescinded technically on grounds of nationality I thought, and still think, that this issue is even more important than that of religious opinions. The growth of national barriers is the greatest source of evil in the modern world. My objection to applying now for American citizenship is not an objection to American citizenship but an inability to concede that the race or nationality to which a human being happens to belong is of any importance. If I were in England I should oppose with all my energy any proposal that professors from America or any other country should be asked to become British subjects.'

Meanwhile, the Philosophy Department had issued a press statement on 13 March, in which it declared that its recommendation of Russell to the City College post was 'a judgment which has the endorsement of hundreds of philosophers including heads of philosophy departments throughout the country'. The statement continued:

'Professor Russell's work in logic has not merely become a classic, but has actually initiated a new era in the development of that science. His writings on the philosophy of the sciences are of major importance. His ethical writings, which have been so violently attacked in the last fortnight, are the fearless attempts of a critically minded philosopher to formulate principles of conduct conducive to human welfare. Disagreement with his specific suggestions for the reconstruction of institutions or personal morals should not lead one to belittle the morally constructive character of his ideas.

'Any revocation of Professor Russell's appointment would lead to the inquisition by laymen into all sorts of personal views held by a prospective teacher instead of the considered judgment of his professional colleagues who are better qualified to know his competence. A college should encourage open consideration of alternatives, honestly held and scientifically reasoned. In the interplay of reasoned opinions, not in the imposition of the dogmas of any specific group, lies the promise of higher education.

'The attack on Professor Russell's appointment is fundamentally an attack upon the liberal democratic tradition, upon which the institutions of our country are founded. On this issue there can be no retreat.'

The department took the initiative in requisitioning signatures from their colleagues throughout the country to attach to a statement addressed to the Board of Higher Education:

'We, members of the American Philosophical Association and teachers of Philosophy in American educational institutions, regard Professor Bertrand Russell as one of the outstanding philosophers of our time, and while not all of us share his personal views on theism and marriage, we consider that these views in no way disqualify him from teaching college students. Indeed, any revocation of his appointment because of his personal opinions would be a calamitous setback to that freedom of thought and discussion which has been the basis of democratic education. . . .'

The Committee for Cultural Freedom contacted Presidents Hutchins and Sproul of Chicago and California, asking them for statements on Russell's record at their universities. Both could confirm that Russell had not spent his time corrupting the young and gave favourable reports which the committee released to the press on 14 March. The committee next drew up a letter which was signed by seventeen prominent professors at Columbia, Harvard, Johns Hopkins, Cornell and New York University, and the president of Brooklyn College. On 16 March, the letter was sent to *The New York Times*, the *Herald Tribune* and to Mayor La Guardia, who was contriving to remain silent on the issue. The letter warned that as a consequence of the campaign against Russell, 'no American college or university is safe from inquisitional control by the enemies of free inquiry.' The seventeen signatories defended Russell's appointment and declared:

'To receive instruction from a man of Bertrand Russell's intellectual caliber is a rare privilege for students anywhere. . . . His critics should meet him in the open and fair field of intellectual discussion and scientific analysis. They have no right to silence him by preventing him from teaching. . . . This issue is so fundamental that it cannot be compromised without imperiling the whole structure of intellectual freedom upon which American university life rests.'

The Russell affair had become a *cause célèbre* amongst the most distinguished intellects of the day, including Albert Einstein, Alfred North Whitehead, Oswald Veblen, Harlow Shapley, Edward Kasner and John Dewey, who played an important part in the campaign. In a communication to Morris Raphael Cohen, Professor Emeritus of Philosophy at City College, whose retirement had occasioned the invitation to Russell, Einstein stated:[13]

'Great spirits have always found violent opposition from mediocrities. The latter cannot understand it when a man does not thoughtlessly submit to hereditary prejudices but honestly and courageously uses his intelligence.'

Einstein was so moved by the persecution of Russell that he penned the following poem:[14]

It keeps repeating itself
In this world, so fine and honest;
The Parson alarms the populace,
The genius is executed.

Fellow English expatriates, Charles Chaplin, Aldous Huxley, G. E. Moore and Alfred North Whitehead, informed Russell of their sympathy and support. Not all religious spokesmen agreed with Bishop Manning's denunciation of Russell. The more enlightened religious leaders supported the Board's appointment of Russell, and among them were Rabbi Jonah B. Wise, Professor J. S. Bixler of Harvard Divinity School, Professor E. S. Brightman, the Director of the National Council on Religion and Education, the Reverend Robert G. Andrus, Counsellor to Protestant students at Columbia University, and the Reverend John Haynes Holmes. Bishop Manning's right to speak for the Episcopal Church was challenged by a fellow clergyman, the Reverend Guy Emery Shipler, who pointed out in the *New Republic*:[15]

'Bishop Manning has been given no authority to represent the Protestant Episcopal Church in such controversies. . . . He has every right to speak for himself; he has no right to speak either for his own diocese or for the national Church. . . . It is unfortunate that the public is under the illusion that every time a bishop . . . bursts into print with a point of view stemming from the Dark Ages he represents the Protestant Episcopal Church.'

Explaining Manning's alignment with the Catholic agitation against Russell, Shipler stated: 'It is not so well known, outside the Episcopal Church, that Bishop Manning is an Anglo-Catholic, that is, one of the comparatively small group in the Episcopal Church whose theological concepts and whose concepts in the field of "morals"—speaking technically—are essentially identical with the official standards of the Roman Catholic Church.'[16]

Warder Norton, of W. W. Norton, the man who had published most of Russell's books in America since 1927, including many of the texts under attack, organised a group of nine major publishers to issue a press statement characterising Russell's appointment as reflecting the greatest credit on the Board of Higher Education. The statement, by way of a publisher's manifesto, appeared on the front page of *The New York Times* on 18 March 1940, and averred:

'We do not necessarily subscribe personally to all the views expressed by those whose books we publish, but we welcome great minds to our lists, particularly now at a time when brute force and ignorance have gained such ascendancy over reason and intellect in many parts of the world.

We think it more important than ever to honor intellectual superiority whenever the opportunity presents itself.'

The New York *Post* was one of the city newspapers most favourably disposed to the Russell cause, and, as the date for the Board's next meeting drew near, requested a statement from Russell on his 'position in the matter'. Russell wired the New York *Post*:[17]

'My position is quite simple. I have been offered and have accepted an appointment as Professor of Philosophy. Neither my views on religion and morality nor those of Bishop Manning are relevant. To prohibit any man from teaching a subject which he is competent to teach because of his religion, race or nationality is of course a familiar proceeding in despotic countries, but the attempt to do so here seems inconsistent with American traditions and professions of free speech and civil liberties.

'I realise that this illiberal action comes from a small but powerful minority and I am glad to find it so widely and emphatically resisted.'

The *Nation* of 16 March carried an editorial which succinctly recounted the unfolding of the controversy and the reason for the attack on the Board:

'Tennessee is far from being the only place in the country where ignorance makes a monkey of education. Hillbillies from Morningside Heights, led by His Most Worshipful Eminence Bishop Manning, and bigots from the backwoods of Brooklyn, mobilised by the Hearst Press, have raised a hue and cry against Bertrand Russell. In the world of education and enlightenment, Mr Russell is a distinguished philosopher, mathematician, and logician, but there must be several hundred thousand New Yorkers who now believe that he is a confirmed lecher, an advocate of adultery, and a believer in the nationalisation of women. . . . The Hearst Press, scenting its favorite journalistic combination, sex and subversion, leaped to the fray. The Knights of Columbus girded on their armor. Behind the uproar is the fact that for the first time in years New York City has a liberal Board of Higher Education. We hope it will repudiate in no uncertain terms an attack which, if successful, would be a serious blow to academic freedom, not only in New York City but throughout the country.'

In the few days prior to the Board of Higher Education's meeting, the campaign for and against Russell intensified. On 14 March, over 2,000 students and faculty members filled the Great Hall at City College to attend a rally called by the Student Union protesting at the attempts to rescind Russell's appointment. From California, Russell wired a message to the meeting: 'Most grateful for your support against clerical interference with academic freedom.'

145

Addressing the rally, Morris Raphael Cohen, declared that if the campaign to debar Russell succeeded, 'the fair name of our city will suffer as did Athens for condemning Socrates as a corrupter of its youth or Tennessee for finding Scopes guilty of teaching evolution.'[18]

The strong sentiment for Russell amongst the students was indicated by the numerous letters they sent to him. William Swirsky, who worked on the College's undergraduate newspaper, the *Campus*, wrote:[19]

'The exaltation I enjoyed upon learning you were coming to teach at my college was as boundless as my sorrow intense when I read and heard the scurrilous attacks on your character . . . of the 6,000 students at the branch [of the college] with which you will be connected, not more than twenty-five have evinced any dissatisfaction whatever with your appointment. . . . As Professor Krikorian said: "his presence within the very walls of our college would be electrifying." If there is anything my paper, the students or the faculty (100 per cent behind your appointment) can do to help you, please let me know.'

Swirsky closed his letter:

'. . . with deep envy of the students who have enjoyed your classes in California and terror that the Board of Higher Education may kowtow to the reactionary but bombastic elements of our city.'

From Bernard Goltz, a member of the Student Council, Russell received the following expression of hope:[20]

'I write this letter on the eve of the meeting of the Board of Higher Education called to reconsider your appointment to the Philosophy Department of C.C.N.Y. If the question of your appointment had been left to the student body, I am positive that there would be no question as to the outcome. The student body is almost unanimously united in supporting the appointment. It is unfortunate that the politicians on the B.H.E. could not resist the pressure placed on them by the bigots and Grundies of our city. . . .

'I do not know what the decision of the Board will be. But it is my sincere hope that they will not deprive the students at the college of the benefit of your great learning. . . .'

In sharp contrast to the dignified campaign waged on behalf of Russell, those who opposed his appointment became even more frenzied in their efforts to intimidate the Board. They, too, held a mass rally at which leading city politicians whipped the audience into a state of near-hysteria. Councilman Charles E. Keegan described Russell as a 'dog' and declaimed: 'If we had an adequate system of immigration, that bum could not land within a thousand miles.'[21] The Registrar of New York

County, Miss Martha Byrnes, recommended that Russell be 'tarred and feathered and driven out of the country'.[22] George V. Harvey, President of the Borough of Queens, threatened the closure of the municipal college by depriving them of their 1941 budget allocation of $7,500,000 if the Board persisted with Russell's appointment. Reminding the Board of its obligations, he said: 'The colleges would either be godly colleges, American colleges, or they would be closed.'[23]

The Board of Higher Education met on 18 March and continued its deliberations well into the night. After intensive debate in which every factor involved was thoroughly considered, the motion brought by Charles Tuttle to rescind the appointment of Russell was defeated by eleven votes to seven. So crucial had the issues become that several Board members made statements defending their voting position. They requested that these be recorded in the minutes of the meeting.[24] Of those who changed their minds, William P. Larkin, the seconder of Tuttle's motion, echoed the objections that had been hurled at the Board from press and pulpit:[25]

'I am opposed to him [Russell] because he is a recognised propagandist against both religion and morality who not only condones, but puts a halo around violation of one of God's fundamental commandments, and advocates a code of morals which self-respecting pagans would repudiate. If appointed, under the shibboleth of "freedom of speech" and "academic freedom" atheism and the ethics of the barnyard would inevitably be preached to the children and youth of New York. I am opposed to an alien propagandist being given the right to use public classrooms to destroy time-honored beliefs of this country and its citizens.'

Larkin concluded:

'It is absolutely unthinkable that the Board of Higher Education would turn over the Chair of Philosophy with all its potentialities for good or evil to the most outspoken foe of religion in the world today.'

Among others casting their votes against Russell were Albert Weiss and Ernest Seelman. Weiss explained:[26]

'I voted in the Administrative Committee as well as on the Board for Mr Russell. I have come to the conclusion I cannot subject the children of our great city to the teaching of the sex philosophy of Mr Russell. I have therefore changed the vote.'

Ernest Seelman voted for reconsideration:[27] 'because I do not believe it is necessary to appoint a man of such questionable views, which have so offended the religious and moral beliefs of a great portion of our community.'

147

It is clear that the campaign to intimidate members of the Board had been partially successful. Speaking as one of those who had not been swayed, Dr Joseph J. Klein declared:[28]

'Aside from every other consideration urged on us so eloquently tonight, I wish to say that I resent the effort of rabbi, priest, or minister, through organised pressure and otherwise, to attempt to influence my official conduct as a member of this public Board . . . organised religion should be told, in unmistakable terms, that it must not attempt to intrude in matters of public education.'

The campaign on Russell's behalf had undoubtedly impressed some of the Board members. Lauson H. Stone, who voted with the majority, drew attention to:[29]

'the numerous communications received from individuals of note and from organisations in academic fields [which] make it perfectly clear that to rescind the appointment of Mr Russell because of his personal views would create an issue involving fundamental educational principles of far greater importance than Mr Russell himself.'

Another Board member who voted for Russell was Joseph Schlossberg, the General-Secretary of the Amalgamated Clothing Workers of America, who wrote to Russell:[30]

'It does not happen often that one is both right and in the majority. My voting for you as Professor in City College has placed me in this privileged position. I am looking forward to the pleasure of meeting you here.'

After the meeting, Ordway Tead, the chairman, made the following statement on behalf of the Board:[31]

'The appointment of Professor Bertrand Russell as Professor of Philosophy was made by unanimous vote of the City College Administrative Committee and the Board of Higher Education. At the time of his appointment, the majority of the Board were fully acquainted with the eminent scholastic position of Professor Russell as embodied in his philosophical and mathematical writings. Professor Russell is one of the two or three most outstanding living mathematical philosophers, with over thirty books to his credit, of which only three or four have been popular treatments of current problems.

'Since coming to this country, he has been for nearly a year at Chicago University, and President Hutchins assures us that Professor Russell made an important contribution there. From there he went to the University of California, and President Sproul writes that he has been "a most valuable colleague". At the College of the City of New York,

Professor Russell will teach logic, the philosophy of mathematics, and the philosophy of science. He brings to this position the reputation of a world-renowned scholar now rounding out a distinguished career.'

The battle, however, was not over. Charles Tuttle sounded an ominous note when, as spokesman for the anti-Russell faction, he said:[32] 'The issue now passes from the Board of Higher Education to the public. Particularly in view of the close vote, public opinion will control in the end.'

Immediately after the decision became known, leading faculty members of the Philosophy Department at City College telegraphed Russell the news. Russell wired back:[33]

'Many thanks for telegram. I am delighted both on public and personal grounds and very grateful for your splendid support. Samson Agonistes 1268–76[34] for deliverer read deliverers.'

With the *sang-froid* he had displayed throughout this period, Russell commented to the Los Angeles *Daily News* of 19 March: 'I would like to lecture in New York, but it is for them to decide. I can't imagine why there should be such a fuss. I believe I was hired to teach philosophy and logic, not morality.'

For the first time since the onset of the controversy, he issued a statement, reported in *The New York Times* of 21 March, and given wide coverage in the national press, defending his views:

'I am, of course, delighted by this victory both on public and private grounds. I came to live in this country because I believed America to be the hope of the world and because I wished my three children to grow up in a land of liberal thought and hope for the future and not in Europe, where all that I care for most seems likely to perish.

'It was distressing to meet in the metropolis of the world's greatest democracy an attempt to establish an inquisition over teachers and a rigorous censorship over students.

'As to "free love", I am far from advocating promiscuity either among students or elsewhere, but I do think that young people should be allowed, if they wish, to live together in unions which may or may not develop into permanent marriage. This would, in fact, diminish promiscuity.

'It is ridiculous to say that I advocate infidelity in marriage, on the contrary, I think that fidelity in marriage is highly desirable.'

Grateful to the City College students for their support, Russell wrote to William Swirsky of the *Campus*:[35]

'I am very glad indeed that the students do not share Bishop Manning's views about me; if they did it would be necessary to despair of the young. It is comforting that the Board of Higher Education decided in my favour, but I doubt whether the fight is at an end. I am afraid that if and when I take up my duties at City College you will all be disappointed to find me a very mild and inoffensive person, totally destitute of horns and hoofs.'

Russell also wrote to Warder Norton,[36] thanking him for the publishers' statement which he had contributed to the controversy. Russell added:

'I am very much impressed by the courage of the Board of Higher Education in upholding my appointment. I did not think they would do so. It still seems to me probable that my enemies will find some way of ousting me; if necessary, by some change in the law. But it is a grand fight and I seem to have recovered with radicals the ground that I had lost by disliking Stalin.'

Norton queried whether Russell had not felt inclined to dismiss the affair with 'one of your good cracks' which elicited the following comment:

'I have not felt tempted to indulge in quips, as the matter was obviously too serious. I should have liked to suggest that no one should be allowed to be a bishop until a Board of Logicians had passed upon his logic, but I am afraid the popular appeal of logic is insufficient.'

Complimenting the Philosophy Department, Russell in a letter to Dr Krikorian stated:[37]

'I am very much impressed by the campaign that my partisans conducted. Obscurantists are always organised, but the friends of freedom, by their very nature, tend not to be. It is obvious that but for a great deal of hard work by the members of the Department of Philosophy, the issue would not have been what it was. I find it hard to believe that the other side will accept defeat, and I am waiting to see what their next move will be.'

NOTES

[1] 27 February 1940.

[2] B. Russell, *Autobiography* (London, 1968), Vol. II, p. 219 (Boston, 1968), p. 334.

[3] See above, p. 113.

[4] Quoted by the American Civil Liberties Union in their pamphlet *The Story of the Bertrand Russell Case* (January 1941), p. 4; and by Paul Edwards in 'The Bertrand Russell Case' which appears as an appendix to Russell's *Why I Am Not a Christian, and Other Essays* (London and Simon & Schuster, New York, 1957), p. 182.

[5] Edwards, loc. cit.

[6] Ibid., p. 183.

[7] American Civil Liberties Union, op. cit., pp. 4–5.

[8] Ibid., p. 5.

[9] To Bernard Goltz, Secretary to the Student Council at C.C.N.Y., on 22 March 1940; B. Russell, *Autobiography*, Vol. II, p. 227; p. 347.

[10] Ibid., p. 219; p. 334.

[11] Edwards, op. cit., p. 185.

[12] Taken from an undated holograph copy. This communication possibly took the form of an overnight cable.

[13] Otto Nathan and Heinz Norden (eds), *Einstein on Peace* (Simon & Schuster, New York, 1960), p. 310; originally published in *The New York Times* (19 March 1940).

[14] B. Russell, *Autobiography* (London, 1969), Vol. III, p. 60 (Boston, 1969), pp. 69–70.

[15] The *New Republic* (8 April 1940); quoted in John Dewey and Horace M. Kallen (eds), *The Bertrand Russell Case* (Viking Press, New York, 1941), p. 152.

[16] Dewey and Kallen, op. cit., p. 153.

[17] Taken from an undated holograph copy; the New York *Post*'s cable was dated 13 March 1940.

[18] Edwards, op. cit., p. 188.

[19] 15 March 1940.

[20] 18 March 1940.

[21] Edwards, op. cit., p. 186.

[22] Ibid.

[23] Ibid.

[24] 'Minutes of the Meeting of the Board of Higher Education of the City of New York' (18 March 1940), see Supreme Court, New York County, Appellate Division, *Papers on Appeal from Order* in the matter of the application of Jean Kay against the Board of Higher Education of the City of New York.

[25] Ibid., pp. 94–6.

[26] Ibid., p. 99.

[27] Ibid., p. 97.

[28] Ibid., p. 93.

[29] Ibid., p. 98.

[30] 29 March 1940.

[31] American Civil Liberties Union, op. cit., p. 5.

[32] Ibid.

[33] 19 March 1940.

[34] 'O, how comely it is, and how reviving/To the spirits of just men long oppressed,/When God into the hands of their deliverer/Puts invincible might,/To quell the mighty of the earth, the oppressor,/The brute and boisterous force of violent men,/Hardy and industrious to support/Tyrannic power, but raging to pursue/The righteous, and all such as honour truth!' (Milton).

[35] 22 March 1940; B. Russell, *Autobiography*, Vol. II, p. 228; p. 348.

[36] Ibid.

[37] Ibid.

CHAPTER 12

THE CHAIR OF INDECENCY

At the very moment when Board Member C. Tuttle was blandly declaring that the Russell controversy would be settled by the public, manoeuvres were being completed to challenge the Board's decision in the courts. On the day after the Board meeting, an order was sought in the State Supreme Court directing the Board of Higher Education as respondent, 'to rescind and revoke the said appointment of the said Dr Bertrand Russell'.[1] The suit was brought, not against Russell, but against the Municipality of New York as the governing authority of the Board of Higher Education. This was presumably the way 'public opinion' was to be consulted.

The papers of the petitioner, Mrs Jean Kay, a taxpayer, living in Brooklyn, and of her attorney, Joseph Goldstein, had already been drawn up on 18 March, in anticipation of the boardroom defeat. Mrs Kay was in no way connected with City College. Her children did not attend the college and when approached by the press neither she nor her legal representative would reveal the source of their funds. Her petition initially alleged that Russell's appointment was illegal and improper on two grounds: that as an alien he could not be legally employed under the State Education Law; and that his teachings were sexually immoral and 'constitute a danger and a menace to the health, morals and welfare of the students who attend the College of the City of New York.' She feared the students 'may follow and make practical application and carry out the teachings of the said Dr Bertrand Russell on sex relationship.' According to Mrs Kay, the practical application of Russell's philosophy would 'result in violations of laws and statutes of the State of New York'.[2]

The supporting affidavit of Joseph Goldstein,[3] an ex-magistrate under the previous Tammany administration, was a masterpiece of character assassination. Goldstein asserted that Russell 'has exhibited practically all his life marked eccentricities and mental quirks, and his conduct throughout his life has been queer and unusual.' The fact that Russell had been married three times was used to illustrate this claim. Goldstein went on to allege that Russell had:

'. . . conducted a school in England, where he taught that children need not respect their parents. He also conducted a nudist school for both sexes of all ages, children, adolescents and adults. He participated in this nudist colony and went about naked in the company of persons of both sexes who were exhibiting themselves naked in public.'

Among Russell's many eccentricities, Goldstein explained, was his 'malicious libel' against the United States expeditionary forces in England, for which offence he served a six-month prison term in 1918. Russell's 'peculiar tactics, mannerisms, eccentricities and queer conduct', Goldstein pleaded, 'are sufficient grounds for an examination by a competent alienist as to his mental condition.' Reviewing Russell's 'philosophy', Goldstein quoted from *Marriage and Morals, Education and the Good Life, Education and the Modern World*, and *What I Believe*, and submitted the four volumes to the court as exhibits. Goldstein claimed that Russell's moral depravity had been sufficiently demonstrated and that his writings exposed him before the entire world 'as a person entirely bereft of moral fiber'. The conclusion was inevitable. Goldstein maintained that:[4]

'. . . he is lecherous, salacious, libidinous, lustful, venerous, erotomaniac, aphrodisiac, atheistic, irreverent, narrow-minded, bigoted, and untruthful; that he is not a Philosopher in the accepted meaning of the word; that he is not a lover of wisdom; that he is not a searcher after wisdom; that he is not an explorer of that universal science which aims at an explanation of all the phenomena of the universe by ultimate causes; that in the opinion of your deponent and multitudes of other persons he is a sophist; that he practices sophism; that by cunning contrivances, tricks and devices and by mere quibbling, he puts forth fallacious arguments and arguments that are not supported by sound reasoning; and he draws inferences which are not justly deduced from a sound premise; that all his alleged doctrines which he calls philosophy are just cheap, tawdry, worn-out, patched up fetishes and propositions, devised for the purpose of misleading the people.'

Goldstein closed his brief with the contention that it was not academic freedom Russell sought 'but license to teach and be the purveyor of filth, obscenity, salaciousness and blasphemy'.

The press reported these dramatic developments with alacrity, quoting extensively from Goldstein's affidavit. Defence of the action was undertaken by the City Corporation, acting on behalf of the Board of Higher Education. Russell was kept in touch with the proceedings by the City College Philosophy Department, but only saw copies of the relevant documents after the court hearing.

Argument on Mrs Kay's petition was heard before Justice John E.

McGeehan of the Supreme Court on 27 March. McGeehan was an Irish Catholic sponsored by Tammany Hall and had 'distinguished himself by trying to have a portrait of Martin Luther removed from a court-house mural illustrating legal history.'[5]

The Board's case was greatly weakened by its legal adviser's decision not to contest the attacks on Russell's character and writings. Their defence was limited to the technical point concerning Russell's citizenship. The assistant corporation counsel, Nicholas Bucci, merely argued that the requirements of the education law as to the employment of American citizens were limited to pre-university teaching and was therefore not binding on the Board of Higher Education. Neither did the defence deal with a third ground of complaint instituted into the proceedings, which charged that the Board had not subjected Russell to a legally required civil service examination to determine 'merit and fitness'.

Throughout the proceedings, Justice McGeehan showed the keenest interest in the evidence on Russell's 'moral fitness', and it was on Russell's character and writings that Attorney Goldstein and the counsel he briefed, William S. Bennet, concentrated their main line of fire. As counsel Bennet prepared to address the court on Russell's writings, he first of all found it necessary to apologise: 'I am confident that your Honor wishes me to omit the salacious portions of his teachings, as far as possible.' To which McGeehan replied: 'Not that it would offend me because I have heard nearly everything that the human ear could have heard in my short and checkered career [sic].'[6] McGeehan clearly expected the worst.

Bennet summarised for the court the immoral nature of Russell's writings and personal life. He then turned to Russell's imprisonment during the First World War for stating that the American army was accustomed to the role of strike-breaking, and, in an angry denunciation declared of Russell:[7]

'It is a lie, a vicious, nasty lie that Russell knew was a lie when he said it, an insult to every American soldier and to every American citizen, and it is against the public policy of the State . . . to employ in its schools or in civil office or any other place a man who in a time when we were fighting for a principle vilified the army of the United States and lied about it. It is the most disgraceful, shocking attempt to appoint a person to the public schools which has ever taken place in the State of New York.'

Supplementing his affidavit, Goldstein elaborated for the court his evidence on Russell's 'nudist colony' in England, again alleging that Russell 'paraded himself nude, together with his wife, in public'. Goldstein concluded:[8]

'The spectacle, your Honor, of our citizens contributing to pay him $8,000 a year to bring his filthy ideas into our colleges is repugnant, and I don't believe it requires too much argument that such a man should not be permitted to be a teacher in school. . . . Furthermore, this old man who is about 70 years of age has gone in for salacious poetry, and we fear he might teach that to the children . . . in his philosophy he quotes, for instance, with approval, such poetry as this:

> Do not mock me in thy bed
> While these cold nights freeze me dead.[9]

'Have we got to pay him $8,000 a year to have such philosophy taught in our schools? I have also adverted in my affidavit and I believe it is borne out by proof that he winks at homo-sexualism; I say, I will go further, that he approves of it.'

Reserving his decision, Judge McGeehan adjourned the court so he could read the books presented in evidence, and remarked: 'If I find that these books sustain the allegations of the petition I will give the Appellate Division and the Court of Appeals something to think about.'[10]

Three organisations were represented at the hearing and were permitted to file briefs as friends of the court—the American Civil Liberties Union, the National Lawyers Guild, and the New York College Teachers' Union. These parties all supported the Board. They contended that the appointment was lawful, that citizenship was not an issue, and that the appointment should not be disturbed because it would be an interference with academic freedom. The brief submitted by the National Lawyers Guild pointed out:

'Dr Russell is said to hold certain views on religion, morality and sex. None of these views is either revolutionary or new. Some of them were advocated by Judge Lindsey twenty years ago. The college libraries are well stocked with Dr Russell's books, and no epidemic of immorality has resulted, as far as the public is aware.'

The attorney representing the American Civil Liberties Union was Osmond K. Fraenkel. He attended the argument before Justice McGeehan and reported to the Civil Liberties Union on 27 March:

'In my opinion the case was very badly handled by the corporation counsel's office. For this I do not blame Mr Bucci, the assistant in charge, who is a very able lawyer. I can only suppose that he acted under instruction. The reason for my criticism is this: The Board put in no answer but made a motion to dismiss, thus giving the judge an opportunity to write an opinion denouncing Bertrand Russell for the charges as made in the petition. Moreover, the Board argued only the technical question concerning the application of the citizenship requirement. No attempt was made to show the extent to which the Board of Higher Education, in its recent session, took into consideration the various criticisms which had been made of Mr Russell or to argue the legal point that its decision on that subject was not subject to review in the courts. . . . It seems to me that it might be desirable to have Mr Russell represented by counsel of his own choosing so that some control over the outcome of the case could be exercised independent of the Corporation Counsel's office. If that is to be done at all, it has to be done very promptly.'

The Director of the American Civil Liberties Union, Roger N. Baldwin, wrote to Russell on 29 March, enclosing a copy of Fraenkel's letter, and stated:

'Because we consider the action against the Board of Higher Education a direct threat to academic freedom, we are vitally interested in the successful defense of the case. If you contemplate having a New York attorney appear in this case for you, we shall be glad to co-operate in every way.'

Justice McGeehan announced his verdict on 30 March. In a lengthy judgement[11] he revoked the Board's appointment of Russell, on all three grounds contested by the petitioner. He agreed that the citizenship requirement was a valid complaint; he upheld the contention that the Board's failure to test Russell's 'merit and fitness' was a sufficient cause to sustain the petition; he found, as the 'most compelling' ground of all, that Russell was morally unfit for the position. In assessing Russell's moral character, McGeehan sustained the view that 'Mr Russell has taught in his books immoral and salacious doctrines.' He proceeded to describe the appointment as 'an insult to the people of the City of New York', and accused the Board of Higher Education of 'establishing a chair of indecency' at City College. By their selection of Russell, the judge declared, the Board had 'acted arbitrarily, capriciously and in direct violation of the public health, safety and morals of the people'.

To those who claimed that academic freedom was under attack, the judge pontificated: 'While this court would not interfere with any action of the Board so far as a pure question of "valid" academic freedom is concerned, it will not tolerate academic freedom being used as a cloak to promote the popularisation in the minds of adolescents of acts forbidden by the penal law.' So enraged was the judge by Russell's 'moral character' that he passed the opinion that Russell would be denied American citizenship if he ever applied for it. McGeehan later remarked that he 'had to take a bath' after reading one of Russell's books, and was of the view that Russell wanted 'to make strumpets out of all our girls'.[12] John Dewey expressed the doubt that the judge had ever read the books at all, and the *New Republic* stated that the judgement must have been 'produced at superhuman speed if the Justice actually wrote it after all the evidence was in'.[13]

There was jubilation among those who had crusaded for Russell's removal. The New York *Sun* proclaimed:[14]

'Mrs Kay carried the day!
'After millions of bitter words had been exchanged between those who assailed the appointment of Bertrand Russell as Professor of Philosophy at City College because of the "advocacy of immorality" contained in his writings, and those who insisted that barring him from the post would be "a blow to academic freedom", Supreme Court Justice John E. McGeehan yesterday granted the Brooklyn housewife's petition for an order revoking Russell's appointment and discharging him from the position.
'Unless the ruling is upset by a higher court—and a number of legal observers insist that it is not likely to be—Professor Russell will be among those absent from the faculty of City College for all time. . . .'

Judge McGeehan received lavish praise from the Jesuit weekly, *America*, which described him as 'a virile and staunch American' who was 'a pure and honorable jurist and . . . rates among the best as an authority on law.'[15] The *Tablet* declared that the decision 'carries a note of simplicity and sincerity that immediately wins acclaim.'[16]

Upon hearing of the decision, Russell described McGeehan as 'a very ignorant fellow'. He added: 'As an Irish Catholic, his views were perhaps prejudiced, but he had no right to make such a statement from the Bench.'[17]

Speaking to newsmen who had descended on his doorstep, Russell remarked: 'I am not as interested in sex as is Bishop Manning, who is greatly concerned with it. Sex is only a small part of what I have written. Bishop Manning and his supporters have noticed only this part. They don't notice that almost all of my writing has been on other subjects.'[18] Of the charges that were brought against him, Russell said: 'Precisely the same accusations were brought against Socrates—atheism and corrupting the young.' Russell added: 'Any person who expresses an opinion without regard to its popularity expects to get in trouble—and I don't like to hold my tongue about important affairs.'[19] However, he sounded a warning: 'All this fuss frightens me. It makes me fear that within a few years, all the intellect of America will be in concentration camps.'[20] In an interview given to a Los Angeles newspaper on his attitude to Christianity, Russell stated.[21]

'The Bible provides texts for many different moods. The good Christians who are attacking me so savagely in New York seem to prefer: "Thou shalt not commit adultery", "There shall be weeping and gnashing of teeth", "Let Him be crucified", and so on.

'My grandmother gave me, when I was a child, a Bible in which she had written her favorite texts, and to these I have added some of my own. I suggest them as required reading for Episcopal Bishop William T. Manning who stands in the front rank of my accusers. They are:

'"Thou shalt not follow a multitude into evil.

'"Thou shalt love they neighbour as thyself. . . .

'"Blessed are ye when men shall revile you and persecute you and shall say all manner of evil against you falsely for my sake. Rejoice and be exceedingly glad for great is your reward in heaven. For so persecuted they the prophets which were before you. . . ."'

Prior to McGeehan's judgement, Russell had issued a statement, on 28 March, expressing his reaction to Mrs Kay's and Attorney Goldstein's pleas in court. Russell had declared:[22]

'I have hitherto kept an almost unbroken silence in the controversy concerning my appointment to City College, and I could not admit that my opinions were relevant. But when grossly untrue statements as to my actions are made in court I feel that I must give them the lie.

'I never conducted a nudist colony in England. Neither my wife nor I ever paraded nude in public. I never went in for salacious poetry.

'Such assertions are deliberate falsehoods which must be known to those who make them to have no foundation in fact. I should be glad of an opportunity to deny them on oath.'

An anonymous correspondent from Newark, New Jersey, wrote to Russell indicating the fierce hatred that had been aroused against him:[23]

'Just whom did you think you were fooling when you had those hypocritically posed "family man" pictures taken for the newspapers? Can your diseased brain have reached such an advanced stage of senility as to imagine for a moment that you would impress anyone? You poor old fool!

'Even your publicly proved degeneracy cannot overshadow your vileness in posing for these pictures and trying to hide behind the innocence of your unfortunate children. Shame on you! Every decent man and woman in the country loathes you for this vile action of yours more than your other failings, which, after all, you inherited honestly enough from your decadent family tree. As for your questions and concern regarding Church and State connections in this country—just what concern has anything in this country got to do with you? Any time you don't like

American doings, go back to your native England (if you can!) and your stuttering King, who is an excellent example of British degenerate royalty—with its ancestry of barmaids, and pantrymen!

'Or did I hear someone say you were thrown out of that country of liberal degeneracy, because you out-did the royal family. HAW!

'Yours

'Pimp-Hater

'P.S.—I notice you refer to some American judge as an "ignorant fellow". If you are such a shining light, just why are you looking for a new appointment at this late date in your life? Have you been smelling up the California countryside too strongly?'

Russell agreed with the American Civil Liberties Union proposal that he should contest the court decision, and Osmond Fraenkel was engaged to lodge an appeal on his behalf. The first opportunity Russell had of study-ing the case against his appointment was when Fraenkel sent him copies of Mrs Kay's petition and Goldstein's affidavit. Russell provided Fraenkel with information relevant to the issues raised by these documents. Concerning Mrs Kay's allegations, Russell wrote to him on 4 April:

'. . . the petition is based on a misunderstanding of the word "philo-sophy" (which I know is often taken by ignorant people to mean theories for the conduct of practical life). . . . The books and opinions men-tioned are no part of my philosophy and cannot be correctly described as philosophy at all. Those of my books mentioned in the petition are on the subject of sociology, which I have never taught in any school or college and will not teach at C.C.N.Y.'

Russell listed for Fraenkel's information those of his books which dealt with philosophy and logic and suggested that they be produced in court. He gave details of his *curriculum vitae* and suggested that 'these facts might be useful in dealing with the proposal of a competitive examina-tion, which would in fact be rather difficult. The only competent ex-aminer would be Dr Whitehead, who would be disqualified as a collabor-ator.'

Regarding Goldstein's affidavit, Russell informed Fraenkel:

'. . . I have never kept a nudist colony. The school which I kept for some time for little children in England could not be so described. The children bathed naked. Otherwise they often played in hot weather wearing little or nothing, as nearly all children do nowadays. They were all under the age of 12.

'I have never myself appeared naked in public. I believe "parade" was the word used. This accusation is equally false with regard to my wife. . . .

159

'The salacious poetry charge is totally unfounded. . . . I have never written a word of poetry in my life. I read a great deal of poetry, both alone and aloud to my family, but none of it salacious, and at Chicago I used to read poetry aloud with my students. But I cannot suppose the charge to be based on knowledge of this custom.'

Fraenkel proposed to counter Goldstein's summations of Russell's writings by comparing them to the books themselves. In a letter of 9 April, Russell approved of this plan and stated: 'I should like emphasis to be laid on the distinction between advocating and not punishing such practices as infantile masturbation.' Russell indicated his willingness 'to submit to examination by a number of eminent alienists, if this would do anything to discredit Goldstein's outrageous affidavit'. He went on to add: 'I understand from Mr Baldwin that you intend to defend me without charge. I appreciate deeply the generous and liberal spirit which you show in this.'

Judge McGeehan's decision was greeted by an outcry of nationwide proportion, led by Russell's supporters. With the battle now revolving around the Courts of Appeal, the campaign to reinstate Russell became dependent upon the Board of Higher Education being allowed to make an effective appeal. The case had become a rallying point for liberal opinion throughout the country, and in order to co-ordinate protest action and raise funds for the appeal, a Bertrand Russell–Academic Freedom Committee was formed. The Committee represented many shades of opinion, with Professor Montague of Columbia University acting as chairman, and a host of college presidents as sponsors, including Sproul and Hutchins. On the executive committee were John Dewey, of the Committee for Cultural Freedom; Dr Franz Boas, the world-famous anthropologist, representing the Committee for Democracy and Intellectual Freedom; Roger Baldwin, of the American Civil Liberties Union; George Countz, of the American Federation of Teachers; Morris Ernst, of the National Lawyers Guild; and Arthur O. Lovejoy, of the American Association of University Professors.

The Philosophy Department at City College had already joined with the Committee for Cultural Freedom and the American Civil Liberties Union in issuing a statement, on 31 March, urging the Board of Higher Education to appeal against the McGeehan decision.[24] The joint statement charged that the court decision ignored convincing testimony of Russell's competence as an educator, and accepted 'without relevant proof . . . allegations that were false with regard to his moral character and fitness'. The statement expressed the fear that the decision had established a 'positively dangerous precedent' for appointment and removal of teachers on grounds other than their fitness as educators.

Numerous bodies wrote to Mayor La Guardia and Ordway Tead, Chairman of the Board of Higher Education, urging them to fight the McGeehan judgement. The American Students Union pledged 'to fight the decision with every resource at our command.'[25]

Among the first to speak out on behalf of Russell were his own students at the University of California. Senior students at U.C.L.A. issued a statement expressing their confidence in Russell and said:[26]

'Far from in any way corrupting the morals of his students, he had, on the contrary, done much to encourage a higher and finer ethical standard by his own personal uprightness, his tolerance, kindliness and complete intellectual honesty.'

U.C.L.A. faculty members also stood by Russell, and Dr Hans Reichenbach, Professor of Philosophy, spoke for them all when he said:[27]

'We all know Professor Russell to be one of the greatest philosophers of our time. He has had great success in his instruction on the U.C.L.A. campus and is well liked by the faculty members. I am astonished at the action taken by the New York Supreme Court.'

Russell was particularly happy with the 'sympathetic reactions' of his students. 'They have been very gracious,' he told the press, 'and the unanimous sympathy they have given me is heartening.' He was also 'gratified' by the extensive support he had received from academics, and remarked: 'They have lived up to their standards of intellect.'[28]

Messages of support from all over America continued to flow into Russell's Los Angeles home. Ohio State University students telegraphed: 'Ready to fight this thing for you and with you.' Sixty faculty members of Northwestern University, Illinois, pledged 'financial aid to defend your rights'.

Students at City College were in a state of great agitation. An emergency protest committee was set up to organise student activity, and William Swirsky, who was on the committee, notified Russell:[29]

'A student protest demonstration is taking place Friday. . . . Wednesday will see the results of a drive for 5,500 signatures on petitions urging your reinstatement. Every student organisation is aroused and the faculty is thoroughly indignant. We've got to win this fight!'

The protest meeting at City College was called by the Student Council, and held on 5 April. Students packed the Great Hall as speakers urged the Board of Higher Education to appeal against the court decision, and warned that attempts to ban Russell constituted a flagrant violation of academic freedom. Messages of support received from distinguished figures were read to the meeting. Thomas Mann, who had been invited to address the assembly, wired:[30]

'Not yet being a citizen of this country I do not feel justified to be the speaker in this cause which only Americans have to decide, but I feel more than compelled to express my sympathy with the aims of your gathering and with the idea of spiritual freedom. Knowing the technique of its destruction from bitter experience, I can but agree with your endeavor not to tolerate intolerance.'

Upton Sinclair, a graduate of City College, wired:[31]

'The judge and the bishop have publicised the fact that England has loaned us one of the most learned and generous men of our time. The advocates of fixed dogmas should not be allowed to rob us of Bertrand Russell's services, nor of our most precious democratic principle, freedom of thought and speech.'

A telegram from U.C.L.A. students stating: 'Your meeting protesting persecution of Bertrand Russell has complete support of U.C.L.A. students who know this great man', received thunderous and sustained applause.
Professor Krikorian wired Russell:[32]

'. . . The student body gave an amazing demonstration in favor of you on Friday. Our morale is high and will fight the case to the bitter end. Both the person involved and the cause have deeply stirred the enlightened groups for academic freedom. Russell Committee to coordinate activity and to be ready for long-drawn fight.'

Russell was prepared to travel to New York and speak in public on behalf of the campaign. In view of the legal proceedings, Fraenkel advised him not to make public statements on McGeehan's decision, and the Committee for Cultural Freedom, who were hoping to invite him East, cancelled their plans. The radical American Committee for Democracy and Intellectual Freedom, however, organised a protest rally at Carnegie Hall, on 13 April, which was addressed by Dr Franz Boas, Professor Walter Rautenstrauch, and others.

Commenting on the campaign for academic freedom that had generated behind him, Horace Kallen wrote to Russell: 'You seem predestined to carry the flag of free thought against its enemies.'[33] Russell replied on 14 April:

'No doubt I ought to consider myself very lucky to be in this privileged position; but it was quite unintentional. I really much prefer abstract work and never expect these fights I find myself in. But the only thing I hate more than fighting is running away.

'The terrific movement to support me is personally very gratifying and publicly very encouraging. I have never seen professors so roused or so united.'

The moves to reinstate Russell through the Appeal Courts were firmly obstructed. Pressure was directed against the Board of Higher Education to dissuade it from proceeding with an appeal. The Tammany politicians were particularly active in the New York State legislature, which was already on record as holding that 'an advocate of barnyard morality is an unfit person to hold an important post in the educational system of our State at the expense of the taxpayers.'[34] More ominously, the State legislature adopted the notorious Dunigan Bill which called for a $50,000 witch-hunt into the New York educational system. Speaking for his bill, Senator John J. Dunigan, the minority leader, declared that the investigation was directed principally at the Board of Higher Education.[35] A resolution was adopted by the New York City Council urging the mayor to reconstitute the Board and appoint more 'creditable' members. The clerical lobby was equally active, and Lambert Fairchild, of the National Committee for Religious Recovery, denounced those members of the Board who supported Russell as 'renegade Jews and renegade Christians'.[36] The Board, despite the minority that lined up behind Episcopalian Tuttle, refused to give way and voted to appeal against McGeehan's decision. Mayor La Guardia, with an eye for the Catholic vote, was embarrassed by the confrontation, and manoeuvred to prevent the Board from appealing.

The reactionary drive to eliminate liberal teaching influences from the colleges was aided by Mayor La Guardia's action, of 5 April, when he removed from the 1941 city budget the financial allocation for the post which Russell was to fill. The mayor justified his action by declaring it was 'in keeping with the policy to eliminate vacant positions'.[37] A few weeks later, the Board of Estimates, the controlling financial body of the city, strengthened the mayor's hand by prohibiting the use of any funds for the employment of Russell. The corporation counsel, appointed by the mayor to handle the Board's legal affairs, in an unprecedented action declined to represent the Board in the matter of their appeal. He strongly urged them against an appeal, which he considered 'would be an unfortunate case upon which to base a legal test of the issues', and advised them instead to accept an offer from Mrs Kay's counsel, which in the event of their dropping proceedings, would mean that 'no order would be entered against the Board upon Judge McGeehan's decision.'[38] The mayor fully supported the corporation counsel, whom he held was the sole authority legally entitled to represent the Board. Russell in a letter to Warder Norton on 27 April 1940 commented: 'I shall be curious to know whether La Guardia is able to prevent the B.H.E. from employing Buckner [private counsel]. His moves to prevent a proper trial of the issue are very mean.' Flouting the mayor, the Board engaged private counsel to handle their appeal, but after several hearings the Appelate Division of the Supreme Court dismissed the appeal on the ground that the Board had no authority to appoint private counsel.

Russell's appeal fared no better. On 16 April, Justice McGeehan refused to allow Russell to intervene, on the grounds that he had 'no legal standing in the proceeding; that he had delayed too long in asserting this right; and that there had been sufficient opportunity for him to answer Mrs Kay's charges at the time of the original hearing.'[39] All further attempts to appeal the case in higher quarters failed, and the McGeehan judgement became final. Speaking of the unsatisfactory disposition of the case, Professor Morris Cohen stated: 'If this is law, then surely, in the language of Dickens, "the law is an ass".'[40] John Dewey commented: 'As Americans, we can only blush with shame for this scar on our repute for fair play.'[41]

The City College controversy was major news in the New York press for several weeks. Most leading New York newspapers took the view that the courts should not interfere with the Board of Higher Education's appointments. The papers most favourably disposed to Russell were the *Post*, the communist party's *Daily Worker*, and the Jewish press. The *Journal-American*, the *Mirror* and the *Sun* were most hostile. The *Herald Tribune* declared that 'no friend of civil liberty and academic freedom'[42] could remain indifferent to the Bertrand Russell case. *The New York Times*, while giving the controversy comprehensive coverage, refrained from editorial comment. On 20 April, however, an editorial was published reflecting on the 'bitterness of feeling' which the issue had generated. Holding that the original appointment was 'impolitic and unwise', *The New York Times* contended that Russell 'should have had the wisdom to withdraw from the appointment as soon as its harmful results became evident. . . .'

A letter from Russell appeared in *The New York Times* on 26 April 1940:

'I hope you will allow me to comment on your references to the controversy originating in my appointment to the College of the City of New York, and particularly on your judgment that I "should have had the wisdom to retire from the appointment as soon as its harmful effects became evident".

'In one sense this would have been the wisest course; it would certainly have been more prudent as far as my personal interests are concerned, and a great deal pleasanter. If I had considered only my own interests and inclinations I should have retired at once.

'But however wise such action might have been from a personal point of view, it would also, in my judgment, have been cowardly and selfish. A great many people who realised that their own interests and the principles of toleration and free speech were at stake were anxious from the first to continue the controversy. If I had retired I should have robbed them of their *casus belli* and tacitly assented to the proposition of opposition that substantial groups shall be allowed to drive out of public office individuals whose opinions, race or nationality they find repugnant. This to me would appear immoral.

'It was my grandfather who brought about the repeal of the English Test and Corporation Acts, which barred from public office any one not a member of the Church of England, of which he himself was a member, and one of my earliest and most important memories is of a deputation of Methodists and Wesleyans coming to cheer outside his window on the fiftieth anniversary of this repeal, although the largest single group affected was Catholic.

'I do not believe that the controversy is harmful on general grounds. It is not controversy and open difference of opinion that endanger democracy. On the contrary, these are its greatest safeguards. It is an essential part of democracy that substantial groups, even majorities, should extend toleration to dissentient groups, however small and however much their sentiments may be outraged.

'In a democracy it is necessary that people should learn to endure having their sentiments outraged. Minority groups already endure this, although according to the principles of the founders of the American Constitution they are equally entitled to consideration. If there is 10 per cent of the population of New York that holds opinions similar to mine, then 10 per cent of the teachers in New York should be allowed to hold those opinions. And this should apply to all unusual opinions. If it is once admitted that there are opinions toward which such tolerance need not extend, then the whole basis of toleration is destroyed.

'Jews have been driven from Germany, and Catholics most cruelly persecuted because they were repugnant to the substantial part of the community which happened to be in power.'

In a somewhat lighter vein, Russell provided a tailpiece to the City College affair in his letter to Warder Norton of 27 April 1940:

'Mrs Kay should have a complimentary copy of "Language, Truth and Fact" [*Inquiry into Meaning and Truth*], with the author's thanks for her help in advertising it. Her counsel asserts that I am "aphrodisiac"— evidently he hasn't the vaguest idea what the word means. I should like to think him right on this point.'

NOTES

[1] Supreme Court, New York County, Appellate Division, *Papers on Appeal from Order*, in the matter of the application of Jean Kay against the Board of Higher Education of the City of New York, p. 40.

[2] Ibid., pp. 35–41.

[3] Ibid., pp. 42–50.

[4] Ibid., p. 49.

[5] John Dewey and Horace M. Kallen, *The Bertrand Russell Case* (Viking Press, New York, 1941), p. 21.

[6] Supreme Court, New York County, Appellate Division, op. cit., p. 71.

[7] Ibid., pp. 76–7.

[8] Ibid., pp. 77–8.

[9] Quoted by Russell in his *Marriage and Morals* (London, 1929), p. 60 (Horace Liveright, New York, 1929), p. 71, to illustrate the forthright character of Renaissance love poetry.

[10] The New York *Herald Tribune* (28 March 1940).

[11] Dewey and Kallen, op. cit., pp. 213–25; see also Supreme Court, New York County, Appellate Division, op. cit., pp. 102–17.

[12] The New York *Herald Tribune* ((?) May 1940).

[13] P. Edwards, 'The Bertrand Russell Case', appendix to Russell's *Why I Am Not a Christian, and Other Essays* (London and Simon & Schuster, New York, 1957), p. 192.

[14] The New York *Sun* (31 March 1940).

[15] Edwards, op. cit., p. 212.

[16] Ibid., p. 213.

[17] Undated and unidentified Los Angeles newsclipping.

[18] The New York *Herald Tribune* (1 April 1940).

[19] Ibid.

[20] The *Daily News*, Los Angeles (29 March 1940).

[21] Undated and unidentified newsclipping.

[22] *The New York Times* (29 March 1940).

[23] B. Russell, *Autobiography* (London, 1968), Vol. II, p. 226 (Boston, 1968), pp. 344–5.

[24] The New York *Herald Tribune* (1 April 1940).

[25] Ibid.

[26] Undated and unidentified Los Angeles newsclipping.

[27] The Los Angeles *Times* (1 April 1940).

[28] Ibid.

[29] 1 April 1940.

[30] The *Beaver* (C.C.N.Y. student newspaper) (5 April 1940).

[31] Sinclair sent a copy of this telegram to Russell on 4 April, with the comment: 'I do not know whether you happen to know that C.C.N.Y. is my *alma mater* . . .'

[32] 8 April 1940.

[33] From Kallen's letter of 2 April 1940.

[34] A resolution, including this statement, submitted by Senator Phelps

Phelps, a Manhattan Democrat, was adopted on 25 March 1940.

[35] *The New York Times* (26 March 1940); a large-scale investigation into the New York educational system followed.

[36] Edwards, op. cit., p. 213.

[37] American Civil Liberties Union, *The Story of the Bertrand Russell Case* (January 1941), p. 8.

[38] Ibid., pp. 9–10.

[39] Ibid., p. 8.

[40] Dewey and Kallen, op. cit., p. 143.

[41] Ibid., p. 60.

[42] Ibid., p. 15.

CHAPTER 13

THE BARNES FOUNDATION

The repercussions of the City College controversy were to make life in America for Russell and his family extremely difficult and uncertain. As Russell has observed:[1]

'A typical American witch-hunt was instituted against me and I became taboo throughout the whole of the United States. I was to have been engaged in a lecture tour, but I had only one engagement, made before the witch-hunt had developed. The Rabbi who had made this engagement broke his contract, but I cannot blame him. Owners of halls refused to let them if I was to lecture, and if I had appeared anywhere in public, I should probably have been lynched by a Catholic mob, with the full approval of the police. No newspaper or magazine would publish anything that I wrote, and I was suddenly deprived of all means of earning a living. As it was legally impossible to get money out of England, this produced a very difficult situation, especially as I had my three children dependent upon me. Many liberal-minded professors protested, but they all supposed that as I was an earl I must have ancestral estates and be very well off. . . .'

Russell's resignation from the University of California was to take effect from the end of the summer term, 1940. Encouraged by the New York lawsuit, a Californian clergyman[2] instituted legal proceedings in Los Angeles on 30 April 1940, describing Russell's teachings as 'subversive' and moving for his immediate dismissal from U.C.L.A. The suit was unceremoniously thrown out of court by a triumvirate of judges who upheld the autonomy of the Board of Regents in determining Russell's fitness to teach 'as it is a matter of international knowledge that the University of California has, under the guidance of the Board of Regents, become one of the great universities of the world.'[3] Concurrent with this Californian action, and whilst the New York court appeals were still to be resolved, a similar threat arose against Russell's William James lectures at Harvard, which were due to commence in September 1940. A Boston legislative agent, Thomas J.

Dorgan, promised to institute legal proceedings against the appointment, and addressing himself to Harvard's president, James B. Conant, declared: 'To hire this man . . . is an insult to every American citizen in Massachusetts.'[4]

The Harvard governing body, comprised of the president and fellows, made it clear that they were prepared to fight any attempted court action, and reaffirmed their decision to engage Russell 'for the best interests of the university'.[5] In a poll conducted among over 200 Harvard undergraduates, only one declared opposition to Russell's appointment.[6] Reaction to his engagement among the Harvard faculty was not quite as unambiguous, which led Russell to hint: 'Perhaps Harvard regretted having made it, but, if so, the regret was politely concealed from me.'[7] William E. Hocking, Professor of Philosophy at Harvard, wrote Russell a 'purely personal' letter on 30 April 1940:[8]

'It would be foolish for me to pretend that the university is not disturbed by the situation. Harvard is not a "State university" in the sense that it draws its major support from legislative grants. . . . But it is a State institution, with certain unique provisions for its government set into the constitution, so that political interference with our working is legally possible. The suit promised by Thomas Dorgan, legislative agent for the City of Boston, has some footing in the law of the Commonwealth, though the university is prepared to meet it. But beyond that, there are possibilities of further legislation which might be serious for an institution already an object of dislike on the part of certain elements of the public.

'As to the suit itself, the university is not proposing to contest it on the ground of "freedom of speech" or "freedom of teaching" (for this would make the university appear as protagonist of a claim of right on your part to teach your views on sex-morals at Harvard, a claim certainly uncontemplated in our arrangements and probably untenable at law). The university is simply holding the ground of the independence of our appointing bodies from outside interference. This is a defensible position, if we can show that we have exercised and are exercising that independence with a due sense of responsibility to our statutory obligations . . .

'We are all terribly sorry that this hue and cry has arisen. . . . For myself, I am equally sorry that you are making the issue one of freedom of speech in the New York situation. For if you lose, you lose; and if you win, you lose also. And the colleges will lose, too: for the impression already in the public mind will be deepened, that the colleges insist on regarding all hypotheses as on the same level—none are foolish and none are immoral: they are all playthings of debate for a lot of detached intellects who have nothing in common with the intuitions of average mankind. Personally I am with the average man in doubting whether all hypotheses are on the same level, or can escape the invidious adjectives.

'Largely because of this, I have had, so far, nothing to say in public on this question. I have been cultivating the great and forgotten right of the freedom of silence, which it is hard to maintain in this country. If I were talking, I should agree in the main with the first paragraph of the editorial in *The New York Times* of 20 April, which you have doubtless seen, and whose refrain is that "mistakes of judgment have been made by all the principals involved".'

Russell replied to Hocking on 6 May:[9]

'Thank you for your letter. It makes me wish that I could honourably resign the appointment to the William James lectures, but I do not see how I can do so without laying myself open to the charge of cowardice and of letting down the interests of the whole body of teachers.

'I almost wish, also, that the president and fellows had not re-affirmed the appointment, since as you say . . . the opposition has considerable basis in law. From my point of view, it would be better to be dismissed now, with financial compensation, than to be robbed both of the appointment and of compensation after long anxiety and distress.

'I did not seek the appointment, and I am not so fond of the role of martyr as to wish continuously and without respite to suffer for a cause which concerns others so much more than me. The independence of American universities is their affair, not mine.

'Someone seems to have misled you as to the line that I and the Board of Higher Education in New York have taken about my appointment there. I have never dreamt of claiming a right to talk about sexual ethics when I am hired to talk about logic or semantics; equally, a man hired to teach ethics would have no right to talk about logic. I claim two things: (1) that appointments to academic posts should be made by people with some competence to judge a man's technical qualifications; (2) that in extra-professional hours, a teacher should be free to express his opinions, whatever they may be. City College and the Board of Higher Education based their defence solely on the first of these contentions. Their defence was therefore identical with that which you say is contemplated by Harvard.

'The principle of free speech was raised by other people, in my opinion rightly. I am afraid that Harvard, like the New York Board, cannot prevent popular agitation based on this principle; though it is of course obvious that in both cases the official defence of the appointment is rightly based on the independence of duly constituted academic bodies and their right to make their own appointments.

'I ask now, in advance, that I may be officially notified of any legal proceedings taken against the university on account of my appointment, and allowed to become a party. This was not done in the New York case, because of the hostility of the corporation counsel, who handled their defence. I cannot endure a second time being slandered and condemned in a court of law without any opportunity of rebutting false accusations against which no one else can adequately defend me, for lack of knowledge.

'I hope that Harvard will have the courtesy to keep me informed officially of all developments, instead of leaving me to learn of matters that vitally concern me only from inaccurate accounts in newspapers.

'I should be glad if you would show this letter to the president and fellows.'

Like Hocking, the Harvard *Crimson*, in reporting the governing body's proposed legal defence of the Russell engagement, incorrectly described C.C.N.Y.'s legal case as being based on 'freedom of speech'. The editor of the *Crimson* published a letter of correction from Russell on 9 May 1940:[10]

'I hope you will allow me to comment on your references in the Harvard *Crimson* of 29 April to the recent proceedings concerning my appointment to City College of New York.

'You say: "Freedom of speech will not be the point under argument, as was the case in the proceedings against City College of New York, when the latter based an unsuccessful defence of its Russell appointment on the assertion that Russell should be permitted to expound his moral views from a lecture platform."

'In fact "freedom of speech" was not the defence of City College and the New York Board of Higher Education. The Board and College based their defence on the principle of academic freedom, which *means simply the independence of duly constituted academic bodies, and their right to make their own appointments*. This, according to your headline, is exactly the defence contemplated by the Corporation of Harvard. Neither the Board of Higher Education nor the faculty of City College at any time made the claim that I "should be permitted to expound my moral views from a lecture platform". On the contrary, they stated repeatedly and with emphasis that my moral views had no possible relevance to the subjects I had been engaged to teach.

'Even if I were permitted to expound my moral views in the classroom, my own conscience would not allow me to do so, since they have no connection with the subjects which it is my profession to teach, and I think that the classroom should not be used as an opportunity for propaganda on any subject.

'The principle of freedom of speech has been invoked, not by the New York Board of Higher Education as their legal defence, but by many thousands of people throughout the United States who have perceived its obvious relation to the controversy, which is this: the American Constitution guarantees to everyone the right to express his opinions whatever these may be. The right is naturally limited by any contract into which the individual may enter which requires him to spend part of his time in occupations other than expressing his opinions. Thus, if a salesman, a postman, a tailor and a teacher of mathematics all happen to hold a certain opinion on a subject unrelated to their work, whatever it may be, none of them should devote to oratory on this subject time which they have been paid to spend in selling, delivering letters, making suits, or teaching mathematics. But they should all equally be allowed to express their opinion freely and without fear of penalties in their spare time, and to think, speak, and behave as they wish, within the law, when they are not engaged in their professional duties.

'This is the principle of free speech. It appears to be little known. If therefore anyone should require any further information about it I refer him to the United States Constitution and to the works of the founders thereof.'

Fortunately, the Boston lawsuit did not materialise and Russell was spared the ordeal of another court case. He managed to find the time to write two specially commissioned articles at the height of the New York and related controversies which were dispassionate analyses of the fundamental issues at stake. They were 'Freedom and the Colleges',[11] published by the *American Mercury* in May 1940, and 'Do I Preach Adultery?' published by *Liberty* magazine in the same month; and were among the few exceptions to the embargo against publishing Russell that was beginning to take force. (A further article of relevance to these issues 'Education in America,'[12] was published by *Common Sense*, in June 1941.) In 'Do I Preach Adultery?', Russell sought to clarify his sexual ethic which, while providing the focal point of the attack on him, had been so crudely distorted. In defence of his views, Russell wrote:

'Love of truth, or (as it may be called) the scientific outlook, is, to my mind, only second to loving kindness as an ethical principle. The man of science knows that it is difficult to ascertain truth, and probably impossible to ascertain it completely. He holds his opinions, not as unalterable dogmas, but only as what seems most likely to be true on the evidence hitherto available. Whatever opinions I have expressed, in regard to sexual ethics as in regard to the most abstruse questions of logic, I hold in this spirit. There is not one of them that I am not prepared to abandon if new evidence of a convincing kind is brought to my notice; but equally there is not one of them that I am prepared to modify or suppress from fear of punishment or hope of worldly advancement. It is difficult not to let one's opinions harden into dogmas when one is attacked by furious dogmatists. But dogmatic resistance and pusillanimous surrender are alike untrue to the scientific spirit. It is for the scientific spirit, not for any conclusions to which it may have provisionally led me, that I am prepared to fight with all my strength. For it is only by the scientific spirit, wedded to loving kindness, that human life can be made less painful and less full of misery than it is now and has always been since the dawn of history.'

It was the war, however, that remained Russell's overriding concern, despite the heavy demands on his time and energy caused by the City College affair. He had finally come to shed his pacifist reservations, although he had 'never held the non-resistance creed absolutely, and I did not now reject it absolutely'.[13] Explaining the difference in opposing the First World War and supporting the Second, Russell wrote:[14]

'. . . I had been able to view with reluctant acquiescence the possibility of the supremacy of the Kaiser's Germany; I thought that, although this would be an evil, it would not be so great an evil as a world war and its aftermath. But Hitler's Germany was a different matter. I found the Nazis utterly revolting—cruel, bigoted, and stupid. Morally and intellectually they were alike odious to me. Although I clung to my pacifist convictions, I did so with increasing difficulty. When, in 1940, England was threatened with invasion, I realised that, throughout the First War, I had never seriously envisaged the possibility of utter defeat. I found this possibility unbearable, and at last consciously and definitely decided that I must support what was necessary for victory in the Second War, however difficult victory might be to achieve, and however painful in its consequences.'

The immediate months following the outbreak of war were possibly among the most difficult in Russell's life. His professional career was entangled in the City College controversy, and he was upset by the personal problems created for his family because of his situation as a virtual social outcast in America. In addition to this burden was the great anguish he experienced as the Nazi threat gathered momentum and seemed on the verge of destroying Britain. Edith Finch, Russell's future wife, who had been introduced to him by Lucy Donnelly while on a visit to England in 1925 and who taught English literature at Bryn Mawr, saw Russell quite frequently during this period and has described his mood:[15]

'I remember the tension with which B.R. awaited the 6 o'clock news when he was with us—tension that we all shared, but that we realised must be very terrible for him. I remember the almost unbearable relief day by day when we heard Big Ben strike 9 and knew that London had not been utterly destroyed. It does not take much imagination to recognise what it must have meant to anyone of such intensity of feeling as B.R., whose love of England was, as he said, "very nearly the strongest emotion that I possess", to have to be a mere looker-on, and a looker-on living amongst people who, even when they cared at all, were also, so far as England was concerned, mere spectators. The anger and pain must have been almost unbearable at hearing such remarks as "Oh, English soldiers are always in retreat; they are always on the run", during the days of Rommel's successes in North Africa and the days of Dunkirk; or the sometimes anxious and sympathetic and sometimes quite careless debates of those not personally concerned as to whether England could or would survive. His whole situation at the time must have been unspeakable—though there is little parade of his feeling in his own writing.'

While Russell had not hesitated in 1939 to advance a neutralist policy for the United States, and although he had since come to support the war, his position as a virtual exile made it difficult for him to urge America to fight. It was to friends in England that Russell conveyed his doubts and anxieties. When Gilbert Murray, with whom he had had sharp differences over the First World War, wrote to him at the University of California on behalf of a German anti-Nazi professor named Jacobsthal, Russell replied on 21 April 1940:[16]

'It is difficult to do much at this date in America for German academic refugees. American universities have been very generous, but are by now pretty well saturated. I spoke about the matter of Jacobsthal to Reichenbach, a German refugee who is a professor here, and whom I admire both morally and intellectually. He knew all about Jacobsthal's work, which I didn't. The enclosed is the official reply of the authorities of this university. I must leave further steps to others, as I am at the moment unable to save my own skin. In view of the German invasion of Norway, I suppose it is only too likely that Jacobsthal is by now in a concentration camp.

'Yes, I wish we could meet and have the sort of talk we used to have. I find I cannot maintain the pacifist position in this war. I do not feel sufficiently sure of the opposite to say anything publicly by way of recantation, though it may come to that. In any case, here in America an Englishman can only hold his tongue, as anything he may say is labelled propaganda. However, what I wanted to convey is that you would not find me disagreeing with you as much as in 1914, though I still think I was right then, in that this war is an outcome of Versailles, which was an outcome of moral indignation.

174

'It is painful to be at such a distance in war-time, and only the most imperative financial necessity keeps me here. It is a comfort that my three children are here, but the oldest is 18, and I do not know how soon he may be needed for military service. We all suffer from almost unbearable homesickness, and I find myself longing for old friends. I am glad that you are still one of them. . . .'

Newspapers in Britain, owing to the war-time scarcity of paper, had given little publicity to Russell's troubles in New York. The *New Statesman* carried a short report on the affair, and on 13 May 1940 Russell wrote to its editor, Kingsley Martin, to take the opportunity of making a public announcement of his support for the war:[17]

'Thanks for your kind paragraph about my New York appointment. We still hope to appeal, but the mayor and corporation counsel, from respect for the Catholic vote, are doing their best to prevent it. A similar fuss is promised over my appointment to give the William James lectures at Harvard in the autumn.

'Actually I am being overwhelmed with friendship and support, but in this country the decent people are terrifyingly powerless and often very naïve. This fuss is serving a useful purpose in calling attention to the sort of thing that happens constantly to people less well known.

'The news from Europe is unbearably painful. We all wish that we were not so far away, although we could serve no useful purpose if we were at home.

'Ever since the war began I have felt that I could not go on being a pacifist; but I have hesitated to say so, because of the responsibility involved. If I were young enough to fight myself I should do so, but it is more difficult to urge others. Now, however, I feel that I ought to announce that I have changed my mind, and I would be glad if you could find an opportunity to mention in the *New Statesman* that you have heard from me to this effect.'

Russell wrote to Robert Trevelyan from Los Angeles on 19 May 1940:[18]

'Thank you very much for the fine volumes of your works, which arrived safely, and which I am delighted to have.

'At this moment it is difficult to think of anything but the war. By the time you get this, presumably the outcome of the present battle will have been decided. I keep on remembering how I stayed at Shiffolds during the crisis of the battle of the Marne, and made you walk two miles to get a Sunday paper. Perhaps it would have been better if the Kaiser had won, seeing Hitler is so much worse. I find that this time I am not a pacifist, and consider the future of civilisation bound up with our victory. I don't think anything so important has happened since the fifth century, the previous occasion on which the Germans reduced the world to barbarism.

'You may have seen that I am being hounded out of teaching in America because the Catholics don't like my views. I was quite interested in this (which involves a grave danger of destitution) until the present battle began—now I find difficulty in remembering it.

'Yes, I have read *Grapes of Wrath*, and think it a very good book. The issue of the migrant workers is a burning one here, on which there is much bitter feeling.

'John and Kate are settling into the university here, and Conrad (just 3) is flourishing and intelligent. We are all desperately homesick, and hope to return as soon as it is financially feasible.

'Give my love to Bessie and tell her it will be very nice to hear from her. John was *most* grateful for Lucretius.'

Russell's appointment at U.C.L.A. was by this time drawing to a close. Because of his reluctance to publicly express himself in America on the war, the press, not surprisingly, sought information about his views from anyone who had contact with him. A United Press despatch caused considerable embarrassment for Russell. The Santa Monica *Evening Outlook* reported on 23 May: 'British Educator at U.C.L.A. says Allied Cause Lost' and continued:

'Bertrand Russell, the British philosopher, today predicted a quick German victory in Europe, followed by an attempt to create a world State, which, he added, would break up like the Roman Empire.

'The Allied cause, he said, is lost. He told his classes at the University of California in Los Angeles that he had "given up hope for the Allies. It would be better for them to win", he continued, "but not much better."'

Russell promptly controverted the story and the following day the same newspaper, under the headline 'Russell Says War Statement Garbled', reported:

'Bertrand Russell, noted British philosopher . . . today emphatically denied making statements on the European war attributed to him yesterday in a United Press despatch.

' "He never has predicted a German victory or said that the Allied cause was lost," Mrs Russell declared in making the correction on her husband's behalf. Russell's statement was as follows:

' "It is as yet impossible to predict the outcome. While the war will leave great misery, whoever wins, I believe that a German victory would be a calamity greater than any in history."

'Mrs Russell added that her husband was "very much distressed" over the fact that his comments on the war had been garbled by students who attended a lecture at which they were made.'

Shortly afterwards, Russell issued a precise statement to the American press, in which he explained his change of outlook towards the war, and indirectly suggested the need for United States commitment:[19]

'This statement is an answer to the many inquiries I have received as to whether I am a pacifist in regard to the present war.

'I have never been an absolute pacifist. I was opposed to the last war because I thought that no important principle was involved. Moreover, we were from the first allied with Russia, then as now a corrupt and brutal tyranny.

'In recent years I was against war, believing that its evils were greater than any Hitler was likely to inflict upon the world. I have now come to realise that I, in common with almost everyone else, under-estimated his power. I did not really believe he could invade England, and the suggestion that he could attack the United States would have seemed to me utterly fantastic. He has now shown that he will go on in his attempt to dominate the world until he is stopped by overwhelmingly superior force.

'Terrible as is the cost of war, whoever wins, I think this is one of those rare cases in which the cost of passivity is even greater.

'If I were of military age I should now be fighting. If there were any other way in which I could take part in the war I should be only too glad, but I have been told that so far there is nothing for me to do. The Allies do not need men, still less old men—they need machines.'

The burden of exile was a great pain for Russell and weighed heavily on his conscience. He wanted to be of service to his country and had approached the British Consul in California, at a very early date, about the possibility of his doing something, however little, to help 'the war effort'. But his offer was brushed aside.

Ironically, while Russell was being frustrated in these efforts, accusations that he was an agent of subversion were being flung at him in America.

The McGeehan judgement had given great encouragement to those forces determined to purge the educational system of liberal influences. A large-scale witch-hunt ensued, with Russell remaining a prime target of abuse. In the New York City Council he was described as a 'fifth columnist' and an 'avowed communist' by Charles E. Keegan who had previously labelled him a 'dog' and a 'bum'. At their national convention in Santa Barbara, California, the Knights of Columbus were urged to concerted action by Joseph Scott, a Los Angeles attorney, 'not only to guard against all subversive activities, but to watch with particular care the type of professors that are employed in our State colleges and universities.'[20] On the eve of the convention, Scott had attacked Russell and charged that 'communism is being taught at the University of California at Los Angeles.' Russell's reaction is conveyed through an unpublished statement which he drafted on 27 May 1940:

'It is unnecessary for me to take notice of all the attacks that are being made upon me; but I wish to protest emphatically against the malicious attempts that are now being made to connect me with some sort of "Fifth Column" or with the communists, or to make me appear an alien political agent. This is going too far.

'For example: in New York recently Councilman Charles E. Keegan asserted that I am an "avowed Communist" and that I can be compared with the "Fifth Columns" which aided Nazi victories. Even while I write this letter a newspaper containing a similar charge against me is brought in.

'For the first of Councilman Keegan's accusations: I am not and never have been a communist. Ever since 1920, when I visited Russia and wrote *The Practice and Theory of Bolshevism* I have been a bitter critic of the Soviet Union. In 1932, when I wrote *Education and the Modern World* I hoped that the early dictatorship in Russia was developing into a more liberal regime and expressed for it a qualified support which I soon saw to have been a mistake. Even in that book, however, there is far more criticism than praise of Soviet methods. I have since come to consider Stalin's government at least as bad as Hitler's, and only less dangerous because less efficient. This view I have frequently expressed in speech and writing.

'The second accusation is deliberately vague. It is not stated that I am a member of a Fifth Column, though it is suggested that I may be. Since I am supposed to be a communist, the Fifth Column to which I might belong would presumably be one of Soviet agents. An accusation of this sort cannot be made openly, since it is demonstrably false and libellous.

'But the words "Fifth Column" have become in the last few days words of terror which can be used to inflame an alarmed populace against any person not a United States citizen. They will be used unscrupulously by persons of all shades of opinions to discredit their opponents. I have talked lately to many inoffensive foreigners, some of them already citizens, some of them hoping to become citizens, who because of a foreign name or accent have begun to tremble in their shoes at the prospects of suspicion, hostility and active discrimination which is opening before them.

'It is indeed necessary for the United States to be vigilant against foreign agents; but I earnestly hope that this vigilance will not entail prejudice against all foreigners and particularly against all Germans, that it will not, as seems all too likely, produce a wave of mass hysteria tossing the words "Fifth Column" here and there until the people become panic-stricken and therefore cruel from an ill-defined fear of foreigners and treachery.

'American patriotism has had this merit: that is has been based not on a common race or creed but upon loyalty to a common enterprise. In American cities millions of people of different racial descent live peaceably side by side who, if they were in Europe, would be at war or on the verge of war. I hope that racial hatred and the persecution of foreigners will never disrupt this loyalty. If foreign agents can disrupt it, fear of foreign agents can disrupt it even more, through fanning old and dormant prejudices.

'I am thinking particularly of German refugees, Jewish and otherwise. The English government has been obliged, by imminent danger, to intern them all. They could not do otherwise; there was no time to distinguish the false from the genuine. I hope that in this country it will be possible by taking the problem in time to avoid punishing the innocent with the guilty. Nothing could be more piteous and bitterly ironical than the position of these unfortunates, who, driven from their homes by Hitler, are suspected everywhere else of being his agents.

'Far from being any sort of political agent I have lately been immersed in entirely abstract work. I have been scrupulously careful to avoid expressing in public any opinion about the relation of this country to European affairs. But it is impossible for a foreigner living in this country not to notice a most ominous change of mood. Since the war began it has been almost impossible to open a newspaper without seeing somewhere the words "Americanism" and "un-American": Americanism is everything good, while everything bad is un-American. This is new, and I cannot think it is to be applauded. The last hope for humanity will be gone if this country allows itself to be frightened into reaction against everything that is new or foreign or strange. Europe is being destroyed by rival nationalisms. Is this a reason for America to take to nationalism too? Italy and Germany and Russia have stamped out everything not Italian or German or Russian. Is this a reason for America to reject everything that is "Un-American"?

'On the contrary, America needs now more than ever to keep alive its traditional ideals of freedom and toleration, regardless of differences of race or creed or opinion. America should uphold, now as in the past thought against dogma, humanism against narrow patriotism, diversity against uniformity, courage against fear.

'I say this not as a hostile critic but as one who deeply appreciates all that is best in this country and dreads any infection of fanaticism and reaction from abroad.'

The summer vacation period of 1940 provided a welcome escape for Russell and his family from the publicity and controversy that had been hounding them since Bishop Manning's outburst. It afforded Russell 'an extraordinary contrast between public horror and private delight', and the opportunity to enjoy some of the natural beauty of America, which left a deep impression upon him. Russell wrote in his *Autobiography*:[21]

'We spent the summer in the Sierras, at Fallen Leaf Lake near Lake Tahoe, one of the loveliest places that it has ever been my good fortune to know. The lake is more than 6,000 feet above sea-level, and during the greater part of the year deep snow makes the whole region un-inhabitable. But there is a three-months' season in the summer during which the sun shines continually, the weather is warm, but as a rule not unbearably hot, the mountain meadows are filled with the most exquisite wild flowers, and the smell of the pine trees fills the air. We had a log cabin in the middle of pine trees, close to the lake. Conrad and his nursery governess slept indoors, but there was no room for the rest of us in the house, and we all slept on various porches. There were endless walks through deserted country to waterfalls, lakes and mountain tops, and one could dive off snow into deep water that was not unduly cold. I had a tiny study which was hardly more than a shed, and there I finished my *Inquiry into Meaning and Truth*. Often it was so hot that I did my writing stark naked. But heat suits me, and I never found it too hot for work.'

During the summer vacation Russell was approached by Dr Albert C. Barnes, the Philadelphia millionaire, with a generous offer to rescue him from his financial dilemma. Barnes was a controversial and out-spoken figure who had made his fortune by inventing and marketing Argyrol, the medicinal compound. He proceeded to accumulate modern French paintings, and had established the Barnes Foundation, which was an art school and gallery that housed his priceless collection. Barnes was a close friend of John Dewey and had a radical reputation. He had publicly denounced Russell's ousting from C.C.N.Y. as 'the work of bigoted authoritarians', and contributed $2,000 towards the publication of Dewey and Kallen's book on the affair. Barnes invited Russell to lecture at his Foundation, where the principles of aesthetics were taught. With no prospect of earning a living, and no hope of an early return to England, Russell was very interested in Barnes's offer. He had been warned that Barnes 'always tired of people before long'[22] and was therefore concerned to obtain a contract covering a fairly definite period. He wrote to Barnes on 18 June 1940:[23]

'Thank you for sending me an account of the Barnes Foundation. I am deeply grateful to you for the suggestion that I should join it. . . . Could you also let me know whether my appointment, assuming that I am free to accept it, would be for a definite or indefinite period? I cannot tell you what an immense boon your offer is to me. One is almost ashamed, at such a moment, to think of personal things, but when one has young children it is unavoidable.'

Barnes promptly offered Russell a five-year contract at $6,000 per annum. He envisaged that the Foundation would provide Russell a democratic sanctuary from authoritarian interference, allowing him ample free time to concentrate on his serious writing. He expressed to Russell the wish 'to do all I can to put you in a position to do the kind of work which only you can do'.[24] Regarding the contribution Russell could make to the Foundation, Barnes wrote again on 24 June 1940:

'If I am not mistaken in your attitude toward life—from "A Free Man's Worship" to *Marriage and Morals*—the hope for a better social order lies in the development of intelligence as a guide to living . . . that general idea is the main root of our enterprise even though we happen to use the material of art to put it over. In doing it, I've had many doses of the same bitter medicine you've been forced to swallow recently; for example, in 1923 the principal Philadelphia newspaper printed an editorial denouncing me as a "perverter of public morals" because I exhibited, wrote and talked about such painters as Cézanne and Renoir. . . .

'I think you'll see in this incident an illustration of how you could function here, granting that life has many phases not many of which have been frankly, honestly and fully presented to people because institutionalised ignorance and prejudice have ganged up on them—as you know, to your sorrow. In short, if you want to say what you damn please, even to giving your adversaries a dose of their own medicine, we'll back you up. We can do it because we are on a par with universities as a chartered institution and we ask no financial support from the politically controlled public treasury. . . .'

Russell wrote to Barnes from his summer retreat at Lake Tahoe, on 20 July, to clarify the nature of his proposed lectures:[25]

'All that you say about the work sounds most attractive, but it certainly needs conversation. I do not know whether you want me to lecture on philosophy or on social questions. I should be very reluctant to lecture on sexual ethics, which have quite wrongly been supposed to be my special field. Actually the subject interests me much less than many others and I should be sorry to be diverted from philosophy and history to sociology. I could, if it suited you, lecture on different philosophies of the past, and their influence on culture and social questions: for example, Platonism and its influence, or the Romantic movement of the nineteenth century.

'Details we could discuss later, but I would be very glad if you could give me some idea now of the sort of subject you are thinking of.

'We would be delighted to see you here at any time before the end of August, though I am afraid we could not offer you hospitality, as we are living in a tiny log cabin. There are however hotels all round.'

Barnes flew out to California in August and a contract was agreed to. Russell was to give one lecture a week during the school year, along the lines he had suggested in his letter, and to begin his duties in January 1941. Russell hoped to base a book on the subject matter of his lectures, which were to comprise a single course running over the five-year term of his engagement, and Barnes was very much taken up with the idea. While Barnes was performing a great service to Russell he was well aware of the benefit accruing to the Foundation from the appointment. He acknowledged this fact in a letter to Patricia Russell on 28 August 1940:

'. . . Bertrand can put us on the intellectual-educational map in a manner I have long wished for; we can give him an opportunity to fulfil his heart's desire; and woe be to those who attempt to pull off another stunt like that of recent times in New York.'

Russell was relieved to have solved his problems, and wrote to Lucy Donnelly:[26] 'I have accepted the Barnes institute; there was no other prospect of any post, however humble. No university dare contemplate employing me.'

Russell revealed the state of his anxiety, at this time, in his *Autobiography*:[27]

'Until he [Barnes] gave me this appointment I had seen no way out of my troubles. I could not get money out of England; it was impossible to return to England; I certainly did not wish my three children to go back into the Blitz, even if I could have got a passage for them, which would certainly have been impossible for a long time to come. It seemed as if it would be necessary to take John and Kate away from the university, and to live as cheaply as possible on the charity of kind friends. From this bleak prospect I was saved by Dr Barnes.'

As the war progressed, Russell became more certain of his own attitude towards it, and he found that he was able to give clearer expression to his views as a result of the German–Soviet non-aggression pact of

August 1939. In reply to a letter from Gilbert Murray[28] Russell wrote on 6 September:[29]

'I quite agree with what you say . . . The issue became clear when Russia turned against us. Last time the alliance with the Tsar confused the issue.

'Sympathy in this country is growing more and more emphatic on our side. My belief is that, if we pull through this month, we shall win. But I am not optimistic as to the sort of world that the war will leave.'

Meanwhile, Barnes was eager to be of whatever service he could to Russell. On his return to Philadelphia he immediately launched into the practical activity of arranging a house and furnishings for the Russells. Russell wrote to Barnes on 24 August; in a tactful attempt to restrain his enthusiasm:[30]

'Thank you very much for your kind letter of 21 August. It is very good of you to be taking so much trouble on our behalf, and when we come East your preliminary search [for a house] will be a great help to us.

'There are, however, some points that I should like to put to you, as I am afraid that your enthusiasm for lovely places may lead to your not quite realising my circumstances. In the first place, it is *impossible* for us to buy: I cannot get money from England, and have here only what I have saved during the last twenty months. In the second place, I shall, out of $6,000 a year, have to keep my two older children at the university, and perhaps spend money on refugee children; I must therefore have a house which not only has a low rental, but is cheap to run and requires little service. I should not know what to do with sixty or seventy acres of farmland. It is much more important to my happiness to live within my means than to live in a beautiful house; and it is essential both to my wife and to myself to reduce the machinery of life to a minimum.

'Choosing a house is a very personal matter, like choosing a wife. I know that in China the latter is done by proxy, but although people make mistakes, we are apt to prefer our own folly to the wisdom of others. We should neither of us wish to decide on a house until we have seen a considerable selection. I am deeply touched at your even contemplating spending $35,000 on the matter, but I am sure we can be happy at very much lower cost, and we could not possibly pay a rent corresponding to such a price, so that, in effect, you would be paying me a bigger salary than was agreed upon.

'Your offer to pay the fare of one of us to fly East is, again, extraordinarily kind. But we are leaving here very soon, and my wife, at least, will be in Philadelphia about 13 September. . . .

'Buying furniture is great fun and I hate to disappoint your kindly impulse, but we have enough furniture coming from England. . . .

'I am very much afraid all this may sound ungracious, but it is not so intended. . . . What you have already done in giving me the post is so much that no more is needed to secure my life-long gratitude. . . .

'P.S. . . . When my wife first gets to Philadelphia, she will be staying with some very old friends of ours.'[31]

Relaxed from his summer holiday, and with the Barnes Foundation appointment to look forward to, Russell arrived at Harvard at the beginning of October to deliver his course of William James lectures. The Harvard *Crimson* of 2 October 1940 reported:

'Spick and span in gray suit, blue shirt and tie, and looking in the best of ruddy British spirits, Bertrand Russell came back to Harvard yesterday for his first long visit since 1914. . . .'

Russell's lectures at Harvard derived from *An Inquiry into Meaning and Truth* which was the fruit of his successive courses at Oxford, Chicago and California. In the book's preface, Russell acknowledged his debt to both professors and pupils at the two American universities who, 'by detailed friendly criticism, helped (I hope) in the avoidance of errors and fallacies'. On the title page of the book, he took the unusual step of listing at length his academic qualifications and honours,[32] and concluded with the declaration: 'Judicially pronounced unworthy to be Professor of Philosophy at the College of the City of New York (1940).'

Barnes continued to provide for Russell's arrival at the Foundation. During October, he raised Russell's salary to $8,000 to relieve him of the necessity of touring the country giving public lectures;[33] although this did not preclude Russell from giving such lectures if he wished. Barnes wrote to Russell on 1 November, informing him of the interest in his lectures, and apologising for a disagreement he had with Patricia Russell (who was called 'Peter' by her friends), over his efforts to assist with the Russells domestic arrangements:[34]

'. . . I'm in a quandary about your classes—we're swamped with applications from outsiders, some of them of the right sort. What I'd like you to tell me is—how many students do you prefer to have? We limit our classes to twenty, but prefer fifteen. I'll leave the decision entirely in your hands. Another question: would a rapid-fire stenographer to take down what you say, help you in the later job of the book? If it will, I'll engage one. . . .

'P.S. I had a fight with Peter. Kiss her for me and tell her I hope to make amends for all the crimes I've committed.'

Russell arrived at the Barnes Foundation on the first day of 1941, with Barnes reiterating: 'the sky's the limit on what you may say here.'[35] Russell settled down to perform his duties:[36]

'We rented a farmhouse about thirty miles from Philadelphia, a very charming house, about 200 years old, in rolling country, not unlike inland Dorsetshire. There was an orchard, a fine old barn, and three peach trees, which bore enormous quantities of the most delicious peaches I have ever tasted. There were fields sloping down to a river, and pleasant woodlands. We were ten miles from Paoli (called after the Corsican patriot), which was the limit of the Philadelphia surburban trains. From there I used to go by train to the Barnes Foundation, where I lectured in a gallery of modern French paintings, mostly of nudes, which seemed somewhat incongruous for academic philosophy.'

Russell had his lectures moved to a smaller gallery explaining that 'so many nudes are distracting to a philosopher lecturing on philosophy'.[37]

Russell was clearly pleased with his position and wrote to Gilbert Murray from his new home, Little Datchet Farm, Malvern, on 18 January 1941:[38]

'. . . I am now established in a small country house, 200 years old— very ancient for this part of the world—in lovely country, with pleasant work. If the world were at peace I could be very happy.

'As to the future: it seems to me that if we win, we shall win completely; I cannot think the Nazis will survive. America will dominate, and will probably not withdraw as in 1919; America will not be war-weary, and will believe resolutely in the degree of democracy that exists here. I am accordingly fairly optimistic. . . .

'Opinion here varies with the longitude. In the East, people are passionately pro-English; we are treated with extra kindness in shops as soon as people notice our accent. In California they are anti-Japanese but not pro-English; in the Middle-West they were rather anti-English. But everywhere opinion is very rapidly coming over to the conviction that we must not be defeated.

'It is rather dreadful to be out of it all . . .'

During the period of American neutrality in the war, Russell's views were often misconstrued, and he wrote a letter to *The New York Times* which was published on 27 January 1941 under the heading: 'Dr Russell Denies Pacifism':

'You print today [23 January] an Associated Press report saying: "Although I have preached pacifism all my life, I am now convinced for the first time that freedom cannot be preserved without military struggle."

'This report is seriously inaccurate. In fact, I did not make this statement or any having the same meaning.

'It is not true that I have preached pacifism all my life or that I have ever been what is called a pacifist. I have not changed my opinion about war. My opinion about war is exactly what it always was: that war is sometimes justified and sometimes not.

'I am weary of hearing it stated, even by my friends, that I was imprisoned in the last war "for my faith". I opposed the last war because it appeared to me that it was one of the wars which are unjustified. Both sides had imperialist aims, no important principle was at stake and the effects would be disastrous for the world.

'Throughout the war of 1914–18 I attempted to make it clear that there were wars in the past, for example the War of American Independence, which I considered worth fighting and beneficial in their effects, and that I could imagine wars in the future in which I should be prepared to fight.

'With regard to the present war: I opposed it in advance because although I thought that in this case there was a principle worth fighting for, the information that I had been able to collect convinced me that this principle could not be preserved by war. Many Englishmen shared this view. It appeared likely that modern war would be so frightful as to be worse than conquest by Hitler. But while the war, though bad enough, has proved less terrible than we expected, conquest by Hitler has in many countries proved even worse.

'It was soon after the conquest of Poland that I decided and publicly announced that I wished to support the war in any way that I could. If I were younger I would have volunteered.'

Because he was too old to enlist, Russell endeavoured in this period, as he had on many previous occasions, to make a contribution to the war effort. Edith Russell (née Finch), looking back on that time, recalls Russell telling her how his persistent offers of his services to British officials had been rejected:[39]

'It seemed to many of us odd that he was not used as a speaker, since he was in much demand as such. And, of course, when he returned to England he was used. However, in all cases he was turned down flat. When he discussed with the said consuls and officials the possibility of his returning to England to help, he was turned down even flatter, being told that he was far too old to be in any way useful and would merely be an added liability and another mouth to feed, etc., etc. He was, in short and in slightly more polished terms, advised that the only way for him to help was to shut up and keep out of it. It is not hard to imagine the burning pain that all this must have caused him.'

Although Russell's feelings were centred upon Britain's imperilled situation, he managed to exercise immense self-discipline in applying himself to his daily professional tasks.

Barnes, well pleased with Russell's lectures at the Foundation, wrote to him on 13 March 1941:[40]

'My associate . . . told me of his conversation with you and asked if I had anything to suggest to facilitate your wish to get a "closer contact with the students" in your class. I know of nothing better than what you are doing but if you would like to try any other plan, you have only to do it without consulting anybody here.

'One thing I can say in all sincerity is that your lectures are doing more for those students than you think or what I thought anybody could do—it's no easy job to jump into a group of mixed and very different backgrounds and create in all of them a genuine interest that makes [them] go into the subject further on their own in an effort to link up what you give with what the other teachers put over in their own classes. Moreover, you've endeared yourself to all of them and if I were a Frenchman I'd kiss you on both cheeks for the benefit you've brought to our efforts to do something worthwhile. Don't you worry about your work here: take it in your stride of living a peaceful, carefree life, and if I can further that wish in any way, you may count on me to do it.'

The congenial conditions of Russell's life only served to sharpen his intense feelings for war-stricken Britain. He wrote to Gilbert Murray on 18 June 1941:[41]

'. . . Life here, with the job I have, would be very pleasant if there were no war. . . . My work is interesting and moderate in amount. But it all seems unreal. Fierceness surges round, and everybody seems doomed to grow fierce sooner or later. It is hard to feel that anything is worth-while, except actual resistance to Hitler, in which I have no chance to take a part. We have English friends who are going back to England, and we envy them, because they are going to something that feels important. I try to think it is worth-while to remain civilised, but it seems rather thin. I admire English resistance with all my soul, but hate not to be part of it.'

If Russell was in any way consoled by his pleasant surroundings, subsequent events at the Foundation were to mar whatever advantages he enjoyed. In his introduction to *The Bertrand Russell Case*, which was first published in June 1941, John Dewey reported that Dr Barnes had engaged Russell and that 'Russell's lectureship is now progressing successfully and to the satisfaction of all concerned.'[42] But Russell found his benefactor 'a strange character' who 'demanded constant flattery and had a passion for quarrelling'.[43] Since Russell tended to keep very much to himself (according to *Time* magazine he 'did not intend to become as cosy as John Dewey', who the magazine, consistent with its style, alleged was Barnes's 'favorite, and frequent drinking companion'),[44] it is perhaps understandable that Barnes should have become disappointed over his relationship with the Russells. A rift opened between Barnes and Russell, but the situation that developed between Barnes and Russell's wife approached the level of a feud. When she used her title in her dealings with the Foundation, Barnes publicly retorted: 'She seems to have difficulty swallowing the impressive title of Lady Russell. It evidently gets stuck just below her larynx for she regurgitates it automatically.'[45] Patricia Russell began to take her husband to work by car, and on occasions stayed on to be present at his lectures. Her presence caused a great deal of irritation at the Foundation; a major irritant was the fact that she was accustomed to knit during the lectures (which she did for destitute children in England). According to Barnes:[46]

'On one occasion she burst into the building and created a scene by a loud and imperious command to one of the members of the Board of Trustees. This tantrum was one of a series of disturbing events which began soon after Mr Russell's course started and recurred frequently. A rising tide of complaints from members of the class testified that the normal management of the Foundation's affairs was being disrupted by her disorderly conduct. . . .'

The Trustees of the Foundation wrote to Patricia Russell on 31 October 1941, claiming that 'your constant movements in knitting during the course of the lecture were annoying and a distraction from attention to the speaker'. It was also noted that 'your occasional attendance at the class was a violation of the regulation governing that matter.' The letter went on to prohibit her from entering the Foundation's premises:[47]

'The Foundation has never been a place where people may drop in occasionally, at their own volition, nor is any person whosoever allowed to do things that interfere with the rights of others or are harmful to the Foundation's interests. Admission to the gallery is restricted to persons enrolled in the classes. . . .'

In reply to the Foundation, Patricia Russell wrote on 1 November:[48]

'. . . As for my knitting: it was with some hesitation that I took it with me—on two or perhaps three occasions—to the Barnes Foundation; but when I consulted my husband he remarked that I had disturbed no one by knitting at far more difficult and technical lectures at the Universities of Oxford, Chicago, California, and Harvard, and that therefore I might assume that I would be giving no offence. I am distressed that in fact I did disturb someone, and would be glad if you would convey to all the students my sincere apologies.'

The letter concluded: 'I marvel . . . that anyone should wish, in a world so full of mountains of hostility, to magnify so grandiloquently so petty a molehill.'

Russell also wrote to the Trustees on 1 November 1941:

'The letter written on your behalf to my wife is astonishing by its incivility. I fail to see why what you wished to convey could not have been said orally without formality and completely unnecessary rudeness. I had not before understood that my wife was not allowed at my lectures; I do not now understand why I was not informed of this. I regret that by asking her to be present I infringed, by ignorance or by oversight, the rules of the Foundation.'

The Board of Trustees, in the person of its secretary, Miss N. E. Mullen, replied to Patricia Russell on 5 November, addressing her as 'Dear Madam':[49]

'. . . It was sweet of you to tell us . . . how low-class the Foundation is compared to Oxford, Harvard, etc.—in short, that a superior, well-bred, learned, charitable, kind-hearted soul should not be informed by barbarians that her presence in their midst is undesirable. How to bear up under the disgrace is our most serious problem at the moment.'

Russell apologised to his class for his wife's knitting, mentioning that they had encountered no objection to her presence at the various universities he had lectured at. Barnes, who was generally present at all Russell's classes, asked: 'Mr Russell, in saying that Oxford, Harvard and Chicago did not object to your wife's presence at your lectures, do you mean to imply that there is something wrong with the way the Foundation conducts its affairs?'[50] Russell replied in the negative.

Somehow, Barnes hoped to remain on good terms with Russell. He wrote to Russell assuring him that everyone at the Foundation liked him, but asked him to understand 'that when we engaged you to teach we did not obligate ourselves to endure forever the trouble-making propensities of your wife.'[51]

Russell lost no time in replying:[52]

'. . . I shall continue to do all in my power (including utilisation of my wife's valuable help in research) to make my lectures as good as I am able to make them, but so far as any personal relationship is concerned, you are mistaken in supposing that there is no quarrel with me, since whoever quarrels with my wife quarrels with me.'

Barnes closed the exchange of letters with the parting shot:[53]

'Your statement "including utilisation of my wife's valuable help in research" is a pure gratuity in the present controversy, unless you mean by that, that your wife will, if you so wish, perform that service on our premises. If that is what you mean, I feel that you should be informed beforehand that if your wife ever enters the door of our gallery, the "whitehaired lady" whom she tried to bully on 27 February[54] has been informed officially how to deal with the situation.'

Barnes summed up his handling of the situation by declaring, for all those who were interested, that: 'the question Mrs Russell forced us to settle was whether autocracy or democracy was to prevail in the conduct of the Foundation's affairs.' And he concluded: 'we voted unanimously in favor of democracy.'[55]

Russell continued to lecture throughout 1942. With Patricia Russell barred from the establishment, Dr Barnes's one cause of complaint had apparently been removed. The *Saturday Evening Post* in covering Dr Barnes's life story, ran an article by Carl W. McCardle, in four weekly instalments, from 21 March 1942, entitled 'The Terrible-Tempered Dr Barnes'. The 4 April instalment was devoted to the Russell–Barnes controversy, and the solution that had been arrived at. McCardle commented: 'If you suppose that this ended the Russell lectures, you are mistaken; he goes on quite merrily. And it has not altered Barnes's estimate of the quality of Russell's teaching or its value to the Foundation.'

McCardle gave the *Post*'s readers an account of Russell's lectures, and a view of the manner in which 'democracy' was practised at the Foundation:

'In English that is a model of simplicity, Russell makes his subject understandable and rather exciting to those even who may never have heard of Pythagoras or can't tell Aristotle from Plato. He painstakingly writes out difficult names and subject matter on an old-fashioned blackboard like a rural pedagogue. Now and then he discusses the sex life of some ancient civilisation with frankness. After his lectures, the class besieges him with questions. One of Barnes's assistants keeps close tab on these questions. If a student persists in asking flippant or irrelevant questions, his membership in the class is short-lived.'

According to William Schack, author of *Art and Argyrol*, a biography of Barnes, an 'uneasy truce' prevailed between the two men. 'Economic necessity' compelled Russell to remain at his post, and: 'If the thought inevitably occurred to Barnes to let Russell go, he was deterred by the [legal] contract and, more strongly perhaps, by what Dewey and his friends might say of him. . . .'[56]

After America's entry into the war, Russell at last found a way of contributing to the war effort. In the United States there was at this time a good deal of anti-British sentiment over Britain's policy in India. The Americans, fighting a desperate battle against the Japanese, saw the need to totally mobilise India for the allied cause. This was of course not possible while Britain refused to grant India independence. Russell who had always argued that 'India should be free of all foreign domination', nevertheless felt that under war-time circumstances, India's leaders 'should be persuaded to end the civil disobedience movement and co-operate in negotiations',[57] with the British. With the encouragement of the writer Pearl Buck, who informed Russell that 'here in America we have not been allowed to hear dissenting voices in England and the sort of official Englishman we have here, and all his propaganda, does little or nothing to mend the rift in the common man',[58] he began to give public lectures on India which aimed at promoting Anglo–American understanding at a time when unity was imperative.

Russell's view was that international government was 'far and away the most important question at present before the world' and that the 'nucleus of any practicable plan will be Anglo–American co-operation.'[59] Russell also wished to bring pressure to bear on the British government to negotiate with the Indian leaders, and sought to do so via his liberal American audiences. Earlier in 1942 he had written to Gilbert Murray:[60]

'. . . You wrote about post-war reconstruction. I think the irruption of Japan has changed things. Anglo–American benevolent imperialism won't work: "Asia for the Asiatics" must be conceded. The only question is whether India and China shall be free or under Japan. If free, they will gravitate to Russia, which is Asiatic. There will be no cultural unity, and I doubt whether Russia and the U.S.A. can agree about any form of international government, or whether, if they nominally do, it will have any reality. I am much less hopeful of the post-war world than before Japan's successes.

'Very interesting struggles are going on in this country. The government is compelled to control the capitalists, and they, in turn, are trying to get the trade unions controlled. There is much more fear here than in England of "planned economy", which is thought socialistic and said to lead to fascism; and yet the necessities of the war compel it. Everybody in Washington realises that a great deal of planning will be necessary after the war, but the capitalists hope then to get back to *laissez-faire*. There may be a good deal of difficulty then. There is a great deal of rather fundamental change going on here, which is worth studying. But I wish I could be at home. . . .'

Russell lectured on India at Temple University and at the Rand

School of Social Science, which booked him to deliver weekly lectures of a popular nature from October to December 1942. One of the most important of the lectures he delivered at the Rand School was 'The Problem of Minorities'.[61] The lecture demonstrates Russell's intimate knowledge of America as well as his deeply felt concern for the plight of its minority groups. Russell was especially interested in the position of black Americans about whom he stated:

'The Negroes . . . represent the greatest failure of democracy in the United States, and until some justice is accorded to them it cannot be maintained that democracy exists here.'

Suggesting the remedies by which minorities could be fully and democratically integrated into American society, he proposed such measures as Federal protection; equal voting opportunities; industrial organisation as a means to achieving equality of opportunity and wages; equal education; a programme for abolishing social prejudice; and minority association. Russell strongly held the view:

'. . . what is vital is to bring about recognition of the solidarity of labour, whether white or black; for until there is this solidarity, employers can always defeat both the Negroes and white labour.'

He reminded his audience that: 'The war cannot be won by discriminatory methods, and it is a partial victory for Hitler when we imitate his race discrimination.' In summing up, Russell declared that 'the evils to be combated have two sources, on the one hand an imperfect acceptance of democracy, on the other hand a wrong understanding of it.' He asserted that every American citizen was a democrat in the sense of 'I am as good as you', but very few in the sense of 'you are as good as I am'.

Barnes, who had been looking for an opportunity to get rid of Russell, decided to regard these lectures as a breach of contract, explaining that in the view of 'legal experts', Russell 'had broken his contract by popular lecturing and by his upholding of Mrs Russell's disorderly conduct'.[62] On 28 December 1942, Russell received a letter from the Barnes Foundation giving him four days' notice:[63]

'For a long time past, our Board of Trustees has had under consideration certain events which have occurred since your contract with us was executed, and which seem to bear directly upon its validity. One of these events concerns the conditions which determined the modification of the terms of original contract with you.

'The details of the matter referred to have been carefully studied in their legal and ethical aspects by properly qualified disinterested persons. The legal factor in the situation—breach of contract—is the basis upon which our Board decided that the existing contract with you be terminated as of 31 December 1942. . . .'

Russell was 'reduced once again from affluence to destitution'. He consulted his lawyer and found that 'there was no doubt whatever of my getting full redress from the courts. But obtaining legal redress takes time, especially in America, and I had to live through the intervening period somehow.'[64] The Philadelphia *Record* quipped that Barnes should 'subsidise Russell so that a controversy enjoyed by all might be continued without undue hardship upon one of the principals'.[65]

Russell issued a statement to the press in which he made public his original letter of contract with the Barnes Foundation, and declared:

'In October 1940, Dr Barnes raised my salary by $2,000 to relieve me, as he said, of the *necessity* of touring the country giving public lectures. A new contract was drawn up, verbally identical with the old, but guaranteeing a salary of 8,000 instead of $6,000. No stipulation was ever made that I should refrain from doing such outside lectures as I wished to do. In November last, some newspapers, reporting my arrangements with Dr Barnes, stated, quoting him as their authority, that my contract precluded my doing outside lecturing. Dr Barnes contradicted this publicly at my request, and wrote to me that any outside lecturing I chose to do was entirely my own affair and had nothing to do with my contract with him.

'During the last year especially, I have done a good deal of lecturing largely unpaid or for nominal fees, on questions that seemed to me of public importance, especially the Indian problem, and have regarded this as war work. On 28 December of last year, I received a letter from the Secretary of the Barnes Foundation, terminating my contract as from 31 December, stating that I had broken the contract, but not explaining how, though it was implied that I had done so by doing other lecturing. I have carried out my contract exactly and have never missed a lecture. I have been told repeatedly both by Dr Barnes and the students that my lectures gave entire satisfaction. The only complaint that Dr Barnes has ever made against me during the two years that I have been in his employment was an objection to my having taken my wife to two or three of my lectures, when she sat at the back of the room knitting sweaters for bombed-out children. Since, however, my wife has not been to the gallery since she was told that her presence there was unwelcome, that is, since October 1941, this complaint, which was in any case absurd, can have no relevance to his having terminated my contract now.

'I intend to take legal action against the Barnes Foundation, and the matter is the hands of Mr Thomas Raeburn White, of White and Staples, in Philadelphia.'

Two years previously, Russell had written to the editor of *The New York Times*, clarifying his contractual arrangement with the Barnes

Foundation; Barnes had not found cause to contradict Russell's statement at the time. Russell's letter was dated 20 October 1940:

'In your issue of 20 October you state that I have accepted another appointment which makes an appeal in the matter of my College of the City of New York appointment unnecessary. You further state that I have entered into a contract with Dr Barnes which precludes my lecturing elsewhere.

'Both of these statements are untrue and I would be obliged if you would correct them. I have accepted Dr Barnes's invitation to lecture once a week for five years at the Barnes Foundation at Merion near Philadelphia. My duties at the Barnes Foundation would in no way conflict with the holding of a professorship at the College of the City of New York; and my contract with the Foundation leaves me complete freedom outside my weekly lecture there.'

Dr Barnes also issued a public statement, which he distributed to the press on 16 January 1943:

'It is true, as Mr Bertrand Russell says, that the Barnes Foundation has discharged him from its staff. It is true also that his lawyer has threatened to sue the Foundation for breach of contract: in reply to this, we told his attorney to go ahead with the suit.

'Mr Russell, in his statement to the press, runs true to his familiar form of presenting himself to the public as a martyr—just as he did when the British government put him in jail during the First World War. In the present case, he tells the public that he is a poor man deprived of his bread and butter by an arbitrary act; the *facts* are that he was dismissed for reasons which he really knows—for they are part of the record—but does not disclose. The letter of 23 December 1942, which discharged him, shows that both the legal and ethical phases of the matter were considered and approved by persons other than ourselves; it shows also that his alleged financial predicament is purely of his own making. . . .'

Alleging that 'Mr Russell's departure from the scene has been a welcome relief not only to the best of his students but to all members of our official and teaching staffs', Dr Barnes concluded:

'I did all that was possible to prevent Mr Russell from again opening the closet and once more parading his skeletons in public. However, since he insists, it would be un-American to put obstacles in his way.'

Russell sued Barnes for $24,000—the three years' earnings outstanding under his contract. Barnes attempted to show that Russell's external commitments had adversely effected his work for the Foundation. According to Russell:[66]

'When my case came into court, Dr Barnes complained that I had done insufficient work for my lectures, and that they were superficial and perfunctory. So far as they had gone, they consisted of the first two-thirds of my *History of Western Philosophy*, of which I submitted the manuscript to the judge, though I scarcely suppose he read it. Dr Barnes complained of my treatment of the men whom he called Pithergawras and Empi-Dokkles. I observed the judge taking notice, and I won my case. Dr Barnes, of course, appealed as often as he could, and it was not until I was back in England that I actually got the money.'

The court awarded Russell $20,000; the amount he had sued for, less his expected earnings from public lectures for the remaining period of his contract. Barnes reacted by publishing a pamphlet which he called *The Case of Bertrand Russell versus Democracy and Education*, in which he asserted that Russell 'had no conception of democracy as a sharing in significant experience', and that if his students learnt anything about democracy from him, 'it was because he presented them with the perfect example of its antithesis'.[67] Russell 'never read this document' (which Barnes sent to the Master and all the Fellows of Trinity College), but commented: 'I have no doubt it was good reading.'[68]

Despite Barnes's claim about the attitude of Russell's students, many, notwithstanding their dependence on the Foundation, offered Russell their sympathy and, in some cases, their support. Barrows Dunham, the philosopher who on the invitation of Barnes had been attending Russell's lectures, wrote to Russell on 24 January 1943:

'. . . I have talked with several members of your class who feel that something should be done, but are not in a position to appear publicly on the issue themselves. They have, however, been energetically spreading abroad the true facts of the case. . . . Please be sure that I will do anything I can to help you. There is nothing that Dr Barnes can do, short of murder, that I would be afraid of.'

Looking back on that period, over thirty years later, Barrows Dunham describes the events that took place at the Barnes Foundation during the period of Russell's lectureship:

'The first of these lectures, if I remember correctly, was sometime in January of 1941. There were about sixty people in the class, of whom I was the only "professional" philosopher. Russell talked for about an hour, and then asked if there were any questions or remarks. Silence. He asked again. Again silence. We were all in awe of the great man—I perhaps more than any of the others. Nobody wanted to risk saying something silly. So then Dr Barnes proclaimed an end to the proceedings. Russell was taken into an office to be interviewed and photographed by the press. Meanwhile, Dr Barnes came over to me, took me by the lapels, hammered on my chest, and said: "Why didn't you fight him?" This was meant as banter in Barnes's heavy style (he was no wit). I suppose he could hardly have guessed what a youngish professor would do in the presence of fame.

'I'm not clear about dates any longer, but I think it was sometime early in 1942 that Barnes fell out with Patricia Russell. The story was that she had expressed dislike or incomprehension of the paintings in the collection. The collection is, to be sure, magnificent, but one was required to regard the things in it as if they had been the relics of saints. Barnes was an anarchist as against other authority, but a tyrant within his own realm. This tyranny rather obscured the fact that his taste in painting (or in painting from Manet to Matisse) was very nearly impeccable.

'Barnes had an extraordinary lack of talent (if one can have a "lack") for explaining or justifying his actions. I think that any psychoanalyst would have recognised at once that he was a hostile man, and no doubt you'd have to dig into his childhood to find the source. My guess is that the primitive hostility blighted his exegetical powers. At any rate, the reason he publicly gave for forbidding Patricia access to the Foundation was that her knitting disturbed the lectures. This was nonsense, and, even if it had been true, was trivial. She sat on the back row, on a folding chair (Barnes sat enthroned in a large armchair); and the only distraction she can have caused was due to her beauty. I am free to admit that I looked back more than once. Anyway, the newspapers had a fine time about this, and for a while Patricia would drop Russell off at the gate she was not allowed to enter. Then, during the last months, Russell would take the "Paoli Local" (a famous series of trains in these parts) from Paoli to Merion, walk to the Foundation (perhaps half a mile), and walk back when he did not have a ride (as I sometimes gave him). There was a painful afternoon when he arrived breathless and red in the face, not quite on time. The climax was approaching, and he feared giving Barnes a more convincing reason for dismissing him. I did not then know how far the struggle had gone, but I well remember the dismay I felt at seeing the leading philosopher of the English-speaking world in such a plight.

'One then had to offer support. My wife and I had had the Russells to tea during the series, and we now had them again. They talked about the abusive letters that Barnes had written them. . . . Some time later, we had tea with the Russells at their home in Malvern. Barnes was the owner of this house, and they were paying rent. They said that Barnes wanted them to buy it on a twenty-four-year mortgage. Russell was then seventy. The odd thing is that he lived long enough to have paid that off, whereas Barnes would have died long before collecting it. Anyway, the Russells refused to buy, and, since that was a crossing of the Barnes will, the refusal may have been one other cause of the ultimate dismissal.

'When the dismissal came, Barnes made use of his henchmen, who were all henchwomen (an odd lot, mostly with bulldog faces), to abuse Russell in the press. One of these was a lady named R. D. Bulley (one never knew what the initials stood for). She said the lectures had been dull. I thereupon thought that somebody in the class ought to say something publicly, and it seemed obvious that the somebody had to be myself. That's what my letter of 24 January 1943 is about. I thereupon sent a letter to the Philadelphia newspapers, only one of which printed it (the *Philadelphia Inquirer*). The letter concluded with a remark that: "Other people have found Russell to be dangerous, but R. D. Bulley is the first to find him dull." When this letter had appeared, one of my colleagues at Temple University came to me to say that Dr Barnes was very angry. Well, nothing came of that.

'My own position in the affair was a little awkward. Barnes had been extremely kind to me. I was in his debt. But it was of course quite impossible to think that such an indebtedness could outweigh the defense of a great philosopher.'

Russell's *History of Western Philosophy*, which formed the basis of his lectures at the Barnes Foundation, was published in America in 1945. It was one of his most important and successful works, 'and proved the main source of my income for many years . . . even, for a time, shining high upon the American list of best sellers'.[69] In the preface to the book, Russell wrote:

'This book owes its existence to Dr Albert C. Barnes, having been originally designed and partly delivered as lectures at the Barnes Foundation in Pennsylvania.

'As in most of my work during the years since 1932, I have been greatly assisted in research and in many other ways by my wife, Patricia Russell.'

NOTES

[1] B. Russell, *Autobiography* (London, 1968), Vol. II, p. 219 (Boston, 1968), pp. 334–5.

[2] Rev. I. R. Wall.

[3] The *Daily Bruin* (U.C.L.A. newspaper) (3 May 1940).

[4] P. Edwards, 'The Bertrand Russell Case', appendix to Russell's *Why I Am Not a Christian, and Other Essays* (London and Simon & Schuster, New York, 1957), p. 189.

[5] Ibid., p. 220.

[6] The Harvard *Crimson* (29 April 1940).

[7] B. Russell, *Autobiography*, Vol. II, p. 221; p. 337.

[8] Ibid., pp. 229–31; pp. 351–3.

[9] Ibid., pp. 231–2; pp. 353–5; see also Dewey's letter to Hocking, ibid., pp. 233–5; pp. 358–60.

[10] Ibid., pp. 232–3; pp. 355–6.

[11] See below, pp. 299–307.

[12] See below, pp. 308–14.

[13] B. Russell, *Autobiography*, Vol. II, p. 192; p. 288.

[14] Ibid., p. 191; p. 287.

[15] From Edith Russell's letter to Barry Feinberg of 16 April 1972.

[16] B. Russell, *Autobiography*, Vol. II, pp. 246–7; pp. 379–80.

[17] Ibid., p. 233; p. 357.

[18] Ibid., pp. 240–1; pp. 369–70.

[19] The New York *Daily News* (11 June 1940).

[20] The Los Angeles *Times* (22 May 1940).

[21] B. Russell, *Autobiography*, Vol. II, pp. 220–1; pp. 335–6.

[22] Ibid., p. 221; pp. 337–8.

[23] William Schack, *Art and Argyrol: The Life and Career of Dr Albert C. Barnes* (Thomas Yoseloff, New York, 1960), p. 324.

[24] From Barnes's letter to Russell of 22 October 1940.

[25] Part of this letter appears in Schack, op. cit., pp. 324–5.

[26] From Russell's letter of 25 August 1940.

[27] B. Russell, *Autobiography*, Vol. II, p. 220; p. 335.

[28] Ibid., pp. 247–8; pp. 380–1.

[29] Ibid., p. 248; pp 381–2.

[30] Schack, op. cit., pp. 326–7.

[31] Lucy Donnelly.

[32] See Illustrations, Plate 24, p. 212.

[33] Russell's letter to *The New York Times*, see below, p. 194.

[34] Part of this letter appears in Schack, op. cit., p. 327.

[35] Carl W. McCardle, 'The Terrible-Tempered Dr Barnes', *Saturday Evening Post* (4 April 1942).

[36] B. Russell, *Autobiography*, Vol. II, p. 221; p. 338.

[37] McCardle, op. cit.

[38] B. Russell, *Autobiography*, Vol. II, pp. 248–9; pp. 382–4.

[39] From Edith Russell's letter to Barry Feinberg of 16 April 1972.

[40] Schack, op. cit., pp. 327–8.

[41] B. Russell, *Autobiography*, Vol. II, pp. 249–50; pp. 384–5.

[42] John Dewey and Horace M. Kallen, *The Bertrand Russell Case* (Viking Press, New York, 1941), p. 7.

[43] B. Russell, *Autobiography*, Vol. II, p. 221; p. 337.

44 *Time* magazine, 'Russell Tussle' (1 February 1943), p. 56.

45 Ibid.

46 Schack, op. cit., p. 329.

47 McCardle, op. cit.

48 Ibid., pp. 330–2.

49 Partly quoted by McCardle, op. cit.

50 Ibid.

51 Ibid.

52 Schack, op. cit., pp. 333–4.

53 Partly quoted by McCardle, op. cit.

54 The 'whitehaired lady' was Miss Mullen, the Barnes Foundation secretary. The incident on 27 February is also referred to by Barnes (see above, footnote 46, p. 188). For Patricia Russell's version, compare Schack, op. cit., pp. 330–2.

55 McCardle, op. cit.

56 Schack, op. cit., p. 343.

57 B. Russell, *Autobiography*, Vol. II, p. 256; p. 395.

58 Ibid., p. 255; pp. 393–5; the letter is dated 23 October 1942.

59 From Russell's letter to Ely Culbertson, the bridge expert, of 12 January 1942. For full text, see B. Russell, *Autobiography*, Vol. II, pp. 253–4; pp. 390–3.

60 From Russell's letter of 23 March 1942. For full text, see B. Russell, *Autobiography*, Vol. II, pp. 250–1; pp. 385–7.

61 Previously unpublished; see below, pp. 315–27.

62 Schack, op. cit., p. 347.

63 Ibid., p. 328.

64 B. Russell, *Autobiography*, Vol. II, p. 221; p. 338.

65 Quoted by *Time* magazine, op. cit.

66 B. Russell, *Autobiography*, Vol. II, p. 222; p. 338.

67 Schack, op. cit., p. 351.

68 B. Russell, *Autobiography*, Vol. II, p. 222; p. 339.

69 Ibid., p. 223; p. 340.

CHAPTER 14

GETTING BACK TO ENGLAND

While he was completing *History of Western Philosophy*, Russell spent considerable time at Bryn Mawr College, where the library facilities were made available to him. His immediate problems, following his dismissal from the Barnes Foundation, were financial, but these he managed to overcome:[1]

'In the early months of 1943 I suffered some financial stringency, but not so much as I had feared. We sub-let our nice farmhouse, and went to live in a cottage intended for a coloured couple whom it was expected that the inhabitants of the farmhouse would employ. This consisted of three rooms and three stoves, each of which had to be stoked every hour or so. One was to warm the place, one was for cooking, and one was for hot water. When they went out it was several hours' work to get them lighted again. Conrad could hear every word that Peter and I said to each other, and we had many worrying things to discuss which it was not good for him to be troubled with. But by this time the trouble about City College had begun to blow over, and I was able to get occasional lecture engagements in New York and other places. The embargo was first broken by an invitation from Professor Weiss of Bryn Mawr to give a course of lectures there. This required no small degree of courage. On one occasion I was so poor that I had to take a single ticket to New York and pay the return fare out of my lecture fee. My *History of Western Philosophy* was nearly complete, and I wrote to W. W. Norton, who had been my American publisher, to ask if, in view of my difficult financial position, he would make an advance on it. He replied that because of his affection for John and Kate, and as a kindness to an old friend, he would advance five hundred dollars. I thought I could get more elsewhere, so I approached Simon and Schuster, who were unknown to me personally. They at once agreed to pay me two thousand dollars on the spot, and another thousand six months later. At this time John was at Harvard and Kate was at Radcliffe. I had been afraid that lack of funds might compel me to take them away, but thanks to Simon and Schuster, they proved unnecessary. I was also helped at this time by loans from private friends which, fortunately, I was able to repay before long.'

At Bryn Mawr Russell found the relaxed atmosphere he needed for his work. In addition, he enjoyed the friendship of Lucy Donnelly and Edith Finch. Apart from *History of Western Philosophy*, Russell had become occupied with an extensive study of epistemology[2] which formed the subject of his course of lectures at Bryn Mawr. Professor Paul Weiss, writing for the *Bryn Mawr Alumnae Bulletin*, of December 1943, drew attention to an anonymous gift which helped sponsor Russell's lectures:

'Bertrand Russell, an old friend of the College—Bryn Mawr was the first college in this country he ever addressed—has been living in this vicinity for the last few years. He could be seen occasionally sitting under the ash in front of the library reading detective stories or in the library stacks looking up more esoteric works and sometimes could be encountered by an occasional student or member of the faculty at the home of his old friend, Miss Lucy Donnelly. But his presence was not known to the College at large.

'The Philosophy Department was, however, recently the fortunate recipient of an anonymous gift from a generous and interested alumna, permitting it to invite Bertrand Russell this semester to give a series of five lectures on the Postulates of Scientific Method. Russell has the great gift of speaking on difficult issues with great clarity and persuasiveness, enlivening the whole with flashes of wit and striking illustrations. The lectures were a tremendous success. Despite torrential rains, students, faculty and others came from Swarthmore, Haverford and Philadelphia in considerable and increasing numbers. His ideas and personality, his comments and illustrations have been discussed widely and vehemently in the classes and in the halls.

'The present series, a portion of a large work with which Russell is now occupied, attempts to find the presuppositions on which a reliable physics can be built. . . . The Philosophy Department is grateful for the opportunity it had to enable Bryn Mawr once again to be a center of thought and discussion for the community.'

By this stage Russell had been in the United States for five years, after having only planned for a stay of short duration. His situation was becoming easier; his two elder children, almost independent; and he was more than ever resolved to return home. Some of his friends in England, with whom he had infrequent contact, were under the impression, reinforced by inaccurate reports, that he had settled permanently in the United States. Beatrice Webb had written to Russell on 17 December 1942:[3]

'I was so glad to see in that remarkable book—*I Meet America*—by W. J. Brown, M.P., that you were not only intent on winning the war but wished to reconstruct the world after the war. We were also very much interested that you had decided to remain in the U.S.A. and to encourage your son to make his career there rather than in Great Britain. If you were not a peer of the realm and your son a possible great statesman like his great grandfather, I should think it was a wise decision but we want you both back in Great Britain since you are part and parcel of the parliamentary government of our democracy. Also I should think teachers who were also British peers were at some slight disadvantage in the U.S.A. so far as a public career is concerned as they would attract snobs and offend the labour movement? But of course I may be wrong....

'Whether you stay in the U.S.A. or not, I do hope you and your two clever young people will pay a visit to Great Britain and that we shall have the pleasure of seeing you and your wife. Pray give her my greetings; I wonder how she likes America.

'P.S. I don't think you know our nephew Sir Stafford Cripps—but he represents a new movement growing up in Great Britain. . . . He left the Cabinet over India!'

Russell, then still at Little Datchet Farm, replied to Beatrice Webb on 31 January 1943:[4]

'. . . I don't know what gave W. J. Brown the idea that I meant to settle in America. I have never at any time thought of doing such a thing. At first I came for eight months, then jobs came in my way. Then, with the war, I thought it better for Conrad (now aged 5) to be here. But all these reasons are nearing their end.

'John (Amberley) is finished with Harvard, and returning to England in a few days to go into the navy if he can, and, if not, the army. My daughter Kate is at Radcliffe; she always does as well as possible in everything she studies. Her hope, after the war, is to get into some kind of relief work on the Continent. I myself am kept here for the moment by various engagements, but I may come home fairly soon, leaving Peter and Conrad here till the end of the war.

'I was much disappointed that India rejected Cripps's offer. People here are ignorant about India, but have strong opinions. I have been speaking and writing to try to overcome anti-English feeling as regards India, which in some quarters is very strong.

'Thank you very much for your most interesting booklet on Russia. Whether one likes the regime or not, one can't help immensely admiring the Russian achievement in the war.

'I do hope to see you again when I get back to England. . . .'

In his book, W. J. Brown, a British trade unionist who had visited

America, diarised a meeting with Russell on 29 November 1941:[5]

'I go for lunch to Culbertson's,[6] where Bertrand Russell joins us. His spare figure is shrunken, and he has aged a good deal since I last saw him. But the fine precise mind and the measured articulation are as pronounced as ever. He is hungry for news and impressions of life in Britain, and is conscious that he is missing a great experience in being out of it. But he says that economic circumstances make it necessary for him to stay here. . . . Russell's old pacifism is completely gone. He would like to see America in the war, preferably via Japan, and is quite reconciled to the view that any world order must be imposed by force and rest on force as its final sanction.'

Russell wrote to Gilbert Murray on 9 April 1943 with news of his intention to return to England and of his desire to continue working for Anglo–American understanding:[7]

'Thank you for your letter . . . about Barnes. He is a man who likes quarrels; for no reason that I can fathom, he suddenly broke his contract with me. In the end, probably, I shall get damages out of him; but the law's delays are as great as in Shakespeare's time. Various things I have undertaken to do will keep me here till the end of October; then (D.V.) I shall return to England—Peter and Conrad too, if the danger from submarines is not too great. We can't bear being away from home any longer. In England I shall have to find some means of earning a livelihood. I should be quite willing to do government propaganda, as my views on this war are quite orthodox. I wish I could find a way of making my knowledge of America useful; I find that English people, when they try to please American opinion, are very apt to make mistakes. . . .

'One reason for coming home is that we don't want to send Conrad to an American school. Not only is the teaching bad, but the intense nationalism is likely to cause in his mind a harmful conflict between home and school.[8] We think submarines, bombs and poor diet a smaller danger. But all this is still somewhat undecided. . . .'

Russell began to grapple with the problem of Britain and America's relationship, and the requirements for securing international peace. The *New Leader* of 4 December 1943 published an article of his, entitled 'England and America—The Problem of Unity or Imperialist Rivalry', in which Russell discussed the reasons leading the British to side with the United States. He supported the consultations between the Allied leaders and stated: 'If peace is to be secure, a bargain will have to be struck between the three rival imperialisms of America, England and Russia. A beginning has been made at Moscow. . . .' Regarding the movement for independence in Asia, Russell declared:

'Russia will probably support this movement, and will thereby acquire a great advantage over England and America in all negotiations concerned with the Asiatic questions. It is possible, however, that the pan-Asiatic movement may become hostile to Russia as a white Power. I do not think this will happen, but it is a possibility to be borne in mind.' Russell was optimistic about the prospect for agreement between the Allied Powers, and wrote:

'There is reason to believe that the United States, the British Commonwealth, Russia and China will remain in alliance when peace is concluded, and will invite the other United Nations to join the alliance. Out of this, if all goes well, an effective international government may in time develop.'

Another article, 'Citizenship in a Great State', published the same month by *Fortune*, examined America's potential role to forge peace and progress in the world, but carried a warning:

'Under the guise of the pursuit of security, new-style imperialism is acquiring influential advocates in the U.S.A. Take, for example, the proposals submitted by Clarence Budington Kelland to the Republican Post-War Advisory Council. He proposes that America shall have a five-ocean navy, a big standing army, naval and air bases everywhere, and as many islands in the Pacific as may seem convenient. He says: "The Pacific Ocean must become an American lake." Mr Kelland's belief, no doubt sincerely held, is that the adoption of this policy would make America safe from attack. Unfortunately, as is the custom of imperialists the world over, he has not considered the reaction of other nations to such proposals, if they were ever put forward by the American government. It is obvious that Great Britain, Russia, and China would strenuously object: "We fought", they would say, "against enslavement by the Axis, and are equally ready to fight against enslavement by anybody else." In this they would have the sympathy of the whole world outside the U.S. The consequence would be that the five-ocean navy would prove too small and a new world war would result, with America in the role now played by Nazi Germany. I am convinced that very few Americans favor such tragic folly.'

Russell argued in favour of an alliance between the United States and Britain, which he foresaw as a step towards a truly international government. But the alliance should not remain exclusive for longer than was necessary:

'If it stood alone, it would substitute Anglo–American for pure American imperialism; those nations that did not profit by the alliance would oppose it, and the world would revert to the tug of war of balance-of-power politics. In this, as the history of four centuries has shown, there is no hope of lasting peace. While, therefore, an Anglo–American alliance may be a very useful step in the right direction, it should not be regarded as an end in itself. The alliance ought to be open to other nations on certain specified terms, and these terms should avoid every appearance of domination by the U.S. and Great Britain. . . .

'An Anglo–American alliance would not be so good a starting-point as an alliance including Russia and China, but it might be the best that would be possible. What is important is that there should be a group of Powers—as a minimum, the U.S. and the British Commonwealth; as a maximum, the United Nations—which should form itself into an organisation for the preservation of peace, intended to grow gradually and ultimately to become worldwide. This alliance should have a constitution, and should be at liberty to admit new members provided they were willing to abide by this constitution.

'The constitution should be mainly concerned to prevent war. It should be agreed that any State guilty of aggression against a member of the alliance should be the enemy of the alliance, and should be attacked by the collective forces of the alliance. If the guilty State were a member of the alliance, it should be expelled, and attacked by the rest of the alliance. In this way it would be secured that aggression anywhere would bring collective punishment.'

Considering America's options, if the future peace of the world was to be preserved, Russell counselled:

'The conclusion of the whole matter, as regards America, is not one that, if I were an American, would cause me regret. America is in the position of a man who has hitherto lived in rural seclusion, but now finds himself called upon to administer great affairs in his country's capital. The U.S. greatly exceeds all other countries in power, both the actual power of armaments and the potential power of industrial resources. This situation brings with it new problems, both internal and external, and new responsibilities, which cannot be shirked except at the risk of a series of great wars. If America exercises its power wisely, firmly, yet moderately, keeping in view always the paramount aim of world peace, our distracted epoch may give place to one of ordered progress. The opportunity exists; it rests with the statesmen and the public to use it for the equal benefit of their own country and mankind.'

Arranging a passage home to England was a protracted process, and after completing the *History of Western Philosophy*, Russell lectured for a short while at Princeton, where he was very happy:[9]

'The last part of our time in America was spent at Princeton, where we had a little house on the shores of the lake. While in Princeton, I came to know Einstein fairly well. I used to go to his house once a week to discuss with him and Gödel and Pauli. . . .

'The society of Princeton was extremely pleasant, pleasanter, on the whole than any other social group I had come across in America. By this time John was back in England, having gone into the British navy and been set to learn Japanese. Kate was self-sufficient at Radcliffe, having done extremely well in her work and acquired a small teaching job. There was therefore nothing to keep us in America except the difficulty of obtaining a passage to England. This difficulty, however, seemed for a long time insuperable. I went to Washington to argue that I must be allowed to perform my duties in the House of Lords, and tried to persuade the authorities that my desire to do so was very ardent. . . .'

Russell's prospects of finding employment in England had improved. His decision to return home was considerably reinforced by welcome news from Cambridge. He informed an American friend:[10]

'We are living at Princeton which we find very pleasant. I had lectures there and now have a seminar. I still come to the Rand School every Wednesday. I have been elected a Fellow of Trinity College, Cambridge, probably for life, which solves my problems. I plan to go home during the summer.'

At last Russell managed to convince the British Embassy to grant him a sailing permit; 'dates were fixed, for Peter and Conrad first, and for me about a fortnight later. We sailed in May 1944.'[11]

Russell wrote a farewell letter to Lucy Donnelly, on 14 May 1944:[12]

'This is a good-bye letter, with great regret that I can't bid you good-bye in person. After months of waiting, we are being suddenly shipped off at a moment's notice—Peter and Conrad are already gone and I go in two or three days. It was nice being your neighbours, and your house seemed almost a bit of England. Please tell Helen [Flexner] I am very sorry not to write to her too—and give my love (or whatever she would like better) to Edith [Finch].'

Russell's sojourn in America had been eventful and tempestuous; *Time* magazine referred to him as 'the philosophical hot potato of U.S. campuses'.[13] Yet he made no complaint that America had been unkind to him. Years later, he summed up this period of his life with the remark that on his tombstone he would have the words inscribed: 'He lived for six years in America, and did *not* write a book about it.'[14]

Appropriately, Russell's final piece of journalism before leaving America was an article for the *Saturday Evening Post*, entitled 'Can

Americans and Britons be Friends?'[15] which was published on 3 June 1944. The article, in which Russell discussed the divergent customs and manners of the Americans and British, and the distorted picture each cherished of the other, aroused considerable response from the *Post*'s readers, one of whom informed him: 'your article has raised quite a hornet's nest'; and scores of letters pursued Russell to England. 'It is extraordinarily difficult to go against these prevailing misconceptions', Russell had written, and the majority of letters tended to confirm this. Russell had regarded his article 'as my modest contribution towards Anglo–American co-operation', and it reflected his hopes for the post-war situation:

'The world needs the co-operation of America and England, not only in formal ways but in the way of genuine friendly feeling. Each nation, like every other, has its faults, and it is only irritating to make a pretense of perfection. But broadly speaking, the international ideals of the two are identical.'

Russell continued to express his wish that this special relationship would grow between the two countries. In 1945, he wrote two articles on this theme; addressed to the British public they were part of Russell's attempt to make 'my knowledge of America useful'.[16] These were 'British and American Nationalism'[17] and 'Some Impressions of America',[18] and reflected on half-a-century's personal experience of the United States. 'My first visit to America was in 1896, when there were as yet no motor-cars in the country', he wrote; and observed:

'I have had innumerable contacts with individuals, almost all of them pleasant, and not a few very delightful; I have had also some contacts with institutions which were decidedly less agreeable. From my impressions, I have come to feel that many things in America are very different from what they are supposed to be.'

As with the *Post* article, Russell discussed the national differences that existed between Americans and British, how this affected their behaviour and attitudes, and their concepts of democracy and politics. He was careful to point out: 'Obviously, sometimes one system is better, sometimes the other. I am not concerned to praise either at the expense of the other, but merely to point out ways in which America and England differ.'

Russell reiterated his view, first expressed many years previously, on the way power was wielded in America:

'One of the things that struck me most forcibly in 1896, and that subsequent experience has confirmed, is that America is much more monarchical than England. In every direction there is more one-man power and less government by committees. It is true that England has a King, but there are very few things that he can do. But in America institutions are so organised that many individuals have a personal power to which there is no analogy in England.'

Russell had many critical things to say about America, including warnings about the 'poison' of anti-Semitism and racialism; the 'vociferous' national sentiment; the 'excessive respect for executive ability' and its detrimental effect on the educational system; the inadequacies of family life. But in summation, he stated: 'Every country has its defects, but in relation to the world, I believe those of America to be less than those of any other country.' And whilst he had frequently experienced a great longing for England during his stay in America, he now remarked: 'Americans are more generally kindly and friendly than English people, and when one comes home one misses the warmth of American friends.'

Russell's principal theme was: 'Hatred between nations is an evil thing; hatred between Allies is very dangerous; and hatred between Great Britain and America is suicidal on the part of both.' He expressed his hope that 'the broad identity of interests between Great Britain and the United States will gradually soften the hatred of us which undoubtedly exists. It is of course the duty of every Englishman to do what he can towards this end. . . .'

Russell was in a buoyant mood at the beginning of 1945, and concluded the 'Impressions' article by stating: 'I have considerable confidence that American influence will, on the whole, be exercised wisely and humanely. . . . I look to the Empire of America for the best hopes that our distracted world permits.'

As the war drew to a close, with new forces emerging that were to shape the course of world events over the next twenty-five years, Russell's mood changed considerably, and on 2 September 1945 he wrote to Dora Sanger from Cambridge, where he was once more lecturing in philosophy:

'Thank you very much for your letter. Yes, the Atomic Bomb makes one have to reconsider all sorts of things. I have never, not even in 1940, felt the outlook as gloomy as now. Everything is working up for a war between the U.S.A. and the U.S.S.R., with us a satellite of the U.S.A.; both sides will use Atomic Bombs, and very little will be left at the end. . . . In the interval between the general election and the Atomic Bomb I had been feeling rather happy; but at the crack of Truman's whip, the British government will have to relinquish all its projects. . . .'

With the end of the war, the world was a greatly altered place, and the period of international tensions known as the Cold War was ushered in. The bombs that fell on Hiroshima and Nagasaki cast their shadow over post-war reconstruction and re-alignments; and over the aspirations of the people of the entire globe. Russell had hopefully contemplated the development of a special relationship between Britain and the United States. In time he became a severe critic of the alliance that emerged. At first, Russell responded to the changed situation a little uncertainly; but he was soon to become totally involved in the unfolding dramas of the next twenty-five years. His interest in American policy was to embrace all his fundamental concerns; and Russell was to be both internationally acclaimed and reviled. On 28 November 1945, in a House of Lords debate on foreign affairs, Russell, addressing the House for only the second time in his life, declared:[19]

'The Atom Bomb is in its infancy. It is certain that it will become more destructive and cheaper to produce.

'The question is: Is it possible for a scientific society to continue to exist, or must such a society inevitably bring itself to destruction? It is not possible to exaggerate the gravity of the possibilities of evil that lie in the use of atomic energy.

'I go about the streets and see the monuments of our civilisation, and in my mind's eye I see a vision of heaps of rubble and corpses all around. That is what we have to face as a real possibility throughout the cities of the civilised world unless we find a way of abolishing war. . . .'

NOTES

[1] B. Russell, *Autobiography* (London, 1968), Vol. II, pp. 222–3 (Boston, 1968), pp. 339–40.

[2] Published in 1948 as *Human Knowledge: Its Scope and Limits* (London and Simon & Schuster, New York).

[3] B. Russell, *Autobiography*, Vol. II, p. 256; pp. 395–7.

[4] Ibid., p. 257; pp. 397–8.

[5] W. J. Brown, *I Meet America* (Routledge, London, 1942), pp. 115–16.

[6] Russell had discussions with Culbertson on a formula for international government (see above, footnote 59, p. 191). For his views on Culbertson's schemes see his *Autobiography*, Vol. II, pp. 253–4; pp. 390–3; see also 'The Key to Culbertson' by Russell, in *The Saturday Book* (October 1950), pp. 81–5.

[7] B. Russell, *Autobiography*, Vol. II, pp. 251–2; pp. 387–8.

[8] In *Education and the Social Order* (London and W. W. Norton, New York, 1932) Russell had stated: 'Children of immigrants in the United States become patriotic Americans, and usually despise their parents' country of origin; this is mainly the effect of the schools.'

[9] B. Russell, *Autobiography*, Vol. II, p. 224; pp. 341–2.

[10] From Russell's letter to Miriam Reichl of 2 February 1944.

[11] B. Russell, *Autobiography*, Vol. II, p. 224; p. 342.

[12] B. Russell, *Autobiography* (London, 1969), Volume III, p. 40 (Boston, 1969), p. 39.

[13] Alan Wood, *Bertrand Russell, the Passionate Sceptic* (London, 1957), p. 196 (Simon & Schuster, New York, 1957).

[14] Ibid., p. 145.

[15] See below, pp. 328–37.

[16] Russell's letter to Gilbert Murray, see above, p. 203. Certain passages from 'Can Americans and Britons be Friends?' are repeated in variant form in these articles. These sections have not been edited out as we wished to keep the articles intact.

[17] *Horizon* (January 1945); see below, pp. 338–49.

[18] Previously unpublished, see below, pp. 350–5.

[19] The *Daily Telegraph* (29 November 1945).

ILLUSTRATIONS

1. Bertrand Russell at the age of 21, shortly before his marriage to Alys Pearsall Smith of Philadelphia.
2. Alys Russell featured in the *New York American*'s report on Russell's election campaign at Wimbledon in May 1907.
3. At the end of 1916 Russell wrote an open letter to President Woodrow Wilson urging him to use his influence to stop the war. Because of the prevailing censorship Russell had an American friend smuggle the letter out of England into America, where it received nationwide publicity.
4. America's declaration of war on Germany in April 1917 was a great blow to the pacifist cause which Russell espoused. Russell commented on the event in an editorial published in the official organ of the No-Conscription Fellowship.
5. The First World War caused Russell to become a socialist. Shortly before his visit to Soviet Russia in May 1920 he wrote an article for the New York *Liberator*, expressing support for the Bolshevik government. Excerpts from his article were quoted in the June 1920 issue of *Current Opinion*.
6. Russell in Japan, 1921. His visit to the Far East made him anxious about the fate of China which was then being decided at the Washington Conference.
7. Russell in America, 1924. The main purpose of his visit was to propagate the cause of socialism and world peace.
8. Americans were interested in Russell's views on a variety of subjects. By the late 1920s he had become generally popular in the country. (*Forward* was a Yiddish-language newspaper in New York City.)
9. Russell debated before large American audiences on social and political themes. Here he poses with the novelist Sherwood Anderson before their debate on 'Shall the State Rear Our Children?', 1 November 1931.
10. Russell inspired American radicals. He is seen here with a group of pacifists in New York during his 1931 tour. From left to right: *front*, Rosika Schwimmer, Russell, and Zola Lief; *rear*, Alfred Lief, Pierre Loving, Warder Norton (Russell's publisher), and William Floyd.
11. Russell's notes for his debate with the philosopher Will Durant on 'Is Modern Education a Failure?' in New York's Mecca Temple, October 1931.
12. Russell with some children at his experimental school. John Russell second from left: Kate Russell immediately to the right of Russell. His

lecture tours of America in 1927, 1929 and 1931 were mainly concerned with earning money to run the school. Russell's views on child education created great interest in America.

13. Russell's sexual ethic was considered too advanced for the times, particularly in America. A 1932 cartoon lampoons his *Marriage and Morals*.

14. A caricature of Russell which appeared in the New York *Herald Tribune* of 2 October 1932.

15. Russell arriving in New York, September 1938, to take up a visiting professorship at the University of Chicago.

16. Russell aged 67, Professor of Philosophy at the University of California at Los Angeles.

17. The house at 212 Loring Avenue, Beverley Hills, Los Angeles, where the Russells lived from 1939 to 40.

18. The Russells at Loring Avenue. Russell and Patricia with, left to right, Conrad, Kate and John.

19. Mrs Jean Kay, a Brooklyn housewife, successfully petitioned the State Supreme Court to revoke Russell's City College appointment. She is seen here with her family.

20. Russell and Patricia reading about the uproar caused by his appointment to the College of the City of New York.

21. *New York Post* cartoon of 2 April 1940. Justice John E. McGeehan, in upholding Mrs Kay's petition, accused the Board of Higher Education of 'establishing a chair of indecency' at City College.

22. Justice McGeehan interviewed by the press after delivering his judgement. He found Russell to be 'morally unfit' to teach New York students.

23. A mass meeting of students in the Great Hall at the College of the City of New York, 5 April 1940, protesting at the revocation of Russell's appointment.

24. The unusual title page to *An Inquiry Into Meaning and Truth*, which was the fruit of Russell's successive lectures at Oxford, Chicago and California. Note the reference to the College of the City of New York.

Photo by Messrs Stearn, Cambridge

American Girl Spoils a
Walkover for Parliament

The former Miss Alys Smith, of Philadelphia, who is trying to elect
her husband to the House of Commons.

A "C.O."
IN PRISON
By W. J. CHAMBERLAIN

"Socialism for Pacifists."
By
A. HAMILTON REMMAY

THE TRIBUNAL

"Tribunal. A Court of Justice."—Webster's Dictionary.

EDITED BY B. J. BOOTHROYD

THURSDAY, APRIL 19, 1917

No. 55

One Penny

AMERICA'S ENTRY INTO THE WAR: By Bertrand Russell

Two recent events have robbed Pacifists in this country of some of the adventitious arguments by which we have been in the habit of buttressing our central position. The two I mean are the Russian Revolution and the entry of America into the war. It is worth while to take stock of our position afresh in view of these two events.

The Russian Revolution, although it has robbed Pacifist opponents of Allied diplomacy of certain debating points, obviously brings peace nearer and improves the outlook for human liberty. The solemn renunciation by the Provisional Government of all annexationist ambitions immensely hastens the day when it will be possible for the Allies and the Central Powers to begin negotiations. It also strengthens the hands of those German Liberals and Socialists who are working for the overthrow of Prussian militarism by means which have a better hope of success than those which our Government prefers to employ.

But the entry of America into the war is a phenomenon much more complicated in its probable effects, and much more difficult to appraise truly. Many Pacifists undoubtedly deplore it. It is worth while to understand what is to be said for this attitude.

It is possible that the entry of America into the war may make peace come sooner. Undoubtedly President Wilson's demands, if he is not overborne by public opinion, will be moderate, and his diplomatic influence will be exerted in favour of asking such terms as the Germans might grant without humiliation. Moreover, the resources of America in men and money must destroy any hope that the Germans may have had of winning the war through the exhaustion of the Allies. For my part, I think what is of most importance to the world at present moment is that the war should be ended as soon as possible. If the nations were not blinded by hatred and pride, they would end it without waiting for victory or defeat, or a degree of suffering that only victory or defeat, appears to be necessary before they will abandon mutual slaughter. If America's entry were certain to shorten the war, I should be glad then that it has occurred, whatever might be said against such a view from the standpoint of theoretical pacifism.

But in the uncertainty of all human affairs there is much to be remembered on the other side. We have in the first place the almost certain growth of militarism and a bellicose outlook in the United States. It is perfectly true that the motives which have led the United States to participate in the war, as set forth by President Wilson, are high-minded, idealistic, and disinterested. So were the motives alleged by our states-

men, no doubt in some cases sincerely, when we entered into the war. It is perfectly true that America is the freest and least military of all Great Powers, but it is also true that before August, 1914 we were the freest and least military of the Great Powers of Europe. We know from bitter experience what becomes of love of justice and liberty when a war is in progress. We have watched step by step the growth of those institutions in this country, whose existence in Prussia was supposed to justify our part in the war. We see the United States already embarked upon measures for universal liability to military service, with, presumably, the same treatment of conscientious objectors in which this country has acquiesced. We see the growth of hatred against Germans in the United States, based upon an ounce of fact to a ton of myth. We know how enjoyable to the Anglo-Saxon mind is the position of moral superiority, and we see the Americans indulging with gusto in all the cruel delights which this position allows. These things make us doubt whether America will be at the end of the war the support of liberal and humane principles in international affairs which she has been in the past.

And the help of America is quite as likely to lengthen the war as to shorten it. Without America, universal exhaustion might have driven all the nations to a compromise peace—obviously the best in the interests of international concord. With America, it may be possible for us, if we choose, to go on for another three years in the hope of final and crushing victory which we have all along announced as our object. It is not improbable that the bellicose version of the American public, which is likely to be now in the ascendancy, will desire the war to last long enough for America to raise a powerful army and to make herself felt in proportion to her resources. The part which we have played toward France, America may play towards us. And, if so, Europe which will be left at the end will be so weak and so exhausted as to have lost all importance for mankind, and the nature of the peace will not matter a jot.

All such considerations are doubtful, and can be argued in either sense according to man's bias. But accidental circumstances cannot touch the position of the whole-hearted opponent of war, which does not rest upon attributing virtue to the "enemy" or wickedness to one's own side, but upon a profound conviction that human welfare is not to be achieved through violence. The war may help the weary populations of the world to see that force is not the road to a secure peace or to friendly relations between the nations. If so, good may come out of it in the end. But it will come through revulsion against war, not through continued belief in punishment, destruction and death.

The New York Times

NEW YORK, SATURDAY, DECEMBER 23, 1916.—SIXTEEN PAGES.

MYSTERIOUS GIRL
TORREON

BRINGS RUSSELL'S
PEACE PLEA HERE

GERMANY LIKELY TO
ASKING WILSON TO A
MUST PUSH WAR, Sa

Germany U Boat Is Sunk
By French Destroyers

Famous English Philosopher and
Mathematician Asks Wilson to
Stop War Ere Europe Perishes.

"YOU, SIR, CAN END IT"

Says Soldiers of All Armies Are
Eager to Quit Fighting—Wilson's Duty Like Lincoln's.

WOMEN TOILERS IN DURESS

Must Work or Negroes Will, He
Charges—Was Puzzled at
His Pacifist Activities.

FIRM WORDS TO PARLIAMENT

But Prorogation Speech
Ignores Berlin Proffer
and Wilson Note.

AN IDENTIC ANSWER TO US

Bonar Law Tells Commons Allies Will Confer Before Making Reply to the President.

VIEWS WIDELY VARYING

Opinion Gains Ground That Wilson's Step Was Due to Expectation of Wider U-Boat War.

ASKS INQUIRY INTO
PEACE TIP PROFITS

Congressman Wood Wants to
Know If Any One High in the
Administration Benefited.

MANY RUMORS IN WALL ST.

Dark Stories of Heavy Winnings
by Persons in Washington Political Circles.

FRENCH PREMIER
RECEIVES NOTE
AT

Paris Press Comments on Mr.
Wilson's Communication
in Friendly Tone.

SEES HIS GOOD INTENTIONS

The Intransigeant Says Germany Cannot Escape on
Request for Terms.

BER
BEI

GERM

Annou

Peat

Confe

To Vindicate the Rights So Rubli
Should Be Our One Endeavor, I

hould support the Bolsheviks and
o-operate with them. And I think
hat Guildsmen, in particular, ought
o pay great attention to Bolshevik
ethods of organization, not only
ecause of their power and prestige,
ut because of their partial adop-
ion of an industrial instead of a
eographical basis for the Soviets.
ut I do not mean to suggest that
e, in this country [England], where
onditions are exceedingly different
om those in Russia, should blindly
llow in the footsteps of the Bol-
heviks. With other Guildsmen, I
ecognize the importance of organ-
ation by trades, but at the same
me believe that the territorial
arliament still has useful functions
perform, and therefore I am not
ersuaded that, for us, the complete
uppression of Parliament as op-
osed to Soviet forms is desirable.
nd I am strongly of opinion that
hatever in the way of Socialism is
asible in this country can be
ccomplished without armed revo-
ution."

A LIBERAL TURNED RADICAL

Prof. Bertrand Russell, lately reinstated in his position as teacher
of mathematics in Cambridge University, England, declares: "I am
one of those who, as a result of the war, have passed over from
Liberalism to Socialism."

Bolshevism has temporarily flouted two
deals which most of us have hitherto
trongly believed in, namely, democracy
nd liberty. Are we on this account to
iew it askance? Bertrand Russell replies
o this question in the negative:

"The dictatorship of the proletariat is pro-
essedly a transitional condition, a war-time
neasure, justified while the remnants of the
ld bourgeois classes were still struggling to
romote counter-revolution. Lenin, following
Marx, regards the State as in essence the domi-
ation of one class in the community. As soon
s communism has abolished the distinction of
lasses, the State is to wither away. When
here is no longer any class except the prole-
ariat, the dictatorship of the proletariat will
pso facto cease, and the State, in the sense in
vhich Lenin uses the word, will disappear. Are
ve to object to this process on the ground that
t may involve for a time the seizure of power
y a minority? And are we to object on the
ame ground to direct action for political ends,
n our own country? Lenin's defence of his
ction is broadly that the opposition to com-
nunism is essentially temporary, and that,
when once communism has been established, it
vill command universal support. An argument
f this sort can only be judged by the outcome.
f the outcome shows, as it seems to have done

in Russia, that the opposition was largely ignorant, and that experience of the new *regime*
leads people to support it, it may be said that
the forcible transition has been justified. The
arguments in favor of democracy and liberty,
it may be said, are arguments applicable to
normal times, not to cataclysms and world
revolutions. In these terrific epochs, a man
must be prepared to back his own faith;
whether he is right or wrong in doing so, only
the issue can show. I think there is something
a trifle pedantic in applying to the circumstances of Russia the sort of arguments and
principles which are valid for ourselves in
ordinary periods. Russia could only be saved
by a strong will, and it is doubtful whether a
strong will could have saved it without dictatorship in some form."

The upshot of the argument is that vital
progress in the world depends upon the
victory of International Socialism, and
that it is worth while, if it is necessary, to
pay a great price for that victory. "I feel
convinced," Mr. Russell concludes, "that
there will be no peace in the world until
International Socialism has conquered, and
that to strengthen its forces, and to weaken
those of the opposition, is the quickest way
to end the conflict."

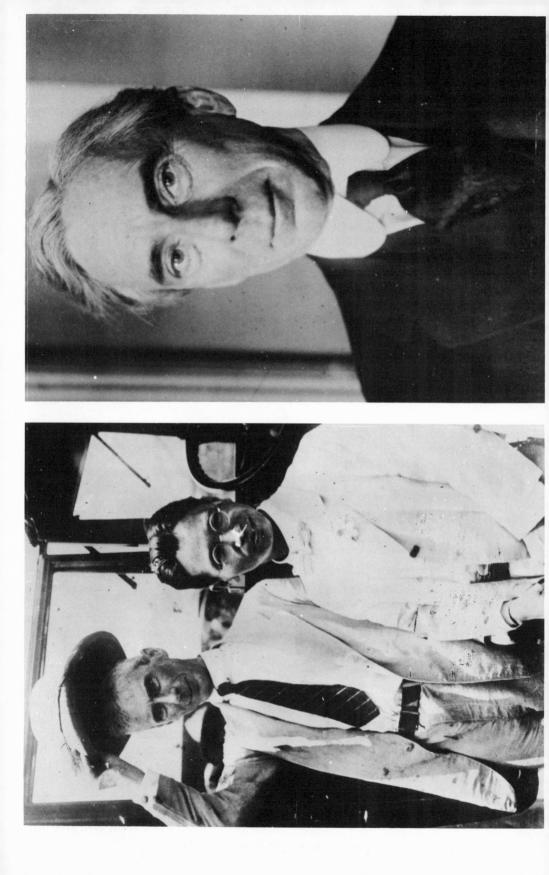

English Section

FORWARD

SUNDAY, MARCH 24, 1929

WHEN BERTRAND RUSSELL GOES TO THE MOVIES

Famous Philosopher-Scientist Writes Whimsically About His Taste in Movies—American Movies Manage to Make America Appear Silly in the Eyes of the Rest of the World—The Morality of the Nursery Tale and the Simplicity of the Fairy Story Seem to be Demanded in America by Grown Men and Women

Written Especially for The Forward

By BERTRAND RUSSELL

Everybody knows that America is more virtuous than Europe, and that the middle west of America is the most virtuous portion of that country. There is a perfectly simple test of virtue which proves the justice of this common opinion: if A wants to persecute B, while B does not want to persecute A, then clearly A is more virtuous than B; he has a higher moral standard and is more inclined to moral indignation. Consequently where a large public has to be appealed to, its most virtuous portions determine the nature of the appeal, for while the vicious can tolerate virtue, the virtuous cannot tolerate vice. Hence every increase in the size of the audience means an increase in the virtuousness of the appeal.

These observations apply with especial force to the cinema. The productions of Hollywood are exhibited in all parts of the world, with the possible exception of Greenland and the Antarctic continent. In the middle west, they seem natural; in the rest of America, intelligible; in other continents, interesting because they are so curious. Moreover much can be done by altering the captions: I saw at Locarno an American film about bootleggers and rum-runners being caught by virtuous policemen, but in order to make it sympathetic to a Southern wine-drinking population all the captions had been altered so as to make it appear that cocaine was the substance in dispute. To an Italian-speaking population the American objection to alcohol seems just as strange as the Hindu objection to beef; it is a fact concerning which sociologists could speculate, but for which one would not seek a rational ex-

BERTRAND RUSSELL

Noted Professor of Homiletics

DR. DAVID PHILIPSON—PATRIOT

By EDWIN ROBINS

I Attend A Spiritualistic Seance

By STANLEY J. HOWARD

9   Associated Press Photo

10   Associated Press Photo

Modern Educⁿ: failure?   1

Not all modern education failure.

Dewey: modern schools: my own.

Great publicly supported systems bad,
    because aims political, not good of child.

Till 19ᵗʰ century, education for few only.

Grandfather, arⁱᶜ character of vicinity.

Now, all Western nations built on literacy.

─ ─ Education first advocated for idealistic reasons,
now, hard-headed practical men.

More harm than good? Future will show.
Love of individual child: not political propaganda.
Education should make men

        INTELLIGENT
        SELF-RELIANT
        CO-OPERATIVE

    Does it do so? Fruits of tree of
officially permitted knowledge?

11

Associated Press Photo

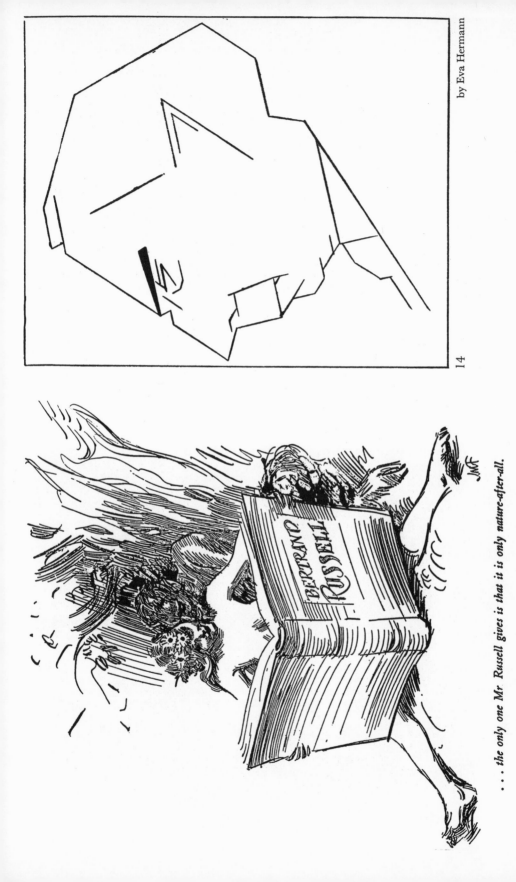

by Eva Hermann

14

. . . the only one Mr. Russell gives is that it is only nature-after-all.

From *Virgins in Cellophane* by Rett Hooper

13

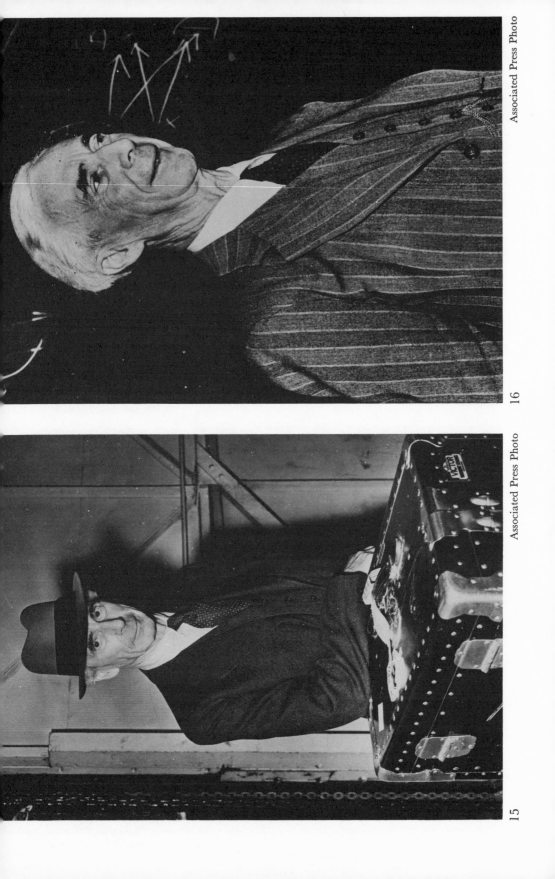

16

15

17

18

19   United Press International Photo

United Press International Photo

21

22

AN INQUIRY
INTO
MEANING AND
TRUTH

BY

BERTRAND RUSSELL

M.A., F.R.S.

Holder of the Nicholas Murray Butler Medal of Columbia University (1915), the Sylvester Medal of the Royal Society (1932) and the de Morgan Medal of the London Mathematical Society (1933). Honorary Member of the Reale Accademia dei Lincei. Fellow (1895–1901) and Lecturer (1910–1916) of Trinity College, Cambridge. Herbert Spencer Lecturer at Oxford (1914). Visiting Professor of Philosophy at Harvard University (1914) and at The Chinese Government University of Peking (1920–1921). Tarner Lecturer at Cambridge (1926). Special Lecturer at the London School of Economics and Political Science (1937) and at The University of Oxford (1938). Visiting Professor of Philosophy at the University of Chicago (1938–1939). Professor of Philosophy at the University of California at Los Angeles (1939–1940). Occasional Lecturer at the Universities of Uppsala, Copenhagen, Barcelona, the Sorbonne, etc., etc.

Judicially pronounced unworthy to be Professor of Philosophy at the College of the City of New York (1940)

LONDON
GEORGE ALLEN AND UNWIN LTD

24

PART II

PRESIDENT WILSON'S STATEMENT

Russell's editorial for the *Tribunal* (London, 1 February 1917)

'The question upon which the whole future peace and policy of the world depends is this: Is the present a struggle for a just and secure peace, or only for a new balance of power? If it be only a struggle for a new balance of power, who will guarantee, who can guarantee the stable equilibrium of the new arrangement? Only a tranquil Europe can be a stable Europe. There must be, not a balance of power, but a community of power; not organised rivalries, but an organised common peace. . . .

'It must be a peace without victory. . . .

'Victory would mean peace forced upon the loser, a victor's terms imposed upon the vanquished. It would be accepted in humiliation, under duress, at intolerable sacrifice, and would leave a sting, a resentment, a bitter memory upon which terms of peace would rest, not permanently, but only as upon quicksand. Only a peace between equals can last—only a peace the very principles of which is quality and a common participation in a common benefit. The right state of mind, the right feeling between nations is as necessary for a lasting peace as is the just settlement of vexed questions of territory or of tactical and national allegiance'—President Wilson to the Senate, 22 January 1917.

The Times, on this passage in the President's speech, retorts:
'There can be no "drawn war" between the spirit of Prussian militarism and the spirit of real peace which the Allies, the Americans, and indeed all neutrals, desire. "Militarism" cannot be exorcised except by defeat in the field, and therefore the Allies can hear of no peace which is not a "victory peace"' (23 January 1917).

We have here side by side, in dramatic contrast, the view of the neutrals and the view of the belligerents. The official excuse which the Allies offer for continuing the war in spite of Germany's desire for peace is that 'militarism cannot be exorcised except by defeat in the field'. If this were indeed true, it is impossible to see how militarism could ever be exorcised, since only militarism on our part can possibly enable us to inflict defeat upon Germany. If *The Times* is right, the only way to end militarism in Germany is to establish it among the Allies. And then they in turn will need a defeat in order that the evil spirit may be exorcised from among them, and so on in an unending chain of tragedy and destruction.

The belief that spiritual gains are to be achieved at the point of the bayonet is the very heart of militarism. When the war began, the writings of Bernhardi[1] were held up to execration among us, because he contended that the Germans had a mission to civilise the world by war. Now, his doctrines are universally accepted among ourselves, and it is illegal to disagree with him except on the one minor point that it is the Allies, not Germany, that must spread civilisation from the cannon's mouth. This is what two-and-a-half years of war without victory have achieved towards exorcising militarism among ourselves. Certainly, so far the result does not encourage a belief in the recipe of *The Times*.

President Wilson rejects this recipe, and states in simple, emphatic language the view for which pacifists have contended. 'Only a peace between equals can last—only a peace the very principle of which is equality and a common participation in a common benefit.' Such a peace is not extorted by force, but must be the outcome of a recognition that war is folly. Out of this recognition a secure peace may spring. But out of a victory won by an unstable combination, affording a standing argument to show how much glory and territory and trade may be won by war, and a standing incentive to the vanquished to seek revenge through the shifting diplomatic groupings of the Powers, nothing can come but a perpetuation of the old bad system and a feverish preparation for greater and more scientific devastation in years to come.

It is against this danger that President Wilson seeks to provide. The truth of what he says is evident to all who are not caught up in the madness of war, as a study of neutral opinion shows. But during war it is difficult for either side to believe that there is anything more important than victory. On both sides in this war, the nearly universal belief is that the nations on one's own side are saints, and those on the other side are devils. If this were true, only victory for one's own side would be needed to insure the rule of the saints. But the neutrals remain inexplicably sceptical, not so much of the crimes of the enemy as of the virtues of one's friends. Each side finds, with astonishment, that its moral superiority is not unhesitatingly admitted by those who can form an impartial judgement. In leading us to understand and respect this neutral view, President Wilson is performing the inestimable service of contributing to heal the bitternesses that the war has produced.

[1] Friedrich von Bernhardi; German general and military writer.

AMERICA'S ENTRY INTO THE WAR

Russell's editorial for the *Tribunal* (London, 19 April 1917)

Two recent events have robbed pacifists in this country of some of the
adventitious arguments by which we have been in the habit of buttressing our central position. The two I mean are the Russian Revolution
and the entry of America into the war. It is worth-while to take stock of
our position afresh in view of these two events.

The Russian Revolution, although it has robbed pacifist opponents
of Allied diplomacy of certain debating points, obviously brings peace
nearer and improves the outlook for human liberty. The solemn renunciation by the provisional government of all annexationist ambitions
immensely hastens the day when it will be possible for the Allies and the
Central Powers to begin negotiations. It also strengthens the hands of
those German liberals and socialists who are working for the overthrow of Prussian militarism by means which have a better hope of
success than those which our government prefers to employ.

But the entry of America into the war is a phenomenon much more
complicated in its probable effects, and much more diffcult to appraise
truly. Many pacifists of proved sincerity welcome it. Some militarists
undoubtedly deplore it. It is worth-while to understand what is to be
said for this attitude.

It is possible that the entry of America into the war may make peace
come sooner. Undoubtedly, President Wilson's demands, if he is not
overborne by public opinion, will be moderate, and his diplomatic influence will be exerted in favour of asking such terms as the Germans
might grant without humiliation. Moreover, the resources of America
in men and money must destroy any hope that the Germans may have
had of winning the war through the exhaustion of the Allies. For my
part, I think what is of most importance to the world at the present
moment is that the war should be ended as soon as possible. If the nations
were not blinded by hatred and pride, they would end it without waiting
for victory or defeat, but in their present mood only victory or defeat, or

a degree of suffering far exceeding any so far endured, appears to be necessary before they will abandon mutual slaughter. If America's entry were certain to shorten the war, I should be glad that it has occurred, whatever might be said against such a view from the standpoint of theoretical pacifism.

But in the uncertainty of all human affairs there is much to be remembered on the other side. We have in the first place the almost certain growth of militarism and a bellicose outlook in the United States. It is perfectly true that the motives which have led the United States to participate in the war, as set forth by President Wilson, are highminded, idealistic, and disinterested. So were the motives alleged by our statesmen, no doubt in some cases sincerely, when we entered into the war. It is perfectly true that America is the freest and least military of all Great Powers, but it is also true that before August 1914 we were the freest and least military of the Great Powers of Europe. We know from bitter experience what becomes of love of justice and liberty when a war is in progress. We have watched step by step the growth of those institutions in this country, whose existence in Prussia was supposed to justify our part in the war. We see the United States already embarked upon measures for universal liability to military service, with, presumably, the same treatment of conscientious objectors in which this country has acquiesced. We see the growth of hatred against Germans in the United States, based upon an ounce of fact to a ton of myth. We know how enjoyable to the Anglo-Saxon mind is the position of moral superiority, and we see the Americans indulging with gusto in all the cruel delights which this position allows. These things make us doubt whether America will be at the end of the war the support of liberal and humane principles in international affairs which she has been in the past.

And the help of America is quite as likely to lengthen the war as to shorten it. Without America, universal exhaustion might have driven all the nations to a compromise peace—obviously the best in the interests of international concord. With America, it may be possible for us, if we choose, to go on for another three years in the hope of that final and crushing victory which we have all along announced as our object. It is not improbable that the bellicose section of the American public, which is likely to be now in the ascendancy, will desire the war to last long enough for America to raise a powerful army and to make herself felt in proportion to her resources. The part which we have played towards France, America may play towards us. And, if so, the Europe which will be left at the end will be so weak and so exhausted as to have lost all importance for mankind, and the nature of the peace will not matter a jot.

All such considerations are doubtful, and can be argued in either sense according to man's bias. But accidental circumstances cannot touch the position of the whole-hearted opponent of war, which does not rest upon attributing virtue to the 'enemy', or wickedness to one's own side, but upon a profound conviction that human welfare is not to be achieved through violence. The war may help the weary populations of the world to see that force is not the road to a secure peace or to friendly relations between the nations. If so, good may come out of it in the end. But it will come through revulsion against war, not through continued belief in punishment, destruction and death.

HOPES AND FEARS AS REGARDS AMERICA

The *New Republic* (Washington D.C., Part I, 15 March 1922, and Part II, 22 March 1922)

I

Apart from the Russian Revolution, the most striking result of the war has been the world-supremacy of the United States. While England and Germany fought for hegemony, America, almost by accident, acquired it. For some time after the war, there was reason to fear that the British government might not recognise the inevitable, but might endeavor, by means of the Anglo–Japanese alliance, to retain command of the seas. Happily this danger is at an end. The Washington Conference has shown our government, for the first time since the days of Cromwell, quietly accepting a position of naval equality with another Power. Although on paper there is equality, in fact there is overwhelming superiority on the side of America, chiefly because of: (1) our dependence upon overseas trade; (2) Canada; (3) the greater financial strength of America; (4) the Panama Canal. Our government will therefore do all in its power to remain on good terms with the United States. To this end we have already accepted the naval ratio, abandoned the Anglo–Japanese alliance, and granted freedom to Ireland; and it may be assumed that for a long time to come our policy will be in harmony with that of Washington.

As the British empire possessed the one thing lacking to America as a world Power, namely naval bases and coaling stations in all parts of the eastern hemisphere, the combination of the two will be irresistible unless and until the whole of Asia, including Russia, unites against them. In the combination, America will be the dominant partner. Therefore the hopes and fears of the world, probably for the next fifty years at least, depend upon the use which America makes of her vast power.

There are in this situation immense possibilities for good, but also immense dangers. The dangers will not be avoided unless Americans become conscious of them. So far, many American radicals seem to me insufficiently aware of the dangers lurking in national self-esteem—

dangers which European radicals have had forcibly brought home to them by the outcome of the war. I wish, if I can do so without offense, to suggest that the disillusioning experiences which we in Europe have undergone are likely to be repeated for those who expect America to pursue idealistic ends, unless they become more critically minded toward their government and their financiers.

I wish first of all to say that I regard America as definitely better, in international affairs, than any other Great Power. The crimes of Versailles were crimes of the Old World, not of the New. America made no secret treaties, and in fact had cut herself off from the possibility of making any by the constitutional powers of the Senate. America alone has stood for the independence and integrity of China. At Washington, America made a sincere attempt to diminish the expense of naval armaments, which might have had even more success but for the secret understanding between France and Japan. America showed, after the war, a complete absence of that hunger for territory which distinguished all the other victors. These are very great moral assets, and they make me, in common with most European radicals, feel that, if any one Power is to be supreme in the world, it is fortunate for the world that America should be that one.

Having stated these excellences, I am compelled, nevertheless, to notice certain facts and tendencies which make me less hopeful of the future than many American radicals. If I could bring them to share my fears, my fears would be much diminished, but it is their optimism which I find one of the most disquieting features of the situation.

European radicals, since the war, differ from those of America chiefly in two respects: first, that they are more disillusioned, and second, that they are more socialistic. Their disillusionment and their socialism are often connected as cause and effect. They are aware that they were taken in by noble professions, and that their support was used to increase the strength of hypocritical scoundrels. They remember their many friends who were lured to death on the battlefield by the lies and trickery of statesmen who battened on the blood of Europe. From this personal experience, with the backward light which it sheds on history, it is natural to conclude that, except by some rare accident, only knaves can succeed in politics. But this is not the final outcome of reflection on war hypocrisy. The final outcome, so far as I am concerned, is a Spinozistic moral philosophy. To apply moral terms to human beings—to call them knaves or scoundrels or what not—is unscientific, expressing only our own ignorant surprise at what we should have foreseen if we had been a little wiser. 'Each thing,' says Spinoza, 'in so far as it is in itself, endeavors to persevere in its being' (*Ethics*, III, 6). It follows that a politician will try to stay in office. One might as well blame the earth for sticking to its orbit though other parts of the universe would be more agreeable to us.

If men are, by their very nature, egoistic, various conclusions follow. The first is that, where this view is not accepted, men will be driven to hypocrisy by the desire to retain the respect of their fellows. In England and America, where it is still believed that quite a number of people are altruistic, it is safe to say that every public man would lose his political influence if the truth were known about him. Hence politics become surrounded by an atmosphere of deceit and hocus-pocus. Even in the height of party strife, politicians usually refrain from accusing each other of those crimes which are necessary for the agreeableness of the profession, such as dining while important matters are being debated; yet when the public does hear of these things it is shocked, because it has a sentimental and unreal view of its representatives. The public thus makes it almost as difficult for a politician to be an honest man as for a parson. Driven into lying by the ridiculous expectations of his supporters, the unfortunate statesman soon acquires the habit of regarding the world at large as fools whom it is his business to deceive. This is especially the case in democratic countries. It is useless to object to hypocrisy in politics while we continue to hound out all who are not hypocrites.

The second conclusion to be drawn from the natural egoism of man is that when nations act 'well', *id est*, for the good of the world, that is because their self-interest happens to coincide with the interest of mankind. It is probable that they will themselves believe that they are acting from altruistic motives; but all students of psychoanalysis know what amazing self-deception takes place below the level of consciousness. There is an easy practical test: do these people who believe themselves to be altruistic continue to pursue the interests of the world at large when such interests clash with their own? I am afraid it is only very rarely that experience provides an affirmative answer to this question. If, then, we wish to create a world where people will act 'well', we must create a policy in which the interest of the individual man or nation is as often as possible in harmony with the general interest.

This brings me to socialism. The American commonwealth is built upon the belief (which is shared, apparently, by a great majority among the radicals) that the ideal polity is a combination of political democracy with economic autocracy. The theory of the virtuous despot was rejected, as regards politics, in 1776, and I do not think the men of that day would have accepted it in economics. But nowadays men are sent to prison for putting an extract from the Constitution (without comment) on a banner, and carrying it through the streets.[1] In fact, the opinions of the Founders have become as inconvenient in America as the opinions of Christ have been found in all Christian countries since the time of Constantine. When the Standard Oil Company was still young, it was possible to publish such books as Lloyd's *Wealth Against Commonwealth*. But nowadays the very men who applauded that book when it appeared will expatiate on the virtues of Mr Rockefeller as displayed in his generous benefactions to universities and research, as a result of which a very large proportion of the intellect of America is directly or indirectly in his pay. The theory that economic despotism is desirable, and that American economic despots would never use their power against the public interest, appears to have been finally established as a result of the White Terror during and after the war. But European radicals believe that economic democracy is as important as democracy in politics. And they do not believe that a country like America, which concentrates enormous financial power in very few hands, can be trusted to act for the good of mankind except when such action furthers the interests of high finance.

I have referred to Spinoza to show that the view which I am advocating is neither cynical nor novel. The view is that men's purposes, in fact, though often without their own knowledge, are egoistic—not quite invariably, but so preponderantly that the exceptions do not count in dealing with large numbers, as in politics. The belief that this is not so is the cause of hypocrisy, of moral indignation, and also of the theory that a benevolent despotism is possible. If men, with few and rare exceptions, are egoistic, the only way of securing justice is by democracy, since a despot will almost always seek his own advantage. But if democracy is to be effective, it requires two extensions beyond the present American practice. The first of these I have already touched upon: economic power is now at least as important as political power, owing to the growth of vast industrial organisations; therefore democracy must be extended to economics, which can only be done by socialism. The second point is that democracy will not be genuinely established until it is international, which requires some sacrifice of sovereignty on the part of separate States. Until there is international government, strong States can bully weak ones, and will do so whenever it is to their interest. To this rule I see no reason to admit exceptions.

The moral drawn by Americans from the war and its outcome is different. They have concluded that the Western hemisphere is virtuous and the Eastern hemisphere is wicked. They are hesitating whether to embark upon the government of the Eastern hemisphere for its own good, or to leave it to suffer the consequences of its crimes. Owing to their failure to recognise the fundamental part played by economic power in the modern world, they will probably think they are deciding to let the Old World alone, when they will be in fact undertaking to govern it through finance. Whatever they may nominally decide, their desire to invest capital abroad is too strong for them to let us alone, and I should be the last to suggest that we deserve to be let alone. But so long as self-righteousness and an antiquated morality of disapproval govern the American outlook, self-deception will be easy and tyranny inevitable.

In a second article, I propose to give concrete illustrations of the danger that American finance may impose a new tyranny upon the world.

[1] Probably a reference to Upton Sinclair; see above p. 87.

II

Before embarking upon controversial topics, I wish to say once more, with the utmost emphasis, that I consider the American government the best (*id est*, the least harmful) of the Great Powers in its international relations, and that I have the profoundest admiration for the American people. The American government is in the van of progress among governments; but, perhaps for that very reason, American radicals (if I am not mistaken) are somewhat less radical than those of some other countries. In Tsarist days, the radicals of Russia were the most thorough-going in the world; and it would seem that bad governments are a necessary condition of good oppositions.

There is one other preliminary point that I wish to make clear. I do not believe in the application of moral epithets in politics, whether of praise or blame. In a former communication, my love of monosyllables led me to speak of 'knaves and fools', in a passage which you quite justly criticise. Instead of 'knaves' I should have said 'men who judge correctly as to their own interests'; and instead of 'fools', 'men who judge mistakenly as to the public interests'. Moral epithets represent, I believe, an insufficient analysis and understanding; when men's actions are understood, they appear inevitable, and therefore no more worthy of praise or blame than sunshine or a thunderstorm.

European radicals for the most part believe that the liberal ideals which prevailed in Europe in the 1860s, and survived in England down to the death of Gladstone, are no longer applicable to the modern world. These old ideals, so far as economics are concerned, may be summed up in free competition. In America they retain a hold over advanced political thought which they have lost in Europe. We observe that free competition within a nation tends to be extinguished by the formation of trusts, and is then transferred to the international sphere. In that sphere, it is one of the most potent causes of modern wars; especially when it takes the more recent form of competition for the possession of raw materials rather than for markets. Since the end of the war, the competition of oil between America and Great Britain must have caused anxiety to every friend of peace; I understand that it is now happily ended, as a part of the general settlement exemplified at Washington. The new tendency is toward international agreements among the financiers and industrialists. *The Times* (London) of 10 January tells how a set of German financiers are in treaty with Messrs Morgan for the rehabilitation of Russia; and the American policy of the Consortium for China is universally known.

This new policy of international capitalism is not on the lines of traditional liberal ideals. It would have shocked Montesquieu or Jefferson or Cobden. Nevertheless, it is a policy offering certain definite hope for the world, because it is constructive and international. Nationalism is, to my mind, the worst evil of our time, and the one which must first be cured before any essential progress becomes possible. The big financiers are, in the modern world, the men who have most to gain pecuniarily from internationalism, because of the danger of ruin and bankruptcy throughout the Eastern hemisphere; they have therefore become, for the moment, the exponents of the international idea. As they are immensely powerful, one may hope that they will overcome the nationalist opposition which exists everywhere, and is especially dominant in backward countries such as France and Japan. In so far as they stand for breaking down the barriers between nations, substituting international for national trusts, and restoring the machinery of production and exchange, the big financiers are attempting a work which is necessary if we are to recover from the effects of the war. In particular, they are doing a work which should be welcomed by socialists, because nationalism, both in feelings and in organisations, is the great enemy to socialist propaganda and to the creation of a true socialist government.

All this, however, leaves untouched the reasons which lead us to prefer socialism to capitalism. Assuming the utmost possible success for the schemes of international finance, they might give the world peace and an abundance of material goods. But they could not give it freedom, and it is very unlikely that they would give any high degree of prosperity to the ordinary wage-earner. Capitalist industrialism concentrates immense power in the hands of a few men; the remainder are robbed of their fair share of control over public affairs and over their own lives, even if, politically, the country they live in is a democracy. When I read what Americans write about political questions, I usually feel an insufficient realisation of the control of politics by finance. Those who emphasise it, like Upton Sinclair, are thought to be muck-rakers, cynics and cranks. Even to suggest that when a big financier makes an investment, he usually does so in order to obtain a return for his money, is thought to be in very bad taste. The emissaries of the Consortium in China, for example, were mortally offended by the hint that the welfare of China was not the *only* thing American bankers were seeking. This attitude, naturally, greatly increased the suspicion with which they were regarded by the Chinese.

Economic determinism as an absolute doctrine appears to me to be mistaken. For one thing, it does not explain the passions which generate the groups toward which men feel herd-instinct. For another thing, I think the passion for power or for superiority to a rival is wider than economic self-interest. And I do not by any means deny that a certain percentage of mankind, in a certain percentage of their actions, are not egoistic. Politics, however, is concerned in the main with the average passions of large numbers of men, and as concerns individuals it is occupied almost exclusively with those who have exceptional power. In the modern capitalistic world, power belongs to the great financiers, who are not likely to be indifferent to economic self-interest, since those who are do not become very rich. At present, therefore, we are not likely to go very much astray in taking economic determinism as a practical guide to what is likely to happen. Certainly we shall go less astray than if we expect much idealism in the holders of power.

An extraordinary object lesson has been afforded by Russia. I suppose it is now generally known that the Bolsheviks were no worse than any other Russian party as regards atrocities or morals, and that they were making an honest attempt to establish a system which they, in common with many other people, believe to be better than capitalism. But they repudiated the Russian debt. Therefore, Great Britain, France, Japan and America were willing to inflict death by slow starvation upon the population of Russia. (Great Britain, it is true, drew back when we saw that the Bolsheviks could menace our position in India; but this can hardly be called an idealistic motive.) When the failure of the harvest made it clear that the powers *could* inflict death by starvation, the Bolsheviks announced that they would assume responsibility for the debt and abandon the parts of their system which were most offensive to the big capitalists. Immediately the scene changed, and we find the nations tumbling over each other in their eagerness to relieve starving Russia. In view of this history, how can it be pretended that there is any country where idealistic motives outweigh a threat to the pocket? I presume readers of the *New Republic* know what happened when the Chinese government recently failed to meet an obligation of five and a half million dollars to a Chicago bank. America behaved exactly as any other Power would have behaved in similar circumstances.

Practically all advanced opinion in Europe believes that the world's ills can only be cured by socialism. Nothing that we can find out about America makes us think that America has discovered any other way. On the contrary, we find in your semi-philanthropic commercialism the survival of a phase of incipient imperialism which we believe we have passed through. We think that America before the war had a liberal foreign policy because Americans had few investments abroad; that since the war, the pressing need of American finance has been to prevent European bankruptcy, which has led to an endeavor to restore peace and order. We infer that the very real merits of American foreign policy hitherto can all be explained by motives of self-interest, and are not likely to survive when self-interest turns against them. We think, in particular, that increase of power for American financiers means increase of persecution for socialists, since in America they are regarded with more intolerance than in any other country. We feel that this could be prevented if American radical opinion were more in harmony with that of Europe. But that is impossible so long as you continue to advocate the combination of political democracy with benevolent despotism in the sphere of economics.

This applies with especial force in international affairs. Western capital, with Germany as broker, is apparently to govern Russia; France, through reparations, governs Germany; England and America have, if they choose to exercise it, a hold on France through French indebtedness, and America similarly could obtain a hold on us. As things stand, I think our influence on France, and American influence on Great Britain would probably be beneficial, but I cannot say as much as regards Western influence on Germany and Russia. That, however, is not the point. The point is that, under the present economic regime, the rich countries have immense power over the poorer ones, and also are able to drain the poorer countries of a very large part of the produce of their labor. The power of the richer countries will, of course, be used, as it has been in Russia, to prevent the propaganda, inauguration, or success of any system which robs the richer countries of their toll. To my mind, this regime is by its very nature contrary to justice, freedom and democracy, all of which form part of liberal (as well as of socialist) ideals, in America as elsewhere. If I am wrong, I shall be glad to be shown my error.

IMPRESSIONS OF AMERICA:

LABOUR AND A THIRD PARTY

The *New Leader* (London, 22 August 1924)

The impressions of a lecturer who travels to a new place every day are necessarily very superficial, and I lay no stress on my own, which may have been all wrong. There are only two points on which I can speak from adequate experience: one, that the trains are amazingly punctual; the other, that people have a fondness for lectures which is, to an Englishman, quite unintelligible. In England, if people admire an author, they read his books; in America, they want to hear him lecture, but they do not dream of reading him. It is impossible to read in America, except in the train, because of the telephone. Everyone has a telephone, and it rings all day and most of the night. This makes conversation, thinking, and reading out of the question, and accordingly these activities are somewhat neglected.

The press in America is much more mendacious than the Rothermere Press. I lectured in Boston to a large and enthusiastic audience, and the lecture passed off without a hitch. At the same moment, a general was addressing the American Legion, and urging them to break up my meeting with violence. Although they did not take his advice, the Boston newspapers next morning reported that my meeting had ended in disorder caused by the outraged patriotism of the American Legion.

The prosperity of the American wage-earner, which sounds like a fable, is a fact. It is very common for wage-earners to own motor-cars, in which they go to their work. There is poverty, but it is among the immigrants who can hardly speak English and are at the mercy of exploiters. Organised labour in America is in favour of restricting immigration, and this attitude is in no way surprising. The standard of life is higher in America than anywhere in Europe, and immensely higher than in Eastern Europe. Consequently the immigrant appears as a blackleg. His ignorance of the language makes him difficult to organise, and he is usually a tool in the hands of the Catholic priesthood. Oddly

228

enough, reactionary opinion in America is also in favour of restricting immigration, because Bolshevism chiefly flourishes among immigrants. One of the difficulties that socialistic opinions have to contend against in the United States is the general feeling that socialism is something 'foreign', advocated chiefly by alien Jews. The well-to-do American wage-earner is easily induced to regard the immigrant rather than the capitalist as his enemy, so that he becomes far more conservative than the wage-earners of Europe. This explains why it is possible for Gompers,[1] the President of the American Federation of Labor, to go on thundering against any recognition of the Soviet government, in a way which would be quite impossible for any man in an analogous position in Europe.

America is cursed by religious and racial troubles, some of which will probably grow less with time, while others seem insoluble. The worst, of course, is the Negro question. The way in which Southerners speak of Negroes, to this day, is so horrible that it is difficult to stay in the room with them. There are immense numbers of Negroes in New York, Chicago, and other northern cities, and wherever they come white antagonism creates a terrible problem. No issue is visible, since white people do not become more tolerant, and the Negro population is rapidly increasing.

Moreover, the violence generated by the suppression of Negroes finds outlets in other directions. The Ku-Klux-Klan, originally Southern and anti-Negro, has spread into many Northern regions, and has become anti-Jew, anti-Catholic, and generally anti-foreign. It is an immense organisation, embracing, at least in the South, most of the clergy of the denominations which we should call nonconformist, and having as its purpose the spread of an illegal reign of terror which shall make life intolerable for all but native, white, Protestant Americans. The prolonged deadlock in the Democratic Convention recently was a struggle between the Ku-Klux-Klan and the Catholic Church; the former supported Mr McAdoo, the latter Governor Smith (who is himself a Catholic).[2] When it became clear that neither could obtain the necessary majority, they compromised on a representative of the Trusts.

The number and prominence of Jews in America is astonishing. In New York they practically control the city politically, municipal contests being between them and the Catholics. Boston is firmly controlled by Catholics, but in Chicago the Jews are again powerful, though less so than in New York. I had the impression that throughout the Eastern States everything that is best in politics, in intellect, and in art, is Jewish. The Jews are mostly the children of immigrants from Germany, Poland, or Russia; they form a large percentage both of the very poor and of the very rich, but they do not, as a rule, remain very poor for long after their arrival in the United States. Owing to their merits and their numbers, there is a very strong anti-Semitic feeling, which takes an English visitor by surprise.

Politically, the most hopeful part of America is the North-West, particularly such States as Wisconsin, Minnesota, and North Dakota. This is an agricultural region, settled very largely by Germans and Scandinavians. Since the Armistice, the agriculture of the North-West has been in a very depressed condition; the farmers have had to mortgage and borrow, so that they have fallen under the power of the banks. The little banks are controlled by the big banks, so that ultimately the financial power derived from the harvests of grain is wielded by a few firms in Wall Street, among which Messrs Morgan and Co. are the chief. This situation has caused the farmers to be more open to socialistic arguments than they are in most parts of the world. A Farmer-Labour party has been formed, with a view to co-operation between progressive farmers and socialist wage-earners. The party, however, has fallen under the sway of the communists, and is therefore not likely to achieve much electoral success.

More important is the presidential candidature of Senator La Follette.[3] His constituents being mostly Germans or Swedes, he was able, without political extinction, to take a more or less pacifist line during the war. Since then, he has been the foremost man in progressive politics in America. He has no chance of being elected President, but his defection from the Republican party increases the chances of the Democrats, and makes the Republicans afraid to be as reactionary as they wish to be. All progressive opinion in America recognises the need of a third party, analogous to our Labour party, and Senator La Follette's candidature represents an important step in that direction. His programme involves many socialistic items, such as public ownership of railways. To my mind, he is more deserving of support than any other public man in America.

On the whole, from the point of view of Labour politics, America is about where we were thirty years ago. This is due to several causes. In the first place, industrialism is more recent than with us; it did not become important until the Civil War, seventy years ago. Even to this day, America is predominantly agricultural. Consequently, industrial habits of thought are less ingrained in America than in Lancashire and Yorkshire and the Clyde. In the second place, immigration and race problems have prevented the growth of a sense of working-class solidarity. In the third place, prosperity has prevented discontent, and has made the existing economic system seem good enough.

The prosperity of America is only partly due to skill; many other factors have contributed. The country has more natural wealth than any other; almost all the raw materials required in industry are obtainable within its borders, except rubber and tin. The area of the country is vast, with unrestricted internal free trade, and a population not nearly so dense as the natural resources would serve to support. There has been a constant influx of able-bodied adults, whose infancy and education have been paid for by the countries of their origin. And there has not been the burden of militarism and war which has oppressed Europe. Even America's share in the Great War was a trivial burden compared to that borne by European belligerents.

The richer and more conservative classes in America are still bitterly anti-German, and consequently pro-French. They are militaristic and patriotic, and wish to deprive America of the advantage hitherto derived from the smallness of the army. Military training is introduced in schools and colleges, and imperialist sentiment is encouraged as much as possible. It seems probable that, under the guidance of finance, America will embark upon a career of imperialism not so much territorial as economic. The opportunity exists, and no nation yet has resisted opportunity when it occurred. It is probable that the Pacific will be the first sphere of American expansion. This is what the Japanese fear, and it is a reason for being tolerant of their chauvinism. There are, however, great forces in America which are opposed to imperialist ventures, and it is possible that they may be able to exercise a restraining influence.

The future development of America is of immeasurable importance to the world, since America is stronger than any other Power, and is bound to exert an immense influence on the history of the next hundred years. It is permissible to hope for the best, since, especially among the youth of America, there is a very definite revolt against the ideals of business success which have been the curse of civilisation in the Western hemisphere. But there is reason for fear as well as for hope, and no man can say whether fear or hope will be justified by the event.

[1] Samuel Gompers, conservative trade union leader.

[2] William G. McAdoo and Alfred E. Smith; the latter was governor of New York State and the first Catholic to be seriously considered for presidential nomination.

[3] Robert M. La Follette received one sixth of the vote in the 1924 presidential election.

THE AMERICAN INTELLIGENTSIA

The *Nation and the Athenaeum* (London, 11 October 1924)

Having not seen America since the spring of 1914, I was expected, during my recent visit, to notice many changes. Americans find it necessary to their self-respect to believe that their country changes fast, and no doubt in the main the belief is true; but naturally the changes are not so readily perceived by strangers as by those who take the constant background of Americanism for granted. Nevertheless, I did notice some rather interesting changes. Ten years ago, I saw mainly universities and university teachers. Certainly their attitude then was in many respects different from that of many teachers at the present time. Ten years ago, the majority were doing their work with no strong consciousness of outside interference; now many of them seem to feel that they have to choose between hypocrisy and starvation.

There are two quite different kinds of tyranny to which university men are exposed in America: that of boards of trustees in the privately endowed universities, and that of the democracy in the State universities. The former is primarily economic, the latter primarily theological; both, of course, combine on moral persecution, and dismiss any man who becomes involved in a scandal, however innocently. Moreover, methods exist of fastening scandals upon those whose opinions are disliked.

The tyranny of boards of trustees is part of the power of capitalism, and is therefore attacked by socialists. Upton Sinclair's book, *The Goose-Step* consists of a long series of instances with names and dates. This book naturally roused great interest in academic circles. As a rule, the principal of a university denounces it as a gross libel, and quite unreliable in its facts; but the younger teachers, in a quiet corner, will whisper that it is quite correct, at any rate so far as *their* university is concerned. An outsider cannot, of course, form a well-informed judgement on this matter without a much longer study than I was able to make. But obviously it is a bad system to make learned men dependent for their livelihood upon a collection of ignorant and bigoted business-men. Some of our provincial universities have tended to imitate America in this respect; but so far, the prestige of Oxford and Cambridge has prevented the bad effects that might have been feared.

The tyranny of the democracy raises more interesting problems, and is much less discussed, because those who dislike tyranny are apt to like democracy. In the South and in some parts of the Middle-West, Protestantism is as fierce as in Belfast, and the whole intellectual atmosphere is reminiscent of the seventeenth century. Since the taxpayer's money supports the State universities, he feels that these institutions ought to magnify his ego by teaching what he believes, not what is believed by those who have taken the trouble to form a rational opinion. Hence the all but successful attempts to make it illegal to teach evolution in certain States. In the East, in some States, the Catholics are sufficiently powerful to enforce an inquisition on State teachers. This atmosphere of theological persecution makes many State universities quite as destitute of freedom as those that depend upon private endowments. And it is in fact a more serious matter than capitalist tyranny, for two reasons. First, the tyranny of a majority is harder to endure and to resist than that of a ruling oligarchy, because the latter, but not the former, rouses the sympathy and admiration of the public for the victim. Second, theology interferes more intimately than politics with the matters concerned in university teaching. It is very difficult to think of a single subject where the teacher can avoid conflicting with those who believe in the literal truth of the whole of the Bible, as the Fundamentalists do. Not even the pure mathematician is exempt, because a value of π which he cannot accept is given in 1 Kings, vii, 23.

Psychoanalysis, which is much more influential in America than in England, has had a disintegrating effect upon the Puritanism of the younger intellectuals. This influence seems to have penetrated more widely than others that might have been expected to be more effective. Being connected with medicine and such practical matters as the cure of insanity and hysterics, psychoanalysis is not dismissed as unimportant by 'practical' men. The emotional upheaval of the war, and the increase of economic independence among women, have both favoured its spread. It has had, conversationally, a remarkable effect in breaking down Victorian pruderies and reticences. Ten years ago, these were far stronger in America than in England; now, if anything, the position is reversed, so far as the private talk of educated people is concerned.

The result of all these causes is that the intelligentsia, as in pre-war Russia, have remarkable social and private freedom, combined with complete public enslavement. In Russia, there was always the hope of revolution. It is true that, when the revolution came, it enslaved the intelligentsia far more thoroughly than the Tsars had ever done, but that was not foreseen. Consequently, the hope of revolution prevented the intellectuals from feeling out of touch with the community; they were (so they imagined) only out of touch with the government. In America, it is much more difficult to entertain this illusion. There is no opportunity for revolution in America. The only strong revolutionary movement is the Ku-Klux-Klan, which is more reactionary than the government. America is essentially a country of pious peasants, like Russia. The peasants in America control the government, but delegate much of their power to certain very rich men, on condition that these men pose as the champions of religion and morality, which they are only too willing to do. It is obvious that, in such a community, intellectual freedom can only exist *sub rosa*.

This whole state of affairs, however, is probably transitory. The worst elements in America are some of those representing the original British stock, which has persisted almost pure in the South. The immigrant Jews form a vast community, with great intellectual and artistic vigour. The Italians, South Slavs, etc, are difficult to assimilate, but when assimilated they are likely to contribute valuable artistic and anti-Puritan elements to the national life. It is true that the immigration of these groups is being severely restricted, but they are already so large in America that they can hardly fail to have a permanent influence.

What is probably more important than all these causes combined is the fact that industry is continually gaining on agriculture in America, and even agriculture is becoming assimilated to industry in its methods. This makes it almost certain that the industrial outlook will, in time, prevail over the agricultural. When this happens, seventeenth-century theological bigotry is likely to lose its influence.

But no merely economic change will bring liberty in America. Economic change, by itself, will merely bring some new form of tyranny. America has not, as we have, strong institutions inherited from the Middle Ages, and has, therefore, no tradition of group autonomy. All through Western Europe, medieval anarchy led to a considerable degree of independence for guilds, monasteries, universities, learned professions, etc. Such freedom as exists in Western Europe is largely the result of these conditions. It has been produced also by political con-tests, between Church and King, King and aristocracy, aristocracy and middle class. In America all these reasons for regarding the community as a collection of groups have been absent. Every man is regarded simply as a citizen, and is expected to submit to the decision of the majority. Democracy, as understood in America, is not softened by any freedom for groups or individuals to decide their private concerns as may seem good to them. This fact, combined with the Puritan tradition of moral persecution, accounts for the extraordinarily small degree of self-determination permitted to the individual in America.

The chief harm done by this state of affairs is the hampering of individual achievement. Biologically speaking, America must produce as large a percentage as Europe of people with artistic or intellectual talents. But the output of America, in art, literature, and science, is singularly inferior to that of Europe. If Einstein had been an American —as he would have been if his father had happened to emigrate—he would have been put on to so many boards and committees that he would have had no time to do original work. Administrative work is valued in America out of proportion to its importance, because the individual is nothing and the community is everything. And yet propagandists for Americanism assert that America is the home of individualism!

IS AMERICA BECOMING IMPERIALISTIC?

Unpublished (1925)

Imperialism, in its early stages, is a natural force rather than a senti-ment. It arises when a poor country with military strength comes in contact with a rich country with military weakness, as happened with the Spaniards in Mexico and Peru; or when a country possessed of in-dustrial arts comes across one with natural resources but undeveloped technique; or when a country with a low rate of interest comes across a country with a high rate. War expenditure has sent up the rate of interest throughout the Old World, and has therefore stimulated foreign investment on the part of Americans. It has also left the Americans im-mensely stronger than any other Power as regards capacity for waging war. The inevitable consequence is the rapid growth of American imperialism, not by design, but merely from force of circumstances. Americans themselves are, for the most part, unaware of what is happening; they know that America is more concerned than formerly with what goes on in various parts of the world, but they imagine the motives of this concern to be purely benevolent. So, to a great extent, they are; but it is that kind of benevolence which thinks it a kindness to make other countries as like America as possible. This is the same kind that is practised by the Bolsheviks, and in both cases it lapses by easy gradations into imperialism.

Let us not, on this account, fall into a nationalist prejudice against America. Americans who contrast themselves with the British advance three propositions: (1) that our imperialism is very bad; (2) that their foreign and colonial policy is better than ours; (3) that their attitude to less developed nations is purely philanthropic. Of these propositions I admit the first two. In the Philippines, the Americans have carried out an educational programme which puts to shame anything that we have attempted in India or the Crown Colonies. In China they have opposed territorial aggression, given their share of the Boxer indemnity to educa-tion, and favoured the progressive elements in public opinion. We, on the other hand, because we desired to go on oppressing India, were anxious that China should remain weak; we continued our alliance with Japan, apparently in order to prevent Japanese pan-Asiatic propaganda in India; we thereby became accomplices in all the Japanese aggressions against China, until veiled threats from America and our dominions caused us to abandon this sinister policy, with the result of freeing Shantung and Eastern Siberia from their Japanese garrisons. All this I admit.

But when I am asked to regard American policy as benevolent, or as differing from our own in anything except method and stage of development, I find myself unable to do so. I propose to set forth some of my reasons in what follows.

There is in New York a small monthly called *The World Tomorrow: A Journal Looking Toward a Social Order Based on the Principles of Jesus.* The issue of December 1924, deals with Gandhi, and suggests that his practice is more in accord with the principles of Jesus than that of his Christian persecutors, a view which I recommend to British missionaries in India. The issue of November 1924, deals with the imperialism of the United States in Latin America. I read there, for example, in an article on Mexico by a Mexican:

'Mexico is now surrounded to the east and south by invaded nations, small defenseless nations on whose soil the military boot of a northern army has left dishonorable footsteps. But, at present, the principal aspect of the imperialistic policy of the United States toward Latin America is not militaristic. It is a subtle life-controlling scheme that the American empire is carrying out to bring about the dreaded fulfillment of the significance of the words of Mr Taft[1] on 22 February 1906: "the borders of the United States virtually extend to Cape Horn." The subterranean invasions that threaten the independence and sovereignty of the Latin American republics are made by powerful financial and industrial interests in the United States. . . . The United States government is responsible to this economic impetus, and in faithful co-ordination with the plans of capitalists brings into play in their favor the skill and craftiness of its diplomatic dueling, and the pressure of military and political power.'

It should be said, in justice, that, admitting this indictment, the United States has shown itself less illiberal towards Mexico than our own late Labour government, which broke off diplomatic relations with Mexico because that Republic attempted to put into operation some of those socialistic principles which our own government professed. (When Mrs Evans was killed she was engaged in armed resistance to the law and authorities of the country in which she lived.) And because this was done by a Labour government, no friend of freedom in this country protested. 'Latin America', the same article continues 'looks with intense eagerness, with life and death interest, on the valiant struggle that young Mexico is making to safeguard her independence and gain her economic emancipation.'

Not only the mineral wealth, but even the pastoral areas of Latin America are mainly in the hands of United States magnates. 'The great plains of Venezuela, Argentina, Brazil, Paraguay, Uruguay and Chile are cattle ranches, owned in areas of millions of acres to a company, by the Armour, Swift, Morris, Wilson, and Liebig companies, which operate tremendous packing establishments.'

An article by Lewis S. Gannett, associate editor of the New York *Nation*, sets out some interesting facts about Central America.

'We do not want to annex these countries; but we insist that they shall do our bidding without annexation. Modern imperialism is subtler than the old, but no less effective. We have had 100 marines in the Nicaraguan capital since 1919—meanwhile Nicaragua has converted her currency, enacted an election law (made in America), and been "developed"; we have marines in Honduras at this moment, and we have on occasion landed marines to "help" the Guatemalans. In Nicaragua, Americans collect the customs and have at times handled the internal taxes; Salvador has just gone under the blight of an 8 per cent loan, guaranteed by 70 per cent of her customs receipts, which a group of New York bankers will collect for her; and if differences arise between Salvador and the bankers, Mr Hughes[2] has arranged to have the Chief Justice of our Supreme Court settle the affair.'

And again:

'On trivial excuses we landed our armies in Haiti in 1915, in Santo Domingo in 1916. The rest of the world was at war; we had a free hand. It is a dirty tale. We seized the customs houses, cut off the salaries of recalcitrant ministers or replaced them with naval officers, invaded the country, shot down the patriots (navy reports call them bandits) who dared oppose us.'

The British have been doing this sort of thing for three centuries. When we find the Americans taking to it, it makes us feel that Anglo–American friendship is being greatly facilitated. The author continues:

'It is plain that an election would force out of office the docile President whom we unconstitutionally put in office and who has done our imperial bidding; so there have been no elections since we invaded the country nine years ago. There will be none until the Haitians are willing to recognise the acts of the occupation, and to elect a government which will do the will of the National City Bank.'

'The United States is the center of one of the greatest economic fires of history.' So Mr Gannett sums up the facts about Latin America. All this happened without the knowledge of the immense majority of the American people. It is an automatic result of the economic system called capitalism. It should not be the object of moral indignation. It goes to prove that Americans are human beings like ourselves, and to disprove the view, commonly held in America, that to cross the Atlantic from east to west, in the proper latitude, infallibly makes a man beget virtuous children, exempt from the ordinary frailties of Europeans. Nationalistic and geographical ethics are foolish; the only way to improve men in the mass is to remove the temptation to greed and the occasions for fear which are unavoidable in a world governed by competition and monopoly based on armed force.

But we must now turn to an even more important field for American imperialism, namely China. Here we cannot point to accomplished facts but only to tendencies and aspirations. These, however, are sufficiently alarming. The first Western imperialism in China—apart from the early efforts of Spaniards and Portuguese—was that of England; then came France, then Germany, and then Japan—the worst, because the nearest. America traditionally held aloof, on idealistic grounds, except for periodically causing the Powers to declare their platonic devotion to the open door. The Washington Conference, however, marked a new departure. Japan had utilised the war period to establish almost a protectorate over China, and had succeeded, by the help of secret treaties with England and France, in securing Shantung for herself at Versailles, as China's reward for participation in the war. Japan's position in the Far East was unassailable so long as the Anglo-Japanese alliance lasted. America therefore decided to use her power to break this alliance. The British government realised the danger; it reluctantly abandoned the devastation of Ireland, the furtherance of Japanese oppression in China, and the non-payment of interest on the American debt. All these three changes of policy, of which only one occurred actually at the Washington Conference, were dictated by the desire to stand well with America. As a result, the Japanese have evacuated Shantung and Vladivostok, and have shown some tendency to liberalise their foreign policy. All this is to the good; but there is another side.

The most illuminating account that I have read of American high policy in the Far East is Thomas F. Millard's *Conflict of Policies in Asia*. Mr Millard knows China well, and was for a long time editor of the leading American review on the Far East. He has been in close touch (not always amicable) with those who direct American foreign policy. He is frank to the point of indiscretion, and says what others only think. His thesis is that the Americans are altruistic in their dealings with backward nations, while the English are not; that the Americans are able to defeat the English in war; and that therefore it is their duty to force the English to abandon thier own policy and support that of the United States. His book consists largely of reprints of memoranda written at various times from the Paris negotiations onwards. Specially interesting are his suggestions to the American government as to methods of causing the abrogation of the Anglo–Japanese alliance. He takes it as probable that there must sooner or later be a war between America and Japan, and points out reasons why this must involve the British Empire if the alliance is still in being at the time, since he holds that even if England preserved neutrality, the just resentment of the Americans at the alliance would lead them to invade Canada. He is much impressed by the fact that Canada constitutes a weakness of the British Empire as against the United States. He thinks it perhaps unwise to allow the Canadians separate diplomatic representation at Washington, since this might enable them to declare neutrality in a war between the British and the Americans. He points out that we could not remain long in arrears with the interest on the debt, because America could seize Canada as security. It is to be observed that he is an ardent champion of self-determination, but apparently this principle does not apply to Canada.

In a memorandum written before the Washington Conference, he urges that the United States must have a secure naval base in Eastern waters. By the Washington Treaty, they agreed not to make such a base; but he consoles himself with the thought that, in view of the new friendship between England and America, Singapore may do just as well. His words are: 'Japanese naval strategists and Japanese diplomats . . . pondered the fact that, although the American government had consented for ten years not to add to its fortified positions in the Western Pacific, it had not objected to the exclusion of Singapore from the limitation by an obscure phrase written into the Treaty.' Is Singapore part of what we pay to secure American friendship? He works out in some detail the strategy and politics of a war with Japan, assuming England neutral. China and Russia, he says, would be needed as allies, but should be advised at first to remain neutral:

'Japan is thus forced at the very beginning of the war to take action which must have the effect of estranging Chinese and Russian sentiment; viz., by violating the neutrality of both China and Russia in the seizure of railways and occupation of territory. This act of Japan can also be used by American propaganda as showing the unscrupulousness of Japan, and comparisons can be made with Germany's invasion of Belgium and Luxemburg. Thus Japan will begin the war by a series of attacks affronting Chinese and Russians, and also the enlightened opinion of civilisation. [It is only at a later stage that the Americans are to begin the unprovoked invasion of Canada, mentioned above, if, England, though neutral, is still Japan's ally.] America, next to Japan, has the best nucleus for an effective intelligence organisation in China. The 8,000 Americans in China (*many of them missionaries*) are distributed in every part of the country; many of them speak the Chinese language, and their relations with the people are on the whole friendly and cordial. The means to organise them into a good intelligence force at once suggests themselves, and need not be given in detail.'

'Propaganda', he adds, 'is the *publicity* methods employed to accomplish the same things that the intelligence division does privately.'

As for the reduction of naval armaments effected at Washington, Mr Millard is commendably frank. 'A status of complete disarmament', he says, 'relatively enhanced the position of the United States because of the superior industrial and financial resources of America and their capacity for rapid warlike energisation and mobilisation.' And again: 'As an abstract proposition, it is probable that the most advantageous position for the United States to commence a war against any power is for both nations to be completely disarmed at the beginning.' If a European had suggested these reasons for America's action, he would have been denounced as a cynic. But Mr Millard dots the i's:

'The measures devised by the American government to get the strategical position in the Pacific on a satisfactory basis for the United States were simple, and had only two points: (1) to break the Anglo–Japanese combination; (2) to limit armaments in a proportion reasonably to secure, with a new political status, the American position.'

Mr Millard deserves our gratitude for not mentioning any supposed humanitarian motive.

Now that America has secured the supreme position in the Far East (or will have done, as soon as the Singapore base is completed), what use is she to make of her power? Here there are two fundamental propositions laid down: (1) International action is required to stabilise China; (2) China should 'make close relations with the United States the keystone of China's diplomacy, and subordinate all other diplomatic relationships to that'. To come to details: China owes money to European Powers, which themselves owe much more to America. Let America write off the amount of China's debt to Europe from Europe's debt to America; then America will become the sole foreign creditor of China, except Japan. At this stage the number of Americans in the administration of the customs and similar services is to be increased. China is to have a moratorium, and the accruing customs revenue (by this time under American management) is to be used to create a strong central government in China, which, once established, is likely to recognise America's remarkably philanthropic disposition by affording a safe field for American investment. If Japan opposes this process, the Open Door principle is to be urged, if necessary to the point of war. There is no reason to dread such an accession of power to one country, because, 'so far as this may be true of any national policy, the policy of the American government indicated at Washington is altruistic, in that a widely beneficent purpose and a kindly sentiment for other nations and peoples is within the purview of whatever is proposed.'

The difficulty of sincere friendship between English and Americans is, says Mr Millard, that the Englishman is not genuinely democratic. 'At home the Englishman is a democrat; East of Suez he assumes the airs and prerogatives of the proconsuls and citizens of Imperial Rome with respect to barbarians. . . . Americans think of American political liberty as belonging to all peoples. . . . Americans are not in favor of continuing indefinitely or of perpetuating political science on a double-standard basis.'

I assure the reader that these words really occur in Mr Millard's book. Yet he knows all about Japanese exclusion from California; presumably he knows about the exclusion of socialists from the New York legislature; I can hardly suppose that he has never heard of the Negro question in the Southern States. Does he know, to take one instance, that, as reported in the *New Republic* at the time, in the presidential election of 1920, a village was burnt to the ground, causing the death of a number of women and children, because one of its Negro inhabitants had endeavoured to exercise his undoubted legal right to vote? He boasts that the Philippines are better treated than India, which is true; it is equally true that the Negroes of Jamaica are better treated than those of the Southern States. The reason in each case is the same: the smaller subject population inspires less fear in the tyrants.

Americans generally believe that they are conferring a favour on 'backward' nations by making them as like America as possible, *id est*, by introducing modern industry and stable government. They overlook several things. In America, the capitalist is American; in the 'backward' countries, he is also an American. The political government, which is unimportant, is left to natives; the real government is in the hands of American banks. Art, leisure, traditional culture are swept away when a country is Americanised. Long hours, low wages, economic enslavement to the foreigner, take their place. There are those who do not think this is a gain.

Nations and groups are maleficent in proportion to their power. While we were supreme in the Far East, we forced opium on China. While Japan was supreme, she fomented dissension and indulged in military conquest. Now that America is supreme, the palm of evil-doing must soon pass to America. There is no hope for mankind except in diminishing the power of one individual or group over another. To suppose that power can be long possessed without being abused, is to show ignorance of history and human nature. The just distribution of power, even more than that of wealth, is the problem which our age must solve if we are to escape a grinding tyranny, a desperate revolt, and a universal cataclysm.

[1] William Howard Taft, Secretary of War, later President.
[2] Charles Evans Hughes, Secretary of State.

THE NEW PHILOSOPHY OF AMERICA

The *Fortnightly Review* (London, May 1928); originally published in *The New York Times Magazine* (22 May 1927), as 'The New Life that Is America's'

In Europe since the end of the war there has existed towards America an attitude of dislike based upon our financial and moral obligations to the United States. We like those whom we benefit and hate those who benefit us. Owing to the Lafayette tradition, France loved America until America was able to repay that debt. Then French sentiment changed because the sense of obligation was galling.

The dislike of America which has grown up in England is due to the fact that world empire has now passed from Lombard Street to Wall Street. The British navy, it is true, is still nominally ours, but we dare not employ it in any way displeasing to Washington. Nothing can alter this situation unless Great Britain should become self-supporting in the matter of food, which seems scarcely possible. Neither the English nor the French, therefore, view America impartially; both tend to emphasise defects and minimise merits.

For my part, while I am conscious of the defects, I think the merits are more interesting, more novel and more important. America is achieving certain things of great moment which have never been achieved before, and is developing a philosophy of life which, whether we like it or not, is obviously more suited to the modern world than that of most Europeans.

Western civilisation is derived from three sources—the Bible, the Greeks, and machinery. The reconciliation between the Bible and the Greeks was a slow business achieved in the course of centuries by the Catholic Church. The Renaissance and the Reformation undid the synthesis and left the two elements again at war, as in antiquity. On the whole, Protestantism represented the Bible and free thought represented the Greeks. But pre-industrial America was Biblical rather than Hellenic. For reasons which I have not now space to set forth, the Judaic and Protestant outlook has been found far easier to adapt to modern

244

industrialism than the outlook of either Catholicism or free thought.

In America, transplantation gradually weakened even those elements of medieval culture which the Pilgrim Fathers had been most anxious to preserve. The new outlook appropriate to machinery was thus enabled to become more nearly completely dominant than in the Old World. Whether we like this new outlook or not is a question of little importance. What is important is that the new outlook is increasingly displacing the old, not only in Europe and America but also in the greater part of Asia. In formulating this new outlook and in creating a community living in accordance with it, America takes the lead.

The dominating belief of what may be called the industrial philosophy is the belief that man is the master of his fate, and need not submit tamely to the evils which the niggardliness of inanimate nature or the follies of human nature have hitherto inflicted. Man, since he became capable of forethought, has been dominated by fears—fear of starvation, fear of pestilence, fear of defeat in war, fear of murder by private enemies. Elaborate systems, partly rational, partly magical, have been built up to minimise these dangers. In the early ages of agriculture, men dealt with the fear of starvation by means of human sacrifice, which was supposed to invigorate the Corn Spirit. It is only very gradually that scientific agriculture has displaced this attitude.

Pestilence also was viewed superstitiously down to our day, and is still so viewed in India. The fear of war has only just begun to be treated rationally, and those who so treat it still labour under the suspicion of being cranks. The fear of murder by private enemies is supposed to be dealt with by the criminal law, but this also was in its origin superstitious, being based upon the notion of blood pollution, and even now the retributory element prevents it from being as effective an engine of prevention as it could easily be made.

I think it could be maintained that, in regard to the elimination of three, at any rate, of these major evils, the United States leads the way. Not only starvation but even poverty is practically non-existent among white men born in America. The problem of making labour sufficiently productive to provide material comfort for all has been solved for the first time in the world's history. As regards pestilence, American scientific medicine is, I believe, second to none, and the general level of sanitation and hygiene is extraordinarily high in most parts of the United States. With regard to war, America is certainly the least bellicose of the Great Powers, and the League of Nations was founded by an American,[1] although for various reasons his countrymen refused to follow him.

To the philosopher, the outlook on life which accompanies these achievements is quite as interesting as the achievements themselves. To my mind, the best work that has been done anywhere in philosophy and psychology during the present century has been done in America. Its merit is due not so much to the individual ability of the men concerned as to their freedom from certain hampering traditions which the European man of learning inherits from the Middle Ages.

Perhaps these traditions can be summed up in the one word—contemplation. European universities were originally places for the training of monks, and monks, though they tilled the soil, existed primarily for the sake of the contemplative life. A modern European professor does not till the soil, but he continues to believe in contemplation. In him this belief takes the form of admiration for pure learning, regardless of its practical applications. I am myself sufficiently European to feel this admiration in a far higher degree than it is felt by the typical American. Nevertheless, I perceive that it is psychologically connected with an attitude of reverence towards the universe which is hardly compatible with the belief in man's omnipotence through the machine. We do not contemplate the flea, we catch it. The modern point of view is in its infancy, but we may foresee a time when it will lead men to regard the non-human world with as little reverence as we now feel towards the poor flea.

American philosophy is sweeping away the static conception of knowledge which dominated both medieval and modern philosophy, and has substituted what it calls the Instrumental Theory, the very name of which is suggested by machinery. In the Instrumental Theory there is not a single state of mind which consists of knowing a truth; there is a way of acting, a manner of handling the environment which is appropriate, and whose appropriateness constitutes what alone can be called knowledge as these philosophers understand it. One might sum up this theory by a definition: to know something is to be able to change it as we wish. There is no place in this outlook for the beatific vision nor for any notion of final excellence.

What applies to our non-human environment applies also to man himself. In old days, there was something called 'human nature' which was supposed to be an unchangeable datum. Probably even in America medieval influences are still sufficiently strong to lead uneducated people to assert that human nature cannot be changed, at any rate when they are arguing with socialists; but for this view they will find no support in their leading psychologists and educators.

Professor Watson[2] has discovered that human nature contains only three ingredients, which are as follows: babies cry when they hear a loud noise and when their cot gives way; they are angry if you hold their limbs; and they are pleased if you stroke them. The rest of what we call human nature in an adult is the result of education, intentional or unintentional. It is difficult to set limits to what could be done by carefully devised education in the way of producing freaks. Possibly, education might even produce people better than ourselves, though this hypo-thesis is, of course, painful to our self-esteem.

Belief in the omnipotence of man is, of course, not wholly true. We must all die, though medical men may postpone the moment. The human race itself will presumably perish when the sun grows cold, if not before. But in spite of these limitations, the new view has become during the last 100 years far more nearly true than the older views which were inherited from the long period of man's bondage to nature. We may say that at last man is achieving mastery and becoming able to realise his purposes without intolerably arduous labour.

Both in the practice and the theory of this emancipation, America leads the way. It involves a change in our values—religious, moral and aesthetic. Traditional art is impregnated with emotions which men's new powers are rendering antiquated. In a situation of danger, it is possible to feel fear or rage or heroic courage; it is possible also to feel nothing, but to take the steps which are necessary to avert the danger. This last is useless for literary purposes, whereas the other three attitudes lend themselves to blank verse. We must suppose, therefore, that the older art forms will lose their vitality as the newer attitude to life acquires strength.

There is no reason to suppose that art will die out, though it must change. Skyscrapers and railway bridges are already beginning to develop aesthetic forms appropriate to the pride of scientific men. But the other arts lag behind because they have no immediate economic motive for adaptation to industrialism. Wells's *Outline of History* might perhaps be turned into an epic or exhibited in the movies; there is no reason in the nature of things why the result should be aesthetically inferior to the first chapter of Genesis. But good aesthetic results will not be achieved until men with the requisite artistic capacity have lived from early infancy in a modern atmosphere. For it may be said broadly that an artist can only express the attitude which he learnt during the first few years of life.

Probably poetry as an art has too strong a tradition to acquire a vigorous modern life. With few exceptions, nothing can be mentioned in poetry that was not known in the time of Shakespeare.

One may sing the praises of wine, but not of tea. It is probable that the art forms will change completely and that during the transition period art will be too experimental to achieve much positive success. America's artistic barrenness is often made a reproach, but I think it is only due to the fact that America has entered upon this experimental period sooner than the Old World. We may expect, therefore, that America will also emerge sooner, and will be the first to create the new art forms appropriate to modern life.

There is one aspect of scientific civilisation which I personally find painful, and that is the diminution in the value and independence of the individual. Great enterprises tend more and more to be collective, and in an industrialised world their interference of the community with the individual [sic] must be more intense than it need be in a commercial or agricultural regime. Although machinery makes man collectively more lordly in his attitude towards nature, it tends to make the individual man more submissive to his group. I do not know whether this has anything to do with the fact that herd instinct is much more insistent in America than in England, and that individual liberty is less respected both politically and socially. Although I cannot but think this regrettable, I do not see how it is to be avoided, and I hold that the mastery over nature is so great a boon that it is worth-while to pay even a high price in order to achieve it.

1 Woodrow Wilson.
2 John B. Watson, the Behaviourist; see above p. 102.

OPTIMISTIC AMERICA

The *Herald Tribune Magazine* (New York, 6 May 1928)

'Felicity', says Hobbes, 'consisteth in prospering, not in having prospered.' In modern language, it is not the amount of your income that makes you happy, but its rate of increase. The man who enjoys life is the man who, with habits adjusted to one standard of life, finds himself continually in a position to adopt a slightly higher standard. That is why, on the whole, England was happy under Queen Elizabeth and Queen Victoria, and America is happy at the present time. I shall be told that I am taking a too materialistic view of the causes of happiness, but before tackling this question let us see in what sense America is more optimistic than Europe.

When I say that America is optimistic, I am not saying that America is altogether happy, for although optimism tends to promote happiness it does not always succeed in actually producing it. I may illustrate the point by the comparison of two novels, one English and one American. The English novel is Miss Lehman's *Dusty Answer* and the American novel is Dreiser's *An American Tragedy*.

Both novels are exceedingly gloomy, but in the English novel the misfortunes result from pessimism, whereas in the American novel they result from optimism. In the English novel the heroine has various love affairs, all of which come to nothing because neither she nor her lovers can persuade themselves that even love lends any real savor to life, which appears to them all an insipid and hopeless business.

In the American novel, on the contrary, the young man's misfortunes result from the intensity of his conviction that happiness is to be obtained from wealth and fashionable women. A little of his zest would have saved the heroine of *Dusty Answer*; a little of her detachment would have saved the hero of *An American Tragedy*.

This difference is, I think, illustrative of the difference between American and post-war Europe. The general inability to believe in anything, which characterises the young European of the present day, has no doubt a variety of causes. On the part of those who were in the war, nervous exhaustion was and is still a potent factor. On the part of most people, there is a cynicism resulting from having made a stupendous effort, which in the end turned out to be of no value. And in all circles, there is the discouragement due to the difficult economic situation— aristocrats have to sell their estates to the New Rich; the sons of business- men who have expected affluence find themselves compelled to work for small salaries with little hope of promotion; wage-earners in spite of Herculean efforts, both political and industrial, find unemployment still prevalent and wages still declining. And everybody in Europe has the somewhat discouraging feeling that through the war political pre- eminence has passed from Europe to America.

The exact contrary of all this is the case in America. America's effort in the World War was brief and successful, at no enormous cost in American lives. The sins of the Treaty of Versailles were not America's sins, and therefore produced in America only cynicism about Europe which is, of course, a pleasant emotion. In spite of a brief depression in 1920, America has been on the whole extraordinarily prosperous since the war and everybody has the sense of being on the up-grade. This economic prosperity has, for example, two important effects in the lives of young men as contrasted with young men in Europe: first, a man can marry at an earlier age than he can in Europe; and second, he can change his profession if, after a few years, he finds it disagreeable, where- as in Europe a man is married to his profession by an utterly indissoluble monogamic marriage.

But in addition to all these considerations, there is perhaps something that goes deeper. America is a pioneer in building up the new mechanical civilisation, and the immense majority of Americans are proud of this civilisation and happy in it. There is nothing in the new civilisation that conflicts deeply with American habits or values. Almost the only thing in the European tradition that Americans have preserved is theology, which is held to be not inconsistent with machines.

Europe, on the other hand, is impregnated with habits derived from feudalism and monasticism. Belief in tradition and historic continuity is connected with feudalism, while belief in art and disinterested learning is connected with monasticism. Sensitive Europeans suffer because the modern world is intolerant of such values. In America, likewise, one meets men with this kind of sensitiveness, but they are fewer and they generally retire to Paris. The whole movement of American life, apart from these rare exceptions, is toward something that can be achieved and that is felt to be important.

For my part, I find my reactions to this situation somewhat contra- dictory; while my feelings are those of a European, my beliefs are on the whole on the side of America. The things that I instinctively value are things for which America has little use; they are such things as theoretical science, art, enjoyment of beauty, lyric love, and historic continuity. I find it very difficult to be enthusiastic about plans for making two automobiles grow where one grew before; I do not feel in my bones that the countryside is improved by the smell of gasoline. But when I try to take an objective view, I perceive that America must be judged not by what I like but by what Americans like. The civilisation that they are producing does, so far as I can judge, produce a higher level of average happiness than has ever existed before in the history of the world.

The chief question in my mind is whether American success is psychologically permanent. The economic prosperity of America is due, of course, very largely to her natural resources, but also to Puritanism. This is evident when one compares what the Spaniards made of Latin America with what the Puritans made of the United States, for in Latin America also the natural resources are very great. Puritanism taught men to forgo present pleasure for a future reward; originally this reward was to be in another life but the habits of discipline which had been generated survived when the reward sought became affluence in old age. The Puritans' power of resisting the solicitations of present pleasure was a vital factor in causing those habits of saving required to produce the capital needed for industrialism.

There was also another way in which Puritanism operated. Religions, which condemn the pleasures of sense, drive men to seek the pleasures of power; throughout history power has been the vice of the ascetic. American civilisation is built more than any previous civilisation upon the will to power, more especially power over the material environment. As Puritanism decays in America, it is to be expected that men will be less content with power and more anxious for the other pleasures that wealth can buy. When that happens, the mechanical civilisation will grow at once less successful and less satisfying.

Something of the same sort happened in the Italy of the Renaissance. The businessmen who built up Italian prosperity in the twelfth and thirteenth centuries were Puritans of the American type: on this ground they were persecuted by both Pope and Emperor, who agreed on nothing else. With Boccaccio, one enters upon a new atmosphere of easy-going hedonism, and from that time onward rich Italians devoted themselves more to enjoying life than to augmenting their wealth, with the result that in the end the wealth disappeared and the enjoyment of life along with it.

It is very difficult to preserve a tradition of stern moral discipline in an atmosphere of great material prosperity, and it remains to be seen whether the discipline which a mechanical civilisation demands can be preserved without theological sanctions. I sincerely hope that it can, but if this is to be done it will be necessary to create and teach in early youth an ethic which shall be wholly of this world and yet not too soft and self-indulgent.

The practical basis of such an ethic should be, I think, a more civilised conception both of happiness and pleasure than one is likely to find in the atmosphere of decaying Puritanism. Ascetic morality condemns all pleasure alike, and thus leads all who are not saints to seek the grosser pleasures rather than those that have some refinement and aesthetic or moral value, since the grosser pleasures are more easily concealed from the stern eye of the moralist. And under a Puritan regime, happiness as well as pleasure tends to be sought in anything that the Puritan condemns.

True happiness is not, in fact, to be obtained through a life of gross indulgence, nor without a certain consistency and self-discipline in action. It is not very difficult to make this fact plain to the young through appeals to their ambition, but it cannot be done by means of prohibitions, the theological reason for which no longer wins the same belief as it once did. Educational reformers have perhaps been a little too much inclined to rely upon the pupil's own impulse as contrasted with the discipline of habit formation.

This covers perhaps the most interesting part of the psychological development of the child, but it does not suffice to generate certain dull virtues which are nevertheless essential to the success of a machine civilisation. I am thinking of such things as punctuality, exactitude and faithfulness to obligations undertaken. Such things are best acquired as habits in youth and continued in later life with the unquestioning automatism that habit produces, but no educational system can be regarded as satisfactory unless it succeeds in generating the modes of behavior required for a co-operation in a machine civilisation.

If education can successfully tackle this problem, the optimism of America may continue indefinitely; but if not, there is a risk that with the breakdown of Puritanism, men may cease to value certain good things which it has produced as an accidental by-product and may, therefore, cease to be happy in the civilisation that they have taken such pains to produce.

I do not expect this result, for I have a great belief in the strength of the constructive impulse in America. But there is a danger, and it cannot be met unless those who have serious purposes in life can learn to divorce them from an out-worn tradition and from an attempt to bully and coerce the young into outward acceptance of conventional standards which in their hearts they reject. The creation of a rationalist ethic is the great need of our time.

THE CINEMA AS A MORAL INFLUENCE

Forward, English-language section (New York, 24 March 1929); published as 'When Bertrand Russell Goes to the Movies'

Everybody knows that America is more virtuous than Europe, and that the Middle-West of America is the most virtuous portion of that country. There is a perfectly simple test of virtue which proves the justice of this common opinion: if A wants to persecute B, while B does not want to persecute A, then clearly A is more virtuous than B; he has a higher moral standard and is more inclined to moral indignation. Consequently, where a large public has to be appealed to, its most virtuous portions determine the nature of the appeal, for while the vicious can tolerate virtue, the virtuous cannot tolerate vice. Hence every increase in the size of the audience means an increase in the virtuousness of the appeal.

These observations apply with especial force to the cinema. The productions of Hollywood are exhibited in all parts of the world, with the possible exception of Greenland and the Antarctic continent. In the Middle-West, they seem natural; in the rest of America, intelligible; in other continents, interesting because they are so curious. Moreover, much can be done by altering the captions: I saw at Locarno an American film about bootleggers and rum-runners being caught by virtuous policemen, but in order to make it sympathetic to a southern wine-drinking population, all the captions had been altered so as to make it appear that cocaine was the substance in dispute. To an Italian-speaking population, the American objection to alcohol seems just as strange as the Hindu objection to beef: it is a fact concerning which sociologists could speculate, but for which one would not seek a rational explanation.

The movies have had one effect which may hereafter prove of some considerable importance: they have persuaded the populations of all other civilised countries (quite unjustly, of course) that Americans are silly. The morality of the nursery tale and the simplicity of the fairy story are, if one were to judge by the cinema, demanded in America by

253

grown men and women. In this respect, America is peculiar. The British appear to be incapable of producing films, but the Germans and Russians can utilise the cinema to produce things that are really admirable, and are only prevented by political considerations from being popular throughout the continent.

For my part, I am a person of simple tastes: I like to see a race between a motor-car and an express train; I enjoy the spectacle of the villain gnashing his teeth because he has just failed to pick off the engine driver; I delight in men tumbling off skyscrapers and saving themselves by telegraph wires; I am thrilled by a sheriff's posse galloping through a sandstorm in the alkali desert. And the enjoyment of these unsophisticated delights is enhanced by the feeling that in that matter at least one is in harmony with the great world democracy. I am too old to have enjoyed the experience, which younger Europeans have on first landing in America, that the movies have suddenly come to life. In old days, cultured persons arriving in Italy had an analogous sensation; they saw Italian opera and Italian painting exemplified by living men and women. Nowadays, for the great mass of mankind, it is America that gives this sensation, since it is only Americans who are represented in the cinema. America has thus become the classic land of art for all simple souls.

The cinema will lose its international character by the introduction of the 'talkies'; one cannot imagine the characters in the movies talking French, Italian, German, or Russian; American is the only language compatible with their acts, gestures, and sentiments. The cinema is perhaps the most heart-rending of all the many examples of artistic barbarism. Its possibilities in a thousand directions are immeasurable; it is capable of an epic sweep which is quite impossible to the 'legitimate' drama; it can deal with such a theme as Shaw's 'Methuselah' far better than Shaw has dealt with it; it can present great movements in history; it ought to be used in all schools for the teaching of history, geography, and zoology. But all these things are impossible so long as the whole of the technique is in the hands of men whose taste has been degraded by the necessity of making an appeal to the most ignorant and stupid parts of the population, and who are themselves so ignorant and stupid that they can do this without cynicism. Many countries have State opera and State theatre, but not State cinema, because the cinema is modern and has not yet been dignified by tradition and great artists long since dead. Nor do I altogether desire the creating of State cinemas in the different countries, since they would inevitably be used to further nationalism. The power of the cinema as propaganda is almost boundless, and the propaganda of nationalism by the State would certainly be more harmful than the propaganda of mere silliness by commercial promoters. If the nations were in earnest to avert wars, those which belonged to the League of Nations would spend money in the promotion of first-rate films to illustrate the ideals which inspired the creation of the League and to promote loyalty to the League as a means of averting war. This of course is out of the question, because the will to peace exists only in those small northern nations which cannot hope to gain anything through war. The Americans, the British, the French, the Italians, the Germans, and the Russians all in their various ways desire war, provided it is the right war. Not one of them has any real will to peace, and not one of them would spend a cent to promote the ideals of pacifism. Perhaps American producers could be induced to engage in pacifist propaganda throughout Europe on condition that no film having this object should be allowed to be shown in America. This might be suggested to the Senate as a means of carrying out its intentions in ratifying the Kellogg pact.[1] The power which the cinema has placed in the hands of Americans for purposes of foreign propaganda has hardly as yet been realised by Americans. When they do realise it, the effect may be curious.

The passion of this age for doing things by mechanism which are not worth doing at all is one which I do not wholly share. When the 'talkies' were new, I went to London by invitation to see and hear a professor in America giving a lecture on 'The Marvels of Science'. It was not nearly so good a lecture as hundreds of other professors could have given, and there was not a word in it which to me personally there was any advantage in hearing. I would not have walked across the street to hear the actual professor in person giving the actual lecture. The sole point of the lecture was the mechanism by which it was produced.

I suppose in time we shall have mechanical knives and forks which will shovel the food into our mouths at precisely the best rate from the point of view of digestion and mastication. Conversation at meals will of course become impossible, since the fork will not wait for the end of a sentence; but it will be a marvelous invention. I suppose also that old gentlemen will produce their favorite anecdote out of a gramophone instead of taking the trouble to speak it. In time we shall all become too lazy to think of a new remark of which we have not already a record. Instead of writing love letters, a man will obtain an eloquent set of records from the shop, and anyone who trusts to his own unaided invention will be thought mean. Individual initiative will be confined to crime; those who are plotting a burglary or bank robbery will no doubt still have to rely upon their own invention, but all legitimate activities will have become stereotyped. I do not look forward to this state of affairs with any pleasure, but I do not see how it is to be avoided.

[1] Ratified in July 1929; U.S.A. and France undertook to settle all disputes by peaceful means.

HOMOGENEOUS AMERICA

Outlook and Independent (New York, 19 February 1930); reprinted as 'Modern Homogeneity' in *In Praise of Idleness and Other Essays* (London and New York, 1935)

The European traveller in America—at least if I may judge by myself— is struck by two peculiarities: first, the extreme similarity of outlook in all parts of the United States (except the old South), and second, the passionate desire of each locality to prove that it is peculiar and different from every other. The second of these is, of course, the cause of the first. Every place wishes to have a reason for local pride, and therefore cherishes whatever is distinctive in the way of geography or history or tradition. The greater the uniformity that in fact exists, the more eager becomes the search for differences that may mitigate it. The old South is in fact quite unlike the rest of America, so unlike that one feels as if one had arrived in a different country. It is agricultural, aristocratic and retrospective, whereas the rest of America is industrial, democratic and prospective.

When I say that America outside the old South is industrial, I am thinking even of those parts that are devoted almost wholly to agriculture, for the mentality of the American agriculturist is industrial. He uses much modern machinery; he is intimately dependent upon the railway and the telephone; he is very conscious of the distant markets to which his products are sent; he is in fact a capitalist who might just as well be in some other business. A peasant, as he exists in Europe and Asia, is practically unknown in the United States. This is an immense boon to America, and perhaps its most important superiority as compared to the Old World, for the peasant everywhere is cruel, avaricious, conservative and inefficient. I have seen orange groves in Sicily and orange groves in California; the contrast represents a period of about 2,000 years. Orange groves in Sicily are remote from trains and ships; the trees are old and gnarled and beautiful; the methods are those of classical antiquity. The men are ignorant and semi-savage, mongrel descendants of Roman slaves and Arab invaders: what they lack in intelligence to-

256

wards trees they make up for by cruelty to animals. With moral degradation and economic incompetence goes an instinctive sense of beauty which is perpetually reminding one of Theocritus and the myth about the Garden of the Hesperides.

In a Californian orange grove, the Garden of the Hesperides seems very remote. The trees are all exactly alike, carefully tended and at the right distance apart. The oranges, it is true, are not all exactly of the same size, but careful machinery sorts them so that automatically all those in one box are exactly similar. They travel along with suitable things being done to them by suitable machines at suitable points until they enter a suitable refrigerator car in which they travel to a suitable market. The machine stamps the word 'Sunkist' upon them, but otherwise there is nothing to suggest that nature has any part in their production. Even the climate is artificial, for when there would otherwise be frost, the orange grove is kept artificially warm by a pall of smoke. The men engaged in agriculture of this kind do not feel themselves, like the agriculturists of former times, the patient servants of natural forces; on the contrary, they feel themselves the masters, and able to bend natural forces to their will.

There is therefore not the same difference in America as in the Old World between the outlook of industrialists and that of agriculturists. The important part of the environment in America is the human part; by comparison, the non-human part sinks into insignificance. I was constantly assured in Southern California that the climate turned people into lotus eaters, but I confess I saw no evidence of this. They seemed to me exactly like the people in Minneapolis or Winnipeg, although climate, scenery and natural conditions were as different as possible in the two regions. When one considers the difference between a Norwegian and a Sicilian, and compares it with the lack of difference between a man from, say, North Dakota and a man from Southern California, one realises the immense revolution in human affairs which has been brought about by man's becoming the master instead of the slave of his physical environment. Norway and Sicily both have ancient traditions; they had pre-Christian religions embodying men's reactions to the climate, and when Christianity came, it inevitably took very different forms in the two countries. The Norwegian feared ice and snow; the Sicilian feared lava and earthquakes. Hell was invented in a southern climate; if it had been invented in Norway, it would have been cold. But neither in North Dakota nor in Southern California is Hell a climatic condition: in both it is a stringency on the money market. This illustrates the unimportance of climate in modern life.

America is a man-made world: moreover, it is a world which man has made by means of machinery. I am thinking not only of the physical environment, but also and quite as much of thoughts and emotions. Consider a really stirring murder: the murderer, it is true, may be primitive in his methods, but those who spread the knowledge of his deed do so by means of all the latest resources of science. Not only in the great cities, but in lonely farms on the prairie and in mining camps in the Rockies, the radio disseminates all the latest information, so that half the topics of conversation on a given day are the same in every household throughout the country. As I was crossing the plains in the train, endeavouring not to hear a loud-speaker bellowing advertisements of soap, an old farmer came up to me with a beaming face and said: 'Wherever you go nowadays you can't get away from civilisation.' Alas! How true! I was endeavouring to read Virginia Woolf, but the advertisements won the day.

Uniformity in the physical apparatus of life would be no grave matter, but uniformity in matters of thought and opinion is much more dangerous. It is, however, a quite inevitable result of modern inventions. Production is cheaper when it is unified and on a large scale than when it is divided into a number of small units. This applies quite as much to the production of opinions as to the production of pins. The principal sources of opinion in the present day are the schools, the churches, the press, the cinema and the radio. The teaching in the elementary schools must inevitably become more and more standardised as more use is made of apparatus. It may, I think, be assumed that both the cinema and the radio will play a rapidly increasing part in school education in the near future. This will mean that the lessons will be produced at a centre and will be precisely the same wherever the material prepared at this centre is used. Some churches, I am told, send out every week a model sermon to all the less educated of their clergy, who, if they are governed by the ordinary laws of human nature, are no doubt grateful for being saved the trouble of composing a sermon of their own. This model sermon, of course, deals with some burning topic of the moment, and aims at arousing a given mass emotion throughout the length and breadth of the land. The same thing applies in a higher degree to the press, which receives everywhere the same telegraphic news and is syndicated on a large scale. Reviews of my books, I find, are verbally the same from New York to San Francisco, and from Maine to Texas, except that they become shorter as one travels from the north-east to the south-west.

Perhaps the greatest of all forces for uniformity in the modern world is the cinema, since its influence is not confined to America but penetrates to all parts of the world, except the Soviet Union, which, however, has its own different uniformity. The cinema embodies, broadly speaking, Hollywood's opinion of what it is like in the Middle-West. Our emotions in regard to love and marriage, birth and death are becoming standardised according to this recipe. To the young of all lands, Hollywood represents the last word in modernity, displaying both the pleasures of the rich and the methods to be adopted for acquiring riches. I suppose the talkies will lead before long to the adoption of a universal language, which will be that of Hollywood.

It is not only among the comparatively ignorant that there is uniformity in America. The same thing applies, though in a slightly less degree, to culture. I visited bookshops in every part of the country and found everywhere the same best sellers prominently displayed. So far as I could judge, the cultured ladies of America buy every year about a dozen books, the same dozen everywhere. To an author, this is a very satisfactory state of affairs, provided he is one of the dozen. But it certainly does mark a difference from Europe, where there are many books with small sales rather than a few with large sales.

It must not be supposed that the tendency towards uniformity is either wholly good or wholly bad. It has great advantages and also great disadvantages: its chief advantage is, of course, that it produces a population capable of peaceable co-operation; its great disadvantage is that it produces a population prone to persecution of minorities. This latter defect is probably temporary, since it may be assumed that before long there will be no minorities. A great deal depends, of course, on how the uniformity is achieved. Take, for example, what the schools do to southern Italians. Southern Italians have been distinguished throughout history for murder, graft, and aesthetic sensibility. The public schools effectively cure them of the last of these three, and to that extent assimilate them to the native American population; but in regard to the other two distinctive qualities, I gather that the success of the schools is less marked. This illustrates one of the dangers of uniformity as an aim: good qualities are easier to destroy than bad ones, and therefore uniformity is most easily achieved by lowering all standards.

It is, of course, clear that a country with a large foreign population must endeavour, through its schools, to assimilate the children of immigrants, and therefore a certain degree of Americanisation is inevitable. It is, however, unfortunate that such a large part of this process should be effected by means of a somewhat blatant nationalism. America is already the strongest country in the world, and its preponderance is continually increasing. This fact naturally inspires fear in Europe, and the fear is increased by everything suggesting militant nationalism. It may be the destiny of America to teach political good sense to Europe, but I am afraid that the pupil is sure to prove refractory.

With the tendency towards uniformity in America, there goes, as it seems to me, a mistaken conception of democracy. It seems to be generally held in the United States that democracy requires all men to be alike, and that, if a man is in any way different from another, he is 'setting himself up' as superior to that other. France is quite as democratic as America, and yet this idea does not exist in France. The doctor, the lawyer, the priest, the public official are all different types in France; each profession has its own traditions and its own standards, although it does not set up to be superior to other professions. In America all professional men are assimilated in type to the businessman. It is as though one should decree that an orchestra should consist only of violins.

There does not seem to be an adequate understanding of the fact that society should be a pattern or an organism, in which different organs play different parts. Imagine the eye and the ear quarrelling as to whether it is better to see or to hear, and deciding that each would do neither since neither could do both. This, it seems to me, would be democracy as understood in America. There is a strange envy of any kind of excellence which cannot be universal, except, of course, in the sphere of athletics and sport, where aristocracy is enthusiastically acclaimed. It seems that the average American is more capable of humility in regard to his muscles than in regard to his brains; perhaps this is because his admiration for muscle is more profound and genuine than his admiration of brains. The flood of popular scientific books in America is inspired partly—though of course not wholly—by the unwillingness to admit that there is anything in science which only experts can understand. The idea that a special training may be necessary to understand, say, the theory of relativity, causes a sort of irritation, although nobody is irritated by the fact that a special training is necessary in order to be a first-rate football player.

Achieved eminence is perhaps more admired in America than in any other country, and yet the road to certain kinds of eminence is made very difficult for the young, because people are intolerant of any eccentricity or anything that could be called 'setting oneself up', provided the person concerned is not already labelled 'eminent'. Consequently, many of the finished types that are most admired are difficult to produce at home and have to be imported from Europe. This fact is bound up with standardisation and uniformity. Exceptional merit, especially in artistic directions, is bound to meet with great obstacles in youth so long as everybody is expected to conform outwardly to a pattern set by the successful executive.

Standardisation, though it may have disadvantages for the exceptional individual, probably increases the happiness of the average man, since he can utter his thoughts with a certainty that they will be like the thoughts of his hearer. Moreover, it promotes national cohesion and makes politics less bitter and violent than where more marked differences exist. I do not think it is possible to strike a balance of gains and losses, but I think the standardisation which now exists in America is likely to exist throughout Europe as the world becomes more mechanised. Europeans, therefore, who find fault with America on this account should realise that they are finding fault with the future of their own countries, and are setting themselves against an inevitable and universal trend in civilisation. Undoubtedly, internationalism will become easier as the differences between nations diminish, and if once internationalism were established, social cohesion would become of enormous importance for preserving internal peace.

There is a certain risk, which cannot be denied, of an immobility analogous to that of the late Roman Empire. But as against this, we may set the revolutionary forces of modern science and modern technique. Short of a universal intellectual decay, these forces, which are a new feature in the modern world, will make immobility impossible, and prevent that kind of stagnation which has overtaken great empires in the past. Arguments from history are dangerous to apply to the present and the future, because of the complete change that science has introduced. I see, therefore, no reason for undue pessimism, however standardisation may offend the tastes of those who are unaccustomed to it.

THIRTY YEARS FROM NOW

The *Virginia Quarterly Review* (University of Virginia, Charlottesville, October 1930)

An Englishman in touch with the British Labour party cannot but be struck, in visiting America, by the profound difference between the outlook to which he is accustomed at home and that which he finds among American 'radicals'. To begin with: the word 'radical' has, to British ears, an old-fashioned Victorian flavor—it suggests a series of men extending from Francis Place, the wire-pulling tailor of the Reform-Bill time, through John Stuart Mill, to Joseph Chamberlain in his youth. Since the beginning of the present century, the word has been obsolete. But in America it lingers, like many other archaic forms of speech and thought. To an Englishman visiting America, I should say: 'Study the language of Shakespeare and the thought of Montesquieu. Then you will be able to understand such words as "chores" and such beliefs as that America is dedicated to Liberty, both of which you might otherwise find unintelligible.'

To obtain a first rough outline of a comparison between the advanced movements in American and British politics, it is necessary to remember that industrialism, as a dominant factor in the national life, is much more recent in America than in England. The serious development of American industrialism hardly goes further back than the Civil War, whereas that of England goes back to the Napoleonic wars. Now the technical side of production—the machinery, the processes, and so on—can be quickly developed in a new environment, and may positively gain from the absence of old plant and old methods. Accordingly, on the technical side American industry is, in the main, more advanced than that of Great Britain. But the psychological side of industrial life is a slower growth. Certain habits of mind inherited from agriculture, handicrafts, and commerce persist in the early phases of industrialism, causing friction in the political machinery. There is no country where the industrial habit of mind is completely dominant or completely developed, but

262

it is perhaps natural that it should be nearest to complete development in Great Britain, where alone it is common to find industrial workers whose grandfathers and great-grandfathers were also industrial workers in the same industries and the same localities. Think of the Lancashire proverb: 'Three generations from clogs to clogs', meaning that when a working man rises to be an employer, his son or grandson will sink back to the level of the wage-earner. This implies a stable environment which is industrial, whereas in America no industrial environment is stable and every solution must be provisional.

Before going further, it is necessary to guard against a possible misunderstanding. I spoke a moment ago of commerce along with agriculture and handicrafts. Now commerce in the sense of interchange of goods is, of course, promoted by industrialism. But commerce in the old sense, in which the merchant was a prince who ruled the economic life of nations, is a thing of the past, or at any rate, is rapidly becoming so. In olden days, both sellers and buyers were unorganised. Between them stood a small group of great merchants whose economic strength far outweighed that of both sellers and buyers. Hence the wealth of Venice, Holland, and London. But with the growth of industrialism, the situation changed. The seller became, in regard to many commodities, a great and powerful corporation, able to dictate terms and to dispense with the middleman. Take, as an extreme case, the marketing of oil: this is undertaken almost wholly by the producers, and leaves no scope for the merchant. There is a tendency, as yet far less developed, for buyers also to organise; this is, in fact, part of the case for socialism. It is clear that while sellers are organised and buyers unorganised, the producer is in a position superior to that of the consumer. Equality of economic strength in an industrial world demands organisation of each economic interest, and not only of some. And wherever there is inequality of economic strength, there will be exploitation.

The elimination of commerce as an independent factor in economic life is, of course, far from complete, but we can already see that it belongs to the inherent tendencies of industrialism, which must gradually substitute for the merchant, direct negotiations between a group of sellers and a group of buyers. In a socialistic world, each of these groups would be a State; in a capitalistic world, one at least would be a trust or combine.

The importance of the elimination of commerce, from our point of view, is that commerce has always been the chief promoter of what are called 'liberal' ideas—such ideas as religious toleration, free speech, free press, democracy, etc. If these ideas are to survive in an industrial world, they will have to take new forms and be thought out afresh. How, for example, shall we combine a free press with the socialist program of State control of industry, including the newspaper industry? For such a problem, nineteenth-century liberalism has no answer to offer.

In passing from these generalities to the actual comparison of American radicalism with the British Labour party, the first thing that strikes an observer is the more backward conditions of American trade unionism. In America, doubtless partly owing to the influence of Mr Gompers, organised labor still hesitates to take an independent part in politics. It is still believed by many that industrial action—the attempt to raise wages and reduce hours by strikes and the threat of strikes—can be pursued independently of political support. I remember attending an international socialist congress in London in 1896, where the more conservative section of British trade unionists advocated this view, as against what was then known as the 'new' unionism. Opinion was almost exactly what one may expect it to be in America two years hence. Trade union development in America is now just about at the stage which British unionism reached thirty years ago.

In England, the next stage in development was forced on the unions by the law courts. The Taff Vale decision showed that unionism could be made safe only by a change in the law, and therefore political action was necessary if industrial action was to continue possible. The Liberal government of Sir Henry Campbell-Bannerman in 1906 passed an Act reversing the Taff Vale decision, but there is little doubt that this Act would not have been passed but for the menace of the newly formed Labour party. Mr Asquith, in common with most of the lawyers in the Liberal party, was very loath to support the change, and was driven into doing so only by the knowledge that unless he did, organised labor would give no support whatever to the Liberal party.

The British Labour party owes its existence to the reactionary decisions of the law courts, and probably the same cause may be relied upon to produce the same effect in America. When once labor is adequately organised, it is only a question of time before the opposition of conservatives forces political action upon the unions. If I were an American radical, I should devote the bulk of my energy to persuading trade union leaders of the necessity of forming a political labor party to safeguard the political interests of their followers. This is clearly the next step at the present time.

It would, however, be a mistake to expect the labor movement in America to develop exactly along lines which Europe has made familiar. There are three principal causes of difference which it will be well to consider successively. The first is the immigrant population; the second, the immense prosperity of America; the third, the importance of agriculture and the fact that it is semi-industrialised.

In New York and along the eastern seaboard generally, the strength of radicalism, such as it is, appears to be mainly derived from immigrants, supported and more or less led by a few Europeanised intellectuals. The result of this situation seemed to me to be—though I saw too little to speak at all positively—that the conceptions and program of the radicals were unduly European. Men—especially Jews—who have been socialists in the countries from which they came, remain socialists in America until they become well off; then they become persuaded that their socialism was merely traditional, part of the habits they brought with them from the Old World, which they have to unlearn in the new environment. Meanwhile, those who have been born in America look upon radicalism as something foreign, tainted, unsuitable to a hundred-percenter. While this situation persists, a strong radical movement in the East is impossible. The restrictions on immigration will, however, cause it to change rapidly. Some conservatives, seeing that the radicals are mainly immigrants, think that the restriction of immigration will kill radicalism. This seems to me a profound error. I hold, on the contrary, that American radicalism will be immensely strengthened by diminishing the supply of immigrants. At present, everybody in America, with few exceptions, grows continually richer, and does so because there is a continually new supply of immigrants to exploit. If they are stopped, there will begin to be native-born Americans who are not improving their economic position. Such men will grow discontented and will supply material for a labor party far more formidable than recent immigrants, who are easily suppressed and easily branded as disloyal. Restriction of immigration, I am convinced, will be an immense gain to American radicalism.

Comparison with the British labour movement strengthens this conviction. The foreign-born population of Great Britain is negligible; the Labour party derives its strength from men and women whose ancestors have lived in the country from time immemorial. It is therefore difficult to accuse them of being unpatriotic, which in fact they are not. They cannot easily be persecuted, because no race-antagonism can be invoked against them. Liberty and toleration are perhaps scarcely possible except in a homogeneous nation. If America continues to restrict immigration, it seems probable that within thirty years almost all the foreign elements except the Negroes will have been thoroughly assimilated. That will give a new strength and a new respectability to the American labor movement. The process will, of course, be gradual, and will presumably begin at once; but its completion may be expected to take something like a generation. Thirty years seems, therefore, about the right length of time to allow for it to mature.

In spite of the immigrant element in the American radical movement, it is less international than the Labour and Socialist parties of Europe.

This is a natural effect of geography. Internationalism and militarism are both caused by experience of war—the former as a means of preventing wars, the latter as a means of winning them. But America, remote and powerful, turns naturally to one or other of two different policies: isolation . . . or economic imperialism. Isolation is the traditional policy, economic imperialism the policy suggested by the post-war situation, and capable of being used either for reactionary or for progressive ends. I do not propose to argue the question as to which is best, either for America or for the world, but I have little doubt that isolation will be more and more abandoned. Advocates of America's entry into the League of Nations, protagonists of disarmament conferences, philanthropists who desire loans to impoverished nations are all helping to bring about a new world government in which the moving power will be American finance. Perhaps it is just as well—but who knows?

If a labor movement is to succeed in America, it will have to differ in its appeal from the corresponding movements in Europe. In Europe, there is an acute problem of poverty; there are large sections of the population who obviously earn too little for well-being. The contrast between these sections and the very rich raises a feeling of injustice which always has made the major part of the driving force for socialism in Europe. In America, apart from recent immigrants, there is little poverty as a European understands it. Almost all wage-earners born in America earn quite as much as anyone really needs. Important things are lacking in their lives, but among these, purchasing power is not to be included. They lack liberty, leisure, education, culture, but not material goods. There is therefore not much force in the simple argument of the European proletarian: 'Why should I starve while the millionaire's idle son lives in luxury?' And this makes it necessary to have a new philosophy behind the American labor movement if it is to win any sweeping success.

The prosperity of the American workingman is calculated to bring despair to the heart of any labor leader who follows European models. Yet in former times, material prosperity only increased the demand of the prosperous for equality. The revolt of the commercial classes against the feudal aristocracy grew more and more formidable as the commercial classes grew richer. Cromwell's Ironsides were not men suffering from destitution. The old battles, however, were political, and political privilege has practically disappeared. With the coming of political democracy, it is supposed that everyone has acquired his due share of power, and that unjust discriminations have ceased. Wage-earners will see through this device only when they have learnt to understand the part played by economic power (as opposed to political power) in the modern world. This will require a slow education by means of voluntary propaganda; but when once that education has been completed . . . wage-earners, however prosperous, will demand the democratisation of economic power also. When that time comes, the American labor movement will lead the world.

This brings me to the farmer–labor movement of the North-West— a movement which, whatever its immediate future, appears to me to contain something genuinely new, with more promise than anything yet existing in the Eastern States. In Wisconsin, Minnesota, and North and South Dakota, I seemed to find a type of economico-political thought which does not fit into the traditional categories but is more adapted than they are to modern economic conditions. From the traditional socialist point of view, a farmer is a capitalist and an employer—he must count with the enemy. The attempt to co-operate with him, which is being made in the Middle-West, can only succeed if it is accompanied by a new economic philosophy . . . less remote from facts than that which many socialists have uncritically inherited from the 1860s. There are, of course, inherent difficulties in the farmer–labor combination. A few prosperous years might cure the farmers of their discontent and make them again friendly toward the banks and railways. The mentality of a man who lives on the land is bound to be rather different than that of an industrial wage-earner. For these reasons, the combination may not last. But if it does, its results may be surprising.

Agriculture in Europe has hitherto proved a fatal stumbling-block to the Labour and Socialist parties. Where it is carried on by small peasant proprietors, they are intensely conservative—terrified lest social-ists should nationalise their land. Where it is carried on by aristocrats employing virtually serf labor, it is bound up with feudalism. Where, as in England, it is carried on by large tenant farmers employing labourers, the farmers feel the labourer their enemy rather than the landowner, and are therefore conservative, while the labourers are usually too terrorised to vote against their employers. The war has intensified the opposition of town and country. The conservatism of the peasants forced the new economic policy on the Bolsheviks, defeated the socialists in Germany, Austria and Hungary, and kept Poincaré in power in France until he took to imposing taxes. This conservatism is largely traditional, the instinctive adherence to old ways common among settled agricultural populations. It is a dead weight which Europe has found great difficulty in moving.

In America, except to some extent in the South, nothing of this kind exists. There is no peasantry because those who cultivate the soil have not been settled on it for generations. The pioneers who developed the West were necessarily men of adventurous disposition, totally unlike the typical, timid, stay-at-home peasant of agricultural Europe. Ever since the time of Columbus, the American continent has drained Europe of her most enterprising sons, selecting the vigorous and imaginative and leaving only the stolid and stupid. Consequently, the agricultural population of America is temperamentally different, on the average, from that of the countries which supplied it. And it is free from the inhibitions due to ages of feudalism and the fear which they generated among serfs and underlings.

This cause, however, might have been insufficient to produce any marked effect if it had stood alone. What has given it strength is its combination with economic causes.

The American agriculturist works, as a rule, for a distant market in Europe or in the Eastern States. He uses the most modern machinery, is free from tradition, and remembers with pride the pioneer work of his father. He undertook farming under the impression that he would be an independent economic unit. It turned out, however, that he was under the thumb of the railways and the banks, especially the latter. The little banks, in turn, are in the hands of the big banks, and the ultimate economic power produced by the work of innumerable western farmers is concentrated in the hands of a few big men in Wall Street. All this operates through credit. Sooner or later a man wants a loan, and when he does, the economic power represented by his land passes into the hands of those from whom he borrows. Theoretically, he might abstain from borrowing; but practically, a bad harvest is likely to leave him no alternative except to sell his farm. As soon as he has been compelled to borrow, he becomes virtually an employee of the banks. Economically, he no longer counts as a landowner or as an employer, but as a mere intermediary. That is why it is possible for him to co-operate with wage-earners.

This case illustrates the industrialising of agriculture which has resulted from modern methods. Lenin, in his contest with the peasants, hoped to give them the industrial mentality by means of his grandiose scheme of electrification, which was to supply them with inexpensive power. This particular scheme has perished with him,[1] but American agriculture has suffered a transformation not unlike that of which Lenin dreamt. The agriculturist is not an isolated unit who can ignore economic conditions in the world at large. In addition to his dependence on machinery and the banks, he depends upon the European market, and is hard hit by the loss of European purchasing power due to the war. He cannot therefore live in a closed circle like the traditional peasant. This situation combines with the selected temperament of the pioneer to produce an agricultural mentality which is quite new in the history of the world and a vast improvement upon what has gone before.

To meet the case of American agriculture, and to make the farmer—

labor combination permanent, American radicalism needs new formulae and a new analysis. Henry George[2] made the attempt long ago, but not in a form quite applicable to modern conditions. The nominal possession of land, which he regarded as the sole source of economic power, may not amount to much: it does not in the case of the farmer who has had to borrow from his bank. The power of the bank rests on credit, and credit (when it is well-founded) rests upon some peculiarly lucrative monopoly, such as oil, railways, coal mines, etc., or possibly upon urban land. It is the holders of ultimate economic power who control our fate to a degree surpassing what was possible for any absolute monarch of former times. The goal which socialists have set before themselves will be reached when ultimate economic power is in public hands, instead of being, as now, in the hands of individuals who are responsible to no one.

The capitalist, as such, is not necessarily a holder of ultimate economic power. Mr Henry Ford, for example, who owes his wealth to skill, not to monopoly, injures no one (except those who are run over by unskillful drivers).[3] There is no good reason why he should be interfered with. But the gains which result from monopoly are in a different class. Socialists have paid too little attention to this distinction, and that is why some of them feel that there is something unnatural in the farmer–labor combination. In this view, however, they seem to me wholly mistaken.

The American labor movement is still in its infancy as compared with the British movement. But I do not doubt that, in view of the economic development of America, the movement will grow rapidly and will take new forms for which Europe offers no precedent. Imitation of Europe is to be deprecated because American conditions are different from those of Europe. Nevertheless, the formation of a Third party is imperative if anything is to be achieved. I make no doubt that within thirty years such a party will be as powerful, and as little destructive, as the British Labour party is now. For the sake of America, and for the sake of the world, I shall rejoice in every step toward that goal.

[1] Russell was clearly mistaken in this view since the Soviet government's 15-year electrification plan, proposed by Lenin in 1920, was to be fully realised and in 1929, was fulfilling its expectations.

[2] Nineteenth-century economist and land reformer; author of *Progress and Poverty*.

[3] Compare with Russell's later view of Mr Ford; see below, pp. 290–1.

THE END OF PROHIBITION

The *New York American* (6 December 1933)

Quite apart from the particular question of the consumption of alcoholic beverages, the end of Prohibition is important as marking the defeat of a certain kind of morality. Broadly speaking, moral sentiment is of two sorts: the first wishes to make others happy, the second wishes to make them unhappy—of course for the sake of their true welfare. Social reformers have been of both types: some wished the poor to have more to eat, others wished them to have less to drink. The psychological root of the reformer's sentiment is, in the one case, sympathy; in the other, envy. It is a good thing when the restrictive morality inspired by envy suffers a resounding defeat, as it has done in the failure of Prohibition. Many men desire the glow of moral self-satisfaction, and such men may be forced, when restrictions on freedom fail, to fall back upon behavior which might have been inspired by kindly feelings. For this reason, I am glad that Prohibition has been judged a failure.

The distinction between the two types of morality is, however, by no means clear-cut, because very often what people wish to do is genuinely harmful to themselves or others, and may be prohibited from entirely benevolent motives. Few reformers have been more wholly of the sympathetic type than Jefferson, yet he frequently deplored the excessive drinking of his time. Among the pioneers of Lincoln's youth, whisky-drinking was an appalling evil, which inflicted untold suffering upon their wives and children. The evils due to alcohol are very real. But the reformer who is unconsciously actuated by envy of the drunkard will not stop to inquire whether worse evils may not result from his methods of taking drink from those who want it. In the case of Prohibition, as every one knows, the evils were very serious: corruption of the police, diversion of their energies from the pursuit of serious criminals to investigation of bootlegging, habitual law-breaking by almost all well-to-do people, with a consequent serious increase of drunkenness, especially among women. Above all, a weakening of self-control and self-respect: in Paris, on the

Atlantic, at Tia Juana, one sees behaviour which causes Americans to be less respected by other nations than they ought to be.

The evils brought about by Prohibition will not cease suddenly. Bootleggers will no doubt still find scope for their activities, and speak-easies will survive as night-clubs do in London, but gradually these evasions of the law will probably come to assume manageable dimensions. It may be expected that, at first, those who can still afford it will become intoxicated somewhat more openly than at present, but this also will in all likelihood be only a passing phase. In the end, the evils due to the state of mind fostered by Prohibition will disappear, and the country will be the better for the abandonment of an attempt which could not succeed.

There is one incidental good effect which has resulted from the era of Prohibition. In the nineteenth century, women everywhere—but most emphatically in America—were considered morally superior to men; this was not only claimed by themselves, but conceded by their husbands. The twice guardians of their virtue were the saloon and the prostitute. The effect of Prohibition, among the richer classes, was to bring drink into the house, with the result that women shared in it. In the days of women's moral superiority, there was little companionship or real intimacy between men and women. Men felt constrained in the presence of women, and women regarded men as coarse brutes whose behavior was uncivilised and unrefined. The modern relation of equality between men and women is more wholesome, more honest, and more companionable. The change is due to many causes, but among them Prohibition has borne a part.

ON EQUALITY

The *New York American* (8 January 1934); published as 'Equality'

From the beginning of their history as an independent nation, the people of the United States have held up equality as an ideal. Jefferson and Jackson aimed at a great continent of small freeholders, where those who would naturally become plutocrats—that is the bankers—should be kept down by periodical repudiation. It proved, however, impossible to carry out this ideal: manufactures, urban land, railways, mines, and oil made some men enormously rich, and gave them an influence in the affairs of the country about equal to that of all the poorer citizens put together. At present a new effort is in progress, in line with those of democrats in earlier times, but more scientific, better equipped with economic knowledge, and therefore not so certain of defeat by the forces that stand for inequality.

Although equality was, from the moment of the Declaration of Independence, proclaimed as a principle, it was only applied in such directions as were politically convenient. For a long time, nobody thought of it as including Negroes or women. Even now, although women have political equality with men, they do not, as a rule, have economic equality, which is in many ways more important. Among the rich, a wife usually has money of her own, but in other classes she depends upon her husband's earnings. The law gives her a right to a share of his income, and to alimony when she gets tired of him or he of her; but it does not give her the economic power that belongs to the person who earns money.

Superficially, among the well-to-do in America, it has often seemed to foreign observers as if women had more power than men, but this is only true in those departments of life which most men regard as of secondary importance. A businessman's love of power finds its outlet in his office and his work, so that he is content to abdicate in the home. In fact, the province which he reserves to himself is more important, as an element in the national life, than that which he leaves to his wife.

272

But his wife, not wishing to acknowledge this fact, is apt to take up culture or philanthropy or some other fad, and to regard business as only suitable for the less refined and sensitive male. With this goes, quite naturally, a tendency to under-estimate the importance of the economic side of life, since the economic reality is at war with the social pretense of women's equality or even superiority. Acceptance of this pretense gives, as acceptance of pretense always does, a certain superficiality and unimportance to much feminine culture, besides having a regrettable effect upon the psychology of women.

Democracy, whether taken as equality between classes or as equality between men and women, has not much reality, so long as it is merely political and not also economic. It is small consolation to be able to vote against a political program if its advocates have the power to make you starve. Political democracy has its importance, since it prevents certain extremes of oppression, and is a necessary step toward the more equitable distribution of economic power. But without economic justice, political justice is incomplete. This was more or less recognised by the founders of American democracy, but their method, which was the creation of vast numbers of independent economic units, is no longer available in our industrial age. Just as political democracy consists, not in complete political independence for each citizen, but in joint management of political affairs, so economic democracy must consist, not in economic independence, but in collective control over economic affairs. If democracy is ever to become a reality, this extension from politics to economics must be made. It is only because so many of our ways of thought are still pre-industrial that this is not obvious to everyone. But experience is rapidly making it obvious, and the battle for economic democracy will be the next great struggle for justice in human affairs.

THE ROOT CAUSES OF THE DEPRESSION

Unpublished (c. 1934)

The gallant attempt now being made in America to promote economic recovery is one which should have the whole-hearted good wishes of all nations. The depression is world-wide, and recovery also is likely to be so, though it may be earlier or more complete in some countries than in others. Will President Roosevelt succeed? I sincerely hope so, but the disease is too deep-seated for sudden cure. There will be need of patience, both on the part of the administration and on the part of the people; and there may prove to be need of measures more drastic than any yet officially contemplated.

In this article, I shall attempt only a diagnosis of the trouble, remembering that, since all countries are depressed, the cause of the depression is not to be sought specially in any one country.

The root of the matter is very simple. Labour is enormously more productive than it used to be, but wages have not risen in proportion to what the labourer produces. This is true not only of manual workers, but also of all except those who possess ultimate economic power—the owners of minerals, the men who control credit, in short, the industrial magnates. Everybody else is producing more than his salary or wages allows him to consume.

Suppose, for example, that you are one of a hundred men employed in a shoe factory. For every hundred pairs of shoes made, the wages and salaries, let us suppose, represent the price of fifty pairs, and the other fifty belong to the financier. But as he is not a centipede, he cannot wear them all. He is therefore left with shoes that he cannot dispose of. The only solution that occurs to him, in bad times, is to dismiss some of his employees, improve his machinery, and make as many shoes as before while there are still fewer people to buy them. This, of course, only makes matters worse. In good times, he has another method: he pays people to buy the shoes that otherwise he could not sell. This is called the beneficent operation of the credit system. He does this in the hope of

274

being paid back some day, but obviously there is no possibility of this, unless some other financier can be induced to pay the debtors to pay back the first financier.

Of course, matters are not quite so simple in real life as they are in our illustration. Men make other things besides shoes, and spend their wages on other things. But the end result is the same. The men who work produce a great deal more than their earnings allow them to consume; the surplus of what they produce goes mainly to very rich men who cannot consume it all, and therefore invest part of their income. But investments, in the long run, can only be made profitable if the produce can be sold at a suitable price, and this is impossible because wages and salaries have not risen in proportion to the productivity of labour.

The thing is obvious if, for a moment, we consider the world's production and consumption as a co-operative enterprise. Suppose ten men set out jointly, one to produce food, another clothes, another shoes, another houses, and so on, their produce to be divided equally among them. Obviously if they discover how to produce more than before with the same amount of labour, they will all have either more goods or more leisure, whichever they may prefer. But in the actual world each of them is told to go on working as hard as before, although the result is more of everything than is wanted. When this result becomes plain, some of them are told their work is no longer needed, and they can go and starve patiently; others are told that, although they produce more than formerly, they are not to earn more. The result is misery to themselves, and impoverishment even for the very rich. The very rich, who were in control throughout Mr Hoover's administration,[1] do not understand their own economic system, and until they are deprived of power no lasting improvement will be possible.

[1] 1928–32.

275

CAN THE PRESIDENT SUCCEED?

Unpublished (*c.* 1934)

Not only to America, but to the world, the experiment now being tried by the government of the United States is of incalculable importance. From the end of the war until the inauguration of Mr Roosevelt, the financial and industrial magnates had a free hand, and they brought the country to a worse pass than it had ever known before. Whatever else may be open to question, it is incontrovertible that to intrust power to the very rich is to court widespread ruin and starvation. The nation, realising this, gave the President an unprecedented degree of control over the economic life of the country. He has used his power with energy and vision, and has at the same time shown skill in minimising friction. He is attempting, without abolishing the capitalist system, to subject it to regulations which will cause it to work in accordance with the public interest, and to produce prosperity instead of disaster. If he succeeds, we shall know that the world's economic troubles can be overcome without violent revolution or civil war. If he fails, some undemocratic form of dictatorship is not unlikely to result, and a new form of servitude may be fastened upon the great majority of ordinary citizens. Every man capable of public spirit must, therefore, wish him well.

He has great difficulties to contend against. Quick success is, in the nature of things, hardly possible, and the nation may grow impatient before his remedies have had time to take effect. His popularity may diminish, and without popularity he cannot retain the necessary driving force.

Great driving force is necessary since he must, if he persists, come into increasing conflict with very powerful forces. When minimum rates of pay are fixed, employers regard them as maximum rates, and by hook or by crook, by a technicality if possible, but, if not, by a direct breach of the law, they reduce all rates of pay to the legal minimum. In like manner, they find ways of diminishing the number of their employees. As the ending of the depression depends upon increasing the total sum spent in wages and salaries, these devices on the part of employers retard recovery. Big business, of course, expects to be able, as always hitherto since the day the Constitution was adopted, to outwit the popular forces, by bribery, by intimidation, by raising false issues, and by the mere weight of obstruction.

Sooner or later, it will be necessary to have a pitched battle with the financial magnates, to ensure that the aggregate of wages and salaries shall be increased actually, and not only on paper. All the forces of reaction, up to and including the Supreme Court, will have to be made to submit to the popular will. It will probably be necessary to take drastic action against employers who have deliberately set to work to defeat the purposes of the N.R.A.[1] It may be necessary, in the worst cases, for the government to take over the management of a business, on payment of compensation based upon the profits of the last two years, as shown by income-tax returns. It may be that a much greater degree of public management than is now contemplated will, in this way, become gradually unavoidable.

Already, the old individualism is a thing of the past; hours, wages, prices, and output are regulated in the public interest. Will it be possible to stop short at this point? Or will it be found that the motive of private profit needs to be wholly superseded as the motive in production? Perhaps recovery will be possible without such extreme measures, but not unless public opinion is prepared for them in case obstruction should make them indispensable.

[1] National Recovery Administration.

ON STATES RIGHTS

Unpublished (*c.* 1934)

In the early days of American history, men of liberal outlook favoured the greatest possible extension of the power of the several States, and the most restrictive interpretation of the constitutional rights of the Federal government. From the very first, circumstances compelled an evolution which increased the powers of the President and diminished those of the States. Few Presidents did more in this direction than Jefferson himself, at the time of the Louisiana Purchase. The Civil War placed the reformers on the side of the Federal government; but Lincoln would be surprised by the powers now conceded to a Democratic President. All this is to the good. The greater mobility of persons and goods in the modern world makes the old, small territorial units an anachronism. Almost the only good thing Hitler has done is the abolition of the Federal Constitution of Germany.

The independence of the separate States in America is less than it was, but—at least as an outsider views the matter—it is still greater than it ought to be. The outside world is shocked when the Governor of California refuses to release Mooney and Billings,[1] whom every non-American who has heard of them believes to be innocent. He is still more shocked when he finds this same governor speaking in praise of lynching, and refusing to punish those who are guilty of this crime. He naturally supposes that there must be some authority superior to the governor, which can take action when that official insists on punishing the innocent and applauding the guilty. When he finds that nothing is done, the good name of America suffers. He probably does not know that, so long ago as 1917, a legal commission appointed by President Wilson inquired into Mooney's case, and decided that there was no good evidence of his guilt, but that the President, under the Constitution, was powerless to take any action. He probably also does not know that President Roosevelt is equally powerless in the matter of the governor's attitude as to lynching.

278

The separate sovereignty of each of the original thirteen States had historical justification at one time, since each had existed as a separate entity before their union. But such arguments do not apply to a State like California, conquered by Federal armies from a foreign Power, and admitted as a State by the Federal legislature. Nor can they now apply to any State. There can be no sound reason, at the present day, for placing the authorities of a single State above the law, and denying to the Federal government and judiciary the right to take cognizance of lawless acts which militate against the general interests of the United States.

It may be said that, at the moment, America has more important matters to think about. I doubt, myself, whether anything is more important, in the present state of the world, than respect for law. Nothing else stands in the way of the naked rule of force by a reckless minority, of which examples are occurring in some of the most important countries. When the constituted authorities set the example of contempt for law, it is to be expected that all the violent elements of the community will follow suit. The Federal government ought to have power to compel the State authorities to obey and enforce the law, even when the law concerned is State law. For indifference to law, when it becomes widespread, means an end of civilisation.

[1] Warren K. Billings, trade unionist, who was sentenced to life imprisonment when Mooney was condemned to die.

INDIVIDUAL FREEDOM IN
ENGLAND AND AMERICA

Unpublished (*c.* 1938)

The first impression of an English traveller in the United States is likely to be that he has come to a country where there is certainly more democracy, and perhaps more individual liberty, than there is in Great Britain. There is far more democratic *sentiment*. Shop assistants, though very obliging, treat customers as equals; there is very little of 'Sir' or 'Madam'. The haircutter has the same manner as a university man, of solicitude based upon kindness, not upon a sense of the monetary value of your patronage. There is no cringing, no oily subservience, no touching of hats. All this is refreshing and agreeable. It results from the fact that feudalism and aristocracy have been unknown in the United States since 1776, and were felt to be alien even before that time.

As for liberty, there is no doubt that the law interferes less with people's activities than it does in England. Before the New Deal, the difference was very marked, except for Prohibition. But even now there is more *laissez-faire* than in any European country.

To all this, however, there is another side, though it is not obvious to the casual traveller. *Laissez-faire* means, in practice, tyranny by employers. Even the casual traveller, if he reflects at all, must be struck by the long hours in shops and the absence of early closing. The speed at which men have to work is regulated by the speed of the machinery, and is such that, in some important industries, the workers become prematurely old. Trade unions, although it has lately been made illegal for employers to refuse collective bargaining, are still detested by employers, of whom some of the most important openly defy the law. Battles for the recognition of collective bargaining have, in recent years, been frequent and bloody, being often conducted, on the employers' side, by means of organised gangs of roughs. Propaganda for trade unions is still, in many places, both difficult and dangerous. In all these ways, America is more like the England of Peterloo and the Dorchester labourers than like the England of the present day.

There is one respect in which there is much more political liberty than in England, and that is as regards libel. I do not think there is much difference in the law, but there is an enormous difference in the practice of the courts and the sentiments of juries. The result is that it is easier than in England to say both true and false things about public men. Important Republican newspapers print obvious falsehoods, of a libellous sort, about the President; in England, even during a Labour government, such things could not be said in print concerning the Prime Minister. On the other hand, in England, many things which ought to be publicly known cannot be published for fear of a libel action. It is difficult to judge which practice is more in the public interest.

The power of the police is very much greater in America than in England. Not only do they take a much more militant part in labour disputes, but their treatment of men suspected of crime is apt to be totally lawless. Arrested men are often held for long periods without being allowed to communicate with their families or their lawyers; during these periods they are treated with great brutality, and sometimes subjected to actual torture with a view to extorting a confession. All this, though publicly known, arouses only sporadic and ineffectual protests.

The power of the leading men in finance and industry in America is astounding. At present, they do not control the Federal government, but they have done so at most times since the Civil War. They still control most of the State governments, and can invoke the aid of the State militia in labour disputes except where the governor is exceptionally liberal. Most of the great newspapers support them. All the best universities live on their benefactions and have powerful motives for not offending them. The outlook of the very rich is so reactionary and dictatorial that they look askance at any approximately impartial treatment of economics and social questions, and suspect all supporters of the New Deal of communism. Their hostility to the President is inconceivably bitter.

Life in America is both more violent and more vital than life in England: what is bad is worse than with us, and what is good is better. There is a great deal more lawlessness and crime in the United States than in Great Britain. The homicide rate in the large cities of America is almost twenty times what it is in England and Wales. This is partly due to the practice of carrying revolvers, and partly to the mixture of races; there are far more murders in the South, by whites as well as Negroes, than there are in the North.

On the other hand, the vigour of the New Deal puts to shame all that has been attempted in the way of progressive politics in post-war England. The trade union movement, after a long period of feeble and reactionary somnolence, has suddenly sprung into new life under the leadership of Lewis,[1] and has achieved spectacular victories against some of the most powerful corporations.

America is not oppressed, as Europe is, by the fear of war. The great majority of the population does not think of war as something in which the United States will have to participate. Those who do expect to be dragged into the next war know that it will take place in other continents, and will not fundamentally affect American life. It is still possible, in the Western hemisphere, to deal with internal problems on their merits, and not as part of the nightmare of international insanity. The young can look forward to the future with rational optimism, and with the feeling that existing evils are not irremediable. Whether or not there is more freedom in America than in England, there is certainly more scope for individual initiative. On the whole, in spite of the violence and brutality and economic oppression, it is probable that the average American is considerably happier than the average Englishman; but this is due less to merit than to geography.

[1] John L. Lewis, president of the Congress of Industrial Organizations (C.I.O.).

THE AMERICAN MIND

Unpublished (*c.* 1938)

Europe, divided as it is politically, has certain mental characteristics which are not so often found in the U.S.A. Recently, my wife and I met a European family settled in America. After talking all the time of how happy they are here and how kind and friendly the people are, they remarked as we were leaving: 'It's nice to meet Europeans. Even when they are of a different nation, one somehow feels at home with them.' (Actually this family was German.) The common traits among Europeans depend, I think, entirely on persistence of certain old traditions in education and social life. There are important elements of the monastic tradition (with the emphasis on the study of ancient culture that went with it) which are especially found in higher education. The American outlook is more practical, more concerned with morals and less with creeds. Since the *Encyclopaedia Britannica* became American it has become (as one can see by comparing different editions) much more informative on scientific and practical matters concerned with the modern world, less good on history and cultural subjects. The habit of using machinery and mechanical devices has penetrated more deeply into the minds of Americans than of Europeans, and has given men more sense of mastery over their environment. Europe looks backward, America forward. When Europeans attempt to think creatively of the future, they produce something crude and harsh, like fascism or communism, because of the effort required to break with the past, which makes them throw away all that is good as well as all that is bad. The Americans, on the other hand, being less imprisoned by old ways of thought, are able to see what is good in them. For these reasons, and because of the greater security of life in America, Americans are more vigorous mentally than Europeans, but less subtle. Europeans, weighed down by the burden of history, tend to be over-subtle and to lose vigour. Americans are much more warm-hearted and friendly, and therefore tend to be unselective. I was told recently by a young American who had

283

lived in Europe that in America he knew many people well, with mutual liking, but had few intimate friends. In Europe, most people were aloof and difficult to know, but there he had been able to form one or two really intimate friendships. Europeans are too selective. They seem, and are, indifferent to the point of hostility and suspiciousness, but at the same time the intimacy of close friendships seems to mean more to them.

These are generalisations, but experience of many people indicated that there is much truth in them.

AMERICA: THE NEXT WORLD CENTRE
Unpublished (*c.* 1938)

Almost every country in the world exaggerates its own importance; America alone does just the opposite. To every intelligent European who comes to the United States fresh from the distractions, despairs, and insanities of the Old World, it is evident that the future of civilisation, and the chief possibility of hope for mankind, is to be found in America. But among Americans, a surprising modesty prevents the realisation of this inevitable destiny.

Yet history should lead us to expect this development. From Babylonia and Egypt, where civilisation began, it travelled westward—first to Greece, then to Italy, then to France and England. Wars destroyed civilisation in its ancient homes: the Turks expelled it from the Levant, the Teutons from Italy, and now once more the descendants of those who destroyed Rome are preparing to do the same to France and England. From a military point of view, the attempt may fail, but it cannot fail to lower the cultural level of the countries that have led the world in recent centuries.

To one who, like myself, grew up during the Victorian age, in a family steeped in history and tradition, the instability of the modern world is bewildering. In 1911, I wrote a book in which, for purposes of illustration, I mentioned the Emperor of China as a person whom I knew to exist although I had never seen him.[1] There had been an Emperor of China since before the dawn of history, but while the book was in the press he was abolished. In the second edition, I altered 'China' to 'Germany'; the German Emperor fell, and I altered 'Germany' to 'Japan'. I hope it may not be long before another alteration will be needed. But it is not only emperors who are subject to vicissitudes. Throughout Europe, old families become impoverished, centres of industry decay and new centres grow up, the morals, manners, and beliefs of daily life change like fashions in dress. A vast expenditure of energy is needed to avoid becoming antiquated, and the future, even in its broadest outlines, is almost wholly unpredictable.

Apart from the world-wide causes of rapid change, which have their origin in scientific technique, Europe is oppressed by fear of the changes that war may bring—changes, not to this or that more modern form of social organisation, but to chaos, anarchy, or military tyranny. All long-term constructive effort seems useless in such an environment. Preparations for large-scale slaughter absorb the energies of the nations, but civilised men, even if they are convinced of the necessity of these preparations, cannot find in them any satisfaction for their humane or constructive impulses. And so, from despair, they grow less civilised, and take refuge in some fierce creed that hides or seems to justify a descent into barbarism. All that we have valued—not only property, not only life, but the things that have made life seem worth preserving—is threatened with destruction, and Europeans scarcely dare hope to transmit to their children, if they survive, more than a fragment of the civilisation that Europe has created.

America alone in the modern world has stability. It has the advantage of distance from the other Great Powers, giving that immunity from invasion that the sea formerly gave to Great Britain. It has the largest white population of any country except Russia. It has an overwhelming preponderance in raw materials. It is not hampered, as are most European countries, by remnants of medievalism and feudalism. Its agriculture and its political life are not weighed down by a mass of ignorant peasantry, wedded to the old ways, and an easy prey to the oppression of the landowner and the money-lender. There is in America a capacity for unregimented co-operative enterprise which is not equalled anywhere else in the world. All these factors produce a sense of security and stability combined with a determination not to rest content with what has been already achieved, which existed in Western Europe in the nineteenth century, but which has there been destroyed by wars and rumours of wars. A young man in America has a reasonable prospect of earning a sufficient livelihood, and of leaving his children at least as prosperous as he will have been himself.

In spite of all this, when I speak to Americans of the great role that their country is bound to play for at least the next 100 years, I am met, almost invariably, by modest disclaimers of fitness for such responsibilities, based upon a rooted belief that America is politically incompetent. Men grumble against the government, forgetting what an inestimable advantage it is to be allowed to grumble. Political competence is an ideal, but where on the surface of the globe is it to be found? Do the Nazis show competence? No doubt they perform miracles of organisation, and have constructed a great air force more quickly than anybody supposed possible. They have concentrated the productive forces of their nation, with great skill, upon one vast enterprise. But the enterprise is one which rouses the self-preservative instincts of the rest of the world, and which must end in ruin to Germany as well as to those whom she turns into enemies. Political competence is shown as much in the choice of objectives as in the means for achieving them, and is lacking in those who attempt the impossible, whatever cleverness they may show in the detail of their hopeless enterprise.

Although the Nazis are the most conspicuous example of unwisdom in Europe, other nations also, in varying degrees, have shown themselves incapable of statesmanship. At the end of the Great War, there was an unexampled opportunity for putting an end to the national rivalries that lead to wars. President Wilson wished to seize the opportunity, but France and England cajoled him into acceptance of an unjust and vindictive treaty, which led, by steps that could easily be foreseen, to all that is bad in modern Germany. Versailles was a very Bedlam of folly, and the only statesman who preserved any sanity was President Wilson. His sanity, it is true, was ineffectual, and grew gradually less in the atmosphere of lunacy; nevertheless, he stands out as the only eminent man who showed wisdom at that time. In later years—at the Washington Conference in 1921–2, and when the Japanese invaded Manchuria in 1931—the United States showed more statesmanship than any European nation. All the available evidence points to the conclusion that, in world affairs, there is more wisdom in America than elsewhere.

It used to be the fashion among educated Europeans to sneer at American culture. Whatever justification this habit may once have had, it has none now. The culture of America has improved, while that of Europe has deteriorated. In Germany, all that was best in culture has been deliberately stamped out, and many of the best individuals, from Einstein downwards, have found a home in the United States, where they transmit to students the free but scholarly use of intelligence which their own country no longer tolerates. In France and England, though intellectual freedom survives so far as institutions and laws can safeguard it, thought and feeling are caught in a new bondage to the danger and tragedy of the international situation. The young know that they are not unlikely to be killed in the next war, and that, if they survive, it will be amid the ruins of all that made a civilised life possible. In such an atmosphere they are apt to become harsh and cynical, or else frivolous as the only way of escaping from intolerable gloom. Culture, if it still survives in these circumstances, becomes lifeless and retrospective.

In America, a contrary process has taken place. I have known American universities since 1896, and have observed a steady advance from that time to the present. Before the Depression, there was apt to be a somewhat shallow optimism, and a belief that the existing stock of ideas sufficed to guarantee continuous progress. The Depression was bad enough to stimulate thought, but not, like disaster in war, bad enough to cause the paralysis of despair. A difficult balance is required to produce the best attitude in matters of culture. There must be a realisation that the dominant ideas of the present age are not likely to prove adequate for any long time in a rapidly changing world, without the kind of fury of revolt that produces a destructive temper. This balance I have found recently among American students in a higher degree than anywhere else. I cannot think that a country where the merits of the young are so great will prove unequal to any responsibility that circumstances may thrust upon it.

The American outlook was formed in the days when a vast continent, almost empty except along the eastern fringe, lay ready for exploitation by energetic men who asked nothing except to be left alone. Europe appeared distant, effete, over-populated, cursed with poverty and kings, and given over to constant wars. In such circumstances, politics seemed unimportant, and isolation the only sensible policy. At the same time, those Americans who cared about culture looked for it in Europe, where leisure and tradition produced an atmosphere more favourable to art and science than that of the frontier. But those days are past. There is no longer any free land for pioneers, but there is also no longer any need to regard Europe as superior in the highest products of civilisation. The self-confidence and the self-depreciation appropriate to the early days are out of place in modern America, especially the self-depreciation. The power to lead the world both politically and culturally will certainly come to the United States, and I firmly believe that with the power will come more of the necessary wisdom than has been shown in the past by nations in a similar position.

[1] *The Problems of Philosophy* (William & Norgate, London, and Henry Holt, New York, 1912).

DEMOCRACY AND ECONOMICS

Survey Graphic (New York, February 1939)

Democracy may be defined as the equal distribution of ultimate power. Immediate power cannot be equally distributed: there must be an executive government, and there must be judicial authorities. There is no reason to suppose that it would be desirable, even if it were possible, to give executive and judicial power directly into the hands of the electorate. The best known example of democracy in judicial decisions is not encouraging: 'Pilate said unto them, Whom will ye that I release unto you? Barabbas, or Jesus which is called Christ? They said, Barabbas. Pilate said unto them, What shall I do then with Jesus which is called Christ? They all say unto him, Let him be crucified.' This was democracy of a sort, but propaganda was not democratic: 'the chief priest and elders persuaded the multitude that they should ask Barabbas and destroy Jesus.' When any one form of power is not democratic, it can be used to vitiate those that are.

In modern democratic countries, economic power remains oligarchic. Democracy, both in Europe and in America, arose at a time when kings were its most powerful opponents, with hereditary aristocracies as their support. Democrats imagined that if privileges of birth were abolished, there would be a general scramble in which the best men would win. There are still people in America who believe this; they include those who have won in the scramble. But in order to believe in it in the present day, it is necessary to shut one's eyes to everything that has happened since the time of Jefferson. In his day, the majority of the population consisted of handicraftsmen and small farmers, each individually possessed of some independent economic power, and it was possible for an idealist to ignore the rising rival plutocracies of Northern manufacturers and Southern slave-owners. One of these plutocracies succeeded in focusing public indignation upon the other, and so escaped censure until it was well entrenched. The same sort of thing happened in England during Cobden's fight for free trade. And so a new aristocracy, wielding new weapons, surreptitiously acquired control of countries that believed themselves to be democratic.

Let us first consider what economic power is. In former days it consisted in ownership of land or capital, but in a developed industrial community ownership does not, as a rule, confer any appreciable share of power. Economic power belongs to large corporations, in which, by various devices, the ordinary shareholder has been deprived of all effective voice in the government, which is in the hands of a small number of self-perpetuating directors. According to Berle and Means, 2,000 individuals control half the industry of the United States. These men transmit their power by heredity or co-option; it is no longer possible, except in the rarest instances, for a man to *force* his way into the inner circle of economic rulers. They are as much a closed circle as the British aristocracy in the eighteenth century. They intermarry, they decide grave matters of policy in informal conversations, and they have no need of any ostensible governing body because of their social solidarity.

What are the powers of this oligarchy? They decide, in the first place, what shall be the wages and hours of practically all industrial workers, since it is always safe for smaller employers to follow in their footsteps. At many times, though not at present, they control the Federal government, both legislative and executive. At most times, they control most State governments, and can invoke the aid of the police and the militia in labor disputes. No attempt is made to cause them to obey the law, even when, like Mr Henry Ford, they openly boast of being lawbreakers. When they organise bands of criminals, who gravely injure unoffending citizens, and even (on occasion) bayonet children, it does not occur to anyone that they should be punished as an ordinary man would be who hired roughs to attack a private enemy. In the Chicago massacre in 1937, as everyone knows (or should know), the police, acting on their behalf, killed 10 and wounded 140 in a crowd of strikers who, according to a Senate investigation, had shown no illegal intentions. Yet the men who profited by this outrage remain respected citizens.

Like the chief priest and the elders, the financial oligarchy controls propaganda. The newspapers, being large capitalistic undertakings, are naturally on their side. In some industrial towns, if a trade union organiser arranges to hold a meeting in a hall or room, the building in which it is, is bought by the corporation concerned and the meeting is canceled. All clashes between labor and the police or hired mercenaries are reported, except in a very few papers, in a manner highly unjust to labor. Apart from those actually engaged in strikes, only people who go to a considerable amount of trouble can ascertain what actually goes on in labor disputes.

To understand the rights and wrongs of the matter, it is not enough to become aware of the detail of barbarism and lawlessness in the actions of the plutocracy; it is necessary, even more, to realise the objects for which they are fighting. They are fighting to preserve their income and to preserve their power, at no matter what cost to the less fortunate populations of the world. Mr Rand, who has done much to perfect the technique of strike-breaking, remarked: 'I am getting sick and tired of these men dictating to me how, when, and where they will work.' The tone reminds one of Henry VIII. They did not dictate to him how, when and where *he* should work, as one might have supposed from his indignation. A world where autocratic individuals can decide irresponsibly how, when, and where large numbers of other individuals shall work, is clearly not a democratic world. In a democratic world, this matter, like others that have to be decided collectively, would be in the hands of a democratic authority. 'A man loses his independence', says Mr Ford, 'when he joins a labor union, and he suffers as a result.' He has not noticed that a man loses his independence in joining Mr Ford. Mr Ford's methods of dealing with propaganda that he dislikes are closely similar to those of the Nazis. When union agents attempt, perfectly legally, to distribute circulars to Ford employees in the street, they are set upon by gangs of hired roughs, and sometimes severely injured. An elaborate secret service spies upon the Ford workers, and those who join unions are dismissed. This policy is successful: Mr Ford is one of the richest men in the world, and his employees are worn out before they reach the age of 50.

It appears to be the fixed policy of all the large corporations that in bad times the loss shall fall mainly upon the poorest, and in good times the gain shall go mainly to the richest. General Motors, for example, in 1935 raised the wages of ordinary employees by 5 per cent, and those of the eleven highest executives by 50 to a 100 per cent. These men had not been starving before, but the fear of destitution was met by raising the incomes of the president and vice-president to $350,000 in 1935 and $500,000 in 1936. During the depression, American wages in general fell 60 per cent, total national income 40 per cent, and interest 3.2 per cent. This shows how effective a plutocratic government in industry can be.

The behavior of the financial oligarchy in nominally democratic countries is in no way surprising. Every class possessed of exceptional power uses its power as ruthlessly as is compatible with retaining it. And it always cloaks its use of power in moralistic phrases which persuade the thoughtless that its opponents are wicked. There is hardly an instance in history of a powerful class shrinking from any cruelty, however atrocious and widespread, in the pursuit of its ends. Fear of rebellion is the only force sufficient to induce some degree of humanity.

The power of the 2,000 leading businessmen in America is very great. Except in so far as the C.I.O. is able to fight them, they determine wages and hours for almost all the industrial workers. They control small businessmen through the banks. They can, as a rule, ruin a professional man whom they dislike. By spending $80,000,000 a year on labor spies and strike-breakers, they compel wage-earners to look at each other with suspicion, since no one knows who is a secret agent. By their control of the press, they can stir up hostility against anyone who attempts to improve the conditions of labor. By corruption and intimidation, they acquire a hold over politicians, and make it difficult for an honest man to succeed in politics, or to remain honest if he does. By their habit of hiring and organising criminals and semi-criminals to fight strikers, they keep alive a dangerous spirit of violence; and by their lawlessness, they do their best to persuade reformers that nothing can be achieved by peaceful means. In order to retain and augment their incredibly large incomes, they do not shrink from poisoning the whole moral standard of their country.

The same situation, in essentials, exists wherever capitalism is combined with political democracy. It is a situation which, if left alone, will inevitably get worse, since it results from the vastness and central control of modern economic organisations which all technical developments tend to increase. There are only two possibilities in an industrially advanced country: either economic power will control the State, or the State will control economic power. In either case, economic and political power coalesce, and become more powerful than either was before. This must, I think, be accepted as a tendency which will be irresistible if technical progress continues.

The advocate of democracy, in these circumstances, cannot be content with democracy in the political sphere. While oligarchy survives in industry, political democracy must be either precarious or impotent if it does not. Let us ask ourselves what is the smallest measure of reform that would suffice to free the population from the tyranny of its present economic masters.

Economic power rests, in the main, upon the control of credit and the ownership of raw materials. If banking, oil, iron ore, and all other crude mineral wealth were in the hands of the State, the power of the plutocracy would be seriously crippled. Foreign trade would also need to be controlled, but that is less important in the United States than it is in smaller countries. Large power stations and large irrigation works, in private hands, confer a dangerous degree of power upon their owners, and should belong to public authorities. The whole question is one of power rather than of income. The existing plutocracy might be given full compensation without greatly diminishing the beneficial effects of the change. They might, that is to say, be transformed into government pensioners, if it were possible to enforce the condition that the pension should cease if they meddled in politics.

In many departments, public control would be sufficient without public ownership. But here we meet the difficulty of corruption. So long as there are very rich men who can become still richer by bribing politicians, it would be foolish to hope that all politicians will resist temptation. Nor are politicians by any means the only men whom it is worth-while to corrupt. This consideration makes it necessary, if economic democracy is to be effective, to extend public ownership to all large enterprises in which success depends upon political favoritism. Only experience can show how far the State would have to go in this direction. But undoubtedly, banking, crude minerals, and foreign trade are the most important sources of economic power, and if they were in public hands it would become less difficult to take whatever further steps might be necessary.

The integration of political and economic power, when it is not democratic, is disastrous. The politicians have acquired economic power in the totalitarian States, and the holders of economic power controlled politics in America from the fall of Wilson to the election of Mr Roosevelt. These examples make many men hesitate to advocate a coalescence which has had such unfortunate results. But this objection fails to meet the point. What is important is the equalisation of power. The concentration of power in the hands of either the State or big business is an inevitable result of modern technique; it is something that happens, not something to be either advocated or resisted. Given modern forms of organisation, there is only one way of equalising power, and that is to concentrate it in the hands of a democratic State. The only practicable alternatives are a political oligarchy or a big-business oligarchy. Each of these alternatives is incompatible with democracy. The latter is less hateful than the former, so long as it is held in check by political democracy; but with the inevitable increase of economic power, political democracy, unless it can conquer the economic field, must become increasingly inadequate and insecure. It might easily, as in ancient Rome, give place to a tyranny which kept the old democratic forms as an antiquarian curiosity. If democracy is to preserve any reality, it must achieve the conquest of economic power.

This change, largely owing to the folly of those who advocate it, has been represented as revolutionary, and as involving loss to all except the proletariat. Consequently it meets with very widespread resistance, and its opponents are able to threaten that it could not be brought about without a social upheaval. This situation, which has been caused by unwise propaganda, must be remedied before the transition can be effected without disaster. The changes that are necessary in order to curb the power of the plutocracy will, if effected peaceably, be beneficial to 99 per cent of the population; and if 99 per cent of the population, or even so many as 70 per cent, can be made to see this, it will be possible to effect the transition peaceably. When the work of persuasion has been adequately performed, whatever measures are necessary can be enacted legally, and carried out with a minimum of force exercised constitutionally by the authorities. But if the work of persuasion has been inadequate, any premature attempt is likely to do more harm than good. For in a contest of force, if the parties are at all evenly matched, it is the most ruthless who win.

The whole question has been enveloped in a red mist through which nothing is seen clearly. But for the fear of corruption, we might suppose, to take a concrete illustration, that all those who have money in oil are given, instead, a government pension of the same capital value. Who would be the worse off? Not ordinary investors, but only those who enjoy the power conferred by control of a great industry. These are few, and they would still have great wealth; they would have lost nothing but the ability to control other men's lives. Is this an object for which disinterested outsiders would think it worth-while to fight and die?

But in fact it is very doubtful whether such a painless method could be successful, again on account of the danger of corruption. If public opinion were sufficiently enlightened and alert, it might be possible to decree effectively that the pensions of ex-magnates should cease as soon as they took any part in politics, but sooner or later they would probably find ways of evading any such law. For this reason, it is very doubtful whether anything effective can be done without greatly diminishing the incomes of the plutocrats.

Moreover, the public would not be allowed to see the issue correctly. The propaganda of the rich in the United States is quite as reckless as Streicher's. We may take as a sample the words of Senator Stephens of Mississippi on the proposed Constitutional Amendment giving the Federal legislature power to regulate the labor of persons under 18 years of age. This august legislator, although the proposal was to confer power upon the body which he adorns, informed the world that: 'This is a socialistic movement and has for its ends purposes far deeper and more radical than appear on the surface. It is part of a hellish scheme laid in foreign countries to destroy our government. Many of the propagandists of the measure are communists and socialists. . . . The child becomes the absolute property of the Federal government.'[1] Again the high priest and the elders! A long and serious educational work will be needed to cause such pronouncements to be received with laughter accompanied by inquiries into the sources of the speaker's income. Until the general public can no longer be stampeded by rodomontade into actions contrary to self-interest no less than to common humanity, all sane advances towards true democracy will be very difficult.

The conquest of economic power by the democracy is an urgent problem for those who wish the democratic form of government to survive. The danger of fascism of the German or Italian variety can easily mislead public opinion as to dangers at home. Socialism and fascism are European products, and in their European forms are not likely to become popular in the United States: both hopes and fears must take new forms when they cross the Atlantic. What is to be feared here is the kind of thing that happened to the medieval Italian republics, which ossified into plutocratic oligarchies. It would be quite possible, by a combination of violence and corruption, to make democratic forms nugatory and freedom of propaganda a lost illusion. As I said before, the coalescence of economic and political power is an irresistible tendency in the modern world. It may be effected in an undemocratic manner by the politicians, as has happened in Russia, Italy, and Germany. It may be effected in an undemocratic manner by the plutocrats, in the countries that are nominally democratic. For the believer in democracy, the only practicable course is to advocate its happening in a democratic way, by the transference of ultimate economic power into the hands of the democratic State.

¹ Quoted from Millis and Montgomery, *Labour's Progress and Problems*. (Russell's note.)

THE CASE FOR U.S. NEUTRALITY

Common Sense Magazine (New Jersey, March 1939)

In America, as in England and France, bellicose opinions have become typical of the Left, while the Right has become more and more favorable for peace at almost any price. Similar situations have existed at other times: in France during the Revolution, in America in the disputes leading up to the war of 1812, and throughout Europe in the days of the Holy Alliance. But throughout the long period from 1870 to the rise of Hitler, it was liberals and radicals who favored peace. I think that their reasons for abandoning this position are fallacious, and that they are mistaken in imagining that the next war will be a Holy War; it will be fought, as other wars have been, for imperialistic aims, such as the control of the Mediterranean and the oil of the Near East. In common with the immense majority in England and France, I wish to see this war averted. But it becomes increasingly clear that it can only be averted at a great price, and that England and France, at some point, will refuse to pay this price. I think, therefore, that, in spite of Munich, war in Europe will come, and probably soon.

War comes only when the opposing forces are roughly equal, for if there is an obvious preponderance on either side the other side gives way. The next great war, therefore, like the last, will probably be long and bitter—more bitter than the last, though perhaps not so long. Whether America is a belligerent or not, air attacks on England and France will effect a vast destruction on life and property, generating a mood of panic rage which can only be kept in order by a severe military dictatorship. Economic hardship in Germany and Italy (if Italy is on the side of Germany) may lead to revolution, but the successful rebels will be fierce men, and are not likely to establish any regime more tolerant than the one that they will have overthrown. In all the belligerent countries of Western Europe, the population will be enormously diminished, large-scale industry will be destroyed, and orderly government, if it survives at all, will survive only in the form of tyranny rendered savage by the fear of murderous anarchy. A war for democracy cannot but end with the disappearance of democracy in Europe, except possibly in Scandinavia.

America, if a belligerent, will not be able to protect the Western democracies from air attack during the first weeks of the war, which will be those of greatest peril. And when peace comes, America, inflamed by war passions, subject, at least for the time, to a governmental autocracy created as a means to victory, will have neither the wish nor the power to secure a sane and liberal treaty: all the mistakes of Versailles will be repeated, but in an intensified form, because the war will have been more destructive and more bitter. Any reconstruction which is attempted will be vitiated by the passions of the war, and by refusal of justice to the vanquished. An impoverished and barbarised Europe will start again on the tragic cycle that has led from Versailles to the horrors of the present day and to the still worse horrors that are to be expected in the near future.

All this will happen because men will have allowed hatred to obscure economic and psychological understanding, as it is already doing among vehement anti-fascists throughout the Western world.

If, on the other hand, America preserves neutrality and therefore remains politically a democracy, there is a considerable possibility that the influence of the United States may be paramount in the reconstruction. Radical war-mongers always speak as though there were good reasons to fear a triumphant victory of the fascist Powers. I think this comes of an under-estimate of the destructiveness of the next great war. It is not to be supposed that the air forces of Germany's enemies would be idle. The industrial regions of the Rhineland would almost certainly be devastated. With luck, we might succeed in destroying all that is most worthy of admiration in Milan, Venice, Florence, and even Rome. The Russians, from the east, would punish the industrial regions of Silesia. Hunger, as before, would undermine the health of German children and the morale of their fathers in the trenches. The nominal victors, almost as much as the vanquished, would be so weakened and destitute as to be completely unable to resist a Power able, as America would be, to relieve distress and aid in reconstruction.

The best hope for the world, if Europe plunges into the madness of another great war, is that America will remain neutral, but will, when the fighting is over, use economic power to further sanity and liberalism, and to restore to the parent continent as much as possible of the civilisation that the war will have temporarily destroyed. Europe will be in so desperate a plight that it will be easy to impose political conditions on American aid in reconstruction. Last time, such conditions were not imposed, and the money involved was lost. I do not see any other way in which, in the event of war, American liberalism can help Europe; for if

America becomes a belligerent, the first effect will be the complete eclipse (at least for the time being) of liberalism, democracy, and free thought in the United States. What will the world gain by the defeat of the fascist Powers if, in the process, the fascist form of government becomes everywhere triumphant?

FREEDOM AND THE COLLEGES

The *American Mercury* (Washington, D.C., May 1940); reprinted in *Why I Am Not a Christian*, (London and New York, 1957).

I

Before discussing the present status of academic freedom, it may be as well to consider what we mean by the term. The essence of academic freedom is that teachers should be chosen for their expertness in the subject they are to teach, and that the judges of this expertness should be other experts. Whether a man is a good mathematician, or physicist, or chemist, can only be judged by other mathematicians, or physicists, or chemists. By them, however, it can be judged with a fair degree of unanimity.

The opponents of academic freedom hold that other conditions besides a man's skill in his own department should be taken into consideration. He should, they think, have never expressed any opinion which controverts those of the holders of power. This is a sharp issue, and one on which the totalitarian States have taken a vigorous line. Russia never enjoyed academic freedom except during the brief reign of Kerensky, but I think there is even less of it now than there was under the Tsars. Germany, before the war, while lacking many forms of liberty, recognised pretty fully the principle of freedom in university teaching. Now all this is changed, with the result that with few exceptions the ablest of the learned men of Germany are in exile. In Italy, though in a slightly milder form, there is a similar tyranny over universities. In Western democracies, it is generally recognised that this state of affairs is deplorable. It cannot, however, be denied that there are tendencies which might lead to somewhat similar evils.

The danger is one which democracy by itself does not suffice to avert. A democracy in which the majority exercises its powers without restraint, may be almost as tyrannical as a dictatorship. Toleration of minorities is an essential part of wise democracy, but a part which is not always sufficiently remembered.

In relation to university teachers, these general considerations are re-enforced by some that are especially applicable to their case. University teachers are supposed to be men with special knowledge and special training such as should fit them to approach controversial questions in a manner peculiarly likely to throw light upon them. To decree that they are to be silent upon controversial issues is to deprive the community of the benefit which it might derive from their training in impartiality. The Chinese Empire, many centuries ago, recognised the need of licensed criticism, and therefore established a Board of Censors, consisting of men with a reputation for learning and wisdom, and endowed with the right to find fault with the emperor and his government. Unfortunately, like everything else in traditional China, this institution became conventionalised. There were certain things that the censors were allowed to censure, notably the excessive power of eunuchs, but if they wandered into unconventional fields of criticism, the emperor was apt to forget their immunity. Much the same thing is happening among us. Over a wide field, criticism is permitted, but where it is felt to be really dangerous, some form of punishment is apt to befall its author.

Academic freedom in this country is threatened from two sources: the plutocracy, and the Churches, which endeavour between them to establish an economic and a theological censorship. The two are easily combined by the accusation of communism, which is recklessly hurled against anyone whose opinions are disliked. For example, I have observed with interest that, although I have criticised the Soviet government severely ever since 1920, and although in recent years I have emphatically expressed the opinion that it is at least as bad as the government of the Nazis, my critics ignore all this and quote triumphantly the one or two sentences in which, in moments of hope, I have suggested the possibility of good ultimately coming out of Russia.

The technique for dealing with men whose opinions are disliked by certain groups of powerful individuals has been well perfected, and is a great danger to ordered progress. If the man concerned is still young and comparatively obscure, his official superiors may be induced to accuse him of professional incompetence, and he may be quietly dropped. With older men who are too well known for this method to be successful, public hostility is stirred up by means of misrepresentation. The majority of teachers naturally do not care to expose themselves to these risks, and avoid giving public expression to their less orthodox opinions. This is a dangerous state of affairs, by which disinterested intelligence is partially muzzled, and the forces of conservatism and obscurantism persuade themselves that they can remain triumphant.

II

The principle of liberal democracy, which inspired the founders of the American Constitution, was that controversial questions should be decided by argument rather than by force. Liberals have always held that opinion should be formed by untrammelled debate, not by allowing only one side to be heard. Tyrannical governments, both ancient and modern, have taken the opposite view. For my part, I see no reason to abandon the liberal tradition in this matter. If I held power, I should not seek to prevent my opponents from being heard. I should seek to provide equal facilities for all opinions, and leave the outcome to the consequences of discussion and debate. Among the academic victims of German persecution in Poland there are, to my knowledge, some eminent logicians who are completely orthodox Catholics. I should do everything in my power to obtain academic positions for these men, in spite of the fact that their co-religionists do not return the compliment.

The fundamental difference between the liberal and the illiberal outlook is that the former regards all questions as open to discussion and all opinions as open to a greater or lesser measure of doubt, while the latter holds in advance that certain opinions are absolutely unquestionable, and that no argument against them must be allowed to be heard. What is curious about this position is the belief that if impartial investigation were permitted, it would lead men to the wrong conclusion, and that ignorance is, therefore, the only safeguard against error. This point of view is one which cannot be accepted by any man who wishes reason rather than prejudice to govern human action.

The liberal outlook is one which arose in England and Holland during the late seventeenth century, as a reaction against the wars of religion. These wars had raged with great fury for 130 years without producing the victory of either party. Each party felt an absolute certainty that it was in the right and that its victory was of the utmost importance to mankind. At the end, sensible men grew weary of the indecisive struggle and decided that both sides were mistaken in their dogmatic certainty. John Locke, who expressed the new point of view both in philosophy and in politics, wrote at the beginning of an era of growing toleration. He emphasised the fallibility of human judgements, and ushered in an era of progress which lasted until 1914. It is owing to the influence of Locke and his school that Catholics enjoy toleration in Protestant countries, and Protestants in Catholic countries. Where the controversies of the seventeenth century are concerned, men have more or less learnt the lesson of toleration, but in regard to the new controversies that have arisen since the end of the Great War, the wise maxims of the philosophers of liberalism have been forgotten. We are no longer horrified by

Quakers, as were the earnest Christians of Charles II's court, but we are horrified by the men who apply to present-day problems the same outlook and the same principles that seventeenth-century Quakers applied to the problems of their day. Opinions which we disagree with acquire a certain respectability by antiquity, but a new opinion which we do not share invariably strikes us as shocking.

There are two possible views as to the proper functioning of democracy. According to one view, the opinions of the majority should prevail absolutely in all fields. According to the other view, wherever a common decision is not necessary, different opinions should be represented, as nearly as possible, in proportion to their numerical frequency. The results of these two views in practice are very different. According to the former view, when the majority has decided in favour of some opinion, no other must be allowed to be expressed, or if expressed at all must be confined to obscure and uninfluential channels. According to the other view, minority opinions should be given the same opportunities for expression as are given to majority opinions, but only in a lesser degree.

This applies in particular to teaching. A man or woman who is to hold a teaching post under the State should not be required to express majority opinions, though naturally a majority of teachers will do so. Uniformity in the opinions expressed by teachers is not only not to be sought, but is, if possible, to be avoided, since diversity of opinion among preceptors is essential to any sound education. No man can pass as educated who has heard only one side on questions as to which the public is divided. One of the most important things to teach in the educational establishments of a democracy is the power of weighing arguments, and the open mind which is prepared in advance to accept whichever side appears the more reasonable. As soon as a censorship is imposed upon the opinions which teachers may avow, education ceases to serve this purpose and tends to produce, instead of a nation of men, a herd of fanatical bigots. Since the end of the Great War, fanatical bigotry has revived until it has become over a great part of the world as virulent as during the wars of religion. All those who oppose free discussion and who seek to impose a censorship upon the opinions to which the young are to be exposed are doing their share in increasing this bigotry and in plunging the world further into the abyss of strife and intolerance from which Locke and his coadjutors gradually rescued it.

There are two questions which are not sufficiently distinguished: the one as to the best form of government; the other as to the functions of government. I have no doubt in my mind that democracy is the best *form* of government, but it may go as much astray as any other form in regard to the *functions* of government. There are certain matters on which common action is necessary; as to these, the common action should be decided by the majority. There are other matters on which a common decision is neither necessary nor desirable. These matters include the sphere of opinion. Since there is a natural tendency for those who have power to exercise it to the utmost, it is a necessary safeguard against tyranny that there should be institutions and organised bodies which possess, either in practice or in theory, a certain limited independence of the State. Such freedom as exists in the countries which derive their civilisations from Europe is traceable historically to the conflict between Church and State in the Middle Ages. In the Byzantine Empire, the Church was subdued by the State, and to this fact we may trace the total absence of any tradition of freedom in Russia, which derived its civilisation from Constantinople. In the West, first the Catholic Church and then the various Protestant sects gradually acquired certain liberties as against the State.

Academic freedom, in particular, was originally a part of the freedom of the Church, and accordingly suffered eclipse in England in the time of Henry VIII. In every State, I repeat, no matter what its form of government, the preservation of freedom demands the existence of bodies of men having a certain limited independence of the State, and among such bodies it is important that universities should be included. In America at the present day there is more academic freedom in private universities than in such as are nominally under a democratic authority, and this is due to a very widespread misconception as to the proper functions of government.

III

Taxpayers think that since they pay the salaries of university teachers they have a right to decide what these men shall teach. This principle, if logically carried out, would mean that all the advantages of superior education enjoyed by university professors are to be nullified, and that their teaching is to be the same as it would be if they had no special competence. 'Folly, doctor-like, controlling skill' is one of the things that made Shakespeare cry for restful death. Yet democracy, as understood by many Americans, requires that such control should exist in all State universities. The exercise of power is agreeable, especially when it is an obscure individual who exercises power over a prominent one. The Roman soldier who killed Archimedes, if in his youth he had been compelled to study geometry, must have enjoyed a quite special thrill in ending the life of so eminent a malefactor. An ignorant American bigot can enjoy the same thrill in pitting his democratic power against men whose views are obnoxious to the uneducated.

There is perhaps a special danger in democratic abuses of power, namely, that being collective they are stimulated by mob hysteria. The man who has the art of arousing the witch-hunting instincts of the mob has a quite peculiar power for evil in a democracy where the habit of the exercise of power by the majority has produced that intoxication and impulse to tyranny which the exercise of authority almost invariably produces sooner or later. Against this danger, the chief protection is a sound education designed to combat the tendency to irrational eruptions of collective hate. Such an education the bulk of university teachers desire to give, but their masters in the plutocracy and the hierarchy make it as difficult as possible for them to carry out this task effectively. For it is to the irrational passions of the mass that these men owe their power, and they know that they would fall if the power of rational thinking became common. Thus the interlocking power of stupidity below and love of power above paralyses the efforts of rational men. Only through a greater measure of academic freedom than has yet been achieved in the public educational institutions of this country can this evil be averted.

The persecution of unpopular forms of intelligence is a very grave danger to any country, and has not infrequently been the cause of national ruin. The stock example is Spain, where the expulsion of the Jews and Moors led to the decay of agriculture and the adoption of a completely mad finance. These two causes, though their effects were masked at first by the power of Charles V, were mainly responsible for the decline of Spain from its dominant position in Europe. It may safely be assumed that the same causes will produce the same effects in Germany, ultimately, if not in the near future. In Russia, where the same evils have been in operation for a longer time, the effects have become plainly visible, even in the incompetence of the military machine.

Russia is, for the moment, the most perfect example of a country where ignorant bigots have the degree of control that they are attempting to acquire in New York. Professor A. V. Hill quotes the following from the *Astronomical Journal of the Soviet Union* for December 1938:

'1. Modern bourgeois cosmogony is in a state of deep ideological confusion resulting from its refusal to accept the only true dialectic-materialistic concept, namely, the infinity of the universe with respect to space as well as time.

'2. The hostile work of the agents of fascism, who at one time managed to penetrate to leading positions in certain astronomical and other institutions as well as in the press, has led to revolting propaganda of counter-revolutionary bourgeois ideology in the literature.

'3. The few existing Soviet materialistic works on problems of cosmology have remained in isolation and have been suppressed by the enemies of the people, until recently.

'4. Wide circles interested in science have been taught, at best, only in the spirit of indifference towards the ideological aspect of the current bourgeois cosmologic theories. . . .

'5. The exposé of the enemies of the Soviet people makes necessary the development of a new Soviet materialistic cosmology. . . .

'6. It is deemed necessary that Soviet science should enter the international scientific arena carrying concrete achievements in cosmologic theories on the basis of our philosophic methodology.'

For 'Soviet' substitute 'American', for 'fascism' substitute 'communism', for 'dialectic-materialism' substitute 'Catholic truth', and you will obtain a document to which the enemies of academic freedom in this country might almost subscribe.

IV

There is one encouraging feature about the situation, which is that the tyranny of the majority in America, so far from being new, is probably less than it was a 100 years ago. Anybody may draw this conclusion from De Tocqueville's *Democracy in America*. Much of what he says is still applicable, but some of his observations are certainly no longer true. I can not agree, for example, that 'in no country in the civilised world is less attention paid to philosophy than in the United States.' But I think there is still some justice, though less than in De Tocqueville's day, in the following passage:

'In America the majority raises very formidable barriers to the liberty of opinion: within these barriers an author may write whatever he pleases, but he will repent it if he ever step beyond them. Not that he is exposed to the terrors of an *auto-da-fé*, but he is tormented by the slights and persecutions of daily obloquy. His political career is closed forever, since he has offended the only authority which is able to promote his success. Every sort of compensation, even that of celebrity, is refused to him. Before he published his opinions he imagined that he held them in common with many others; but no sooner has he declared them openly than he is loudly censured by his overbearing opponents, whilst those who think without having the courage to speak, like him, abandon him in silence. He yields at length, oppressed by the daily efforts he has been

making, and he subsides into silence, as if he was tormented by re-
morse for having spoken the truth.'

I think it must also be admitted that De Tocqueville is right in what
he says about the power of society over the individual in a democracy:

'When the inhabitant of a democratic country compares himself individually with all those about him, he feels with pride that he is the
equal of any one of them; but when he comes to survey the totality of his
fellows, and to place himself in contrast to so huge a body, he is in-
stantly overwhelmed by the sense of his own insignificance and weakness. The same equality which renders him independent of each of his
fellow-citizens taken severally, exposes him alone and unprotected to the
influence of the greater number. The public has therefore among a
democratic people a singular power, of which aristocratic nations could
never so much as conceive an idea; for it does not persuade to certain
opinions, but it enforces them, and infuses them into the faculties by a
sort of enormous pressure of the minds of all upon the reason of each.'

The diminution in the stature of the individual through the hugeness
of the *Leviathan* has, since De Tocqueville's day, taken enormous strides,
not only, and not chiefly, in democratic countries. It is a most serious
menace to the world of Western civilisation, and is likely, if unchecked,
to bring intellectual progress to an end. For all serious intellectual progress depends upon a certain kind of self-respect, a certain kind of independence of outside opinion, which cannot exist where the will of the
majority is treated with that kind of religious respect which the orthodox
give to the will of God. A respect for the will of the majority is more
harmful than respect for the will of God, because the will of the majority
can be ascertained. Some forty years ago, in the town of Durban, a
member of the Flat Earth Society challenged the world to public
debate. The challenge was taken up by a sea captain whose only argument in favour of the world's being round was that he had been round it.
This argument, of course, was easily disposed of, and the Flat Earth
propagandist obtained a two-thirds majority. The voice of the people
having thus been declared, the true democrat must conclude that in
Durban the earth is flat. I hope that from that time onward no one was
allowed to teach in the public schools of Durban (there is, I believe, no
university there) unless he subscribed to the declaration that the round-
ness of the earth is an infidel dogma designed to lead to communism and
the destruction of the family. As to this, however, my information is
deficient.

Collective wisdom alas, is no adequate substitute for the intelligence
of individuals. Individuals who opposed received opinions have been the

source of all progress, both moral and intellectual. They have been un-popular, as was natural. Socrates, Christ, and Galileo all equally in-curred the censure of the orthodox. But in former times, the machinery of suppression was far less adequate than it is in our day, and the heretic, even if executed, still obtained adequate publicity. The blood of the martyrs was the seed of the Church, but this is no longer true in a country like modern Germany, where the martyrdom is secret and no means exists of spreading the martyr's doctrine.

The opponents of academic freedom, if they could have their way, would reduce this country to the level of Germany as regards the pro-mulgation of doctrines of which they disapprove. They would substitute organised tyranny for individual thought; they would proscribe every-thing new; they would cause the community to ossify, and in the end they would produce a series of generations which would pass from birth to death without leaving any trace in the history of mankind. To some, it may seem that what they are demanding at the moment is not a very grave matter. Of what importance, it may be said, is such a question as academic freedom in a world distracted by war, tormented by per-secution, and abounding in concentration camps for those who will not be accomplices in iniquity? In comparison with such things, I admit, the issue of academic freedom is not in itself of the first magnitude. But it is part and parcel of the same battle. Let it be remembered that what is at stake, in the greatest issues as well as in those that seem smaller, is the freedom of the individual human spirit to express its beliefs and hopes for mankind, whether they be shared by many or by few or none. New hopes, new beliefs, and new thoughts are at all times necessary to mankind, and it is not out of a dead uniformity that they can be expected to arise.

EDUCATION IN AMERICA

Common Sense Magazine (New Jersey, June 1941)

An Englishman accustomed to Oxford or Cambridge, when he first comes in contact with academic life in America, is likely to be somewhat bewildered, and to be led by nostalgia into undue criticism. Gradually, however, unless he is excessively prejudiced, he becomes aware of the many points in which the American system is superior to the British. He will still believe that Oxford and Cambridge have certain merits which have not crossed the Atlantic, but he will probably come to doubt whether anything but a lucky accident can preserve these merits in the modern world, or make them more than a by-product of demerits that are perhaps more important.

The outstanding characteristic of American university education, except in a few Eastern institutions, is the attempt to preserve democracy in a sphere which is naturally undemocratic. A much higher percentage of the population goes to the universities in the United States than in any European country. State universities are very cheap, and for those who have the necessary physical and mental vigor, it is possible to work one's way through at almost no cost. The result is that there is in America a much wider diffusion of moderate academic knowledge than is to be found anywhere else, and that university men are not a class apart, but are engaged, in large numbers, in occupations which in England would be left to men at a lower level of culture. With this there goes, both for good and evil, a closer bond between universities and the social life of the nation which exists in England.

The great difficulty, in an attempt to democratise academic institutions, is that *learning*, which they exist to promote, is not felt to be important in most democracies. Respect for learning, in the old sense, has been greatly diminished by the presence of scientific technique. The technician is the modern medicine-man, and whatever knowledge he needs is admitted without question to be important. But what he needs is practical, and has almost no connection with the older ideal of culture. The worst effects of this point of view are to be seen in the schools which are still concerned with academic instruction, but are felt, in this respect, to be performing a not very useful task. The result is that they do not perform it well. The task that they perform well is the one that is *felt* to be important, namely that of turning young people into loyal citizens. But as regards knowledge, Europeans who teach in American universities are surprised by the ignorance of freshmen.

I may be told that the sort of thing I have in mind is provided in post-graduate teaching. To some extent, this is true. There are, however, important limitations. In the first place, in most universities, the clever students are compelled in their first years to go through the same course as the rest; this means that they are kept too busy to think, and too distracted among a multitude of subjects to acquire a sound knowledge of anything. Many of the ablest men, in the second place, are poor, and have to make a living by outside work; this is fatal to health in many cases, and tends to blunt the edge of intelligence. In spite of these drawbacks, I have found more encouragement in post-graduate work in America than in my own country. There is a hopefulness and enthusiasm which is not to be found in the disillusioned atmosphere of Europe.

Nevertheless, the promise of the early years is not often fulfilled. A young man who obtains a teaching post is expected to publish 'original' work in considerable amounts, and is judged on its quantity rather than its quality. Newton was for twenty-one years a Fellow of Trinity before he published; in America, he would have been likely to lose his post for such 'idleness'. To this argument, however, there is a valid retort; that for about 150 years after Newton, neither Oxford nor Cambridge produced anything of value. It may be worthwhile to sacrifice the remote chance of the superlatively excellent in order to make sure of *something*. More serious than the stress on publication are two other temptations to which young teachers in universities are exposed. One of these is the prestige of administration as opposed to learning, and the other is the financial advantage attaching to safe conservative opinions. The first inclines a man to spend his time on matters other than research; the second fills him with fear of the powers that be, and makes him timid, not only where the possibility of subversive opinions is directly involved, but ultimately, from habit, in even the most remote and academic questions. The result is that few men, at 50, have achieved as much as their abilities at 23 might have led one to expect.

This brings us to the question of academic freedom, which has two forms, one collective and one individual. The collective question is: How far should universities manage their own affairs? The individual question is: How far should a teacher be at liberty to profess whatever opinions seem best to him, so long as he performs the duties of his post?

These two have quite different histories, and involve different sentiments.

Collective freedom for universities arose in the Middle Ages as part of the independence of the Church from State interference. A long line of eminent ecclesiastics, such as St Ambrose, Gregory VII, St Anselm, and Innocent III, had successfully resisted the secular power in the name of religion, and the universities, as an offshoot of the Church, had profited. A heretical professor might be condemned, but he would be condemned by men of his own kind and of equal learning. This form of collective freedom still exists at Oxford and Cambridge, but only as a survival; it is not to be found in the newer English universities, or in America. There has been a change of sentiment, which has profound effects of many kinds. The ordinary citizen no longer feels, as he did from the fourth century to the sixteenth, that there is an organised body to which he owes a stronger loyalty than he owes to the State. Consequently, the State's love of power encounters no effective resistance and the islands of collective freedom left over from the Middle Ages are successively submerged.

Moreover, when collective freedom in university matters is claimed in America, it is claimed on behalf of the administration rather than on behalf of the teachers, and the gulf between these is often very wide. There is between England and America a paradoxical difference, namely that American institutions are more monarchical than their English counterparts. This difference impressed me when I first began to know the United States forty-four years ago, and has impressed me increasingly ever since that time. The presidents of railroads and other big industrial or financial corporations wield powers which in England would be exercised by a board. The presidents of universities have an authority which vice-chancellors may envy, but cannot hope to rival. This depends mainly on the fact that, except in rare instances, the president has the power of appointment, and, in the case of the younger teachers at least, the power of dismissal.

I have before me two addresses by presidents of universities, Dr Nicholas Murray Butler of Columbia, and Dr A. G. Ruthven of the University of Michigan, both urging the importance of freedom for universities, and both defining it, in effect, as the right of the administration to curb the activities of teachers. 'University freedom,' says Dr Butler (I quote *The New York Times* of 4 October), 'is as important as academic freedom. Indeed, before and above academic freedom of any kind or sort comes this university freedom which is the right and obligation of the university itself to pursue its high ideals unhampered and unembarrassed by conduct on the part of any of its members which tends to damage its reputation, to lessen its influence or to lower its authority as a center of sound learning and moral teaching. Those whose convictions are of such a character as to bring their conduct into open conflict with the university's freedom to go its way toward its lofty aim should, in ordinary self-respect, withdraw of their own accord from university membership.' What will happen to them if they do not, is left to be imagined.

Dr Ruthven's speech, which was made to a convention of the National Association of State Universities, is in some ways even more interesting. (I quote the *Christian Science Monitor* of 9 November.) He first stated that 'freedom of independent thinking, expression, and assembly in our schools is not licence for students and faculty to work against the very forms of government which allow such rights to exist', and that 'criticism should invariably be sympathetic and constructive'; he then went on to say that 'a well-developed attack upon higher education is in the making' and that the danger of Federal control has been increasingly imminent.' His final statement is that the major objective of the schools should be the training of good citizens. I am a little puzzled as to Dr Ruthven's theory of government. Does he hold that resistance to Federal control is part of the duty of a good citizen, and should be taught in schools? Has his own criticism of the Federal government been invariably 'sympathetic'? Does he hold that the 'good citizen' will advocate acquiescence in the *status quo* of the moment, or a reversion to an idyllic past? For those who wish to retain posts at the University of Michigan, these questions are of considerable practical importance. We, however, must pass them by for others more germane to our subject.

These two addresses have in common the view that it is the business of a school or university to create 'good citizens', and that the university should impose its view of good citizenship upon any teacher who may have a different view. This raises three distinct questions: first, is the creation of 'good citizens' the purpose of a university? Second, should each teacher be free to state his own view as to what constitutes good citizenship, or should a collective decision be enforced? Third, if the latter view is taken, what authority is to make the collective decision? I shall take these questions in reverse order.

When Dr Butler speaks of 'the university' and of 'university freedom,' it is clear that, for him, the university is embodied in its president: *l'état, c'est moi*. The freedom that is claimed is that of the president: neither from within nor from without is his view of what constitutes good citizenship to be interfered with. This view also obviously underlies Dr Ruthven's objection to all resistance to government except his own and that of men who share his views. So long as all the younger teachers are subject to dismissal by the president, he may tolerate the *forms* of democracy, secure that there will be none of the substance. One may see, in

America, assemblies of university teachers listening, in awed submission, while the administration informs them how they are to vote; to one accustomed to the more democratic methods of England, the spectacle is horrifying.

It is assumed, in addresses such as those we are considering, that there can be no honest divergence of opinion as to what constitutes good citizenship. Is it, for instance, contrary to good citizenship in California to call attention to the bad conditions among migrant workers, and to suggest methods of amelioration? To this question, of course, the authorities will not answer 'yes', but they will visit with their displeasure any one who effectively answers 'no'. Their displeasure, of course, will be for quite other reasons: that he is a bad teacher, that he encourages the young not to respect their elders and betters, or that he has failed to produce enough research. (An investigation of conditions among present-day men and women, if it makes any practical recommendations, is not 'research'.)

The view of 'good citizenship' taken by the rich and powerful is sure to be quite different from that taken by the poor and oppressed. Consequently, if every university teacher must teach what his president considers good citizenship, it must happen, in the great majority of cases, that his teaching will have a strong class bias, and will be largely directed to obstructing attempts at the removal of economic injustice. Only security of tenure can remedy this evil.

I come now to the question: Even if perfect democracy existed among university teachers, should a collective decision as to what constitutes good citizenship be enforced? And this at last brings me to the question of individual as against collective academic freedom. The principle of individual academic freedom has no roots in the Middle Ages; it is an outcome of the liberalism of the eighteenth and nineteenth centuries, and, like everything liberal, is now questioned by some champions of democracy almost as much as by fascists and communists. The question of individual freedom in general is not one which I propose to argue, but there are some special considerations in the case of university teachers. These are, in general, men of exceptional intelligence and learning, whose opinions deserve some weight. If they are prevented from expressing their conclusions, either by the democracy or by the plutocracy, it is almost certain that progress, both intellectual and social, will be seriously impeded. Every one admits this as regards the past. Copernicus, from fear of condemnation, published posthumously; Kepler was forced to earn his living by astrology; Galileo recanted under threat of torture; Spinoza was condemned by Jews and Christians alike; Darwin could not have held a university appointment, except perhaps at London. No system of university government, however democratic, would have led universities to endorse these men's opinions in their own day, and if it had been the practice to enforce collective decisions they would have been silenced. But it is supposed—on what evidence, heaven knows—that we have grown wiser than our ancestors, and that now, though not at any previous period in human history, an unpopular opinion is sure to be a harmful one. The obvious falsehood of such a view throughout the past is the basis of the claim for individual liberty of opinion. Where liberty of opinion is stifled, no means remain for combating the tyranny of the powerful or the prejudices of the multitude—except, after sufficient ages of misery, by the wasteful and dangerous method of violence and bloody revolution. I conclude that collective decisions, however arrived at, should not be enforced upon university teachers in matters of opinion.

I come at last to the question: Is the creation of good citizens the purpose of a university? It certainly cannot be the sole purpose, for no one would deny that a man may be a good citizen without having been at a university. The special function of a university, obviously, is to foster learning, while the making of good citizens is a more general matter, in which other institutions are at least equally concerned. In what sense, then, do Doctors Butler and Ruthven understand the words 'good citizen'? It would seem that, in so far as this kind of excellence can be created by a university education, they must mean a combination of two things: right opinions, and effectiveness in propaganda, for only the latter is promoted by learning.

What are *right* opinions, in the view of the average university president? Not majority opinions, for most of them are Republicans. Not educated opinions, for in almost every American university most of the faculty are more highly educated than the president, and should therefore have the right to discipline him, if education were the deciding factor. What, then, remains? Only one thing: right opinions are the opinions of the rich. This view, however, cannot be avowed, since it is necessary to pay lip-service to democracy.

For my part, I do not think a university ought to have a collective view as to what are right opinions. It ought rather to adopt the practice professed by the Platonic Socrates, of following wherever the argument leads; the promotion of free and well-informed discussion, rather than of this or that conclusion, should be its function. Churches and political parties exist for the segregation of men according to their opinion; universities should classify men differently, according to their tastes and pursuits. If a man is fond of learning and good at acquiring it, he is suitable for academic life. If you disagree with his opinions, by all means combat them in argument; but if you cannot succeed by argument, in spite of being his equal in learning, then it is your duty to adopt his opinion, not to proscribe it.

313

The anti-liberal attitude of many educational administrators in America, which is rapidly increasing and becoming a serious menace to an important kind of liberty, is rendered the more dangerous by the fact that men of learning, with few exceptions, are not allowed to acquire power in the educational machine. In privately endowed universities, the power is in the hands of big business; in State universities, it is in the hands of politicians. What would be thought of a proposal to hand over the management of (say) the railroads to a board of university professors? Everyone would point out that they could not be expected to understand the business. But no one seems to think it equally odd to hand over the universities to men of the type of railroad presidents who know nothing of higher education, and can only be induced to concede its utility by having it presented as a means of combating subversive propaganda.

As for the State universities and the politicians, they lead to a different set of considerations, more congenial to the plutocrats. State education is a form of socialism, and the evils that it displays are those to be feared of a bureaucratic and unduly centralised socialistic regime. The essential difficulty, however, is the same in both cases: that a highly technical matter is left to the management of people who know nothing about it. I met in Leningrad in 1920 a professor of pure mathematics, left over from the *ancien régime*, who complained that, under the new system, the charwomen had as much voice as he had in the management of the university. In America, this would seem odd because the charwomen were poor, but not because they were ignorant.

The problem of academic government is part of a larger problem, which it is urgently necessary to consider at the present time. Our half of the world is engaged in a fierce struggle to preserve as much liberty as possible, and success in the struggle demands a great concentration of power and a great unity of effort. These things are inimical to freedom, and may defeat our aims even if, in a military sense, we are victorious. Power-loving individuals use the crisis to urge concentration and unity in fields where they are not necessary. If freedom is to survive, we must preserve whatever islands of autonomy are compatible with self-preservation. Of these, universities are among the least dangerous, since the academic mind, as a rule, is by temperament timid and conservative except when goaded by suppression. I am encouraged by the vehement criticism with which Dr Butler's address was met, to hope that academic freedom, even if it suffers a temporary eclipse, may recover its luster when the world ceases to be a conflict of hysterias, and men have time to remember more permanent goods than victory.

THE PROBLEM OF MINORITIES

Unpublished; delivered as a lecture to the Rand School of Social Science, New York, between October/December 1942

It is generally recognised that 'government by the majority' is not the whole of what should be understood by 'democracy'. Democracy arose in connection with 'natural rights', and was generally accompanied by some 'Declaration of the Rights of Man'. Although the philosophy of natural rights is now discredited, we still think that democracy requires abstention from certain exercises of power against individuals and minority groups. In the American Constitution, the provision about 'due process' expresses a part of this point of view: an individual cannot be imprisoned or executed unless a court of law decides that he has done something previously declared by the legislature to be a crime. This is a very important matter; execution or imprisonment by executive decree is one of the chief weapons of tyranny. Again, the Constitution safeguards religious freedom, as well as freedom of speech and of the press. Such limitation of the power of government over individuals is an important aspect of what most people understand by 'democracy'.

The problem that I wish to consider is cognate, but not identical; it is the problem of the limitations which should be imposed upon majorities as regards coercion of minorities. This question is difficult both in principle and in practice. I propose to say first a few words about the general theory of the treatment of minorities, and then to consider the practical problems arising in this connection in the United States and elsewhere.

A minority may be one of race, or one of opinion; Negroes, in this country, are a racial minority, while communists are a minority of opinion. Again, a minority may be geographically concentrated, or may be diffused throughout the country; the Irish, for example, are a diffused minority in the United States, but were a geographically concentrated minority (in Ireland) when Ireland and Great Britain were under one government. A racial minority generally also has minority opinions on some matters, and if it does not it is likely to be not important from one point of view. But a group defined by race must be separated, in discussion,

315

from one defined by opinion, since it is not increased or diminished by propaganda, and membership of it is not a matter of free choice. The most difficult part of the problem is that of racial minorities not geographically concentrated; this includes Jews and Negroes. But let us begin with the easier parts of our problem.

The easiest problem is that of a geographically concentrated minority which, throughout a certain area, is overwhelmingly in the majority. This was the case with Ireland when it was part of the United Kingdom; it was the case of the Slovaks under the Czechs, the Ukrainians under the Poles, the Croats under the Serbs, and so on. In all such cases the theoretical solution is clear: devolution for certain purposes, and a Federal authority for the rest. But when feeling between the majority and minority groups is very bitter, complete separation may, at least temporarily, be necessary.

In practice there are always difficulties. As a rule, the region of the minority contains some members of the majority who do not wish to lose their dominant position and become in turn the oppressed. The larger group clings to power, and the smaller group is led into acts of illegal violence, or even armed rebellion, in pursuit of independence. There are often border districts where it is not clear which group has the majority. In a few rare instances, the problem has been peaceably solved by the disputants themselves; the most notable case is the separation of Norway and Sweden. But in the immense majority of cases the dominant race (which may be a minority) has continued to oppress the other until compelled to cease by force—either that of rebellion, or that of an external power, or both in combination.

The government of the League of Nations gave minorities the right to appeal to the League against oppression. But in this, as in other matters, the League took no effective action, for fear of offending the States whose action was criticised. The principle, however, was right. Where a majority oppresses a minority, it is clear that there should be some legal method of redress, and that this must depend upon the intervention of some authority external to both disputants. When England gave independence to Ireland, it was in deference to American opinion. If, as seems likely, a move is now made towards Indian autonomy, it will be partly for the same reason, partly to stimulate Indian resistance to Japan.

The whole problem of nationalities can only be radically solved within an international federation. Such a federation will have to give minorities the right to lay grievances before the Federal government, and to make laws according to which decisions are to be reached in regard to such grievances. The general rule must be to allow autonomy in all local concerns, but to have a Federal authority to decide foreign policy, armaments, tariffs, control of raw materials, and other matters that do not concern only either subordinate national group. But as this question belongs to the sphere of international government, I shall not now pursue it further.

Sometimes the same principle, of a comparatively neutral outside authority, can already be applied. The white men in British African possessions are to some extent restrained from oppressing the Negroes by the Home government. In the United States, the Federal government is less biased against Negroes than are the governments of the Southern States, and its intervention in Negro questions, when it occurs, is usually in the direction of justice. (I shall deal with the Negro question shortly.) It is obvious that the rights of minorities, whatever we may consider them to be, can only be guaranteed if there is some authority superior to the local oppressive majority. In the absence of such an authority, there is no remedy except the very doubtful one of rebellion, or the gradual one of organisation and agitation with a view to the growth of a liberal sentiment in the majority.

In regard to minorities of opinion, the general principle is clear: there should be a free field for propaganda, and an equal share per head in voting. There are, however, some minority opinions which cannot be treated adequately by this principle. Communists and fascists agree in the view that an organised minority should seize power by force, and put an end to democracy. Such an opinion, so long as it is that of a minority so small as to be powerless, may be disregarded. But when it becomes enough of a menace to threaten civil war or a *coup d'état*, the majority clearly has a right to take steps for self-protection. This applies generally to organised bodies of which the essential aim is in whole or part illegal. Assassination of statesmen obnoxious to a minority, for example, should not only be punished when it occurs, but should not be tolerated as a purpose to be advocated. The practice of assassinating politicians obnoxious to a minority was common in Japan in recent years, and in Germany during the rise of Hitler. In the sixteenth and seventeenth centuries, Jesuits advocated regicide whenever the king happened to be a Protestant; one cannot, therefore, blame Protestant kings of that time for their refusal to tolerate Jesuits. If a minority is to be tolerated, it must not aim at forcible seizure of power while still a minority, nor must advocacy of illegal acts be part of its programme.

The principle, however, is subject to various limitations. Many reforms—for instance, votes for women—have been won by deliberate law-breaking. In these cases, the law-breaking is an incidental method of propaganda, and the aim is to secure a change in the law by constitutional procedure. In such cases, it is often wiser to change the law than to punish conscientious criminals. No general principle can be laid down for such cases.

There are bodies of opinion—pacifism, for instance—which involve a purely passive breach of the law, that is to say, refusal to act as the law directs. The spectacle of an earnest Quaker being sent to prison because he will not do what he thinks wrong is a painful one. A wise government will do much to avoid such action, but it cannot *always* be avoided. We are here in a region of practical statesmanship, not of abstract considerations.

Hitherto, I have been considering minorities which are oppressed, or seek an opportunity to oppress others. There is, however, in every democracy, another minority problem, that of pressure groups. A pressure group is an organisation which has certain interests other than those of the general public, and which seeks to sell its support of men or measures in return for concessions to its sectional demands. The most obvious example of the working of pressure groups is the tariff. As a rule, a duty on some particular commodity helps the producers of that commodity, but harms the consumers who are usually much more numerous. It does not, however, in most cases, harm the individual consumer as much as it benefits the individual producer. Accordingly, the different groups of producers make a bargain with each other to support each other's interests, and the unorganised interest of the consumer is ignored. This is not government by the majority, but by a coalition of minorities.

Minorities, if sufficiently determined and sufficiently organised, may be able, in a democracy, to impose their will upon majorities on all issues except those that are regarded by the public as the most important. In the United States, the most influential minority of this sort is the Catholic Church. There are several pivotal States in which the Catholic vote holds the balance; therefore no presidential candidate can resist Catholic pressure, unless it goes so far as to unite non-Catholics, or a large proportion of them, in opposition. In this way a minority may get power far in excess of its numerical strength.

Pressure groups cannot be prevented in a democracy, and perhaps serve a useful purpose. The only cure for the evils associated with them is a more complete organisation of interests, so that as a result of conflicting forces, something emerges which is approximately what the majority wants. This, of course, is not a successful cure if some minority is so hated that no others will combine with it. Nor is it democratic in its working if certain groups (for example the richest) have much more power of effective propaganda than their opponents. But, on the whole, pressure groups prevent the grossest forms of oppression of the majority, and a government which abstains from gross oppression of the majority is, as governments go, exceptionally beneficent.

Much the most difficult problem is that of racial minorities which are not geographically concentrated. The most important of these, in the United States, are Jews and Negroes. The Jews are an international problem, more serious in Central Europe than in America. The Negroes, on the other hand, represent the greatest failure of democracy in the United States, and until some justice is accorded to them it cannot be maintained that democracy exists here. I will consider Negroes first, as being the simpler problem.

The problem, of course, starts from slavery, which led to Negroes being considered an inferior caste. At the end of the Civil War they were suddenly emancipated and given the vote, without economic opportunity, without education, and among a white population which had always despised them and now also hated them. The results were of course disastrous, both while the North insisted upon allowing political power to the ignorant enfranchised slaves, and afterwards, when the Southern whites, by various expedients, re-established their supremacy. Negroes in the South are now disfranchised by various devices—poll-tax, literacy tests, questionnaires, etc., administered with a view to disqualification of coloured people. If all these devices fail, sheer violence is used. Nor, in fact, is there any one for the Negroes to vote for; for, while it is unconstitutional to disfranchise them as such, it is perfectly legal to exclude them from the primaries, so that no candidate favourable to them can be nominated. Throughout the South they are as completely devoid of political power as they would be if colour, in itself, deprived them of the vote.

For those who hold democratic principles, it is not wholly easy to decide what *ought* to be done with a group which, on the whole, is culturally inferior to the average. The policy of the North after the Civil War, of giving them the vote and leaving them to sink or swim, is obviously not right. There must first be education, both theoretical and practical, and then a gradual introduction to public responsibility. There must be a careful avoidance of any suggestion that the inferiority is permanent, and there must be every encouragement for talent. The goal should be complete equality of status as soon as possible.

What has been done in regard to Negroes in the United States is very different from this. The immense majority of whites have proclaimed their eternal superiority to coloured people, and have enforced social separation to the utmost. In Northern cities, Negroes are only allowed in certain specified ghettos, unless as servants of white employers. They are compelled by white regulations to suffer appalling overcrowding, making sanitation and cleanliness impossible; they are then reproached for being diseased and dirty. When Hitler does this to Polish Jews, the very people who are doing it to Negroes profess to be shocked. In most

319

Southern States, it is illegal for whites and coloured people to be edu-cated in the same institution, even if it is private. In many places in the South, there are no schools for Negroes, who consequently have no education.[1] Hospitals for white people will not admit Negroes, and hospitals for coloured people are few; there are cases of white people with a coloured chauffeur, all injured in an automobile accident, when the chauffeur has died while the hospital authorities were debating whether they could admit him.

The cruel superstition of Negro inferiority is shown in a peculiarly disgusting form by the recent action of the American Red Cross in regard to blood transfusion. At first, no Negro blood was accepted; then, as a great concession, it was announced that it would be accepted, but only given to coloured people. This was accompanied by a statement that there is no difference between white and coloured blood, and no scientific reason whatever why white men should object to receiving coloured blood in blood transfusions. A population which tolerates or expects such action by the Red Cross has no right to pose as the cham-pion of democracy, or to feel morally superior to Hitler. I shall return to this matter shortly.

Throughout the South, there is no justice for coloured people in the law courts. Once in a way, this is made glaringly obvious by such a case as that of the Scottsboro boys; but in general it passes unnoticed. The police will always suspect a Negro first if possible, and the courts will condemn him more readily. Lynching usually goes unpunished. Although lynching is not very frequent, the fear of it hangs over Negroes perpet-ually. And the Ku-Klux-Klan was always available to establish a reign of terror.

Economic discrimination against Negroes takes many galling forms. They are everywhere allowed only inferior work, and in the South are paid less than white men for the same work. At the end of the Civil War, slave labour on the plantations gave way to the sharecropping sys-tem, which is a form of peonage, in which Negroes and poor whites share.

'A gross cash family income of $250 a year is a liberal estimate not only for the South's 1,832,000 tenant farmers but also for her 600,000 farm wage-hand families, 200,000 stranded rural families, and 200,000 smallest farm owner operators. . . . Averaging nearly four per family, here is a population of over 11,000,000—over one-third of all the people in the South.'[2]

This poverty is partly white, but it is traceable to the evils brought about by the degrading of the Negroes and the land. The degrading of the land has gone on for a long time, and is similar to what has happened in the dust bowl.

The agricultural ruin of the South drove large numbers of Negroes into industry, both in the South and in the North. Many were imported into the North during the last World War. Between 1920 and 1930, 1 million Negroes left Southern agriculture for industry, mostly in the North. In industry they come into competition with white workers; indeed, in many cases, their first irruption is as strike-breakers. In the steel strike of 1919, for instance, 30,000 of them were employed in this capacity. This naturally caused bitter feelings in the trade unions. It has been customary for white workers to insist that only inferior jobs shall be open to Negroes, and to strike if better jobs are given to them. Also, until recent years, the unions pretty generally refused to admit coloured people. Now many unions have realised that this is a short-sighted policy, and that all labour, white and coloured, must stand together if it is to succeed. I shall have more to say on this subject in a moment.

The harm that is done by the oppression of coloured people is not only to them, but also to the white population. The use of Negroes as strike-breakers, which was rendered possible by the illiberality of white wage-earners, made successful trade union action very difficult. The determination not to employ coloured people in skilled work meant that whatever special skill they possessed was lost to the community. At present, when an all-out effort is necessary to win the war, failure to utilise coloured labour to the full is likely to have very serious consequences. In the South, the position of poor whites is obviously depressed by the existence of a Negro population which is prevented, to the utmost extent possible, from bettering its economic position.

Even more serious is the general growth of violence and moral degeneration. In the South, not only Negroes, but radicals of even the mildest sort, are objects of mob hysteria; the suspicion that a man may perhaps be a radical is enough to cause his arrest on some pretext, and to make it necessary for him to leave the neighbourhood, even if it cannot be proved that he is guilty of the crime of possessing decent and humane feelings, or of believing in democracy. The South is the most conservative section of the country; recently it was Southern democrats, almost alone, who persisted in voting against the forty-hour week.

I come now to the question of remedies for these evils. To a large extent, the principles are the same in dealing with other minorities that are oppressed, whether in the United States or elsewhere—for example, the Jews in post-war Germany. There are some important differences, but more similarities. The most important difference is that the Jewish question can only be dealt with by an international authority.

What is needed in regard to Negroes in the United States may be put under five heads:

(1) Federal protection. (2) Industrial organisation as a means to

equality of opportunity and wages. (3) Equal franchise (and voting opportunities). (4) Equal education. (5) Abolition of social prejudice (without which justice from police and law courts is impossible).

Some of these methods are applicable to other minorities, some are not.

(1) *Federal protection*. Racial prejudice is greatest where there are most Negroes. In these regions, local authorities are likely to be exceptionally unfair. The only remedy is Federal interference.

The present administration claims to have conferred certain benefits on Negroes; in fact, most of those who could vote seem to have voted for Roosevelt in 1936 and 1940, in spite of traditional Republicanism. But Federal administration and legislation are constantly hampered by local prejudice and prejudice in the Federal administration itself, and by interference of Congress led by Southern members, or responsive to white pressure. Liberal officials are ousted by Congress refusing an appropriation until they are dismissed.[3]

The Federal government yielded to the pressure of Southern industrialists when it accepted the Steel code perpetuating North-South wage differentials, which Secretary Perkins[4] criticised as both unfair to Negroes and not in the interest of white labour. Cayton and Mitchell in *Black Workers and the New Unions* point out, in this connection, that 'many codes were so written as arbitrarily to tend, for no adequate reason, to distinguish the white and colored labor force of an industry', and that 'this tended to reinforce the already existing tension between these two groups.'

Van Deusen (*The Black Man in White America*) says: 'the Social Security Act is of little service to Negroes since it excludes from benefits under the old age security and unemployment provision, domestic, agricultural, and casual workers. The greater number of Negroes employed fall in these groups.'

All this, as well as the absence of a Federal measure to stamp out lynching, shows that Federal control, while important and essential, is not enough, at any rate at present.

(2) *Industrial organisation*. To my mind, the first step is industrial organisation in unions containing both white and coloured workers. This must precede any campaign for equal political rights, since Negroes cannot win equality except as a pressure group, and can only become an effective pressure group by combination with white workers. This must not exclude organisation of Negro workers as Negroes, both to secure their rights in the unions, and to agitate against discrimination. But what is vital is to bring about recognition of the solidarity of labour, whether white or black; for until there is this solidarity, employers can always defeat both the Negroes and white labour.

Unions formerly excluded Negroes, but, now the American Federation of Labour, and the C.I.O. especially, has made great efforts to organise them, with much success. Cayton and Mitchell say: 'One of the most striking phases of the entire S.W.O.C.'s campaign was the extent to which the union has been able to modify racial prejudice within the ranks of white laborers. The effect of working together for a common goal, of facing a common enemy, and of day-to-day co-operation in union affairs has been to draw white and Negro workers together to an extent perhaps never before equalled in this country.'

When interests are seen to be the same and an effort is made to overcome snobbery, colour prejudice is found to be much less than was expected, and may disappear. On the other hand, anything that emphasises differences, and supplements natural with economic differences, accompanied by competition, enormously strengthens genuine race prejudice. These reflections apply to all racial minorities—Jews, Italians, etc. Employers understand this psychology and do their best—very often— to stimulate race prejudice. Both white and coloured workers, and also immigrants of different races, must be on their guard against these attempts to divide and conquer labour. They have everything to gain by union. There is regrettable discrimination in war industries not only against Negroes and aliens, but against Jews. This cannot in fact go on. We are told that even with the absorption of women into industry in considerable numbers, industry will be forced to employ Negroes in skilled jobs, hitherto withheld from them, at the end of eighteen months at the present rate of industrial expansion. The war cannot be won by discriminatory methods, and it is a partial victory for Hitler when we imitate his race discrimination. It is possible that discrimination cannot be eliminated without Federal legislation, making such discrimination against any racial group a Federal offence. Even then such a rule would be evaded by professing [for example] that it just happened that the most suitable applicants were all White American citizens. It may be necessary in recalcitrant plants to appoint Federal personnel managers. In addition to Negro–White co-operation in unions, Cayton and Mitchell suggest United Negro Trades organisation, on the analogy of United Hebrew Trades, to work among Negroes, organising them into groups which can in turn press for admission to general unions. Such trade organisations should not of course be substitutes for mixed trade unions, but auxiliary thereto.

(3) *Equal franchise (and voting opportunities).* There is necessity for a new party, since Democrats, as a whole, are biased against Negroes as Negroes, while Republicans are biased against them as workers, and, in the South, by need of conciliating Southern whites.

There must be repeal of poll-taxes, etc. But these can only be accomplished by formation of a party representative of interests of blacks and poor whites, and this party can only be formed by strong labour organisation of workers of all colours and creeds.

(4) *Equal education* is essential, but will only come as a result of other reforms (though Federal government has done something).

(5) *Abolition of social prejudice.*

a. By growing realisation of white workers that their own interests demand making common cause with Negroes.

b. By the different movements for Negro advancement, such as the industrial and academic education movements, both valuable, and the National Association for the Advancement of Coloured People.

c. By ceaseless effort on part of liberal and unprejudiced people. Most Americans are too complacent. They think that what needs to be amended is somebody else's business.

I come now to the Jewish question. This differs from the Negro question in being much less acute in America than in various other countries; also in the fact that Jews are culturally at least the equals of their enemies; and thirdly in the fact that it is mainly an international question.

To anyone coming from England, the extent of anti-Jewish feeling in the United States is astonishing. Many employers will not employ Jews;[5] many hotels refuse to admit them; they are often excluded from summer camps and bathing beaches. President Lowell endeavoured, unsuccessfully, to cause Harvard to discriminate against them. I find this sort of thing unintelligible. But at any rate Jews in this country do not suffer any *legal* disabilities. When the war has been won, it will have to be part of the peace settlement to see that such disabilities are abolished wherever they exist. This will only be possible if there is an international Federal government which can interfere in the same sort of way in which the U.S. Federal government can interfere in the South; for otherwise anything stipulated in the peace treaty will be temporary. As a general principle, justice to oppressed minorities is only possible through a Federal government, most constituents of which do not share the illiberal sentiment that leads to oppression. Where such a government is unattainable, only slower methods, such as we have considered in the case of the Negroes, are possible.

In the case of the Jews, it is important to preserve their culture, which has a distinctive contribution to make to the total of world culture. It is a mistake to suppose that internationalism requires us to be all alike. This is an error analogous to that which inspires the determination of American schools to turn the children of immigrants into good Americans by cutting them off from the culture of their home countries. In the case of the Jews, it is one of the valid arguments in favour of Zionism: everybody else is at home somewhere; the Jew, in an unfriendly world, is in some degree an alien wherever he goes. This situation is painful, and must prevent the best development of Jewish culture.

It ought to be agreed in the peace settlement that Jews, everywhere, shall have equal rights with others, guaranteed by international authority. If the nations most hostile to Jews are defeated, this will be possible. We cannot deal with the Negro question in this way, since the U.S. will not submit to being coerced by an international authority; fortunately in the U.S. the Federal government has less colour prejudice than the Southern States. The Federal principle, therefore, has its application to the Negro problem. For the Jewish problem, no other solution is possible, and the federation will have to be international.

As everyone knows, the League of Nations was supposed to protect minorities, but was as ineffectual in this as in everything else. The Jews in Hungary and Poland, and the Ukrainians in Poland, had the right to appeal to the League of Nations, which had guaranteed them civil equality. It did nothing, however, even when proofs of the grossest oppression were presented to it. This raises the question: Can an international authority be so constituted and so administered as to be more effective than the League of Nations? Let us look at the matter realistically. If the Axis Powers are defeated, it will be by an alliance of America, the British Empire, Russia and China. This alliance, if it can be continued after the war, will be the nucleus of any international authority. Obviously nothing will be done to compel justice to minorities in the U.S. or the U.S.S.R. In these two countries, only the growth of international liberal sentiment will cure existing evils. In the British Empire, something may be done to please the U.S., which, while refusing citizenship to Hindus (who in England may be and have been M.P.s), holds (quite rightly) that England ought to be more liberal than the U.S. In China the only important minority is the communists, who will no doubt be protected by Russia. But how about the rest of the world?

I am concerned at the moment especially with the rights of Jews. There ought to be provisions on this subject in the peace treaty; and in the constitution of whatever international authority emerges there should be a provision against all discrimination on the ground of race or religion. But such provisions will be ineffective if the Great Powers are willing to waive them on account of considerations in the game of power politics. If, for example, there are, within the international authority, two groups, one centred on Russia, the other on the U.S., each will buy allies by condoning injustice. Only when the game of power politics has been replaced by a firm international government will treaties protecting Jews become really effective. Meantime, the Germans, if beaten, can be coerced into granting equal rights to Jews. But I have not much hope that a restored Poland would be better than before the present war, unless the victors were strong and resolute enough to use coercion. The principle of self-determination, applied by President Wilson, must be regarded as subject to severe limitations, and one of them should concern the treatment of Jews and other minorities.

Various localised national groups of immigrants are proving difficult to reduce to the common denominator of Americanism. In their case, what is desirable is a recognition, especially in school, of their national culture. The poetry, folk-lore and history of the country from which they come should be kept alive in their memory. It does not make for sound development to tell a child or young person simultaneously that it is the grandest thing on earth to be an American, and that he himself will never be anything but an alien. In earlier days immigrants, at least in the second generation, were easily assimilated, partly because of the welcoming attitude of the community; for some decades now this has been no longer the case, and the old methods need modifying. That there is something wrong with the schools and other apparatus of adjustment in this respect appears from the fact that while immigrants (though more criminal than at home) are slightly less criminal than the general population, their children are more so.[6]

To sum up this discussion of minority problems; the evils to be combated have two sources, on the one hand an imperfect acceptance of democracy, on the other hand a wrong understanding of it.

(1) Democratic feeling in the individual has two aspects. On the one hand, 'I am as good as you'; on the other hand, 'you are as good as I am'. The first is consonant with natural self-assertion, while the second is not. Every American citizen is a democrat in the first sense; very few are democrats in the second sense. Almost all white Americans feel superior to coloured people; very many feel superior to Jews; the rich feel superior to the poor; the native-born to the immigrants. Such feelings, in some degree, are probably inevitable, but they must not be allowed to take oppressive forms. It is essential to successful democracy that there should be a wider appreciation of our common humanity, and of the necessity of friendly co-operation. The essence of the liberal outlook is the belief that co-operation promotes happiness more than fighting does, and this has not been invalidated—quite the reverse—by the developments that have rendered obsolete some parts of the traditional liberal outlook, for example, *laissez-faire*. Every central governmental authority should therefore do all in its power to prevent sectional intolerance.

(2) It is a misunderstanding of democracy to suppose that it sanctions, or even proclaims, the unlimited tyranny of the majority. In matters as to which a common decision is necessary, the majority must prevail; but there are many matters as to which a common decision is unnecessary, and even undesirable. It is not good that men should be all alike. Some

of the most desirable pursuits must, by their nature, belong to a minority. It is good that there should be poets and artists and musicians; but where uniformity is prized, those who might be poets or artists or musicians will be persecuted at school until they abandon their peculiar tastes. It is good that there should be men of unusual opinions, since every true opinion is at first unusual; but where the Rotarian ideal is strongly held, unusual opinions are a grave social and economic handicap.

De Tocqueville, more than 100 years ago, wrote impressively on the tyranny of the majority in the United States, which he regarded as the peculiar danger of a democracy. What he said deserves as much attention now as when he wrote. Let us listen to what he says on this subject [the lecture notes break off at this point].

[1] Even where there are schools, the average expenditure in eleven Southern States is $12.57 a year for a Negro child, as against $44.31 for a white child (1930). (Russell's note.)

[2] Raper and Reid, *Sharecroppers All*, p. 164; 70 per cent of Negroes in agriculture are sharecroppers. (Russell's note.)

[3] The *Nation* (21 February 1942). (Russell's note.)

[4] Frances Perkins, Secretary of Labor, the first woman to hold a cabinet position in the U.S. Administration.

[5] This ought to be made illegal. (Russell's note.)

[6] Brown and Roncek, *Our Racial and National Minorities*, p. 700. (Russell's note.)

CAN AMERICANS AND BRITONS
BE FRIENDS?

The *Saturday Evening Post* (Philadelphia, 3 June 1944)

America and England, at the present time, are engaged in trying to like each other and, in a lesser degree, in pretending that they have always done so. It is very important for both countries, and for the whole world, that they should succeed in liking each other, but I do not think pretense as to the past is any help. It would be better to drag the lingering dislike and suspicion out into the open, to analyze them, and to attempt to deal with their causes. This would be a subject for a book, but in this article I shall confine myself to personal impressions.

Something, however, must be said about the faults of the English in the past. In the present day, it seems to me that the dislike of England in America is commoner and stronger than the dislike of America in England, but this was not always the case. In the nineteenth century, the English regarded America with the same mixture of admiration and hate that has been given to Russia since 1917. It was thought to be a strange, wild, revolutionary country; it was beloved by young radicals and hated by old conservatives. Young people who hoped to reform the world went to America to discover how to do so. On the other hand, some of their elders seemed to think that by so doing they risked perhaps their lives and certainly their morals.

I was astonished to find the strength of this sentiment when editing the letters and diaries of my parents.[1] They were among the young radicals who went to America to learn wisdom, but some among their older relations strongly disapproved. One young cousin wrote: 'Papa still thinks the Americans only half civilised.' One old maiden-aunt wrote letter after letter of pained protest and continued to sigh over them for the rest of her life. But all their younger relations, even the decorous and timid girl cousins, were full of interest and envy. When they returned, my mother met at a garden party the Duchess of Cambridge, grandmother of Queen Mary and great-grandmother of the present King. The Duchess said in a loud voice: 'Let me look at your petticoats to see if they are dirty. I hear you only associate nowadays with dirty radicals and dirty Americans.' And when, in 1851, my grandfather, Lord Stanley, was offered the post of Minister to the United States, he felt that he had been insulted, and declined, telling his wife that he wanted 'something much more tempting than Washington', adding, 'Naples, I own, would have its attractions.' His mother's comment was: 'I never heard anything so impertinent as the offer made you —a stupid place with a stupid business to settle. I am glad you did not hesitate a moment.'

These preposterous anecdotes, which seem as incredible to the modern Englishman as they can to any American reader, illustrate not only an attitude toward America but also a personal arrogance and conceit which no longer exist in England. At least I can say that if there lives in any remote village an ignorant and stupid squire with such manners and such opinions, I am thankful that I have not met him. But the bitter and just resentment aroused by such behavior has been handed down from father to son in the United States, and the present generation of Englishmen suffer from it. It is only when I recall such incidents that I can understand the covert bitterness and readiness to quarrel, and imagine slights that I have often met with in America toward myself and my countrymen.

In those days, Americans were disliked in conservative circles because they were democratic and their example encouraged democracy in England. My uncle, Lyulph Stanley, visited America, and while he was still an undergraduate at Oxford annoyed his father by speaking at the Union in favor of universal suffrage. His father wrote: 'I am sorry that Lyulph spoke at the Union in favour of Universal Suffrage being the only limit to Reform. It is not true, and if we were to see it we should soon repent. America will soon have had enough of it, even if she has not already found it out.' He was wrong in his prognostications. The advocates of democracy had unbroken success, and the aristocratic England that he loved is now as dead as the dodo. Dislike of America for being democratic is now extinct in England; such political dislike as exists is more due to the opposite belief that in America the rich have more power than they have in England. But old impressions of English arrogance and aristocratic intolerance are hard to eradicate, however false they may be to the facts of the present day.

Unfortunately, there are some things about the way in which an Englishman naturally feels and acts and speaks which quite unintentionally give Americans the impression that he is high-hatting them, and that he still has some of that offensive and unjustifiable feeling of superiority that existed a 100 years ago. The English, as a rule, are shy and reticent; they are seldom what Americans would consider good mixers.

Their shyness makes them shrink from talk with strangers, and their reticence makes them unwilling to acknowledge their own emotions, even among friends. An Englishman will often, from sheer timidity, cross the street to avoid conversation with an approaching acquaintance, and he will snub conversational advances from a stranger in a train with a cold indifference which seems appallingly rude, but which often conceals pure terror.

The English visitor in America is often ashamed of his inability to make an adequate return for the cordial friendliness of his hosts. They tell him how pleased they are to meet him, how beautiful his wife is, and how adorable his children. They do everything to put him at his ease, but he often becomes more ill at ease every moment. He tries in vain to make pretty speeches in reply, but the more he feels, the less he can say. Shyness paralyzes him and he becomes silent and apparently cold. However, this habit of social reserve wears off in a year or two if the visitor is young, and many English boys and girls have been cured of it by spending their college years in America.

But our reticence concerning our deeper emotions cannot, I think, be altered. It is not a new characteristic; you will find it in Shakespeare. In *Macbeth*, when Macduff learns that his wife and children have been killed by the tyrant, he says nothing at all. Malcolm, who understands his silence, says:

> What, man! ne'er pull your hat upon your brows;
> Give sorrow words: the grief that does not speak
> Whispers the o'er-fraught heart, and bids it break.

When, in 1940, it looked as if there was a possibility of the destruction of England, many kindly Americans expressed their sympathy to me, but my impulse was to pretend to feel nothing, and I am sure that, in so far as I yielded to this impulse, I must have given offense. Many times during the Blitz, people in America used to say to me: 'You must be glad to be out of it.' I felt as if they had congratulated me on being absent from the death-bed of my wife or one of my children, and I used to wonder whether most Americans were indeed so different from most English people that they would be glad to be out of their country at such a time, or whether it was merely that all people are unable to imagine suffering totally outside their experience. And then I would remind myself that my own reserve had probably given the impression that I did not care. Many English people have the same instinct of silence about their private affections, and even about places and poems that they love deeply. Carried too far, this habit is undesirable and stultifies human relationships.

Even in love, many Englishmen never lose their reserve and can never bring themselves to say explicitly: 'Darling, I love you.' A common form of proposal is: 'You know I'm awfully fond of you and we seem to get on pretty well. What about getting married?' Fortunately, the intimacy of marriage usually breaks down such inhibitions, but in more superficial relationships they are often a great hindrance. Not long ago I sent an English friend in this country, Mr X, to see another Englishman, Y. Afterward, I asked X how they had got on. 'Oh,' said X, 'I thought he was an awfully nice man, but he didn't seem to like me very much.' Whereupon I asked Y for his report. 'Well,' said Y, 'we didn't have much to say to each other. I liked him, of course, but he seemed so bored all the time; didn't take to me, I suppose.' From which the American reader will see that we sometimes have the same effect upon one another as we so often do upon foreigners.

The highest term of praise that many English people ever use is 'not bad'. I remember one of the first dinner-parties my wife and I attended in this country together. When we got home, we sat down to talk it over. I had had a delightful time, but, being English, I was reluctant to admit it. Our conversation ran something like this:

'*B.* (feeling his way): Well, what did you think of it?
P. (as if fearing a snub): I thought it was rather fun, didn't you?
B. (relieved): Yes, I thought it wasn't at all bad.
P. (gaining courage): I didn't see much of the people at your end of the table. That Mrs So-And-So seemed rather nice.
B. (thawing more and more): Yes. And quite intelligent.
P. I'm glad you liked her. I thought she was delightful. She seemed to like us. Do you think she really did?
Both of Us (suddenly laughing at ourselves): How disagreeable we are. Why don't we both admit straightaway that they were delightful people and that we had the time of our lives?'

We went on to consider how foolish the English are to allow timidity to seal them in a wall of ice, and how much most of them would profit from mixing with Americans, for inexpressiveness eats inward; emotions that are never expressed, ultimately die. We say that still waters run deep, but sometimes they are merely stagnant. On the other hand, it must be said that life gains in subtlety and richness if it is kept stratified to a certain extent. When reserves are broken down, the reward is proportionately richer, and Americans have sometimes told me that, while in England, everyone at first seemed to cold-shoulder them, they made, in the end, more intimate friends than they had at home, where everyone said 'Hi-ya' with the same cordiality to all alike.

And there is another side to the question. Though Americans are generally friendly and kind toward strangers, and demonstratively affectionate to those they like, they also do not scruple to express dislike when they feel it, and often show in the process considerable brutality. In England, a man's behavior toward you may be much the same in either case. You may miss the caresses, but you will also miss the blows. And since we are less governed by fashion, in our emotions as well as in our notoriously shabby clothes, active persecution of an unpopular figure is rarer in England than it is in the United States.

It is a misfortune for Anglo–American friendship that the two countries are supposed to have a common language. A Frenchman in America is not expected to talk like an American, but an Englishman speaking his mother tongue is thought to be affected and giving himself airs. Or else he is taken for a German or a Dutchman, and is complimented on his grammatical mastery of the language of another nation. Only his accent, he is told, reveals that English is not his mother tongue. In the amusing film *My Kingdom for a Cook*, the visiting English author is told that he speaks English very well for a foreigner. This has happened to us repeatedly. Only the other day, my wife was lunching in a restaurant with our son, aged six whose precise grammar, large vocabulary and meticulous enunciation are a source of wonder to his adult friends and of ridicule among his American playmates. They shared a table with an apparently cultivated middle-aged lady who asked how long the boy had been in this country, and on being told five years, remarked: 'Really! He doesn't know English very well yet, does he?' It is hard to resist a desire to explain that English is the language spoken by the English. Albanians and Montenegrins are allowed their own language, but the English are thought uppish or uneducated if they exercise a right conceded to the rest of mankind.

Mr Jack Alexander, in a recent article in the *Saturday Evening Post*, remarked that the Americans commit felonious assault on the language, and said: 'I really don't think that the British, in their hearts, forgive us for this, and I don't know why they should. It is their language and we have done it wrong.' There is something in this, but, for my own part, it is not the American modifications of the English language which annoy me. I find much American speech very pleasant to listen to, and much of the slang refreshingly expressive. But I wish they would frankly call it American, and not English. I should not mind being told that I do not talk American very well. I don't.

One of the things that all Europeans find surprising in America is that, from the moment of leaving the boat, they are constantly asked: 'How do you like America?' Except among those who have traveled abroad, the question is purely rhetorical, since it is assumed as a matter of course that the European must like America better than his own country. If he lets it appear that he does not, he gives offense. The effect upon a European is just as if he were asked: 'How do you like my wife?' and were expected to say that he much preferred her to his own. A German refugee of my acquaintance, who lived in England for many years but is now in America, told me that in all his years in England he was never asked how he liked the country. People would feel that, in asking such a question, they risked making the foreigner choose between politeness and veracity.

National arrogance, which used to be a British characteristic, is always an accompaniment of world power. So long as Britannia ruled the waves, the English were inclined to despise other nations, and were not always careful to hide their contempt. But now the American navy is larger than the British, Washington is the governmental center of the world, and New York is the financial center. The English, after being dominant for 200 years, have got to learn to take second place, and to do it as gracefully as possible. The arrogance which formerly was theirs is now rapidly crossing the Atlantic along with sea power. Oddly enough, it takes the same moralistic form. The English used to boast of being more virtuous than Continental nations; now the Americans boast of being more virtuous than Europeans. And as the narrow barrier of the Channel makes the English appear insular to Continental nations, so the Americans seem insular to Europeans, in proportion as the Atlantic is wider than the Channel. It is noticeable that this cannot be said of Americans who have lived for some time abroad. If it were customary for young people to receive part of their education abroad, it is to be hoped that this insularity might be diminished on both sides of the ocean.

The belief of Americans in their own moral superiority sometimes shows an extraordinary imperviousness to evidence and to common sense. Take, for example, this advertisement: 'Why has Winston Churchill been able to fire the courage of Great Britain—fuse its clashing elements? Where does he get his imagination, his wisdom, his magnetism, his strength? Is it because he is part American?' Do Americans really think that these qualities are unlikely to occur in anyone not American?

The following quotation from an editorial in the *Boston Globe* is even more astonishing: 'The American young man is unique. Humane, kindly, instinctively gentle and considerate of women and the weak, the aged and infirm, the idea of using mortal violence against his fellow beings is one which has never entered his honest head.'

I should be the first to admit that many—very many—American young men have these good qualities. But the fact remains that the statistics of murder and rape are higher in America than, for example, in England. But most Americans do not know this. In their over-enthusiastic attempts to produce a deep and warm love of the United

333

States in all its citizens, whatever their origin, many of the organs of public opinion keep up a constant paean of praise of all things American, and 'un-American' has become a comprehensive term of censure. But there are many good things in the world which are not American—for instance, Chinese art—and there are even some bad things which are American. It is impossible for a bystander not to feel a shiver of alarm when he encounters exaggerations of national pride such as those which I have quoted. Patriotism which has the quality of intoxication is a danger not only to its native land but to the world, and 'My country never wrong' is an even more dangerous maxim than 'My country, right or wrong'.

It is interesting that conceit and arrogance are the faults most often complained of on both sides. I cannot help hoping that closer acquaintance may make us more conscious of the many good qualities which we share and less inclined to blame each other for arrogance. We would do well to remember that in this respect we seem to many sensitive and cultivated Orientals equally intolerable.

There are many differences between us in customs and manners, in themselves trivial, but which lead to misunderstanding and disproportionate irritation, because the common language leads us to expect a similarity of ways we would not look for in Italians or Chinese.

One thing that causes difficulties is that, contrary to the general belief, manners are in some respect more formal in America than in England. I was surprised when I discovered that in America a lecturer was expected to appear in evening dress. English people, having heard from Americans that there is less formality in the United States than in England, find themselves giving offense by behaving as if at home. This applies also to debate and argument, which is conducted in America more politely, and with less downright assertion of differences, than is customary in England.

Again, what is considered polite in one country may be impolite in the other. I have heard complaints from English girls that American soldiers sometimes offend them by flattery and by a sort of playful love-making which seems to them almost insulting at a first meeting. An Englishman does not lavish endearing terms on a girl or comment on her beautiful eyes unless he is in love with her, and sometimes not even then. When an American does all this during a dance, the English girl may feel that he is taking liberties. But if she knew more of American customs, she would understand that he is probably merely a kindly soul who wants her to have a pleasant evening.

In America, when you meet a man who has achieved distinction in some direction, it is correct to talk to him about his 'shop', which in England is not done except with caution and on what are considered

334

suitable occasions. The difficulty, to an Englishman, is aggravated by the fact that, owing to the belief that all men are equal, it is thought that everybody can understand anything. A visiting lecturer, at the end of a long day, has an hour's lecture, and then an hour of questioning. At length, dead tired, he is rescued by his host and hostess, and hopes to be able to relax. But he may find that they expect him to explain quantum theory and the theory of relativity, the relative merits of the American and British schemes for an international currency, and so on. To them, it appears to be necessary that they should show a polite interest in their guest's subject, but to him they may appear inconsiderate.

Personal questions are also a stumbling block. In England these are considered impertinent, and we are taught in youth to avoid them to an almost absurd degree, so that one may know a man well for years without asking or being told where he was born and went to school and what his father's profession was. An American in England perhaps feels that the people he meets are indifferent and cold because they ask him none of these things. On the other hand, the English visitor is often surprised by being put through a sort of catechism: what part of England does he come from, where did he go to school, where does he send his children to school, how long has he been in America, does he like it, and what are his plans for the future? These inquiries are made so pleasantly and with such obvious kindliness that it is impossible to resent them, but our different habits make them often embarrassing.

One of the unfortunate results of a common language combined with geographical separation is that the English and Americans have a much larger fund of misinformation about each other than about any other nation. Uneducated English people derive their ideas of America from Wild West movies and gangster films, which make the country seem a paradise for boys, and purgatory for adults. Educated English people know about lynching, about violence in labor troubles and about municipal corruption, but about the better aspects of American life they are not often so well informed. The net result is a picture which is quite out of proportion.

The American picture of England is even more distorted. The English visitor is sometimes so scolded for the sins of George III that he is seized with a bewildered misgiving that he is not himself but the ghost of that misguided monarch. He cannot understand why it should be assumed that, merely because he is English, he must approve of the policy of George III, until he realises that the average American believes that the King was a typical Englishman of his day, and that the country has not changed since. Only yesterday I was flatly contradicted when I mentioned the fact that many people opposed the government's policy toward the American colonies at the time, and that now no one would defend it. Americans know that their own country has changed since 1776, and that Chicago, San Francisco, Big Steel and the New Deal did not then exist. But they do not realise that the political and social change has been greater, even, in England than in America. Many of them picture England as a land of moated castles and downtrodden peasants. Others, more up-to-date, derive their impressions from Victorian novels, particularly those of Dickens, and picture the average urban Englishman groping his way through filthy slums in a perpetual pea-soup fog.

Even the Americans who know England, or think they do, stay at the best hotels, associate exclusively with the rich, visit medieval ruins, and know nothing of British industry, of trade unionism or of the gradual breakup, since 1911, of rural estates. It is extraordinarily difficult to go against these prevailing misconceptions. Evidence against them is rejected as propagandist lies. No one reflects upon the fact that there is close agreement between Mr Roosevelt, who is of the Left, and Mr Churchill, who is of the extreme Right.

The things that the English notice in America are quite different from the things that the Americans notice in their own country, and the same is true of what Americans notice in England. When Americans come to England, they notice that there are those who touch their hats and say 'sir'; they notice that some people have titles. These things give them the impression of a class-ridden country. They do not reflect that customs survive the social structure from which they rose, and that the man who says 'sir' may have an income little less than or even as great as the man he addresses respectfully, and equal political power. The respectful address is accorded nowadays not on the basis of rank or wealth, but on the basis of education, which does not, in America, enjoy the same prestige. When an Englishman lives in America, he notices that trade union leaders are not, as at home, part of the governing class, but are still regarded by the majority of well-to-do people as dramatically wicked. He notices that the rich are surrounded by flatterers, and that scholars and scientists often hold what seems to him a position of degrading subservience to the rich men who control or finance universities, laboratories and observatories. He notices in all parts of the country a love of uniformity, which seems to him very dangerous, since it is akin to the regimentation which is one of the preconditions of fascism. Opinions not held by the majority expose a boy to persecution, and a man to loss of income. There is, in consequence, very much less freedom of thought and speech than there is in England.

All this is connected with what I believe to be a wrong conception of democracy. Democracy demands that no one should have special privileges, but it does not demand that people should be all alike. There is a tendency in America to think that any man who ventures to be different from the majority of his neighbors in any way is setting himself up and claiming to be better than his neighbors.

This view is fatal to excellence. A community requires many different kinds of work, and each kind of work requires, if it is to be well done, its own kind of character and aptitude. Americans have, however, the correlative good qualities in a higher degree than the English. On the average they are—at least so it seems to me—more energetic and more hopeful. The English had these qualities in the nineteenth century, but the two great wars, with the long depression in between, combined with the knowledge that they have lost their dominating position in the world, have caused in many of them a mood of weariness and pessimism. Their long experience of international problems, which will be valuable in combination with American hopefulness and energy, might, without it, not be sufficiently dynamic.

The world needs the co-operation of America and England, not only in formal ways but in the way of genuine friendly feeling. Each nation, like every other, has its faults, and it is only irritating to make a pretense of perfection. But, broadly speaking, the international ideals of the two are identical. British imperialism, the bugbear of American Anglophobes, is milder than most others, and is genuinely intended to give place to self-government in due course, but the problems of the transition are more difficult than they appear to those without the relevant knowledge and experience. There is, at the moment, great friendliness in England toward America, and it is important, both to our own nations and to mankind as a whole, that this friendliness should be reciprocated. United, we have a rare opportunity to move the world in the direction of our common ideals, but if we are kept apart by mutual suspicions, the enemies of our hopes will triumph. It is our duty, at this time more than at any other, to forget our separate fears in the ardor of the hopes in which we are at one.

[1] *The Amberley Papers* (London and W. W. Norton, New York, 1937).

337

BRITISH AND AMERICAN NATIONALISM

Horizon (London, January 1945)

Every age has its typical folly, and that of ours is nationalism. This is of course no new phenomenon. It appeared first among the Jews in the time of the Maccabees: then it went underground until it was revived by the English in their resistance to the Armada. Shakespeare gave it such admirable expression that his readers did not notice its absurdity. The French Revolution made it rampant in France; Fichte, and the war of liberation in 1813, caused it to spread to Germany. Now it exists everywhere: in Mongolia and Monaco, in Equador and among the descendants of the Aztecs, no less than among the Great Powers. It is a centrifugal force, preventing the governmental and economic unification which is called for by modern technique both in industry and in war. If it cannot be prevented from controlling national governments, there is little hope of preserving civilised populations from suicide.

The two nationalisms that I have experienced most vividly have been those of America and England. From 1938 till May 1944 I lived in various parts of the United States; I returned to England on a British boat, and was still at sea on D-Day. The nationalist feeling on both sides was very disquieting, for it is obvious to every sane person in both countries that their co-operation is absolutely necessary if disaster is to be averted. I am the more perturbed since I find in myself a proneness to respond to British nationalism and to condemn that of America, which I can only control by a great effort towards impartiality. Thus, my own emotions help me to know how difficult it is to eradicate this pernicious way of feeling—pernicious because it generates hatred between members of nations that ought to work together.

The highly educated minority in both countries is, on the whole, free from this unfortunate passion. In universities, on both sides of the Atlantic, one finds an attitude of mutual respect, and an ignorance of what is thought and felt by the man in the street. Government officials, and the innumerable unofficial emissaries whom the two governments send to London and Washington respectively, belong to the same social group as the university professors, and seldom encounter the fiercer forms of national feeling. If they did, perhaps even more would be done by the authorities to promote mutual understanding.

There is a great difference in the nature of the patriotisms of the two countries. British patriotism is quasi-biological, and has an affinity with family feeling; American patriotism is more analogous to party or sectarian loyalty. An Englishman may feel that the socialists are subversive, or, alternatively, that the Tories are ruining the country; he may feel this strongly enough to hate the party to which he is opposed. But this feeling is totally unlike the feeling he has towards his country's enemies, and fades away in a time of national crisis. Our patriotism, like that of other European countries, is made up of love of home, the feeling of cosy safety produced by what is familiar, the comfort of known traditions and prejudices, and the instinct that, in spite of superficial dissensions, we are at one on all really serious issues. A hen, terrified by a motor-car, will rush across the road in imminent danger of death, in order to feel the safety of home. In like manner, during the Blitz, I longed to be in England. But all Americans said: 'How glad you must be to be out of it', and were totally unable to understand my contrary feeling.

American patriotism is quite different. The United States is not biologically a nation; a minority of the inhabitants are descended from people who were in America 100 years ago. When an American feels a glow of warmth about his country, he is not thinking, as an Englishman might, of hedgerows and the song of the cuckoo and wild roses in June, of village churches that keep alive what was best in the Middle Ages, or even of the traditional pomp of kings and lord mayors and judges in their wigs. Shakespeare speaks of the English as 'this happy *breed* of men'; Lincoln speaks of the Americans as 'dedicated to a *proposition*'. This contrast sums up the difference. English patriotism, like that of other Europeans, belongs to the instinctive and sub-conscious part of human nature, in which we are little different from the brutes; American patriotism belongs to the intellectual, conscious, reasoning part, which is more civilised but less compelling. To us, our country is part of our birthright; to Americans, theirs is part of a sacred Cause.

This fundamental difference, because it is not understood, is a source of mutual irritation. Every European in America has been worried by the constant question: 'How do you like America?' To us, there is a sort of indecency about the question, as if a man should say, 'How do you like my wife?' We do not think it a mark of virtue to prefer another man's wife to one's own, nor do we think it right to prefer another man's country. I had in America a German friend (a refugee) who had lived many years in England; during that time (so he told me) he had never

339

once been asked: 'How do you like England?' But if a country is 'dedicated to a proposition' the matter is different. If the proposition is true, we all owe allegiance to it; if false, none of us do so. Therefore, the man who prefers his own country to America seems, to Americans, to be finding fault with the fundamental articles of their creed. I could not make it clear to Americans (with only two or three exceptions) why I did not wish to become naturalised. I said that an adopted nation was like adopted children, and could not give the profound emotional fulfilment that is to be derived from one's own children and one's own nation. But my words remained unintelligible, and produced no glimmer of response.

What is this 'proposition' to which America is dedicated? I shall venture to paraphrase and enlarge on Lincoln's few words on this subject, since I wish to set forth what the average American sincerely and profoundly believes. It is hardly relevant that the United States does not realise his ideals. Every clergyman will admit that the Christian Churches fail to realise Christian ideals, but he is none the less genuinely loyal to these ideals and persuaded of their importance. So an American may admit this or that blemish, and still maintain, in all sincerity, that America is striving to go in the right direction, which in his opinion other nations, and especially the British, are not.

England, for most Americans, is still the England of George III. What has happened since may, in part, be known intellectually, but has not been assimilated emotionally. America stands for those things in which Jefferson differed from George III: equality, absence of caste, political and religious freedom, abstinence from foreign conquest—the creed, in fact, of English and American radicals in 1776. The English are disliked because they have hereditary titles, because they have an empire, and because socially they are felt to be haughty. It is also thought that they are effete and inefficient, but at the same time astute and always able to outwit the simple and honest Americans. On the highest moral grounds, therefore, it is the duty of Americans to oppose British cunning, arrogance, and lust of dominion.

The attitude of suspicion of England is sometimes carried to extraordinary lengths. I was assured at a dinner table, by a middle-aged lady who was apparently considered sane, that the aeroplanes which attacked at Pearl Harbor were British, the airmen having dyed their skins and painted their eyebrows to slope upwards; this she had from one in the know at Washington, whose name she was not at liberty to divulge. An American pilot, who had been disabled in North Africa, flatly gave me the lie when I mentioned that, at the time of the War of Independence, many Englishmen were on the side of America. From reading the Chicago *Tribune* it is hardly possible to discover that the nominal enemy is Germany, not England. I have often heard Americans, with gleaming eyes, express the wish that they could fight England instead of the relatively harmless Nazis. When I have made speeches on India, as I have frequently done, everything I said has been discounted as British propaganda, except once, when a Hindu and a Muslim were both on the platform, and displayed their dissension without any need of emphasis on my part.

The nationalism of Americans, owing to the fact that it is not so deeply based on instinct as that of the British, is more vocal, more shrill, and more blatant. There is supposed to be something called 'The American Way of Life', which is so excellent that it ought to be imposed throughout the world. The family, one gathers, was invented by the Pilgrim Fathers; from Adam and Eve to their day it was unknown, and is still unknown on this side of the Atlantic. It is quite useless to point to comparative statistics of divorce or to any other evidence; the belief remains unshakeable. Leading articles in newspapers assure readers that the American young man, in contrast to the European, is sexually virtuous and hates violence. Here again, an appeal to the statistics of rape and homicide is useless. The wife of a Chicago professor assured me that there only *seemed* to be more murders in Chicago than in London because the English police were so inefficient. And if labour troubles are worse in America than England, that is because English employees have no spirit and English employers are cowards.

I do not think Americans can be conciliated by kowtowing to them. If we were to attempt this, we should have to do various things, some good, some bad. First and foremost, we should have to abolish titles. Next, we should have to surrender all the parts of the empire that are not self-governing. Third, we should have to revert to unregulated capitalism, abandon all attempts at planning, and allow the unemployed to starve. Fourth, we should have to adopt the American attitude to Negroes. Last, but not least, we should have to learn to talk American, for nine Americans out of ten believe that our way of speaking is an affectation, only adopted to show our superiority. We found, in America, that strangers in shops or buses at first took us for Germans and tolerated our way of speaking, but when they found that English was our native language they became indignant with us for not speaking as they do. It never occurred to them for a moment that the English have some rights in the English language.

In June 1944, I published in the *Saturday Evening Post* an article called 'Can Americans and Britons be Friends?' It was intended as my modest contribution towards Anglo–American co-operation, and was the very reverse of provocative. The gist of it was that, while of course America is God's own country, still the English have perhaps *some* humble merits, which could be acknowledged without endangering the purity of American morals and patriotism. The result was a shower of violently abusive letters; hardly a single American letter was friendly, though there were friendly ones from Englishmen, Scotsmen, Irishmen, and even Hindus. Here is a typical sample of the American response:

'Sir—In your "Can Americans and Britons be Friends?" you ignore the most obvious fact that the mutual dislike between Americans and "Britons" exists solely for the English, and not for the Welsh, Scotch and Irish who are well liked by the Americans, and vice versa—you also disregard the fact that the Welsh, Irish, and Scotch residents of the United States make sincere efforts to Americanise themselves and become naturalised citizens as soon as possible. You further overlook the fact the Irish and Welsh dislike the English as heartily as we Americans loathe you; and for the identical reasons! If the English do not consider themselves "the master race" why do they insult the American people by refusing to become naturalised citizens (save only to procure jobs in war plants at exorbitant rates of pay)? And why has Russell prevented his young son from learning to speak the American language although the lad has spent five of his six years in the haven of the U.S.? The answer is either obtuseness, or snobbery—it certainly is not sense. This old-stock American of remote British ancestry considers the English to be America's No. 1 enemies as twice within twenty-five years they have made suckers out of us by involving us in costly wars in which we have no vital stake; and are now assiduously sowing the seeds for involving us in a third war (with Russia). According to his scale of values, the modern-day Englishman is the next to lowest form of animal life—the American who toadies to the English being the lowest. No American of personal dignity wants or feels the need of the "friendship" of the English—you are far too expensive "friends"—forty billion dollars 1917–18; 250–300 billion in 1941–45—it would be far cheaper for us to join the Germans (or the Russians) and exterminate your breed.'

This is not an anonymous effusion; the writer gives his full name and address. The name is not Irish, but one familiar and native in England.

Such a letter as this will be dismissed by most educated Americans, and by most English people who have associated with educated Americans, as the mere effusion of a crank, but this is a dangerous error. I have encountered the point of view which it expresses in print, in letters, and in social intercourse too frequently to be any longer able to suppose it rare or politically unimportant. It is the point of view which dominated American policy from the rejection of the Versailles Treaty to the passing of the Neutrality Act. Since 1939, the men who have been in charge of the American government have succeeded, by the exercise of amazing tact and skill, in preventing the United States from signing its own death-warrant by permitting the defeat of the British; but few people on this side of the Atlantic know how difficult it has been to achieve this success—or how powerful are the anti-British forces which may assert themselves when the war is over. British sailors in American ports experience a popular hostility so great as to involve frequent danger to life; this hostility is, of course, partly Irish, but by no means wholly. There is a vast hatred of us on the part of a very large section of Americans. This fact is in the highest degree disquieting—so disquieting that many people refuse to acknowledge it. But I do not think any useful purpose is served by blinking facts, for until the facts are admitted, nothing effective can be done to diminish the evil.

That there are any valid grounds for hating us is not easy to admit in the face of hostility, nevertheless I fear it is true. We have in the past been arrogant and contemptuous towards Americans; no novelist would have written about a European country as Dickens wrote about the United States in *Martin Chuzzlewit*. Something of this attitude still exists. So far as I have been able to judge, medicine is better in America than in England, but I have frequently found English medical men unwilling to consider seriously innovations coming from the other side of the Atlantic. I should not be surprised to find that the same attitude exists towards technical improvements in industrial processes. Nor are stay-at-home English people aware of the misdeeds of our representatives abroad. At the present moment, our actions in Belgium, Italy and Greece are such as to fill every sensible man with deep misgivings. When I lived in China I found that, so long as the British had any influence there, they exerted it almost always in favour of what was decadent and corrupt, and against every movement that gave hope of radical improvement. We have now little power to do harm in China, but we still do harm where we can. Until we undertake a drastic reform of the Foreign Office, friends of mankind abroad will continue to think ill of us, and not without cause.

If we are to be less hated in America, we must admit and amend our shortcomings, without being silent about our virtues. But when we have done everything that is in our power, much will remain to be done by Americans, especially by those who control education in schools.

When one finds oneself or one's country hated, one reacts at first in an instinctive manner which is usually unwise. When the amiable correspondent whom I have quoted, in order to show the freedom of Americans from that arrogance which exclusively characterises the British, expresses the hope that his country will join with Germany or Russia to exterminate us, my first instinctive reaction is to feel in return an equal animosity, and to explore the possibility of a United States of

343

Europe which shall be strong enough to meet hate with hate and force with force. But while a United States of Europe would be infinitely desirable if it were possible, it would not advance the welfare of mankind if the motive of its formation were hostility to the United States of America. Hatred between nations is an evil thing; hatred between allies is very dangerous; and hatred between Great Britain and America is suicidal on the part of both. We must therefore avoid feeling hatred ourselves, and try to find ways of diminishing the hatred of which we are object.

I do not think we can achieve anything by being mousy and humble, or by singing small about what we have done in the war. Americans, almost to a man, consider our loss of Singapore shameful, but their loss of Manila glorious. We do no good by giving in to this belief. They observe that in the battle of Normandy we remained stuck, while they careered over France; here, again, we should insist on explaining the strategical situation. We should shout from the house-tops that our war effort, per head, has been greater than theirs. Only harm is done by being 'tactful' in these respects.

American boastfulness is like that of small boys, and they expect it to be met by boastfulness in return. When we abstain from boasting, it is not from modesty, but from pride; they sense this, and as our pride is what they most dislike, our failure to brag increases their dislike of us. It also causes them to be genuinely ignorant of the facts. Our newspaper publicity in America would be more useful if it were more self-assertive —not as to our virtues, but as to our efficiency. Not that we should ever hint at any shortcomings on their part, but that we should be more blatant about our own exploits.

The source of the trouble lies largely in American schools, which are in some regions exploited as agents for the propagation of nationalism. Education is a matter for each State, not a Federal matter; it is everywhere deeply involved in politics. Public sentiment is such that few politicians would dare to find fault with anti-English teaching in schools; the Federal government might, as a war measure, express opinions as to what is prudent, but has no power to enforce its views.

The educational effect of 'democracy', as understood in America, is curious. Every taxpayer feels that he has a right to object if, in any State-supported institution, anything is taught of which he personally disapproves. If, in a State university, a biology teacher ventures to express a belief in evolution, or a teacher of ancient history throws doubt on the complete historicity of the Pentateuch, or a teacher of astronomy mentions that the Inquisition opposed Galileo, the president of the university in question is inundated with indignant letters from uneducated farmers or fanatical Irishmen, saying that their hard-earned money ought not to be spent on the dissemination of such pestiferous falsehoods. If the president of the university is obdurate, the governor and legislature of the State are approached, by a powerful lobby if the matter is deemed of sufficient importance. Naturally the practical politicians see no reason why professors should insist on teaching any-thing unpopular. 'Democracy' is interpreted as meaning that the majority knows best about everything. Are birds descended from fishes? Are there reasons for doubting whether Joshua made the sun stand still? Has the Church ever been hostile to scientific doctrines subsequently accepted? Is Aristotle's doctrine of the syllogism capable of improve-ment? The prevalent feeling in America, except among the highly educated minority, is that such questions should be decided, not by the opinions of those who have studied them, but by the prejudices of the ignorant majority. This makes the life of a teacher in a State institution somewhat hectic: at every moment he or she has to fear that a pupil will repeat something to his parents, they will repeat it to the priest or the pastor, and there will be the devil to pay.

The pressure of the ignorant multitude is, however, only half of what the teacher has to face. There is also the pressure of the plutocracy, exercised more discreetly, but not less drastically. The condition of im-migrant labour in the State of California has long been appalling; it was set forth in a best seller, *The Grapes of Wrath*. A young instructor in the University of California ventured to investigate the question, and to publish his results, among which was the conclusion that trade union organisation was necessary if conditions were to be improved. He was in consequence dismissed from his post, on the alleged grounds that he was a bad teacher and did insufficient research. (Investigating the conditions of labour in California is not 'research'.) Although the other teachers sympathised with him, they could do nothing, for fear of sharing his fate. If their children were not to starve, they had to acquiesce *in suppressio veri* and *suggestio falsi*.

The position of a teacher in an American university is utterly different from his position at Oxford or Cambridge. The independence enjoyed by the fellows of a college at Oxford or Cambridge is a legacy of the Middle Ages; it is derived from the autonomy of the medieval Church, and owes much to the courage of St Ambrose and the philosophy of St Augustine. Even in England, it is only tolerated as a survival; the modern provincial universities have not been allowed to possess the merit which makes Oxford and Cambridge unique. This merit is that the men who teach also control the finance. The master and fellows of a college have no one above them except the State; and as they belong to the same social caste as the men who (in effect) compose the State, they have seldom had difficulty in coming to terms with Parliament and

345

the government. The master is either elected by the fellows, or is just such a man as they would have elected; moreover, he is a constitutional monarch, possessing only very limited powers. The consequence is that learned men have, in England, an independence and a status which, elsewhere, they have been gradually losing ever since the Reformation. We all know of their subjection in Germany and Russia, but in America there is something similar, though less in degree and less avowed.

An American university is a very different affair from Oxford or Cambridge. Its finances are in the hands of a board of trustees, who are businessmen, usually wholly devoid of academic qualifications. These businessmen appoint a president who may or may not have had some academic education, but is selected for his supposed administrative ability, which, of course, includes agreement with the political and theological prejudices of the trustees. The president, so long as he retains the support of the trustees, has the powers of an oriental despot rather than those of a constitutional monarch. All the younger members of the faculty (roughly speaking, those under about 38 or 40 years of age) hold their posts on a yearly contract; if the president, for no matter what reason, dislikes one of them, his contract is not renewed. And if the cause (avowed or unavowed) of his dismissal is one with which other presidents of universities sympathise, he will find it very difficult, if not impossible, to obtain another post. Consequently, cases in which younger teachers refuse to toe the line are rare. The older men, who have the title of professor, have more security of tenure, but even they would find their position very difficult if they were on bad terms with their president. As a rule, by the time a man becomes a professor he has been tamed, and has learnt the advantages of submission.

The result of this system is that while presidents of universities are part of the governing class, mere men of learning are nobodies, having something of the position of Greek slaves in the Roman Empire. I found that when the president of a university invited me to dinner, if he wished to do me honour the other guests would be businessmen; only social inferiors were invited to meet mere professors. The difference of status is at once apparent to anyone who has to visit both professors and the president in their respective offices. The president's office is in a palatial building, with carpets even in the passages; his rooms are vast and expensively furnished, with all the evidences of insolent luxury, while the professors' little dens are stowed away in stuffy corners. This expresses the relative estimation in which Americans hold administration and learning.

In regard to some subjects, the harm done by this system is not apparent. It does not affect the teaching of mathematics or physics, and it does no harm to the teaching of medicine or chemistry or crystallography or entomology. But whenever a subject is related, even indirectly, to economics or politics or theology, the harm done is immeasurable. Among young students in America, as I have known them, there is a great deal of first-class ability, combined with a degree of enthusiasm and enterprise which is much less common in England. I cannot speak too highly of the best of the young men whom I have taught in America. But owing to the system, very few of them achieved as much as their abilities would have led one to hope. T. S. Eliot, whose acquaintance I made when he was my pupil at Harvard, turned his back upon America; his somewhat reactionary opinions are, no doubt, all due to revolt against the ideals of his native country. Of the rest of my American pupils, some were Jews, and had to combat the anti-Semitic prejudice which makes it very difficult for Jews to obtain university posts; others were radicals, who either surrendered and lapsed into listless cynicism, or stuck to their convictions and therefore abandoned the teaching profession. Those who somehow managed to fit in were so overworked, as a result of the exploiting instincts of the ignorant businessmen whose employees they were, that they lost their resilience and the fine edge of their abilities was blunted. And so, in one way or another, America's immense heritage of idealistic ability is squandered by a system which divides all power between the prejudices of the ignorant many and the ruthlessness of the plutocratic few.

The situation in schools is much worse than in universities. In New York and Boston, the Catholic Church is dominant; New York schoolteachers are taught to speak of the Reformation as 'the Protestant Revolt'. In the Middle-West there is intense local patriotism, and teachers can hardly hope for an appointment except in their own city or its vicinity. They must of course carefully abstain from shocking the prejudices or pruderies of even the most benighted parents, and from saying anything that might conceivably offend the plutocracy. All this is faithfully recorded in *Middletown*,[1] a book which should be studied by all who wish to understand America. The actual instruction, from a technical point of view, is very poor; English young people who were sent to America in 1940 and who are now of an age to go to the university, find that they have to go to school again in England in order to reach the necessary scholastic level. My daughter, then aged 15, came to America to visit me in 1939, and had to stay there because of the outbreak of the war; young as she was, I had to send her to the university, because no school taught anything (except lying plutocratic propaganda) that she had not already adequately learnt.

All this is difficult to reform without a radical reform in politics, of a sort which seems very improbable, since it would have to go against the American conception of 'democracy'. According to this conception, not only are one man's political rights as great as those of another, but his judgement is equally to be respected on all points. On bimetallism or Egyptology or astronomy, the opinion of an up-country farmer is allowed the same weight as that of a man who has spent his life in study-ing the question at issue; indeed, if popular passion is roused, the farmer's opinion has the greater weight, because he can find more people to agree with him. Nor is it only in opinion that conformity is demanded; in dress and manners and speech any departure from what is usual is frowned upon. A learned man must not be absent-minded, or display any of those amiable eccentricities described in Lamb's essay on Oxford in the vacation; he must learn to look and move like a business-man, if he is not to be thought to be setting himself up. This protective colouration gradually goes deeper, and in time, even in his dreams, he comes to prefer executive efficiency to thought and meditation. In Europe, a man's profession can often be guessed from his demeanour, but not so in America, where the whole middle class apes the successful executive. All must be alike; none must be outstanding unless in income.

The intolerable boredom of such a vast uniformity is alleviated by certain tolerated forms of hero-worship; those who excel in athletics or the movies are allowed to be great, and have some of the privileges of aristocracy. But even for them there are strict limits; no movie star, however great, could avow himself or herself an agnostic and still appear on the screen. And as every one knows, an apparently virtuous life is essential, though a new wife or husband every few months is permissible.

There are in America very many individuals who are intelligent, high-minded, and in every way delightful; I have a large number of friends in that country whose friendship I value very highly. But unfortunately the system is such that almost all the most admirable people are devoid of power, and many of them know very little about how affairs are managed. In the public life of America, the best thing is the Federal government, which is also what is most conspicuous; the worst things are those that happen under cover and do not become known. The power of the very rich, even under a government that they abhor, is much greater than the average citizen supposes: they can give or withhold credit and custom and subscriptions, as advertisers they have a hold on the press, and as trustees they control the majority of universities. A man who is in their bad books can succeed as an author, but in hardly any other career; that is why American literature is so largely radical.

It is to be hoped that the new world-wide responsibilities of the United States will lead to more respect for knowledge, and a greater readiness to accept guidance, in practical affairs, from those who have studied the matter in hand. In particular, to return to our earlier theme, we may not irrationally expect that supremacy will make American patriotism less uneasily self-assertive, and that the broad identity of interests between Great Britan and the United States will gradually soften the hatred of us which undoubtedly exists. It is of course the duty of every Englishman to do what he can towards this end, but a great part of the work will have to be done by Americans. The American government is clearly aware of the necessity, and perhaps may find means to promote that friendly feeling without which the outlook for the world must be utterly black.

The problem is part of the larger problem of nationalism throughout the world. Since it has become impossible for even the most powerful nations to hold their own without the help of allies in war, the cruder forms of national self-assertion have everywhere become incompatible with self-preservation. This fact is not at all realised by the general public in America; I have frequently heard it said that, with the largest army, navy, and air force in the world, the United States could easily defeat a coalition of all other Powers. This state of mind is dangerous, and might lead in time to an attempt at world conquest. We in England have learnt (except for a few old men, some of them in high places) that it will not do to offend everybody; but many of us still have towards citizens of other countries the haughty attitude acquired during our period of unquestioned naval supremacy. It is a wholesome exercise to admit your own faults and other people's merits. In private life everyone knows this, but, as between nations, those who claim a monopoly of patriotism are often blind to it. Human beings of different nations do not differ as much as they think they do; they have the same pains and pleasures, similar loves and hates, and an equal admixture of good and bad. Mutaul hatred can only injure both; mutual esteem is enjoined not only by the moral law, but by common prudence.

[1] A classic sociological study by Helen and Robert Lynd.

349

SOME IMPRESSIONS OF AMERICA
Unpublished (*c.* 1944–5)

My first visit to America was in 1896, when there were as yet no motor-cars in the country, and outside the cities the roads were only dirt tracks. In subsequent years I have paid many visits, as lecturer or visiting professor; and from 1938 until last May I lived in the United States, first in Chicago, then in California, and then in the East. I have had innumerable contacts with individuals, almost all of them pleasant, and not a few very delightful; I have had also some contacts with institutions which were decidedly less agreeable. From my impressions, I have come to feel that many things in America are very different from what they are supposed to be. Sometimes the merits of America are not duly appreciated by Americans; sometimes—as happens in every other country—demerits are more readily perceived by foreigners than by those whose perceptions have been blunted by familiarity.

One of the things that struck me most forcibly in 1896, and that subsequent experience has confirmed, is that America is much more monarchical than England. In every direction there is more one-man power and less government by committees. It is true that England has a King, but there are very few things that he can do.

But in America institutions are so organised that many individuals have a personal power to which there is no analogy in England. Railroad presidents, university presidents, and mayors of great cities govern their respective institutions as medieval kings governed, whereas in England there is a board or committee with a formal head who may have pomp but has usually little power. A railway is governed by a board of directors, of which the chairman is not usually the most influential member. Oxford and Cambridge have a chancellor, usually a duke, who is not allowed to do anything, and a vice-chancellor who can do very little, though on formal occasions he has the satisfaction of looking imposing in magnificent robes. But the most striking contrast is between the Mayor of New York and the Lord Mayor of London.

The Mayor of New York can and does decide who is to teach and who is not to teach in the educational establishments of his city; in innumerable questions of policy his word is law. The Lord Mayor, on the contrary, in spite of his show and his banquet, can do very little, and is compelled to devote almost all his energies to eating and digesting enormous dinners. As an individual he is nothing, and few people know his name; he exists as the transmitter of a ritual inherited from the Middle Ages. The English separate pomp from power: the pomp is concentrated in ceremonial persons, but the power is diffused. Americans, having abolished pomp, have left power in the hands of departmental monarchs. In most institutions in America, government is not by discussion, but by the fiat of an elected despot.

The reason for this difference is, I think, that there is in America a greater belief than in England in the importance of getting *something* done, as opposed to getting the best thing done. Government by discussion is slow; that is why, for example, it cannot be employed by an army in the field. Wherever quick decisions are essential, one-man rule is preferable to committee government. But when the matter is one about which there is time to deliberate, the committee system has several advantages: it affords more of a safeguard for democracy, it educates more people into an understanding of administration, and it diminishes the likelihood of capricious, biased, or self-seeking uses of power. Obviously, sometimes one system is better, sometimes the other. I am not concerned to praise either at the expense of the other, but merely to point out ways in which America and England differ.

This difference extends even into family life. In the typical successful marriage in England, the husband and wife form a committee of two, while in America each is monarch in his or her own sphere: the husband rules in the office, the wife rules in the home. I have been struck, in America, by the very small share that fathers usually have in deciding how the children shall be educated, and, conversely, by the very meagre interest of wives in their husband's business. The consequence is that there is not nearly so much mental companionship between husbands and wives as there is where decisions are made by both jointly. The father—especially with the increasing prevalence of divorce—tends to have a continually diminishing role in the children's lives; where this development has gone furthest, his role has become solely financial.

This elimination of fathers, together with the fact that the immense majority of schoolteachers are women, has the result that children in their formative years have hardly any contact with men. The effect on boys is, to my mind, very unfortunate. They come to think that everything connected with culture is feminine; Shakespeare and Beethoven, if they have heard of them, are condemned as 'cissies'. The fear of being

351

'cissy' dominates boys; from a dread of this awful defect they learn to despise poetry and music and all the graces of life; their play becomes violent and destructive, and they come to think that to be uncivilised is to be glorious. Boys may love their mothers or their teachers, but they cannot take them as models to be imitated, because they are going to grow up into men, not into women. If the natural savagery of boys is to be tamed, it must be by men; and in America men, in general, do not perform this function.

The gulf between boys and girls, and between men and women, is much greater in America than in England; to an English observer, it seems as if much more of the Victorian age had survived west of the Atlantic than in Queen Victoria's own country. Girls, from an incredibly early age, are encouraged to be coquettish and to take pleasure in being dressed up; they are seldom tomboys who share their brothers' play. When they grow up, they still for the most part, aim at being as feminine as possible. I am a great reader of detective stories, and I find that in those written in America the heroine is portrayed as helpless and silly, while in those written in England she does her fair share of the tough work. This is not evidence as to the facts, but it is evidence as to what authors believe that readers wish to think about men and women.

To pass to another topic: there is a great difference in the sentiment of national solidarity as it exists in the two countries. In America it is vociferous and ready to become combative; it does not regard itself as patriotism, but as objective recognition of the merits of the United States, in which people of other countries are expected to join. Many Americans are surprised and rather offended when they find that aliens have for their respective countries the same affection that Americans have for theirs. This is a natural result of the fact that most of the aliens whom an American knows are immigrants who have chosen to leave their own countries. The alien who prefers his native land is thought to be insulting the United States. No parent expects his children to be preferred by other parents before their own, and to a European the feeling for one's country is of this sort; but to most Americans, America is a cause rather than a home, and those who (wherever they live) do not embrace the cause are thought to be wrong-headed.

Patriotism in England is at most times dumb and inexpressive, because it is subconscious. It is, I think, stronger and more compelling than American patriotism, but less vociferous, because it is taken for granted. This, of course, is due to the fact that England is a small homogeneous nation, whereas the United States is a very large nation which has been faced with the problem of assimilating immense alien populations. In England, most men, except on public occasions, would blush to express a patriotic sentiment; it would seem a slightly indecent exhibition of something that should be intimate and private, like love for wife and children. Only poets, who are licensed to write about love, may also, if they can, express the feeling for England which in other men remains silent. It never occurs to them that a foreigner could share this feeling; Europeans who have lived both in England and in America say that every American asks how they like America, but no Englishman asks how they like England, any more than he would ask: 'How do you like my wife?'

English patriotism, because it is so universal, is more tolerant of divergent opinions than that of America. There are, it is true, some Englishmen who are not patriotic, as the war has shown, but they are regarded as strange monsters; until a man is absolutely proved to belong to this handful of freaks, it is assumed that, whatever his opinions, he has in his own mind some way of reconciling them with what is regarded as a proper feeling for England. It is the fact that this solidarity exists that makes English freedom possible. In America, as I have seen it, there seems to me much less theological and political freedom than in England. At Oxford and Cambridge, many teachers are avowed communists or atheists; in American universities, it is much more necessary to be discreet about such heretical opinions.

Almost all English people, when they go to America, are amazed by the strength of anti-Semitism. I could hardly believe it when I first discovered that there are hotels and summer camps which will not admit Jews. At one time I wanted to join a swimming club for the benefit of my children. I found one which seemed admirable, but when the management explained that no Jews were admitted, my principles forbade me to join. I failed to find one in my neighbourhood that would admit them. In universities, while it is not impossible for a Jew to become a professor, he must reach a considerably higher level than would be expected of a gentile. I have listened patiently to all the arguments used in extenuation of this imitation of Hitler, but I have not heard one that seemed to me to have any shred or particle of validity. Anti-Semitism and the colour bar introduce a poison of intolerance into the social system, which is very dangerous and threatens to spread to various unpopular minorities, both of race and of opinion.

But there is quite as much to be said on the other side. In the absence of some reason for dislike, Americans are more generally kindly and friendly than English people, and when one comes home one misses the warmth of American friends. If you are an average man or woman, not belonging to some unpopular group, you will be much better treated by your acquaintances in America than in England. But it is unwise to be different from the average, even in directions generally recognised as good. When I was first in America, I knew a lady who had lately had a child, and some friend remarked 'perhaps he will be a genius'. 'Oh I, hope not', said the mother, in pained tones. This, I still think, was typical.

Democracy—a word which we have come to use perhaps too glibly—is a complex matter, compounded of laws, social customs, and sentiments. In America, the sentiment of democracy exists in a somewhat curious form: everybody is persuaded that he is as good as anyone else, but that many people are not as good as he is. The social hierarchy, as it exists in people's imaginations, is like Table Mountain: it has steep sides and a flat top. Oneself is on the top plateau, but many others are at varying heights on the slopes. So all are happy; none need look up, but all can look down, at least upon coloured people.

The existence of such a hierarchy is often vehemently denied in argument, but in novels it is taken for granted. 'The wrong side of the tracks' is a phrase just as damning as the English 'not quite'. One finds people objecting when their daughters want to marry social inferiors, just as much as in England. Nevertheless, the sentiment of democracy does do something important for Americans, since it preserves them from *admitting* social inferiority. The snobbish humility of English people who touch their hats and say 'Sir' is shocking to Americans, and rightly so. I can only say that this aspect of English life is rapidly disappearing.

But when it comes to the distribution of power, the comparison is very different. The inequalities of power are much greater in America than they are in England. I am thinking not of formal political power, as to which there is little difference between the two countries—for the King and the House of Lords have no more structural importance than Gothic ornaments on a skyscraper. What I am thinking of is power behind the scenes—power to control appointments, to win favours from the police, to secure the right kind of newspaper publicity, to practise successful lobbying, and so on. This kind of power determines which among young men shall achieve conspicuous success in business or journalism or education; those who do not have its backing, unless they become authors or trade union leaders, remain throughout life obscure and unsuccessful, whatever abilities they may possess. Except on major political issues, the men who wield this kind of power are the real rulers of America, but they work so unobtrusively that most Americans are almost unaware of their influence.

This unofficial government is composed of very few people: the leaders of big business, the heads of the Catholic hierarchy, and two or three university presidents—though in general, university presidents are servants of big business, and not possessed of independent power. In most universities, the ultimate power is in the hands of certain very rich men, who appoint the president. He, in turn, must please them in his appointments to teaching posts, and those whom he appoints must please him. By means of this system, the best brains in the country are sterilised; the experts whose opinions receive applause and wide publicity are those who are willing to toe the line, while those who give an honest opinion are considered subversive and wrong-headed. The views which it is prudent to profess, in philosophy, history, economics, and social science, are not those of the men who have studied these subjects, but of men whose expertness lies in quite a different field—that of making money for themselves. The consequence is that a great deal of first-class ability is wasted through being given the choice between obscurity and humbug.

This evil is connected with another—the excessive respect for executive ability as compared to all other kinds. In any university, the executive offices are furnished with a luxury and pomp which would be thought excessive for a professor, however eminent. The carpets on the stairs warn the mere man of learning that he is approaching the portals of the great. Sometimes, as a mark of quite special favour, he may be invited to a dinner party to meet interesting businessmen instead of his intellectual equals; this is an honour to which only a few mere professors can hope to attain. The consequence is that professors do their best to look like businessmen, and do not permit themselves the absent-minded unworldliness which characterises the best of their European colleagues.

I am not pretending that sycophancy towards the powerful is any commoner in America than elsewhere, although it is America that coined the word 'yes-man'. What distinguishes America is not sycophancy, but the uniform character of its objects; practically all of them are great executives or their wives. In England, where the social system is more complex, the great are of more varied kinds, and the prevalence of the committee system causes individuals to have less patronage to bestow than they have in the United States.

Every country has its defects, but in relation to the world, I believe those of America to be less than those of any other country. The position of dominance which belonged to England in the nineteenth century will now belong to the United States, except in that large area which will be dominated by Soviet Russia. America will inevitably be forced into a kind of non-territorial imperialism, but I have considerable confidence that American influence will, on the whole, be exercised wisely and humanely. Indeed, in this field I have more belief in Americans than most of them have in themselves. I think their hegemony will be kindly and tolerant to a greater degree than that of any European country would be, and whatever pangs I may feel as a patriot, I look to the Empire of America for the best hopes that our distracted world permits.

BIBLIOGRAPHY

A selection of Russell's writings on, or relating to, America, not included in this volume (Ms/Ts and/or published versions are located in the Russell Archives)

'How America Can Help to Bring Peace' (1915), unpublished

'Is Nationalism Moribund?', *Seven Arts* (October 1917)

'How Washington Could Help China', the *Daily Herald* (16 December 1921)

'Bring Us Peace: An Appeal to American Students', the *New Student* (7 October 1922)

'Slavery or Self-Extermination: A Forecast of Europe's Future', the *Nation* (11 July 1923)

'The Recrudescence of Puritanism', *Outlook* (20 October 1923); reprinted in *Sceptical Essays*

'The Politics of Oil: The Threatened Combine of Combines', a review of *The Oil Trusts and Anglo-American Relations* by E. H. Davenport and S. Russell Cooke, *New Leader* (11 January 1924)

'Bolshevism and the West', a debate with Scott Nearing, League for Public Discussion (1924)

'What is Wrong with Western Civilisation?', a talk delivered to the League for Industrial Democracy (3 April 1924), unpublished

'How to be Free and Happy', a talk delivered to, and published by the Rand School of Social Science (1924)

'Americanization', a review of *Culture and Democracy in the United States* by H. M. Kallen, the *Dial* (August 1924)

'Capitalism—or What?', the *Banker's Magazine* (May 1926)

'Bertrand Russell Thinks America Will Rule the World in Future', *Forward* (12 September 1926)

'What I Think of America', *Forward* (31 October 1926)

'Why Psychoanalysis Is Popular', *Forward* (13 March 1927)

'Education and the Good Life', a talk delivered to the Child Study Association of America (November 1927), unpublished

'Is America Giving a Chance to Individuality?', *Nation's Business* (March 1928)

'The Ostrich Code of Morals', *Forum* (July 1928)

'The Americanization of Europe is Inevitable', *Forward* (9 December 1928)

'Is Modern Marriage a Failure?', a debate with J. Cowper Powys, the Discussion Guild (1930)

'Shall the State Rear Our Children?', a debate with Sherwood Anderson, *Literary Digest* (28 November 1931)

'Do I Preach Adultery?', *Liberty* (May 1940)

'England and America—the Problem of Unity or Imperialist Rivalry', *New Leader* (4 December 1943)

'Citizenship in a Great State', *Fortune* (December 1943)

'Britain—U.S.A.: The Main Differences between Our Way of Life and Theirs', *New Leader* (28 October 1944)

INDEX

357

gives his impressions on the cinema 108-9; after execution of Sacco and Vanzetti he seeks to keep their memory alive 110;

fifth visit to America September 1929 110; lectures on East and West coasts 111; debates with Will Durant on 'Is Modern Education a Failure?', and with John Cowper Powys on 'Is Modern Marriage a Failure?' 112; publishes *Marriage and Morals*; attacked by Bishop Manning, and Columbia University withdraws invitation to Russell 113; returns to England, December 1929; his impressions of the visit 115; writes 'Homogeneous America' and 'Thirty Years from Now', and publishes *The Conquest of Happiness*, 1930 116;

sixth visit to America, October 1931 116-19; debates with Sherwood Anderson on 'Shall the State Rear Our Children?' 117; debates with Jay Lovestone, American Communist, on 'Is Proletarian Dictatorship the Road to Freedom?' 119; begins his weekly articles for the Hearst Press 119; break-up of his marriage to Dora, and he gives up the running of his school 119; the Depression adversely affects sale of his books in America 120; citizens of North Carolina petition against Russell lecturing at State University, 1932 120; supports Roosevelt's peace policy and New Deal programme 120-1; publishes *Education and the Social Order* 1932, and *Freedom and Organization 1814-1914* 1934, the latter containing much commentary on development of American democracy and industrialisation 121-3; maintains his pacifist position throughout 1930s, and

publishes *Which Way to Peace?*, 1936 123; returns to work on technical philosophy, and lectures at Oxford on 'Words and Facts' 126; third child, Conrad, born April 1937 126; beset by financial problems 126; desires post at American university 126-7; appointment at Chicago University 127; seventh visit to America, September 1938 127; impressions of Chicago 128; anxious about threat of war 128; accepts professorship at UCLA from September 1939; short lecture tour 129; writes 'The American Mind', 'Individual Freedom in England and America' and 'America the Next World Centre', criticises financiers and supports New Deal 129; writes 'Democracy and Economics', February 1939, again critical of financiers 130; urges U.S. neutrality in 'If War Comes—Shall we Participate or Be Neutral?' 130; supports Roosevelt's attempts to avert war, April 130; John and Kate arrive in America, summer 130; problems created by outbreak of war 131; impressions of UCLA, and California migrant labour 132-3; accepts CCNY post and resigns from UCLA, February 1940 133, 135; CCNY appointment attacked by Bishop Manning, March 136-7; pressure on Board of Higher Education 137; students defend Russell 138-9; organisations for and against Russell enter the fray 139-40; question of citizenship raised 141-2; led by CCNY Philosophy Department American academics rally to Russell 142-6; mass meetings for and against, Russell viciously attacked by Keegan et al. 146-7; Board upholds deci-

sion on 18 March 147-9; delight at victory 149-50; lawsuit against appointment, March 152-3; case heard before Justice McGeehan, 27 March 154-5; weakness of defence case 155-6; McGeehan revokes appointment on March 30, describes Russell as morally unfit for the position 156; praise for McGeehan, and Russell's reactions 157-8; Russell's attempts to contest the decision 159-60; nationwide outcry and protest 160-2; pressure to prevent Board appealing, and La Guardia's action 163-4; press reaction and *New York Times* editorial of April 20 164-5;

witch-hunt instituted against Russell 168; attempt to have him dismissed from UCLA, April 168; legal proceedings threaten his William James lectures at Harvard 168-72; writes 'Freedom and the Colleges', 'Do I Preach Adultery?' and 'Education and America', in defence of his views 172-3; anguish over Nazi threat to Britain 173-4; finds it difficult to maintain a pacifist position 174; announces his support for the war 175-7;

witch-hunt intensifies, Russell described as fifth columnist 177-9; summer vacation at Lake Tahoe provides welcome rest 180; approached by Barnes, and conditions of employment 180-4; delivers William James lectures in October 184; arrives at Barnes Foundation in January 1941 184-5; further explanation of his support for the war and efforts to contribute 185-6; rift develops between Barnes and Russell, and Patricia barred from premises 187-90; gives public lectures on India with aim of promoting

325, 327n
Soviet government (*see also* U.S.S.R.) 80, 109
Spain 304
Spinoza 221, 223, 312
Spring Rice, Sir Cecil 60–1
Sproul, Robert 132–3, 143, 148, 160
Stalin, Joseph 131, 150, 178
Standard Oil 71, 89, 223
Stanley, Lord 329
Stanley, Lyulph 329
'States' Rights, On' 119, 278–9
State, the 119, 158, 223, 278–9, 292, 303, 310, 345
Stephens, Senator 294
Stone, Lauson H. 148
Streicher, Julius 294
students 13, 44, 97, 104, 111, 137–9, 143, 145–6, 149, 161–2, 177, 187, 193, 194–6, 212, 288, 309, 311
Students Union, American 161
suffragettes 49
suffragists 30
Supreme Court (*see* New York State)
Supreme Court (U.S.A.) 123
Survey Graphic 130, 133n, 289
Sweden 316
Swirsky, William 146, 149, 161
syndicalism 77, 79

Tablet 137, 157
Tahoe, Lake 180–1
Taff Vale decision 264
Taft, William Howard 237, 243n
Tammany Hall 22, 136, 140, 152, 163
Teachers' Union Auxiliary 93
Tead, Ordway 135, 148–9, 161
Telegraph House 102, 117
temperance 21
Temple University 191, 197
Tennessee 145–6
'Terrible-Tempered Dr Barnes, The' (McCardle) 190, 198n, 199n
Theocritus 257
'Thirty Years from Now' 116, 262–9
Thomas, Grace 29
Thomas, Helen (*see also* Helen Flexner) 25, 28

Thomas, James Carey 20, 25, 28
Thomas, Martha Carey 20–1, 24–5, 27n, 29, 33–8, 38n, 42–3
Tibet 111
Time magazine 11, 13, 15n, 187–8, 198n, 199n, 206
Times, The 11, 15n, 60–1, 64, 70, 215–16, 225
'To Bertrand Russell' (Edman) 70
'Tourists, On' 119
Town Hall Club (New York) 103
Toy, Nancy 55
trade unions 123, 132, 191, 264, 280–1, 290, 321–3, 336, 345
Trevelyan, Elizabeth 176
Trevelyan, Robert 131, 175–6
trial marriage (*see also* companionate marriage) 106
Tribunal, the 70–1, 73, 215–16, 217–19
Tribune, Chicago 340
Trinity College, Cambridge (*see also* Cambridge University) 20, 26n, 32, 61–2, 69, 82, 90, 195, 206, 309
Truman, Harry S. 208
Trusts (*see also* big business) 85, 89, 90
Tuttle, Charles H. 137, 147, 149, 152, 163
Twentieth Century Club (Boston) 52
'Two Bertrand Russells, The' (Eastman) 105

un-American 179, 194, 334
United Nations 204–5
Unity (Chicago) 99–100
Unpopular Essays 101n
Unpopular Review 53
Uruguay 238
USSR (*see also* Russia) 178, 208, 258, 269, 300, 305, 325

Vanderbilt, Commodore 123
Vanzetti, Bartolomeo (*see also* Sacco and Vanzetti case) 11, 39, 96, 110
Vatican 136
Veblen, Oswald 32, 143
Veblen, Thorstein 79
'Vegetarians, On the Fierce-

ness of' 119
Venezuela 238
Venice 263, 297
Versailles, Treaty of 174, 221, 239, 250, 287, 297, 342
Victoria, Queen 352
Vietnam 11, 13
Vildrach 45
Villon, François 40, 45
Virginia Quarterly Review 116, 262
Virginia, University of 262
Virginia, West 74
Vladivostok 239

wages 123
Wales 63
Wallas, Graham 21, 81
Wall, I. R. 197n
Wall Street 230, 244, 268
Walsh, Francis W. 140
Wanamaker, John 23, 27n
war 54, 62, 86, 94, 186, 205, 231, 236, 240, 241 255 266, 285, 286, 288, 297–8, 307, 338, 342, 349
'War and Non-Resistance' 57
War Crimes in Vietnam 15n
Ward, James 26n
War Office (British) 51, 63–4
War of Independence, American 116, 186, 340
Washington 41, 53, 60, 68–9, 91, 93, 96, 206, 220–1, 225, 244, 299, 329, 333, 339, 340
Washington Conference (1921) 83–5, 211, 220–1, 225, 239–42, 287
Watson, J. B. 102, 116, 117, 124n, 246
Wealth against Commonwealth (Lloyd) 223
Webb, Beatrice 201–2
Weiss, Albert 147
Weiss, Paul 200–1
Wells, H. G. 51, 107, 247
Wendell, Barrett 28
What I Believe 153
'What is Wrong with Western Civilisation?' 76n, 94, 356
'What I Think of America' 356
'When Lilacs Last in the Dooryard Bloom'd' (Whitman) 29
Which Way to Peace? 124
White and Staples, Philadelphia 193
Whitehead, A. N. 32, 41, 78,